American Accent Training: Grammar

说出正确的口语
——美音达人的语法书

（美）Ann Cook · 著

北京语言大学出版社
BEIJING LANGUAGE AND CULTURE
UNIVERSITY PRESS

图书在版编目(CIP)数据

说出正确的口语：美音达人的语法书／（美）库克
(Cook,A.) 著；樊英波译. —北京：北京语言大学出
版社，2015（2017.1重印）
　ISBN 978-7-5619-4279-6

　Ⅰ. ①说… 　Ⅱ. ①库… ②樊… 　Ⅲ. ①英语—口语—
美国 ②英语—语法 　Ⅳ. ①H319.9 ②H314

中国版本图书馆CIP数据核字（2015）第213770号

版权登记号：图字01—2015—1800号

书　　名：说出正确的口语——美音达人的语法书
　　　　　SHUO CHU ZHENGQUE DE KOUYU——MEI YIN DA REN DE YUFA SHU
编　　著：（美）Ann Cook
责任编辑：李　亮　张　倩
封面设计：大愚设计

出版发行：北京语言大学出版社
社　　址：北京市海淀区学院路15号　　邮政编码：100083
网　　站：www.blcup.com
电　　话：发行部　（010）62605588 / 5019 / 5128
　　　　　编辑部　（010）62418641
　　　　　邮购电话　（010）62605127
　　　　　读者服务信箱　dywh@xdf.cn
印　　刷：北京慧美印刷有限公司
经　　销：全国新华书店

版　　次：2017年1月第1版第4次印刷
开　　本：880毫米×1230毫米　1/16　印张：22.25
字　　数：400千
书　　号：ISBN 978-7-5619-4279-6
定　　价：49.00元

Table of Contents

Chapter 6: Indirect Speech and the Unreal Duo
间接引语和非真实双重时态

Chapter 7: Reverse Modifiers and Opinion Words
后置修饰语和观点词

Overview 概述   **Track 001**

Welcome to *American Accent Training: Grammar*. This book and CD set is designed to teach you to speak standard American English. Everything is explained and a complete answer key is in the back of the text. At any point, you can call（001）800-457-4255 for support.

欢迎使用《美语发音秘诀：语法》，这本书及其配套CD旨在教你学会说标准的美式英语。本书讲解的内容无所不包，并在书后提供了完整的参考答案。你随时可以拨打我们的电话寻求帮助。在中国大陆请拨打001-800-457-4255，在美国本土请拨打800-457-4255。

"I hate grammar. It's boring." "我讨厌语法，因为它很枯燥。"   **Track 002**

Studying grammar rules is, for most people, not fun. This method stays as far away from memorization as possible, and lets you jump right into applying and using the techniques in actual speech. After all, in conversation, you're not going to think, "Was that modifier dangling?" or "Hmm, was that subjunctive pluperfect enough?"

对大多数人来说，学习语法规则并不好玩。本书的学习方法尽可能地避开死记硬背，让你从一开始就直接在实际语境中运用所学技能。毕竟，与人交谈的时候你不会去想"那个修饰语用得恰当吗？"或者"唔，那里用虚拟的过去完成时够了吗？"

"Is this just a grammar book?" "这只是本语法书吗？"

No, this isn't just a grammar book. You will learn vocabulary, sentence types, story order, logic, intonation, word connections, and pronunciation. Your comprehension and listening skills will become sharp and accurate. Your writing will become crisp and detailed, yet concise and to the point. When you apply all the techniques in this book, your writing and speaking will be fluent, logical, and easily understood.

不，这不仅仅是一本语法书，因为你还会学到词汇、句型、故事顺序、逻辑、声调、单词连读以及发音。你的理解力和听力会变得既敏锐又准确。你的作文也会变得干脆利落、细节丰富，并且语言简洁、切中主题。当你把书里介绍的所有技能都用上以后，你的作文和口语都会变得无比流畅、富有逻辑性，并且清晰易懂。

"But I've already studied grammar..."
 "但我已经学过语法了……"   **Track 003**

Studying grammar in the traditional way doesn't do much for many students, and that's why we've come up with an entirely new approach. You know how when you're in a new town or in a shopping mall, there is a map on a pedestal with an arrow indicating "You Are Here"? The problem most students have is that they are literally lost in the language. They know some of the details, but they don't really know how the puzzle pieces fit together. In other words, they lack a good understanding of the big picture of English. This book provides a visual map, so you always know right where you are.

对于很多学生来说，传统的语法学习方法用处不大，所以我们才研究出了这一整套新方法。你有过这种经历吗？当你身处一个陌生的城市或者大型商场时，看到建筑物的基座上画着一张地图，上面有个箭头提示说"你在这儿"。对于大多数学生来说，他们面临的问题是他们其实已经迷失在语言中了。他们只知道其中的一些细节，但却不知道整个拼图是怎样拼出来的。换句话说，他们对英语这张大拼图缺乏整体的理解。本书则为你提供了一张看得见的地图，这样你就始终知道自己的确切位置了。

"English is too hard." "英语太难了。"

English has about half a million words, but nobody uses all of them. The average educated person only uses about 2,500 high-frequency words, many of which you may already know. By starting with the basic structures presented here, along with the high-frequency vocabulary, you will quickly learn how to make simple, 100% accurate sentences. By gradually building on the perfect foundation with different vocabulary, you will soon be able to express yourself easily.

英语总共约有50万个单词，但没人会每个单词都用。一个受过中等水平教育的人一般只使用约2500个高频词汇，而这些词中的很多你都已经知道了。有了这些高频词作基础，在你开始学习本书介绍的基本结构之后，你很快就能写出简单但百分百正确的句子。然后逐渐在这个完美的基础上扩充自己的词汇量，你很快就能表达自如了。

"I can't understand when Americans talk to me." Track 004
"美国人跟我说话的时候我听不懂。"

Although this is a grammar book, it takes a singularly auditory approach. The exercises are also on the CD, so you will learn to hear the sounds, rhythms, patterns, structures, and vocabulary of spoken American English.

虽然这是一本语法书，但它采用了独特的听力训练法。本书的练习题也都在CD上，所以你可以从中学到美式英语口语的发音、节奏、模式、结构以及词汇。

"How long will this take?" "学完这本书要多久？"

The amazing thing about this approach is, because you will quickly understand where you are in the language-learning process—*what you already know and what areas you still need to study*—you will be able to fill in the gaps in a couple of months.

这种训练法的神奇之处在于：因为你会很快知道自己处在语言学习过程中的哪个位置——哪些是你已经知道的，而哪些是你还要继续学习的，所以只要花上几个月，你就可以查完漏、补完缺。

"How do I know what to do?" "我怎么知道要做什么？"

Clear instructions are given for each lesson. Each exercise is reviewed from seven different perspectives: vocabulary, grammar, word order, story order, intonation, word connections, and pronunciation. This is essentially the way you learned your first language as a child.

本书的每一课都给读者提出了明确的指示，而每道练习题也都从以下七个不同的角度对知识进行了复习：词汇、语法、词序、故事顺序、声调、单词连读以及发音。这其实就是你儿时学习母语的方法。

"Where am I now?" "我现在处在什么位置？"

It's natural to wonder where you are in something as big as a language, especially when it's your second language. To help with that, we use the simple icons ◄●► to indicate where you are on the language map. (See page 7.)

想知道自己把一门庞大的语言学习到了什么程度是理所当然的事，尤其当它是你的第二语言时。为了帮助读者，我们用很简单的图标◄●►来指示你在语言地图中的位置(见第7页)。

The structure of the chapters themselves will to orient you to what you already know, what there is to learn, and how the puzzle pieces fit together.

各章节的安排本身也可以帮助你了解哪些是你已经知道的，哪些是你还要学习的，以及大拼图是如何拼出来的。

What Is Grammar? 什么是语法？   Track 005

American Logic	美国人的逻辑
Story Order	故事顺序
Sentences	句子
Words	单词
ABCs	字母

Grammar is a combination of the eight parts of speech: nouns, pronouns, adjectives, verbs, adverbs, prepositions, conjunctions, and interjections. Think of these eight parts as the building blocks that you will use to construct your sentences.

语法就是把八类词组合在一起的方法，这八类词分别为：名词、代词、形容词、动词、副词、介词、连词和感叹词。试着把这八类词看作你造句用的砖瓦吧。

We start out with a very simple three-block foundation（noun-verb-noun）, and, bit by bit, you add blocks until you have a solid, well-constructed sentence. Our goal is clear, direct speech, not flowery language.

我们先从最简单的三块砖结构（名词—动词—名词）开始，然后再一点点往上添砖加瓦，直到造出牢固、结构良好的句子。我们的目标是学会明白、直接的语言，而不是华丽的词藻。

The starting point—the first two building blocks—are nouns and verbs. It's important to realize how many ways these two building blocks can be used.

这个方法的起点——即头两块砖——是名词和动词，知道这两块砖的各种用法非常重要。

How do we fit all the pieces together? The key to English grammar is the nine-grid. It is a synopsis of the most basic structures. Later, you will learn different structures, but if you master this form, you will always be able to communicate clearly and logically, both in speech and in writing.

那我们要如何把这些砖组合到一起呢？学好英语语法的关键是九宫格，它是最基本的结构的总览。在后面你还会学习其他的结构，但只要你掌握了这个表格，你就总能展开清晰且有逻辑的交流，不管是说还是写。

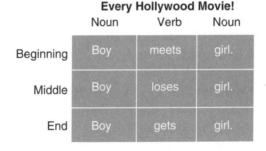

Every Hollywood Movie!

	Noun	Verb	Noun
Beginning	Boy	meets	girl.
Middle	Boy	loses	girl.
End	Boy	gets	girl.

Write down the following as accurately as possible. When you are finished, take the grammar placement tests and complete the initial writing sample.

听下面的录音，并准确记录听到的内容。完成以后，再做第13页的语法摸底测试，并完成第一篇写作练习。

Simplified Terminology
简化的术语

This book presents grammar and accent from a simplified perspective. For instance, you may know that **Bob sees Betty** is an SVO（Subject-Verb-Object）sentence, and that **Bob is late** is SVC（Subject-Linking Verb-Complement）. However, our goal is not to create grammarians, but rather to get you to understand the basic structures in a simplified manner. To this end, both sentences fit in the nine-grid in the same way.

本书采用了深入浅出的方式来讲解语法和语音。比如，你也许知道Bob sees Betty 是SVO（主语－动词－宾语）结构，而Bob is late是SVC（主语－系动词－表语）结构。但是，我们的目标并不是要培养语法学家，而是要让你轻松地明白这一基本结构。为此，我们把这两个句子都放进了九宫格来表示。

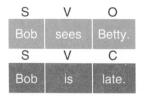

In the same vein, terms such as **intonation, pitch, pitch change, stress, the staircase, up and down, inflection, strong words, emphasis, and peaks and valleys** are all used to indicate that the speaker is highlighting one or two words in a sentence.

同样的道理，诸如声调、音高、音高变化、重音、音阶、起伏、抑扬变化、强势词、强调、音峰以及音谷这些术语，都是用来表示说话人正在强调句子中的某一两个词的。

Chapter Structure
章节结构

Each chapter has six sections.

每一章都有六个部分。

DICTATION	STORY	NOUNS	VERBS	TEST	ESSAY

The **Dictations** start out easy and get progressively more difficult. They are tied in to the grammar topic of each chapter. For example, the first dictation only uses the simple present tense of the verb **to be**, whereas the later ones use all of the structures presented up to that point. The dictations intentionally use contractions so that they resemble standard, colloquial speech. The audio is on the CD.

听写材料开始的时候比较简单，然后变得越来越难。这些材料与各章讲解的语法点有着紧密的联系。例如，第一段听写材料只使用了动词to be 的一般现在时，然而后面的材料则会相应地用上所有已经讲过的结构。听写材料中特意运用了很多缩略形式，这样它们才像标准的口语。所有的音频都在CD上。

The **Story** progresses from the simple nine-grid of the classic Hollywood movie plot to a complete story with various verb tenses and a wide range of sentence structures. It is about a quirky Italian bodybuilder named Max and recounts his life in California.

故事从经典的好莱坞电影情节开始一路发展成完整的故事,而语言也从简单的九宫格不断完善,直到包含各种时态和各种句子结构为止。故事讲述了一位古怪的、名叫Max的意大利健身人士在加利福尼亚的生活。

In each chapter, the **Nouns** section addresses nouns and noun-related concepts, such as *plurals, pronouns, prepositions, conjunctions, comparatives, superlatives, countable/uncountable, articles, adjectives, compound nouns, word order, and reverse adjectives* (traditionally known as relative clauses).

每章的名词部分都会讨论名词或与名词相关的概念,比如复数、代词、介词、连词、比较级、最高级、可数和不可数、冠词、形容词、复合名词、词序以及后置形容词(传统的叫法为关系从句)。

One **Noun**, Many Uses

After you think about what a noun can do, you should turn your attention to *actions* (verbs).
当你思考了名词的作用之后,你就应该开始关注行动(即动词)了。

The **Verbs** section covers all of the tenses, as well as *contractions, negatives, questions, adverbs, tag endings, phrasal verbs, main verbs, linking verbs, and verbs of perception*, as well as verbs that typically cause difficulty such as *do/make, take/have, get*, and so on. A visual verb map shows you where you are and what you need to learn (see page 9).

动词部分不仅讲解了所有的时态,还讲解了缩写形式、否定形式、疑问句、副词、反意疑问句、短语动词、主动词、系动词和感官动词,另外还涵盖了学生普遍学不好的动词,比如 do/make, take/have, get等。动词地图会告诉你自己在什么位置,还需要学习什么(见第9页)。

One **Verb**, Many Uses

In addition to getting as much speaking practice as possible, it's important for you **to learn to write** and **to write to learn**. At the end of each chapter are the **Test** and **Essay** sections. By taking the time to review what you have learned and putting your thoughts down on paper, you will assimilate the grammatical concepts and vocabulary into your writing.

除了要尽可能多说以外，学会写作和在写作中学习也很重要。所以，在每章的最后是测试和写作部分。通过复习前面学过的东西并把所思所想记录下来，你会把语法概念和词汇融会贯通到写作中去。

Student's Before/After Writing Sample
学生使用本书前/后的写作实例

The following is a writing sample from a student before he began using this book. The second sample represents his progress after three months of study.

下面的第一篇文章是某学生在使用本书前写的。第二篇文章体现了他经过三个月的学习后所取得的进步。

Initial Writing Sample 一开始的写作样例

I lives in San Luis Obispo. This isn't a big town but it so beatiful. It have a lot of moutains, hills. We can hiking to the top for see over this town. Here not far from the beach it about 15 minutes drive to beach. So that it have many tourist visit here. In down town we have 2 book stores, fashion stores and restaurants. This town have 3 thai restaurants.

I like thai food restaurant more than another one. It address in down town and test is so delicious. Here we have down town market every thusday. This market have fresh fruit from farmmer dilect to customer. So I think here is a good choise if you wanted to take vacation, I would be your guide.

Three Months Later 三个月以后

Last weekend Steve and I did many things. At first we thought Steve would go to work, but it was raining, so he couldn't go. Saturday morning we went to the donut shop. After we got home we played the puzzle untill afternoon then we went to the beach. In the evening after dinner time we went to the gym. I worked out with the cardiomachine a little bit then I went to the pool, the hot tub and also the sauna. I was reading "a little princess" while I sat in the sauna room. Sunday morning we went to the donut shop again. Actually Steve like to have some sweet in the morning everyday, but we know it isn't good for his health, so he try to have it only the weekend. We were watching TV while we had donuts. Every sunday we have to clean the fish tank. We have 3 gold fish. All of them have a different color. One's gold another one's black and the last one's mix 2 color together(the gold and the back). There aren't different only the color but also diferrent in the charcter too. They are my good friend. They have been eating all the time, it made a lot of poo, so that their house need to be cleaned every week. After took care of our fish, we played the Video-games he's always win me. I had been practicing many times before I played with him, but I never won him. If I won, I would be happy. I believe if I keep go on practicing, I will win in one day.

Visual Grammar
视觉语法

The idea of a visual grammar is a very important aspect of our language-learning approach. The verb map that you'll see throughout this book is similar to the shopping mall map with a large **You Are Here** arrow.

对于我们的语言学习方法来说，视觉语法这个概念是一个很重要的方面。你将看到的贯穿本书的动词地图与商场里的地图很相似，后者通常有一个表示"你在这儿"的箭头。

When you start, you will be using the **simple present tense**. You will learn where the verb belongs in a simple sentence, how to conjugate verbs, and what supporting words go with a particular tense.

刚开始的时候，你将会先使用一般现在时。你要学习简单句中动词的位置，动词的变化形式，以及在某一具体时态下要使用什么辅助词。

Throughout this book, the three symbols are ◀ **past**, ● **present**, ▶ **future**. Whenever you see the dot ●, you will know that you are dealing with some aspect of "now." The two triangles ◀▶ point in the relevant time direction.

贯穿全书的是这三个符号：◀过去时、●现在时、▶将来时。只要你看到这个点●，就知道自己正在处理与"现在"有关的问题。而这两个三角形◀▶也指向相应的时间方向。

Look at the chart below. If this were all you knew—but you used it perfectly every time—you would have a good start in English.

请看下面的图表。假设你就只知道这些，但你每次都能正确地运用，那你的学英语之路就有了个不错的起点。

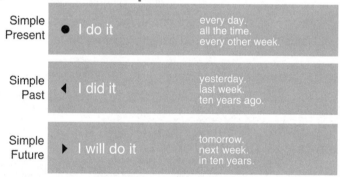

Time relationships are very important in English. We are very interested in the sequence of events, as well as the dependence of one event on another.

时间关系在英语中非常重要。我们对事件之间的前后顺序、一件事与另一件事的依存关系都很感兴趣。

After you work through the various aspects of the **simple** tenses, you will go on to the **duo** tenses. The main thing to remember is that there are always two related events with the duo tenses. The symbols are **present duo** ◀●, **past duo** ◀◀, and **future duo** ▶▶.

当你学完一般时态的各种情况以后，你就要继续学习双重时态了。你需要记住的一点是：在双重时态下，总有两件相互关联的事情。相应的符号为：双重现在时◀●、双重过去时◀◀、双重将来时▶▶。

Notice that the present duo has both a past and a present symbol. This is because you are pulling the past up into the present time. Even if you don't mention the present, it is there. This is a difference between **I didn't do it** and **I haven't done it**. In the first example, the event is over. In the second example, however, there is a strong element of the present, as—even now—you may still do it.

请注意：双重现在时既包含过去时的符号，也包含现在时的符号。这是因为你把过去与现在联系到了一起。即使你没有提到现在，它也在那里。I didn't do it.（我没做过。）和I haven't done it.（我还没做。）这两句话是有区别的。对于第一个句子来说，事件已经结束了；然而，第二个句子却蕴含着很强的有关现在的意味，因为——就算到了现在——你仍然可能去做。

Duo Tenses Are In **Pairs**

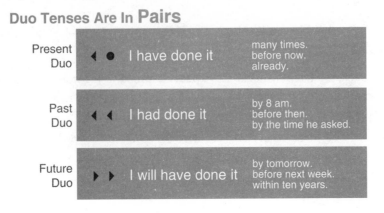

Present Duo	◄ ●	I have done it	many times. before now. already.
Past Duo	◄ ◄	I had done it	by 8 am. before then. by the time he asked.
Future Duo	► ►	I will have done it	by tomorrow. before next week. within ten years.

These are traditionally referred to as the perfect tenses.
在传统的语法体系中，这些被称为完成时。

Once you have a strong understanding of the difference between the **simple** and the **duo** tenses, you are ready to work on the **unreal duos**. You'll notice a black-to-white symbol change to reflect this unreal status. These tenses are called "contrary to fact" because they don't actually happen.

当你充分理解了一般时态和双重时态的区别以后，你就可以开始学习非真实双重时态了。为了反映这一非真实的状态，你会发现我们把黑色符号换成了白色符号。我们之所以说这些时态"与事实相反"，是因为它们实际上并没有发生过。

Duo Tenses Can Be **Unreal**

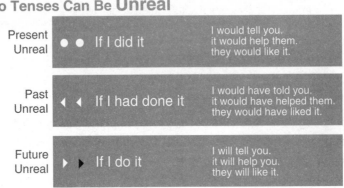

Present Unreal	○ ○	If I did it	I would tell you. it would help them. they would like it.
Past Unreal	◄ ◄	If I had done it	I would have told you. it would have helped them. they would have liked it.
Future Unreal	▷ ►	If I do it	I will tell you. it will help you. they will like it.

These are traditionally referred to as the subjunctive conditional, and they are sometimes considered a mood or mode rather than a tense.
在传统的语法体系中，这些被称为虚拟条件句，有时人们更愿意把它们看作一种语气、一种情态，而非一种时态。

Now, let's pull the three elements together into a verb map. This is a map of statements.
现在，让我们把这三张表格放到同一张动词地图中去。这是一张陈述句地图。

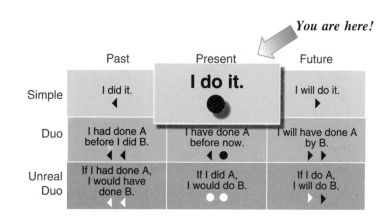

The Verb Map
动词地图

When you have completed this book, you will be familiar with all of the components below. The **T formation** in each box indicates the more commonly used verb tenses.

当你学完本书以后，你就熟知以下每个组成部分了。下列每个表格中都有一个T形区域，它们是使用得相对频繁的动词时态。

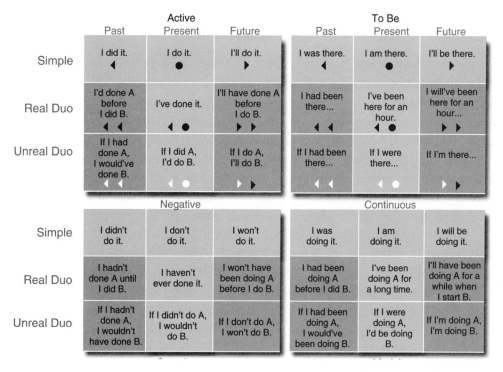

	Questions				Modals		
Simple	Did I do it?	Do I do it?	Will I do it?		I had to do it.	I have to do it.	I'll have to do it.
Real Duo	Have I done A before I did B?	Have I done it before?	Will I have done A before I do B?		I'd had to do A before I had to do B.	I've had to do A many times.	I'll have had to do A before I have to do B.
Unreal Duo	If I had done A, would I have done B?	If I did A, would I do B?	If I do A, will I do B?		If I'd had to do A, I would've had to do B.	If I had to do A, I'd have to do B.	If I have to do A, I'll have to do B.

	Causative				Passive		
Simple	I had it done.	I have it done.	I'll have it done.		It was done.	It is done.	It will be done.
Real Duo	I'd had A done before I had B done.	I've had A done many times.	I'll have had A done by the time I have B done.		A had been done before B was done.	A has been done many times.	A will be done before B is done.
Unreal Duo	If I'd had A done, I would've had B done.	If I had A done, I'd have B done.	If I have A done, I'll have B done.		If A had been done, B would've been done.	If A were done, B would be done.	If A is done, B will be done.

Integrating Grammar and Speech
融合语法和口语

Traditionally, written and spoken English are taught separately. This has the unfortunate consequence that students internalize the grammar with their own accents. They are then faced with the need to go back and try to reconfigure their presentation. With this method, you learn the same way you did with your first language. The words and structure are introduced at the same time as the sounds and rhythms. The goal is to master the foundations in all aspects and then build up to the higher levels. If you only learn grammar, there are times that your accent will make it seem like you haven't mastered the basics. For instance, native Chinese speakers sometimes drop the final consonants in speech, so it seems like they don't conjugate well. Once they are taught to link the words together, they come across with both the correct grammar and the standard accent.

在传统的教学模式下，英语的书面语和口语是分开教的。这就导致了一个不良的后果，那就是学生会把语法内化到自己的发音中去，于是他们需要重新回去解决语音的问题。但如果运用本书的方法，你就能按照学母语的方法来学英语了。在本书中，单词和结构与发音和节奏是放在一起讲的。这样一来，学生就可以先扎实地打好各方面的基础，然后再更上一层楼。如果你只学语法，那么有时候你的发音会让人觉得你连最基本的都还没有掌握好。比如，中国人在说英语的时候有时会发不出单词最后的辅音，以至于听起来好像他们没有掌握词形变化一样。一旦教会他们如何连读，他们就相当于同时掌握了正确的语法和标准的发音。

It's also vital to understand how intonation plays a part in grammar. For example, when you have a **description**, the second word is stressed（cold **milk**）, but when you have a compound, you need to stress the first part of the word（**milk**man）. Adding a suffix like **-y** can give you an adjective（milk**y**）, and adding **to** will often create a verb from a noun（**to** milk）.

了解声调在语法中的作用也是至关重要的。比如，当你描述物品时，第二个单词需要重读（cold **milk**，冷牛奶），但当你说复合词时，就要重读单词的第一部分（**milk**man，送奶工）。milk后面加上后缀-y就变成了形容词（milky，乳状的），而加上to就从名词变成了动词（**to** milk，挤奶）。

In the later chapters, you'll find exercises to help you develop advanced comprehension skills. These exercises will ask you to supply missing information, select an appropriate response, identify if a statement is true or false, identify the gist of a statement, recognize specific facts, and draw logical conclusions.

在后面的章节中，有很多练习可以帮助你培养高级理解技能。这些练习会要求你补充缺失的信息、选择恰当的回答、判断某个说法的正确性、概括某段话的主旨、找出基本的事实，或者得出合理的结论。

Vowel Chart
元音表

Consonant Chart is on page 21.
辅音表见第21页。

There are only five characters that are different from the standard English alphabet: æ, ä, ə, ɛ, and ü.

只有以下的五个符号与标准的英语字母不同：æ, ä, ə, ɛ, ü。

Tense Vowels

Symbol	Sound	Spelling	Example
ā	ɛi	take	[tāk]
ē	ee	eat	[ēt]
ī	äi	ice	[īs]
ō	ou	hope	[hōp]
ū	ooh	smooth	[smūth]
ä	ah	caught	[kät]
æ	ä + eh	cat	[kæt]
æo	æ + o	down	[dæon]
oi	oh + ee	boy	[boi]

Lax Vowels

Symbol	Sound	Spelling	Example
ɛ	eh	get	[gɛt]
i	ih	it	[it]
ü	ih + uh	took	[tük]
ə	uh	sun	[sən]
Semi-Vowels			
r	er	her	[hr]
l	ᵊl	dull	[dəᵊl]
w	wᵊ	quick	[kwik]
y	yᵊ	onion	[ənyᵊn]

SAMPLE CURRICULUM: 4-hour classes / Total 80 hours
课程安排范例：每堂课4小时 / 总共80小时

Week 1: Chapter 1		Week 2: Chapter 2	
Testing Grammar Placement Dictation Writing Sample **Chapter 1 Dictation** **Story** 1-2 to 1-19 **Nouns** 1-20 to 1-27	**Questions** 1-28 to 1-29 **Pronouns** 1-30 to 1-41 **Present Tense** 1-42 to 1-53 **Time Words** 1-54 to 1-57 **Test & Essay**	**Dictation** **Story** 2-2 to 2-3 **High Frequency Words** 2-4 **Nouns** 2-5 to 2-13 **Prepositions of Location** 2-14 **There is / are** 2-15 **Conjunctions** 2-16	**Present Tense** 2-17 to 2-27 **Negatives** 2-28 **Contractions** 2-29 **Questions** 2-30 to 2-33 **Tags** 2-34 to 2-36 **Verb Grid** 2-37 **Commands** 2-38 **Test & Essay**

Week 3: Chapter 3		Week 4: Chapter 4	
Dictation **Story** 3-2 **Syllables** 3-3 **Nouns Countable /** **Uncountable** 3-4 to 3-5 **Comparatives** 3-6 to 3-8 **Prepositions of Direction** 3-9 to 3-11	**Past Tense** 3-12 to 3-24 **Middle I** 3-25 **Get** 3-26 **Time Words** 3-27 to 3-28 **Test & Essay**	**Dictation** **Story** 4-2 to 4-3 **Reduced Vowels** 4-4 **Countable and Uncountable** **Nouns** 4-5 to 4-8 **Prepositions of Time &** **Manner** 4-9 to 4-10 **Modifiers** 4-11 to 4-12 **Intonation** 4-13 **Reading Comp** 4-14	**Tee Aitch** 4-15 to 4-16 **Intonation** 4-17 **Verbs: Continuous** 4-18 to 4-23 **Get** 4-24 to 4-25 **Questions** 4-26 to 4-33 **Test & Essay**

Week 5: Chapter 5		Week 6: Chapter 6	
Dictation **Story** 5-2 **Intonation** 5-3 to 5-4 **Word Order** 5-5 to 5-6 **Conjunctions** 5-7 to 5-8 **Countable Nouns** 5-9 to 5-11 **How** 5-12 to 5-13 **Two** 5-14 to 5-16	**Use** 5-17 to 5-18 **Countable Nouns** 5-19 to 5-23 **Future Tense** 5-24 to 5-36 **Grammar in a Nutshell** 5-37 to 5-42 **Do / Make** 5-43 **Stand** 5-44 **Test & Essay**	**Dictation** **Story** 6-2 **Joiners** 6-3 **Indirect Speech** 6-4 to 6-7 **Question Review** **So / Such** 6-8 **Verbs: Present** **Unreal** 6-9 to 6-12	**Opinion Words** 6-13 to 6-14 **Do / To Do / Doing** 6-15 **Say, Tell, Speak, Talk** 6-16 to 6-17 **Verbs of Perception** 6-18 to 6-22 **Take** 6-23 to 6-24 **Test & Essay**

Week 7: Chapter 7		Week 8: Chapter 8	
Dictation **Story** 7-2 **Linking** 7-3 to 7-4 **Reverse Adjectives** 7-5 to 7-9 **How** 7-10 to 7-12 **Some / Any** 7-13 **Time** 7-14 to 7-20	**Present Duo** 7-21 to 7-24 **P B F V W** 7-25 **There / It** 7-26 to 7-27 **Verb Review** 7-28 to 7-30 **Turn** 7-31 **Test & Essay**	**Dictation** **Story** 8-2 **Intonation and Attitude** 8-3 **L & R** 8-4 to 8-7 **Complex Intonation** 8-8 to 8-16 **How Questions** 8-17	**Noun / Verbs** 8-18 **Prepositions** 8-19 to 8-25 **Unreal Duo** 8-26 to 8-28 **Causative** 8-29 to 8-31 **Test & Essay**

Week 9: Chapter 9		Week 10: Chapter 10	
Dictation **Story** 9-2 **Listening Comp** 9-3 to 9-14 **Review** 9-15	**Reported Speech** 9-16 **Past Unreal Duo** 9-17 **Verb Review** 9-18 **There / Had / Be** 9-19 to 9-23 **Nutshell** 9-24 **Give** 9-25 **Test & Essay**	**Dictation** **Story** 10-2 **Nasals** 10-3 to 10-5 **Word Order** 10-6 to 10-7 **Doubt / Question** 10-8 **Prefixes** 10-9 **Comprehension** 10-10	**Synonyms Passive** 10-11 to 10-13 **Useful Verbs** 10-14 **Past & Future Duo** 10-15 to 10-19 **Verb Review** 10-20 **Test & Essay**

Tests
测试

You'll find three types of **Tests** in this book:
本书共有三种不同类型的测试:

1. Comprehensive grammar **placement** tests（basic and advanced）
   综合性语法摸底测试（基础和高级）
2. **Mastery** tests at the end of each chapter
   每章最后的单元测试
3. A **mid-term** and a comprehensive **final**
   期中测试以及综合性期末测试

Even if you are advanced, you should go through the entire program to make sure everything is in place and in the proper order. Of course, advanced students can go through more quickly, as long as they get 100% on each of the chapter tests.

即使你的英语水平已经很高, 你也应该从头到尾地学习本书, 因为只有这样才能知道自己是否掌握了全部内容, 并且确保各个知识点的先后顺序是对的。当然, 水平高的学生可以更快地学完本书, 只要他们在每个单元测试中都可以拿满分。

"Where do I start?" "我从哪里开始？"

It's important to determine your level, so the first step is to take the four placement tests:
明确自己的英语水平非常重要, 所以第一步就是进行以下四个摸底测试:

- Basic Grammar 基础语法
- Advanced Grammar 高级语法
- Dictation 听写
- Writing Sample 写作

Below are two grammar placement tests. Each one should only take about 15 minutes. The Answer Key is on page 306.

以下是两个语法摸底测试。每个测试要在15分钟内完成。参考答案在第306页。

Placement Test: Basic Grammar 摸底测试：基础语法

1. Circle the correct answer.
   a. I **is / am / are** a student.
   b. They **is / am / are** at a party.
   c. She **is / am / are** out of the office.
2. Change the sentence to the plural.
   a. This test is easy. _____
   b. The tree is tall. _____
3. Change the positive statement to a negative.
   Shelly is in Europe. _____

4. Change the statement to a question.

Your brother is in college. _____

5. Fill in where the **blue text** should appear in the sentence.

a. _____ I _____ am _____ late _____. (**always**)

b. _____ I _____ am _____ late _____. (**every day**)

6. Circle the correct answer.

a. The zookeeper **feed / feeds** the animals.

b. Joe and Ellie **tell / tells** funny jokes.

7. Replace both nouns with pronouns.

a. **Edgar** reads a **book**. _____

b. The **boys** fly the **kite**. _____

c. **Moira** plans her **classes**. _____

8. Fill in the most appropriate word.

a. The ring is _____ her finger.

b. He is sitting _____ a chair.

c. They are working _____ an office.

d. The subway is _____ ground.

9. Circle the most appropriate connecting word. Use each word only once.

a. They speak French **and / but / so** Italian.

b. We eat the cheese, **and / but / so** not the crackers.

c. It is late, **and / but / so** we are in a hurry.

10. Change the positive statement to a negative.

a. Lou knows Ed. _____

b. The cars go fast. _____

11. Change the statement to a question.

a. It rains every day. _____

b. You like it. _____

12. Circle the correct answer.

That plan is **bad / worse / the worst** of all.

13. Fill in the most appropriate direction word.

a. The boys jump _____ the pool.

b. The cat runs _____ from the dog.

14. Convert to the past.

Example: I **watch** TV. I **watched** TV.

a. They think about it. _____

b. We see him at the gym. _____

c. We have enough time. _____

15. Change the positive statement to a negative.

Morgan heard a noise. _____

16. Change the statement to a question.

a. James drove to New York. _____

b. Andrea and Sarah walked to work. _____

14

17. Fill in where the **blue text** should appear in the sentence.

    _____ James _____ drove _____to New York. (**frequently**)

18. Fill in the proper tag ending.

    a. He was funny, _____?

    b. I am here, _____?

19. Indicate the proper tag ending.

    a. They thought about it, _____?

    b. She didn't say it, _____?

20. Circle the correct answer.

    a. There was **a / some** water on the floor.

    b. He took **a / some** bath last night.

21. Circle the correct answer.

    a. What **a / the** surprise!

    b. It's **a / the** only way we can do it.

22. Circle the correct answer.

    a. They poured **a / —** water on the plants.

    b. Did you bring **a / —** water bottle?

23. Circle the correct answer.

    a. Did you have **much / many** trouble?

    b. Did you have **much / many** problems?

24. Circle the correct answer.

    a. He **sleeps / is sleeping** right now.

    b. They **work / are working** hard every day.

25. Change the statement to a question.

    The store is being remodeled. _____

26. Circle the correct answer.

    a. What time do you get **down / up / to** in the morning?

    b. Stop the bus! I need to get **down / off**!

27. Change the statement to the future.

    a. Charlie went to France. _____

    b. Marcus did not order shoes from Italy. _____

    c. Did Larry fix my computer? _____

28. Change the positive statement to a negative.

    Timmy will answer your questions. _____

29. Change the statement to a question. Do not use pronouns or contractions.

    The cell phone will need to be charged. _____

30. Circle the correct answer.

    a. Could you **do / make** me a favor, please?

    b. Try not to **do / make** any more mistakes.

    c. We need to **do / make** a final decision.

31. Circle the correct answer.

    a. What are you **saying / telling / talking** about?

    b. Bonnie **said / told / talked** the truth.

32. Fill in the proper word.

    a.   What does ASAP stand _____?

    b.   What letter does your first name start _____?

Placement Test: Advanced Grammar 摸底测试：高级语法

1.   Respond using **We don't know**.

    a.   Do you know who did it? _____

    b.   Do you know who makes them? _____

    c.   Do you know who will take care of it? _____

2.   Convert from a statement to a question.

    a.   He did it.   What _____

    b.   They will buy that.   What _____

    c.   He did it there.   Where _____

    d.   He did it then.   When _____

    e.   He did it quickly.   How _____

    f.   She paints beautifully.   How _____

3.   Respond using **I'm not sure if**.

    a.   Did he do it? _____

    b.   Do we need one? _____

4.   Convert to a reported statement using **I thought that**.

    a.   He does it. _____

    b.   She will buy one. _____

    c.   We are trying our hardest. _____

5.   Circle the correct answer.

    a.   It's 20 degrees out! You **will be / must be** freezing!

    b.   He has a slight fever. He **will be / may be** getting sick.

    c.   There's a slight possibility that he **will be / could be** telling the truth this time.

    d.   I am required to do this tonight. It **will be / has to be** finished tonight.

    e.   **May / Will** I sit here? Do I have your permission?

    f.   He is very strong. He **can / may** lift 300 pounds.

    g.   I have a cold. I **should / will be** go to bed early tonight.

    h.   I hope **to see / seeing / see** you later.

    i.   How can we avoid **to go / going / go** to that meeting?

    j.   Did he **to manage / managing / manage** to figure it out?

    k.   She promised **to give / giving / give** it careful consideration.

    l.   The landlord asked the tenant **to keep / keeping / keep** the noise down.

    m.   Do you plan on **to go / going / go** on the field trip?

    n.   They refused **to tell / telling / tell** us what happened.

    o.   Everyone insisted on **to leave / leaving / leave** early.

    p.   Did anyone see him **to take / take / taking** the folder?

    q.   You have to let him **to try / trying / try**.

    r.   I didn't **look / see** him at work today.

    s.   Could you **look / see** at this proposal, please?

    t.   Can you **hear / listen** the birds singing?

    u.   We need to **hear / listen** carefully in order to understand everything.

    v.   He's the person **who / whose / that / what** wrote the report.

    w.   That's the idea **who / whose / that / what** changed everyone's way of thinking.

    x.   I'm not sure **who / whose / that / what** idea that was.

    y.   This thing is not **who / whose / that / what** I wanted!

    z.   I hope it **will / is / was / were** work out.

    aa. I wish it **will / is / was / were** possible.

    bb. If there **is / were / had been** time right now, we would take care of it.

    cc. If there **is / were / had been** time tomorrow, we will take care of it.

    dd. If there **is / were / had been** time yesterday, we would have taken care of it.

    ee. You **should be / should have been** there yesterday.

    ff. When I was young, I **could dance / could have danced** really well.

    gg. I'm sorry you had to walk. You **could call / could have called** me.

6.   Fill in the proper tag ending.

    a.   We have to finish quickly, _____?

    b.   They had to redo it, _____?

    c.   She has been there before, _____?

    d.   They had never acted like that before, _____?

    e.   The school will be closed Thursday, _____?

    f.   She has good grades, _____?

    g.   He had better think about it, _____?

    h.   They'd rather play, _____?

7.   Select the proper answer.

    a.   He enlisted in the army two years **for / ago / in**.

    b.   He's been in the army **for / ago / in** two years now.

    c.   He'll be getting out **for / ago / in** a couple of days.

    d.   They thought it over **during / while** the meeting.

    e.   We chatted amiably **during / while** the intermission.

    f.   **During / While** you're up, could you get me a glass of water?

    g.   What do you do **during / while** the day?

    h.   It's not safe to talk on the phone **during / while** driving.

    i.   We plan on working **by / until** 10:00.

    j.   We need to start **by / until** 7:00.

    k.   They have worked here **for / since** ten years.

    l.   They have been here **for / since** 2001.

    m. Let me call you back **in / after** a couple of minutes, OK?

    n.   He had to take another call, but called me back **in / after** a few minutes.

    o.   Have you finished **yet / already / still / any more**?

    p.   They have **yet / already / still / any more** finished.

    q.   The others are **yet / already / still / any more** working on it.

    r.   We don't want to do this **yet / already / still / any more**.

8.   Fill in the blank using the proper form of **to / for / of / about / on / with / from**.

    a.   Did they have a good reason _____ their actions?

b. Have you decided _____ a strategy?

c. I hope you don't object _____ this schedule change.

d. The new employee really reminds me _____ my cousin.

e. They insisted _____ doing it a particular way.

f. We just don't have time to deal _____ this right now!

g. Did you happen _____ find out who will be there?

h. Many people prefer _____ skip breakfast.

9. Convert to the present real duo.

Example: I **watch** TV. I **have watched** TV.

a. They do the dishes. _____

b. Things fall in earthquakes. _____

c. The situation gets better. _____

d. The competitors bring their own gear. _____.

e. Everyone saw that movie. _____

f. The students learned the lessons. _____

g. The CEO was thinking about it. _____

h. Many people forgot the answer. _____

10. Circle the correct answer.

a. He **thought / has thought** about it many times before today.

b. Jennie **bought / has bought** it two years ago.

c. I **never saw / have never seen** such a thing in my life.

d. Do you think he **did / has done** his homework yet?

e. I think he **already went / has already gone** home.

f. He **thinks / has thought** about it for years.

g. We **need / have needed** to start studying for quite some time now.

h. Jennie **lived / has lived** there in 1968.

i. Jennie **lived / has lived** there since 1968.

11. Fill in where the **blue text** should appear in the sentence.

a. _____ they _____ do _____ it _____. **perfectly**

b. _____ they _____ do _____ it _____. **usually**

c. _____ they _____ do _____ it _____. **here**

d. _____ they _____ do _____ it _____. **at night**

e. _____ they _____ do _____ it _____. **definitely**

12. Circle the correct answer.

a. The boy wanted to buy the toy, but his mother wouldn't **let / make** him.

b. My coworker needed the day off, but our boss wouldn't **let / allow** him to leave.

c. Our schedule didn't **let / permit** us to take unplanned vacations.

d. I **let / had / made** my hair cut yesterday.

e. We're trying to **make / get** him change his mind.

f. It's hard to **make / get** him to change in any way, shape or form.

g. That man **looks / sees** just like George Clooney!

h. I love that song; it **sounds / hears** like Liza Minelli.

i. This is so soft, it **touches / feels** like silk.

13. Convert to an active statement. Do not use contractions or pronouns.

    Example: It was chosen by Edward. Edward chose it.

    a. The pyramids were built by the ancient Egyptians. _____

    b. Our friends were stunned by the accusation. _____

    c. The colors were selected by the design committee. _____

    d. Your ideas will be presented by a professional speaker.

        _____

14. Circle the correct answer.

    a. Our friends **are / have always been** very supportive throughout the years.

    b. The press **has reported / had reported** on the story before that article, but this time they gave more details.

    c. I hope we **have thought this through / will have really thought this through** before we finalize the decision.

    d. If they had been more thorough, they **wouldn't miss / wouldn't have missed** that report.

    e. If our campaign is successful, we **would all be promoted / will all be promoted.**

    f. If Lewis were in charge, we **will / would have** more fun at the office.

    g. I **would definitely take / will definitely take** care of that tomorrow.

    h. If you **let / had let** me borrow it, I'll be sure to return it by tomorrow.

    i. If it weren't raining, **we'd walk / we'll walk**.

    j. If it hadn't been raining last week, **we would've walked / we will've walked**.

DICTATION

Placement Test: Dictation 摸底测试：听写

There is a 30-second audio clip on the CD, Track 006. Write down what you hear. The time limit is seven minutes.

_____
_____
_____
_____
_____
_____
_____
_____
_____
_____
_____
_____
_____
_____
_____

ESSAY

Placement Test: Writing Sample 摸底测试：写作

Now, let's establish your writing level.
Write a short essay about yourself.

_____
_____
_____
_____
_____
_____
_____
_____
_____
_____
_____
_____
_____
_____

The **Vowel Chart** on page 11 covers the vowels and diphthongs. Here, you can see the consonants and blends.

第11页上的元音表包含了所有的元音和双元音。在下面的图表中，你可以看到辅音和混合辅音。

Consonant Chart
辅音表

Unvoiced	Voiced
p	b
t	d
f	v
k	g
s	z
ch	j
sh	zh
th	th
h	
	l
	r
	m
	n
	ng
	y
	w

The columns are labeled *unvoiced* and *voiced*. What does that mean?

以上两栏的标题分别为清音和浊音。它们是什么意思呢？

Put your thumb and index fingers on your throat and buzz like a bee, zzzzzzzzzzz. You will feel a vibration from your throat in your fingers.

把你的大拇指和食指放在喉咙处，并像蜜蜂一样发出zzzzzzzzzzz的音。这时，你的手指会感到从喉咙处传来的震动。

If you whisper that same sound, or hiss like a snake, you end up with sssssssssssss. You will feel that your fingers don't vibrate.

如果你轻声地说同样的声音，或者像蛇一样发出嘶嘶声，你实际发出的就是sssssssssssss的音。这时，你的手指就不会感到有震动。

This means that Z is a voiced sound and S is unvoiced.

这里的意思就是：Z是浊音，S是清音。

Telephone Tutoring
电话指导

Preliminary Diagnostic Analysis 初步诊断分析

The preliminary diagnostic is part of a comprehensive analysis to determine your language skills in grammar, vocabulary, writing, comprehension, accent, and pronunciation. If you are studying this book on your own, please contact us toll-free at (**001**) **800-457-4255** or **AmericanAccent.com** for a referral to a qualified telephone analyst. The analysis is designed to let you know where your English is standard and non-standard.

初步诊断是语言技能综合分析的一部分，它可以帮助判定你在语法、词汇、写作、理解、口音、发音等方面的水平。如果你正在自学本书，在中国大陆请拨打001-800-457-4255，在美国本土请直接拨打800-457-4255，或者登录网址AmericanAccent.com来找一位合格的电话分析员。此次分析可以让你知道自己的英语哪里标准，哪里不标准。

Read the following groups of words out loud.
请大声朗读以下不同组别的单词。

1. all, long, caught	5. ice, I'll, sky	9. come, front, indicate	13. out, house, round
2. cat, matter, laugh	6. it, milk, sin	10. smooth, too, shoe	14. boy, oil, toy
3. take, say, fail	7. eat, me, seen	11. took, full, would	
4. get, egg, any	8. work, girl, bird	12. told, so, roll	

A	B	C	D	E	F
1. pin	1. bin	1. wrapping	1. grabbing	1. rip	1. rib
2. fat	2. vat	2. refers	2. reverse	2. half	2. have
3. sip	3. zip	3. doses	3. dozes	3. face	3. phase
4. she	4. den	4. you should	4. usual	4. bash	4. beige
5. ten	5. joke	5. petal	5. peddle	5. not	5. nod
6. choke	6. that	6. etcher	6. edger	6. etch	6. edge
7. think	7. gold	7. with her	7. wither	7. bath	7. bathe
8. cold	8. rip	8. locking	8. logging	8. lack	8. lag
9. yes	9. brain	9. mayor	9. correction	9. day	9. car
10. would	10. me	10. coward	10. prayed	10. how	10. temper
11. his	11. knee	11. reheat	11. dimmer	11. call	11. them
12. lip		12. collection	12. dinner	12. temple	12. then
13. plain		13. played	13. ringing		13. thing

1. Get a better water heater.	1. Try it again.
2. Gedda bedder wader heeder.	2. Put it on.
3. Italian Italy	3. It's not a bus.
4. attack attic	
5. atomic atom	1. Tryida gen.
6. photography photograph	2. Pudidan.
7. let led	3. Its nada bus.

Chapter 1
第一章

Simple Nouns and Verbs
简单的名词和动词

In this chapter, you will learn singular and plural nouns using the present tense of the verb **to be**, pronouns, contractions, negatives, questions, time words, word order and story order, and the basics of intonation and pronunciation.

在本章中，你将要学习以下内容：使用be动词现在时的单复数名词、代词、缩略式、否定式、疑问句、表时间的词、词序、故事顺序，以及最基本的语音语调。

DICTATION | Let's find out exactly what you hear at this point. There are five sentences on the CD. Listen to each one several times and write what you hear. Even if you are more advanced, this is a good exercise to establish a benchmark for your current level.

让我们看看在这里你将听到些什么。CD上有五个句子，每个句子各听几遍后请把听到的内容写下来。即使你的英语水平很高，这个练习也很不错，它可以为你当前的水平确立一个基准。

Exercise 1-1: Dictation   Track 007

Listen to the audio and write the exact transcription in the spaces below. When you're done, check the Answer Key, beginning on page 307.

1. _____
2. _____
3. _____
4. _____
5. _____

Now that you have taken the grammar placement tests on page 13 and completed the initial dictation and essay on page 20, you are ready to start with a simple story.

既然你已经做完了第13页上的语法摸底测试，以及第20页上的第一个听写和写作测试，那你就可以学习下面这个简单的故事了。

STORY | Our story starts in a very basic way. We will use just nine words to tell the entire story. This nine-grid is the most basic structure in English.

我们的故事用最基本的方式开始讲起。只要用九个单词，我们就可以把整个故事讲完。九宫格在英语中是最基本的结构。

Each sentence has three parts—noun, verb, noun.
每个句子都有三个部分——名词、动词、名词。

Each story has three parts—introduction, body, conclusion.
每个故事都有三个部分——开头、主体、结尾。

Later, you will learn different structures, but if you master this form, you will always be able to communicate clearly, both in speech and in writing.
后面你还会学习其他不同的结构，但只要你掌握了这种形式，你就总能清楚明白地与人交流，不管是口语还是书面语。

One of the most important things to do when listening to a story is to ask questions. Memorize these forms:
当你在听故事的时候，有一件事情非常重要，那就是提问。记住以下形式：

What does _____ mean?
What is a _____?
I don't know what a _____ is.
I don't know what that means.
How do you say _____ in English?
Excuse me, could you say that again, please?

Exercise 1-2: Telling a Story — Introduction   Track 008

Listen to the audio and repeat the basic nine-word story five times out loud.

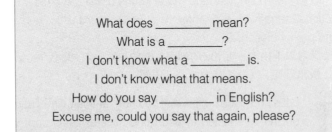

Next, we are going to practice this simple story in eight different ways: vocabulary, grammar, word order, story order, phrasing, intonation, word connections, and pronunciation.
接下来，我们要用八种不同的方式来练习这个简单的故事：词汇、语法、词序、故事顺序、语调、声调、单词连读以及发音。

It's important to ask questions in order to learn new vocabulary. What does **meet** mean? What's a **boy**?
在学习新单词的时候，提问很重要。meet是什么意思？boy指什么？

Exercise 1-3: Telling a Story — Vocabulary

Look up and learn the following words.

boy, girl, meets, loses, gets

24

Exercise 1-4: Telling a Story — Grammar

Memorize the parts of speech.

Boy and **girl** are nouns; **meets**, **loses**, and **gets** are verbs.

Exercise 1-5: Telling a Story — Word Order   Track 009

Listen to the audio and repeat the story five times out loud, focusing on word order.

The word order starts with the *subject* (**boy**), ends with the *object* (**girl**), and is linked with the *verb* (**meets**, **loses**, **gets**).

这里的词序是这样的：以主语(boy)开头，以宾语(girl)结尾，而这两部分又由动词(meets, loses, gets)连接起来。

Every Hollywood Movie!

	Noun	Verb	Noun
Beginning	Boy	meets	girl.
Middle	Boy	loses	girl.
End	Boy	gets	girl.

Exercise 1-6: Telling a Story — Story Order   Track 010

Listen to the audio and repeat the story five times out loud, focusing on story order.

The story order *starts* with the meeting, *changes* in the middle with the loss, and *ends up* with the happy couple.

这里的故事顺序如下：开始是两人相见，中间因为失去而发生变化，最后以幸福的一对结尾。

	Subject	Verb	Object
Intro	Boy	meets	girl.
Body	Boy	loses	girl.
Conclusion	Boy	gets	girl.

When you have a noun-verb-noun sentence, the nouns are stronger than the rest of the words. There is more emphasis on the words **boy** and **girl**. In the second sentence, you have already been introduced to the boy and the girl, so you need to indicate the *contrast* by stressing the verb. Use the staircase intonation for this.

在结构为"名词—动词—名词"的句子中，名词要比其他单词更重要。这里，boy和girl被强调得更多。在第二个句子中，因为你已经认识了这个男孩和女孩，所以你需要重读动词来强调所发生的变化。请使用阶梯状声调进行练习。

Exercise 1-7: Intonation

Listen to the audio and repeat out loud five times. Focus on correct intonation.

	Subject	Verb	Object
Intro	Boy	meets	girl.
Body	Boy	loses	girl.
Conclusion	Boy	gets	girl.

Boy

meets

girl.

Notice the arrows to the right of the box in Exercise 1-8. These indicate the tone of your voice, so you can tell that the first two sentences are not the end of the story.

请注意Exercise 1-8中表格右边的箭头。箭头指示了你应使用的语调，这样你就能判断出前两个句子并不是故事的结尾。

Exercise 1-8: Phrasing

Listen carefully to the audio and repeat out loud five times. Notice the arrows indicating the phrasing.

Boy	meets	girl.
Boy	loses	girl.
Boy	gets	girl.

Exercise 1-9: Pronunciation Intro

ACCENT

Listen to the audio and repeat the sounds out loud five times. These five sounds will be used every time you speak.

æ	ä	ə	r	th
cat	caught	cut	car	the
bat	bought	but	water	this
hat	want	what	her	these
last	lost	lump	real	then
sat	saw	such	roar	they
that	thought	thus	rather	there

Exercise 1-10: Pronunciation

Listen to the audio and repeat out loud five times. Focus on the pronunciation.

Boy	meets	grrrl.
Boy	luz'z	grrrl.
Boy	gets	grrrl.

The three pronunciation points are **meets**, **loses**, and **girl**. Make a clear ee sound in **meets**, so it doesn't sound like **mitts**. The two S's in **loses** have a Z sound. The R should be a clear, throaty sound.

三个发音点分别是：meets，loses，girl。在读meets的时候，ee的声音要发清楚，这样听起来才不会像mitts（拳击手套）。单词loses中的两个s有Z的音。girl中的R音应该是清晰的喉音。

Note: In this book, you will see three symbols used interchangeably— *, ', ə. This is a soft vowel sound that you can almost skip over—poss*ble, poss'ble, possəble.

注意：在本书中，你会看到三个可以交替使用的符号—— *，'，ə。它们都代表一个几乎可以跳过的轻元音——poss*ble，poss'ble，possəble。

Word Connections
单词连读

Word connections, or word flow, are an important aspect of clear communication. In writing, there is a little white space between each word, but these disappear in fluent speech.

想要用英语实现顺畅的交流，学会连读就非常重要。在书面英语中，每个单词之间都有一点白色的间空，但在流利的口语中它们就消失了。

Exercise 1-11: Word Connections   Track 015

Listen to the audio and repeat the text on the right out loud five times. Focus on letting the words run together. Yes, it looks strange, but trust the phonetics!

Looks like...			Sounds like...		
Bob	opens	**an envelope.**	**Bää**	bopən	zə**nänvəlop.**
Bob	**drops**	the envelope.	Bääb	**dräps**	thee⁽ʸ⁾envəlop.
Bob	gets	**angry.**	Bääb	gets	**sængry.**

Here is a quick overview of the main rules of word connections.
下面总结了单词连读的主要规则。

Final Consonant + Initial Vowel	**Jum**p **o**ver sounds like ju**m p**over.
T + Y = Ch D + Y = J	Di**d y**ou pu**t y**our **car away?** Di**d j**u pu**ch**er **car away?**
Y & W Connectors Between Vowels	**He opens** > he⁽ʸ⁾**opens** **Go away** > go⁽ʷ⁾**away**

Once you are fully comfortable with the basic nine-grid and can imitate it perfectly, you are ready to go on to two classic stories: *Goldilocks and the Three Bears* and *Sleeping Beauty*.

一旦你完全适应了这个基本的九宫格，并且能很好地模仿它，那么你就可以开始学习这两个经典故事了：《金发姑娘和三只熊》与《睡美人》。

Exercise 1-12: "Goldilocks"— Intonation and Phrasing   Track 016

Listen to the audio and repeat the story. Notice the intonation of new information and phrasing.

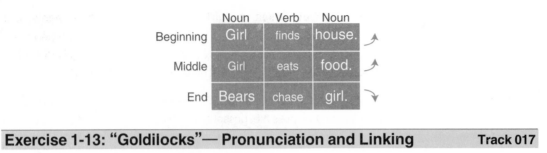

	Noun	Verb	Noun	
Beginning	Girl	finds	house.	↗
Middle	Girl	eats	food.	↗
End	Bears	chase	girl.	↘

Exercise 1-13: "Goldilocks"— Pronunciation and Linking   Track 017

Listen to the audio and repeat the story. Focus on the pronunciation and linking the words.

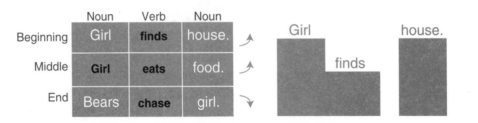

	Noun	Verb	Noun	
Beginning	Girl	**finds**	house.	↗
Middle	**Girl**	**eats**	food.	↗
End	Bears	**chase**	girl.	↘

Exercise 1-14: "Sleeping Beauty" — Intonation and Phrasing   Track 018

Listen to the audio and repeat the story. Notice the intonation of new information and phrasing.

	Subject	Verb	Object	
Introduction	Witch	enchants	girl.	↗
Body	Prince	wakes	girl.	↗
Conclusion	Girl	marries	prince.	↘

Exercise 1-15: "Sleeping Beauty" — Pronunciation and Linking   Track 019

Listen to the audio and repeat the story. Focus on the pronunciation and linking the words.

Wit	chenchants	grrrl.
Prints	wakes	grrrl.
Grrrl	merreez	prints.

Exercise 1-16: Your Own Story

*Using the nine-grid, write a short story with a **beginning**, **middle**, and **end**, also known as an **introduction**, **body**, and **conclusion**.*

	Noun	Verb	Noun
Introduction			
Body			
Conclusion			

Exercise 1-17: "Let's Meet Max" — Intonation   Track 020

Listen to the audio and repeat the story, focusing on intonation.

Max	comes	to America.
He	has	fun.
He	goes back	to Italy.

For pronunciation, listen for the æ sound in **Max**, **back**; the final Z sound in **comes**, **has**, **goes**; the neutral vowels in **come** and **America**(kəm and əmerəkə); and the T in **Italy** that sounds like a D (idəly). An easy rule to remember is if you change the T to D, then the next vowel will be the schwa (or ə). For word connections, put the W connector in **to⁽ʷ⁾America** and the Y connector in **he has**. This can either be **he⁽ʸ⁾haz**, or **he⁽ʸ⁾az** if you speak quickly and drop the H.

听录音时，请特别注意以下发音：Max和back中的æ音；comes, has, goes结尾处的Z音；come和America(kəm and əmerəkə)中的中性元音；Italy中那个听起来像D(idəly)的T。请记住这一简单规则，即如果你把T读成了D，那么T后面的元音就是非重读央元音(或ə)。在单词连读时，要把连接音W放入to和America之间，即变成to⁽ʷ⁾America，并把连接音Y放进he和has之间。后者既可以读作he⁽ʸ⁾haz，也可以读成he⁽ʸ⁾az，后一种情况属于读得太快时省掉了H音。

Exercise 1-18: "Let's Meet Max" — Pronunciation and Linking   Track 021

*Listen to the audio and repeat the story, focusing on pronunciation and word connections. Notice that the H in **has** is dropped.*

Mæx	kəmz	to⁽ʷ⁾ əmerəkə.
Hee	⁽ʸ⁾æz	fən.
Hee	goz bæk	tə idəly.

Exercise 1-19: Your Own Stories

Using the nine-grid, write two short stories with a beginning, middle, and end. You can start adding simple words to complete the sentences.

	Noun	Verb	Noun
Beginning			
Middle			
End			

	Subject	Verb	Object
Introduction			
Body			
Conclusion			

NOUNS

This section tells about *nouns* and how to change them to *pronouns*. A noun is a person, place, or thing. Nouns can usually be represented with a picture. In the nine-grid story, the first and last word of the first sentence is a noun. You will also work with the basic modifiers (*a, the, this, that, these, those, some, many, most, all, my, your, his, her, our,* numbers, etc.).

本部分讲解名词以及如何把名词变成代词。名词可以表示人、地方、事物。名词通常可以用图画来表现。在前面的九宫格故事里，第一句话的第一个和最后一个单词都是名词。你还要学着使用最基本的修饰语(a, the, this, that, these, those, some, many, most, all, my, your, his, her, our 以及数字等等)。

Nouns Are Things

A Person　　　　　　**A Place**　　　　　　**A Thing**

A or *An*

Exercise 1-20: *A* or *An*

Use **a** or **an** for general words or for introducing a noun. **An** is used before a vowel. When you're done, check the Answer Key.

This is _____ bike.　　　　　　This is **a** bike.

This is _____ apple.　　　　　　This is **an** apple.

1. Here is _____ car.
2. There is _____ egg.
3. _____ dog is _____ animal.
4. Sam is _____ honest man.
5. It is _____ nice day today.

Plural Rule: Add an S
复数形式的规则：加S

The nice thing about English is that, generally, you just add an S to indicate that there is more than one thing. These are called *plurals*.

英语有一个非常好的特点，通常你只要在名词后面加上一个S就可以表示数量大于1。这些加了S的名词就叫做复数。

a ♥
2 ♥s

There are a few exceptions to the -s rule.

加-s的规则也有一些例外。

Common Irregular Plurals			
Singular	**Plural**	**Singular**	**Plural**
man	men	foot	feet
woman	women	tooth	teeth
child	children	mouse	mice
person	people	knife	knives

Woman is pronounced **wüm'n** and **women** is **wimmen**.

Woman读作wüm'n，而women读作wimmen。

Pronunciation of the Final S
S在单词末尾的读音

The final S sounds like a Z. **Dogs** sounds like **dogz**.

单词末尾的S通常发Z音。比如，dogs就读作dogz。

Even if you put a Z at the end of a word that ends in a T, K, P, or F, it will still sound like the proper S sound: **eatz**, **lookz**, **popz**, **laughz**.

在以T、K、P、F结尾的单词后面加S要念S音，就算你读的是Z音，听起来照样像S音：eatz, lookz, popz, laughz。

If the word ends in S, SS, SH, ZH, CH, X, Z, J, or O, add **-es**. It will sound like əz.

如果单词以S、SS、SH、ZH、CH、X、Z、J或O结尾，那就要加-es，并读作əz。

If the word ends in Y, the Y changes to I, and you add **-es** (**party/parties**).

如果单词以Y结尾，就要先把Y变成I，然后再加上-es（party/parties）。

Note: This does not apply for **-ey**, or **-ay**, or **-oy** words, such as **key**, **play**, or **toy**.

注意：这一规则不适用于以-ey、-ay或-oy结尾的单词，比如key, play, toy。

Z	əz
reads	buses
sags	misses
rubs	sauces
saves	roses
rows	buzzes
calls	dishes
hums	watches
sins	boxes
sins	judges
	garages

All final vowels are followed by the Z sound:

sees=seez

New or General Things
新事物或一般事物

A and **one** are similar, but **a** is much more commonly used. **One** is very specific and is used with other numbers: one book, two books. The plural of **a** or **one** is **some**. **Some** is one of several common words that can be added before the plural noun: **some** things, **all** things, **two** things, **many** things. Let's look at some of them.

a和one差不多，但a使用得更加广泛。one的指示意思非常具体，并且常和其他数字一起连用，比如：one book, two books。a或one的复数形式是some。some可以用来修饰复数名词，几个经常用来修饰复数名词的单词如下：some things, all things, two things, many things。

Exercise 1-21: A Thing, Two Things Track 022

Listen to the audio and repeat the phrases.

Singular	Plural
a dog	some dogs
one dog	three dogs
a book	some books
a hat	some hats
a dish	all dishes
one watch	two watches
one car	three cars
a person	some people

Exercise 1-22: A Thing, Two Things — Intonation / Pronunciation Track 023

Listen to the audio and repeat the phrases, stressing the nouns and focusing on the pronunciation.

Singular		Plural	
a dog	ə **däg**	some dogs	səm **dägz**
one dog	wən **däg**	three dogs	three **dägz**
a book	ə **bük**	some books	səm **büks**
a hat	ə **hæt**	some hats	səm **hæts**
a dish	ə **d'sh**	all dishes	äll **d'shez**
one watch	wən **wätch**	two watches	too **wätchez**
one car	wən **cär**	three cars	three **cärz**
a person	ə **prsən**	some people	səm **peepəl**

Exercise 1-23: A Thing, Two Things — Plurals Track 024

Make these plural by adding a final S in the spaces. Some sound like S, some sound like Z.

		Pronunciation			Pronunciation
1. a chair	two chair**s**	too chairz	6. a pill	two pill__	too pillz
2. an egg	two egg__	too (w)eggz	7. a lamp	two lamp__	too læmps
3. a day	two day__	too dayz	8. a hair	two hair__	too hehrz
4. a week	two week__	too weeks	9. a letter	two letter__	too ledderz
5. a desk	two desk__	too desks	10. a pencil	two pencil__	too pens'lz

Rule: No Naked Nouns
规则：名词不存在单独使用的情况

You almost always need a word before the noun in English, such as *a book,* **my** *book,* **this** *book.* If someone says, **I want book** or **Book is good**, he sounds like a caveman. This is the No-Naked-Nouns Rule. Remember, the first time use **a**, the second time use **the**. Both sound like ə.

在英语中，你几乎总要在名词前再加一个词，如：**a** book，**my** book，**this** book。如果有人说I want book或者Book is good，那他听起来就好像是山顶洞人。这就是"不单独使用名词"准则。记住，第一次出现的名词用a，第二次出现的用the，且两者的发音都像ə。

Already Known Things
已知事物

You can use **the** with both singular and plural nouns. Remember to add **-s** to the plural noun.

在单、复数名词前都可以使用the。

请记得在复数名词后面加-s。

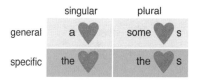

	singular	plural
general	a ♥	some ♥ s
specific	the ♥	the ♥ s

A/An and *The*

Exercise 1-24: *A/An* or *The*

---

*Use **the** for specific or unique words, or when the noun has already been introduced. When you're done, check the Answer Key.*

1. The sun is bright.
2. He is _a_ doctor.
3. Where is _the_ kitchen?
4. It is _a_ falling star.
5. There is _a_ mistake here.

6. _The /A_ car is expensive.
7. Where is _the /a_ bathroom?
8. Is this _a_ mistake?
9. He is _a_ president. _the_
10. She is _a_ child.

This and *That*

This and **these** are close by you, and **that** and **those** are farther from you.

this和these指离你近的事物，而that和those指离你远的事物。

This and **that** are singular, and **these** and **those** are plural.

this和that是单数形式，而these和those则是复数形式。

	near	far
singular	this	that
plural	these	those

Exercise 1-25: This Thing, These Things   Track 025

Listen to the audio and repeat the phrases.

Singular	Plural
the **dog**	the **dogs**
this **dog**	these **dogs**
that **dog**	those **dogs**
the **book**	the **books**
the **hat**	the **hats**
the **dish**	the **dishes**
this **watch**	these **watches**
that **car**	those **cars**

Exercise 1-26: This Thing, These Things — Pronunciation   Track 026

ACCENT

*Listen to the audio and repeat the phrases, stressing the nouns and focusing on the pronunciation, particularly the beginning **Th** sound. Make sure the tip of the tongue is pressed against the back of your top teeth.*

Singular		Plural	
the dog	thə **däg**	the dogs	thə **dägz**
this dog	th's **däg**	these dogs	theez **dägz**
that dog	thæt **däg**	those dogs	thoz **dägz**
the book	thə **bük**	the books	thə **büks**
the hat	thə **hæt**	the hats	thə **hæts**
the dish	thə **d'sh**	the dishes	thə **d'shəz**
this watch	th's **wätch**	these watches	theez **wätchəz**
that car	thæt **cär**	those cars	thoz **cärz**

Exercise 1-27: *Here* or *There*

Fill in the blank with **this**, **that**, **these**, **those**. Then check the Answer Key.

1. This car is near me.
2. That car is over there.
3. These cars are near me.
4. Those cars are over there.
5. These dogs are close to us.
6. Those books are near you.
7. Those books are far from you.
8. These shoes are near you.
9. Those shoes are far from you.
10. That dog is not close to us.

Phrasing
语调

As you know, phrasing gives you important information. When you use a rising tone at the end of a sentence, you are asking a question. When you use a falling tone, you are making a statement.

众所周知，语调可以传递很重要的信息。当你在句尾使用升调时，说明你在提问。当你在句尾使用降调时，说明你在陈述。

Exercise 1-28: Asking Questions   Track 027

Listen to the audio and notice how a statement sounds different from a question. Notice the arrows.

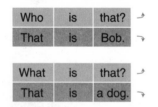

Exercise 1-29: Asking Questions

Put a check mark by the correct answer to each question. Then check the Answer Key.

1. Who is that? 　　　☐ This is Ed.　　　■ That is Ed.
　　　　　　　　　　☐ These are Ed.　　☐ Those are Ed.

2. What is this?　　　☐ This is a garden.　☐ That is a garden.
　　　　　　　　　　☐ These are gardens.　☐ Those are gardens.

34

3.	What are those?	☐ This is a paper clip.	☐ That is a paper clip.
		☐ These are paper clips.	☐ Those are paper clips.
4.	Who are they?	☐ This person is a man.	☐ That person is a man.
		☐ These people are men.	☐ Those people are men.
5.	What is that?	☐ This is a donut.	☐ That is a donut.
		☐ These are donuts.	☐ Those are donuts.
6.	What are these?	☐ This is a coffee cup.	☐ That is a coffee cup.
		☐ These are coffee cups.	☐ Those are coffee cups.
7.	Who is this?	☐ This is my friend.	☐ That is my friend.
		☐ These are my friends.	☐ Those are my friends.
8.	What is this thing?	☐ This is a teapot.	☐ That is a teapot.
		☐ These are teapots.	☐ Those are teapots.
9.	Who are these people?	☐ This is a cowboy.	☐ That is a cowboy.
		☐ These are cowboys.	☐ Those are cowboys.
10.	Who are those people?	☐ This is a teacher.	☐ That is a teacher.
		☐ These are teachers.	☐ Those are teachers.

The first time you mention something, use a *noun*. Then, once the topic is known, replace it with a *pronoun*.

当你首次提到某物时，要使用名词。然后，一旦谈论的主题成了已知信息，就用代词替换名词。

Nouns at the beginning of the sentence are called *subject* nouns. After the verb, they are called *object* nouns. Object pronouns are slightly different from subject pronouns.

位于句子开头的名词叫做主语名词，放在动词后面的则叫做宾语名词。宾格代词和主格代词有一些细微的差别。

Exercise 1-30: Replacing Nouns at the Beginning of a Sentence   Track 028

*Listen to the audio and notice the word order. The **pronoun** is not stressed.*

noun	Tom	is a doctor.
pronoun	He	is very kind.

Pronouns at the beginning of a sentence:

	singular	plural
1st person	I	we
2nd person	you	you
3rd person	he she it	they

Exercise 1-31: Replacing Subject Nouns with Pronouns

*Fill in the blank with the proper pronoun: **I**, **you**, **he**, **she**, **it**, **we**, **they**. Note that the boldface words are stressed. When you're done, check the Answer Key.*

	Nouns	Pronouns	
	My father	**He**	is in the car.
1.	Ben and **Bill**	*They*	are at the **library**.
2.	**Jenny**	*She*	is reading a **book**.
3.	Bill and **Mark**	*They*	are planning a **party**.
4.	Betty and **Jan**	*They*	are **tourists**.
5.	My **friends** and I	*We*	are at **home**.
6.	Those **cars**	*They*	are too **expensive**.
7.	You and your **cousins**	*You*	are in **France**.
8.	This **cheese**	*It*	is **delicious**.
9.	Our **city**	*It*	is **crowded**. (many people)
10.	**Jasmine**	*She*	is not at **home**.

Exercise 1-32: Replacing Subject Nouns with Pronouns — Pronunciation
Track 029

ACCENT	*Listen to the audio and repeat five times. This is how Exercise 1-31 should sound. Focus on the intonation, word connections, and pronunciation. Remember that ə is pronounced **uh**.*

	Nouns	Pronouns
1.	Benen **Bill**er ət thə **librery**.	Therət thə **librery**.
2.	**Jenny**iz reading ə **bük**.	Sheez reading ə **bük**.
3.	Billen **Mark**er plænning ə **pardy**.	Ther plænning ə **pardy**.
4.	Beddyan **Jænn**er turists.	Ther turists.
5.	My **friend** zanäi arət **home**.	Wirət **home**.
6.	Thoz **cärz**er too⁽ʷ⁾**eksspensive**.	Ther too⁽ʷ⁾ **eksspensive**.
7.	Youan yer **cuzin** zerin **Frænce**.	Yerin **Frænce**.
8.	This **cheez**iz dəlishəs.	Its dəlishəs.
9.	Ar **cidy** iz **crowded**.	Its **crowded**.
10.	**Jæzmin**iz nädət **home**.	Sheez nädət **home**.

Exercise 1-33: Replacing Nouns at the End of a Sentence
Track 030

Listen to the audio and notice the unstressed pronoun.

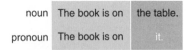

noun	The book is on	the table.
pronoun	The book is on	it.

Pronouns at the **end** of a sentence:

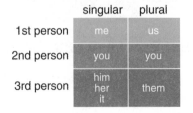

	singular	plural
1st person	me	us
2nd person	you	you
3rd person	him her it	them

Exercise 1-34: Replacing Object Nouns with Pronouns

Fill in the blank with the proper pronoun: **me**, **you**, **him**, **her**, **it**, **us**, **them**. *The boldface words are stressed. Then check the Answer Key.*

		Noun	Pronoun
	The doctor is in	her office.	it
1.	The **news**papers are on	the **table.**	*it*
2.	The women's **shoes** are on	their **feet.**	*them*
3.	This **package** is for	Mr. **Jones.**	*him*
4.	That **letter** is for	my **mom.**	*her*
5.	**Joe** is sitting next to	Mr. and Mrs. **Wilson.**	*Them*
6.	Sam is **reading** to	my **sister** and me.	*us*
7.	The **call** is for	you and your **friends.**	*you*
8.	This **story** is about	you and **me.**	*us*
9.	My **car** is in	the **garage.**	*it*
10.	Her **brothers** are in	**school.**	*it*

Exercise 1-35: Replacing the Nouns with Pronouns — Pronunciation   Track 031

ACCENT

*Listen to the audio and repeat five times. Notice how the stress changes from the object noun to the verb. Notice that the **h** of **him** and **her**, and the **th** of **them** can be dropped.*

	Nouns	Pronouns
1.	th **nooz** paperzrän thə **table.**	thə **nooz** paper zerän it.
2.	thə wimmenz **shooz**erän ther **feet.**	thə wimmenz shoozer**än** em.
3.	th's **pækə**jiz fr mister **jonz.**	th's **pækə**jiz fr **him.**
4.	that **ledd**eriz fr my **mäm.**	that **ledd**erz fer **her.**
5.	**joz** sidding neks t' misteran miss'z **wil**s'n.	heez sidding **neks** too^(w)m.
6.	**sæm**iz reeding to my **sis**terən me.	sæmiz **reed**ing d^(w)s.
7.	the **cäll**iz fr you^(w)an yer **frenz.**	thə **cäll**iz fer **you.** (you guys)
8.	th's **story**izə bout you^(w)and **me.**	th's storyizə bow d**əs.**
9.	my **cär**zin thə gə**raj** (or gərazh or groj).	my cär**zin** it.
10.	her **brə**ther zerin **skool.**	her brəther ze**rin**it.

Earlier, we discussed that when you introduce a thing for the first time, you need to say "a thing." After you have mentioned it once, you say "the thing." There is another pattern to follow when you replace these words with pronouns. **A thing** turns into **one,** and **the thing** turns into **it.**

之前我们讲过，当你首次提到某物时要说"a thing"，而当你再次提起它的时候，就要说"the thing"。当你用代词替换这些词时，可以使用以下形式：用one替代a thing，用it替代the thing。

noun	subject pronoun	object pronoun	possessive modifier	possessive pronoun
Tom Mary the book	I you he she it we they	me you him her it us them one	my your his her its our their	mine yours his hers its ours theirs
the books a book				

Exercise 1-36: Replacing Nouns with Pronouns — *It* or *One*

Fill in the blank with the proper pronoun, it or one. The boldface words are stressed. Then check the Answer Key.

A	The
The man is near a store.	The man is near the door.
The man is near one.	The man is near it.

		Pronouns
Your friend is on	an airplane.	one
1. **My brother** is on	the **phone**.	it
2. **George** is near	a **window**.	one
3. **Joe** is far from	his **hotel**.	it
4. I am in a good	**mood**.	it one
5. This is a very expensive	**present**.	it one
6. Joe's brother and I are so happy to see	**your family**.	it
7. All of the **kids** are still in	the **pool**.	it
8. **Everyone** is talking about	his **idea**.	it
9. The **puppies** are in	a **pile**.	one
10. I have another	**problem**.	one

the first time	a	noun
the next time	the	noun

Exercise 1-37: Replacing Nouns with Pronouns — Pronunciation Track 032

ACCENT

Focus on the intonation, word connections, and pronunciation. Notice how the stress moves off the noun.

Nouns	Pronouns
1. My **brəther** izän thə **phone**.	My **brəther zän**it.
2. **Jorj**iz nir ə **window**.	Jorjiz **nir** wən.
3. **Joz** fär frəm thə hot**el**.	**Joz fär** frəmit.
4. I minnə güd **mood**.	I minnə **güd**wən.
5. Thisizə very expensive **prezənt**.	Thisizə very **expensive** wən.

6. Joz brəthr anai ər so hæppy t' see yer **family**!   Joz brəthr anai ər so hæppy t' **see**^(y)em!

Joz brəthr anai ər so hæppy t' **see**⁽ʸ⁾em!

7. Alləv thə **kid**zer stillin thə **pool**.   Alləv thə kidzer still**lin**it.
8. **Every**wəniz tähking əbow dhiz **ide**ə.   Everywəniz **tähk**ing əbow dit.
9. Thə **pəppee**zerin ə **pile**.   Thə pəppeezer**in** wən.
10. I hævə nəther **präblem**.   I hævə **nəther** wən.

Exercise 1-38: Replacing the Nouns

Rewrite each sentence, replacing all nouns with pronouns. The intonation is marked for you in bold. The stress moves to the verb in the new pronoun sentences. When you're done, check the Answer Key.

My sister is reading a book.   **She** is reading **one**.

1. Ben and **Bill** are in the **pool**.   They are in it
2. **Frank** is watching **TV**.   He is watching it
3. **Debbie** is near the **door**.   She is near it
4. The **bags** are on the **table**.   They are on it
5. **Jim** is holding a **pen**.   He is holding one
6. **Sam** is in a good **mood**.   He is in good one
7. The **dogs** are in the **house**.   They are in it
8. My **family** is in the **car**.   We/They are in it.
9. My **brother** and I are good **friends**.   We are good ones
10. You and your **cousins** are on a **break**.   You are on one
11. His **wallet** is in his back **pocket**.   It is in his back one
12. The **car** keys are in his **hand**.   They are in his ~~one~~ it
13. His **pen** is on the **floor**.   It is on it
14. The **cars** are in a different **garage**.   They are in a different one
15. Their **clothes** are in the **closet**.   They are in it

Exercise 1-39: Replacing the Nouns — Pronunciation   Track 033

ACCENT   *Listen and repeat.*

My **sisterz** reeding ə **bük**.   Sheez **reed**ing one.

1. Ben'n **Bill**er in thə **pool**.   Ther **in**it.
2. **Frænk**s wätching **TV**.   Heez **wät**ching it.
3. **Debbee**ez nir thə **door**.   Sheez **nir**it.
4. Thə **bægz**er än thə **tay-bəl**.   Ther **än**nit.
5. **J'm**z holding ə **pen**.   Heez **holding** one.
6. **Sæm**zinə a güd **mood**.   Heez**in** one.
7. The **däg**zerin thə **house**.   Ther **in**nit.
8. My **fæmlee** zin thə **cär**.   Ther **in**nit.
9. My **brother** an aiyer güd **frenz**.   Wir **güd** wənz.

10. Yoo^(w)ən yer **cəzin**zer ännə brayk.   Yrr **än** wun.

11. His **wället**siniz bæck **päckət**.   Its **in**nit.

12. Th **cär** keezeriniz **hænd**.   Ther **in**nit.

13. Hiz **pen**zän thə **flor**.   Its **än**nit.

14. Thə **cär**zerinə different **gəräzh**.   Therinə **diff**rent one.

15. Ther **cloz**erin thə **cläzet**.   Ther **in**nit.

Possessive Pronouns
物主代词

We have looked at *subject* and *object* pronouns. These are words that replace the nouns at the *beginning* and the *end* of a sentence. Now, we will look at possessives. Possessives indicate that you own something, or that something belongs to a person. Let's start with the modifiers. They are the same at the beginning or the end of a sentence.

我们已经学过了主格代词和宾格代词，它们分别可以替换位于句首和句尾的名词。现在，让我们来学习物主代词。物主代词指你拥有某物，或者某物属于某人。让我们先从形容词性物主代词开始讲起吧，它们在句首和句尾的用法是一样的。

noun	subject pronoun	object pronoun	possessive modifier	possessive pronoun
	I	me	my	mine
	you	you	your	yours
Tom	he	him	his	his
Mary	she	her	her	hers
the book	it	it	its	its
	we	us	our	ours
the books	they	them	their	theirs

Exercise 1-40: Possessive Modifiers

Fill in the blank with the appropriate possessive modifier. Then check the Answer Key.

My sister is reading _____ book.   **She is reading her book.**

1. Ben and **Bill** are in _their_ **pool**.

2. **Frank** is watching _his_ **TV**.

3. **Debbie** is near _her_ front **door**.

4. _Her_ **keys** are in her **hand**.

5. **Jim** is holding _his_ **pen**.

6. **Sam** is in _his_ **room**.

7. _His_ **dogs** are in Joe's **house**.

8. My **family** is in _our_ **car**.

9. My **brother** and I are on _our_ **way**.

10. You and your **wife** are on _your_ **boat**.

11. His **wallet** is in _his_ back **pocket**.

12. My **car** keys are in _my_ **hand**.

13. _Her_ **pen** is on her **desk**.

14. The **car** is in _its_ usual **place**.

15. Their **clothes** are in _their_ **closet**.

Exercise 1-41: Possessive Pronouns

Fill in the blank with the appropriate possessive pronoun. Then check the Answer Key.

My sister is reading her book.　　　　It's **hers**.

1. That's their **pool**. ── It's ___theirs___.
2. It's his **TV**. ── It's ___his___.
3. It's her front **door**. ── It's ___hers___.
4. They're her **keys**. ── They're ___hers___.
5. It's his **pen**. ── It's ___his___.
6. It's his **room**. ── It's ___his___.
7. They're Joe's **dogs**. ── They're ___his___.
8. It's our **car**. ── It's ___ours___.
9. It's our **way**. ── It's ___ours___.
10. That's their **boat**. ── It's ___theirs___.
11. That's his **wallet**. ── It's ___his___.
12. This is my **car**. ── It's ___mine___.
13. They're her **pen** and her **desks**. ── They're ___hers___.
14. It's the robot's **schedule**. ── It's its. **Grammatical but not used.***
15. That's our **closet**. ── It's ___ours___.

∗ To use **its** you need a noun sentence, such as *I am not sure of its use*. Note the apostrophe in the contraction **it's** and the lack of one with the possessive pronoun **its**.

　　its要放在有名词的句子中使用，例如：I am not sure of its use.（我不确定它的用法。）注意：在it's这一缩写形式中有撇号，在物主代词its中没有撇号。

VERBS

Let's go back to the basic grid pattern, but this time, we'll focus on the verbs rather than the nouns. On the chart, the time is indicated with words and symbols: **Past ◄**, **Present ●**, **Future ►**. The name of the verb type is indicated on the left.

　　让我们回到基本的九宫格模式吧，不过这次我们要集中讲解动词而不是名词。在表格中，时间通过语言和符号表示：Past◄（过去），Present ●（现在），Future►（将来）。表格的左侧注明了动词的类型。

　　Simple refers to verbs that are completed in a single action. **Duo** is when an action or situation is linked to a moment in the past. You always need two events for a duo. The symbols for the duo are **Past ◄◄**, **Present ◄●**, **Future ►►**. (These are traditionally called the perfect tenses.) The **Unreal Duo** also requires two events. The symbols for the unreal duo are **Past ◁◁**, **Present ◁○**, **Future ▷ ►**. However, the key is that they don't actually happen because they are contrary to fact (traditionally called the subjunctive conditional). These will be covered in detail in subsequent chapters.

　　Simple（一般时态）指可以用一个动作完成的动词。Duo（双重时态）指某个动作或场景与过去的某个时间点相关联。双重时态的构成始终需要两个事件，其相应的符号为Past ◄◄, Present ◄●, Future ►►。（在传统语法体系中，这些被称为完成时态。）Unreal Due（非真实双重时态）也由两个事件构成，其相应的符号为Past ◁◁, Present ◁○, Future ▷►。不过，最关键的一点是：因为它们与事实相反，所以实际上并没有发生过（在传统语法体系中被称为虚拟条件句）。这些在后面的章节中会详细讲解。

Verb To Be
You are here!

	Past	Present	Future
Simple	I was there. ◀	**I am here.** ●	I will be there. ▶
Duo	I had been there before then. ◀◀	I have been there before now. ◀●	I will have been there by then. ▶▶
Unreal Duo	If I had been there, I would have been happy. ◀◀	If I were there, I would be happy. ●●	If I am there, I will be happy. ▶▶

◀ past   ● present   ▶ future

It's the same pattern!

A = B

A is B

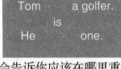

The verb **to be** is the same as an equal sign. **Tom = golfer**.

be动词相当于等号。Tom = golfer。

The emphasis goes on the *nouns*. When there are pronouns instead of nouns, the stress falls on the *verb*. The audio tells where the stress goes: **Tom** is a **golfer**. He **is** one. Notice the pronunciation.

重读要落在名词上。当名词被代词取代后，重读要落在动词上。音频资料会告诉你应该在哪里重读：**Tom** is a **golfer**. He **is** one. 请注意发音。

Tom   a golfer.
is
He   one.

Nouns and pronouns are both important, but pronouns are much more common. It's important for you to understand these patterns, so that you can understand the subject-verb-object (SVO) structure.

名词和代词都很重要，但是代词更常用。理解这些模式对你来说很重要，因为只有理解以后你才能明白"主语—动词—宾语"(SVO)这一结构。

Täm   Bäb.
seez
He   him.

Let's look at the different grammatical persons and see how the verb changes. This is called *conjugating*. You only need three words: **is**, **am**, **are**.

下面让我们来学习不同的人称以及动词的相应变化。这就叫做动词的词形变化。你只需要掌握三个词：is，am，are。

Exercise 1-42: The Simple Present — Now   Track 034

Listen to the audio and repeat until you have mastered the sounds and rhythms.

	Singular	Plural
1st person **Me!**	I am here.	We are here. You and I are here.
2nd person **You!**	You are here.	You (all) are here.
3rd person **Other People**	He is here. She is here. It is here.	They are here.

Exercise 1-43: The Verb *To Be*— *Is* or *Are*   **Track 035**

ACCENT

These sentences follow the subject–verb–object structure. Fill in the blanks with **is** *or* **are***. Then, listen to the audio and pay close attention to the intonation. Check your work using the Answer Key.*

	His hands	**are**	small.	hiz **hæn**zer **smäll.**
1.	**Tom**	*is*	a **golfer.**	**täm**izə **gäl**fr.
2.	The **car**	*is*	**new.**	thə **cär**iz **new.**
3.	The **kids**	*are*	at **school.**	thə **kid**zerat **skool.**
4.	This **hat**	*is*	on my **head.**	this **hæd**izän my **hed.**
5.	Those **dishes**	*are*	in the **sink.**	thoz **dish**'zerin the **sink.**
6.	One **watch**	*is*	**enough.**	wən **wätch**izə **nuff.**
7.	My **shoes**	*are*	green and **red.**	my **shoo**zer gree nän **red.**
8.	Those **ideas**	*are*	**interesting.**	tho zy **dee**⁽ʸ⁾əzer **in**tresting.
9.	**Some** people	*are*	**helpful.**	səm **peep**ler **help**fəl.
10.	That **plan**	*is*	**good.**	that **plæn**iz **güd.**
11.	Not all **jokes**	*are*	**funny.**	nädäll **jok**ser **funny.**
12.	Most **computers**	*are*	PCs.	most **c'mpyoodrz**er pee **ceez.**
13.	Many **cell** phones	*are*	**small.**	meny **cell** phonzer **smäll.**
14.	The sub**marine**	*is*	under**water.**	the səbmə**ree** nizənder **wäder.**
15.	My **friends**	*are*	in the back **seat.**	my **fren**zerin the bæck **seet.**

Exercise 1-44: The Verb *To Be*— *Am, Is, Are*   **Track 036**

Here, fill in the blanks with **am***,* **is***, or* **are***. Then, listen to the audio and pay close attention to the intonation. Check your work using the Answer Key.*

		am	here.
1.	He	*is*	a **student.**
2.	You	*are*	**nice.**
3.	Bob and **Betty**	*are*	**late.**
4.	This **student**	*is*	**ready.**
5.	Your **brother**	*is*	**there.**
6.	I	*am*	**tired.**
7.	This **dancer**	*is*	**good.**
8.	My **brothers**	*are*	hard **workers.**
9.	**Businessmen**	*are*	**busy.**
10.	Your **sister**	*is*	a **cook.**

Now that you have a good understanding of the basic grid order, we're going to shorten some of the words, add a word, and change the word order. This will give us *contractions, negatives, and questions.*

既然你已经很好地理解了这一基本的九宫格，那接下来就让我们缩略一些词、添加一些词、改变一些词的顺序吧。这样做可以分别得到缩略式、否定式和疑问句。

After completing this section, you will be able to make statements (positive and negative) and ask questions. You will have a very strong foundation in English. From here on, you will just need to add more vocabulary to these patterns.

学完这部分内容以后，你就能够陈述事实(肯定的和否定的)或者提问了，而你也就为自己的英语打下了坚实的基础。从现在起，你只需要往这些模式里注入更多的单词就可以了。

Contractions, Negatives, and Questions Are Closely Related
密切相关的缩略式、否定式和疑问句

In the top rows of the following charts, you will see the same sentence three times. Below each one you will see three changes.

在下列三个表格的第一行，你会看到同一个句子出现了三次。在每个句子下面，你分别能看到一种变化。

1. **Contraction** The apostrophe replaces the letter i in the word **is**.
   缩略式　　　用撇号代替单词is中的字母i
2. **Negative** The word **not** is added.
   否定式　　　加上单词not
3. **Question** The first two words are reversed.
   疑问句　　　颠倒最前面两个单词的顺序

Exercise 1-45: Contractions, Negatives, and Questions　　Track 037

Listen to the audio and repeat until you have mastered the sounds, rhythms, and concepts.

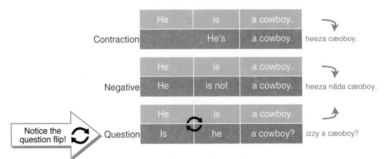

In the contracted form, you can see that the apostrophe replaces the first letter of the verb.
在缩略式中你会看到：撇号替换了动词的首字母。

Full Form	Contraction		Full Form	Contraction
I am	I'm		We are	We're
You are	You're		You are	You're
He is She is It is	He's She's It's		They are	They're

Exercise 1-46: Contractions

Change the nouns to pronouns and put in the verb contraction. Then check the Answer Key.

44

The movie **is** interesting.   It**'s** interesting.

1. The **teachers** are **happy**.   're
2. My **bus** is here.   's
3. The **dogs** are **dirty**.   're
4. My **hair** is **wet**.   's
5. The **boys** are **late**.   're
6. The **clock** is **fast**.   's
7. **Tom** is **French**.   's
8. These **reports** are **easy**.   's
9. **Sally** is your **friend**.   's
10. **Swimming** is **fun**.   's

Exercise 1-47: Contractions — Intonation and Pronunciation   Track 038

ACCENT

Listen to the audio and repeat five times, focusing on intonation and pronunciation.

1. The **teechrz**er **hæppy**.   Ther **hæppy**.
2. My **bəs**iz hir.   Its **hir**.
3. The **dägz**er **dirdy**.   Ther **dirdy**.
4. My **hair**z wet.   Its **wet**.
5. The **boyz**er **late**.   Ther **late**.
6. The **cläcks fæst**.   Its **fæst**.
7. **Tämz French**.   Heez **French**.
8. Theez r'**port**ser **ee**zy.   Ther**eezy**.
9. Sally iz yer **frend**.   Sheez yer **frend**.
10. Swimming iz **fən**.   Its **fən**.

Exercise 1-48: Negatives

*Change the positive to a negative by putting **not** after the verb. Then check the Answer Key.*

The movie is interesting.   **The movie is not interesting.**

1. The teachers are happy.
2. My bus is here.
3. The dogs are dirty.
4. My hair is wet.
5. You are silly.
6. The clock is fast.
7. Tom is French.
8. These reports are easy.
9. I am your friend.
10. This is fun.

There are two ways to make negative contractions. One way is to replace the o in **not** with an apostrophe. The other way is to replace the first letter of **is** or **are** with an apostrophe. The meaning does not change between the two forms. One example of each contraction is highlighted.

否定缩略式有两种写法。一种是用撇号替换单词not中的字母o。另一种是用撇号替换is或are的首字母。虽然这两种写法不一样，但意思是相同的。每种缩略式的范例都用不同的颜色标注出来了。

Full Form	A	B
You are not We are not They are not	You aren't We aren't They aren't	You're not We're not They're not
He is not She is not It is not	He isn't She isn't It isn't	He's not She's not It's not

Exercise 1-49: Negative Contractions

Change the positive to a negative contraction. Change all nouns to pronouns. Then check the Answer Key.

The movie is interesting.	**It is not** interesting.	It **isn't** interesting.

1. The teachers are happy.
2. My bus is here.
3. The dogs are dirty.
4. My hair is wet.
5. You are silly.
6. The clock is fast.
7. Tom is French.
8. These reports are easy.
9. I am your friend.
10. This is fun.

Rule: The Question Flip ↻
规则：疑问句的词序颠倒

As mentioned, you can ask a question by flipping the subject and the verb.
正如前面所说，只要颠倒主语和动词的位置就能得到疑问句。

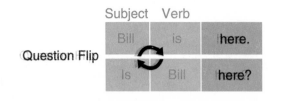

Exercise 1-50: Questions ↻

Change the statements to questions, using the question flip. Move the verb to the front. Then check the Answer Key.

The movie is interesting.	**Is the movie** interesting?

1. The teachers are happy.
2. My bus is here.

3. The dogs are dirty. _____
4. My hair is wet. _____
5. You are silly. _____
6. The clock is fast. _____
7. Tom is French. _____
8. These reports are easy. _____
9. I am your friend. _____
10. This is fun. _____

Exercise 1-51: Questions with Pronouns ⟳

Change the statements to questions and the nouns to pronouns. Then check the Answer Key.

The movie is interesting.   **Is it** interesting?

1. The teachers are happy. _____
2. My bus is here. _____
3. The dogs are dirty. _____
4. My hair is wet. _____
5. You are silly. _____
6. The clock is fast. _____
7. Tom is French. _____
8. These reports are easy. _____
9. I am a student. _____
10. This is fun. _____

Now let's talk about **tag questions**, which are used to confirm or verify. They are common in spoken English, but you don't see them as much in writing.

现在我们来学习反意疑问句，它们通常被用来确认前面的话。在口语中，反意疑问句很常见，但在书面语中并不常见。

Note: The tag for **I am** is irregular. It is: **aren't I**?
注意：I am 的反意疑问句比较特殊，其形式是：aren't I?

Exercise 1-52: Making a Tag Question ⟳

*Reverse the order and the polarity to form a tag question. If the verb is positive, the tag is negative. If the verb is negative, the tag is positive. Use the **question flip** to create the tag ending. When you're done, check the Answer Key.*

+ − **Sam is lazy,**   **isn't he?** ⟳
− + **Sam isn't lazy,**   **is he?** ⟳

1. The teachers are happy,   *Aren't they*
2. My bus isn't here,   *is it*
3. The dogs are dirty,   *Aren't they*
4. My hair is wet,   *isn't it*
5. You are silly,   *Aren't you*

6. The clock is fast, _____ *isn't it*
7. Tom is French, _____ *isn't he*
8. These reports aren't easy, _____ *are they* [they]
9. I am your friend, _____ *Aren't I*
10. This is fun, _____ *isn't this it*

Exercise 1-53: Contractions, Negatives, and Questions ♺

*Complete the grid using the verb **to be**. Then check the Answer Key.*

	Statement	Negative [am not]	Question ♺
I	I am here	I aren't here	*Am I here?*
You	You are here	You aren't here	Are you here?
He	He is here	*He isn't here.*	Is he here?
She	She is here	She isn't here	Is she here?
It	It is here	It isn't here	Is it here?
We	We are here	We aren't here	Are we here?
They	*They are here.*	They aren't here	Are they here?

Time Words: Mid and End Position
时间副词：放在句中或句末

Some time words come in the middle of the sentence and some come at the end. Let's start with the ones in the middle.

有些时间副词放在句中，有些则放在句末。我们先从放在句中的讲起。

Exercise 1-54: Time Words, Mid（Before the Adjective） Track 039

Listen to the audio and repeat until you have mastered the sounds and concepts.

		◀ Mid ▶	Adjective
1.	I'm	always	**late**.
2.	You're	almost always	**tired**.
3.	Bob and **Betty** are	generally	**confused**.
4.	He's	usually	**ready**.
5.	It's not	often	**sunny**.
♺ 6.	Are they	frequently	**hungry**?
7.	She's	sometimes	on **time**.
8.	We're	hardly ever	**worried**.
9.	You are	almost never	**satisfied**.
10.	**Some** people are	never	**focused**.

Exercise 1-55: Time Words, End (After the Adjective)　　　Track 040

Listen to the audio and repeat until you have mastered the sounds and concepts. Notice that the ending time words all have a noun.

		Adjective	◄ End
1.	I'm	late	every **day**.
2.	You're	tired	all the **time**.
3.	Bob and **Betty** are	confused	on a daily **basis**.
4.	He's	ready	every **time**.
5.	It's not	sunny	all **day**.
↻ 6.	Are they	hungry	once a **week**?
7.	She's	on time	every **Monday**.
8.	We're	worried	twice a **day**.
9.	You are	satisfied	every **morning**.
10.	**Some** people are	focused	almost every **day**.

Exercise 1-56: Time Words, Mid — Pronunciation　　　Track 041

Listen to the audio and repeat until you have mastered the sounds and concepts.

	Grammar and Spelling	Pronunciation and Intonation
1.	I'm always **late**.	äimäweez **lay**-eet.
2.	You're always **tired**.	yeräweez **täi**-yrrd.
3.	Bob and **Betty** are generally **confused**.	bäb'n **bed**dyer gen-rəlly c'n**fyu**zd.
4.	He's usually **ready**.	heez yuzhlly **reddy**.
5.	It's not often **sunny**.	its nädäffen **sənny**.
↻ 6.	Are they frequently **hungry**?	är they freekwently **həngry**?
7.	She's sometimes on **time**.	sheez səmtimzän **ty**-eem.
8.	We're hardly ever **worried**.	wir härdly ever **wrr**-eed.
9.	You are almost never **satisfied**.	yer ähmost never **sæd**əsfyd.
10.	**Some** people are never **focused**.	səm peepler never **fouc**əst.

Exercise 1-57: Time Words, End — Pronunciation　　　Track 042

Listen to the audio and repeat until you have mastered the sounds and concepts.

	Grammar and Spelling	Pronunciation and Intonation
1.	I'm **late** every **day**.	äim **lay** devery **day**.
2.	You're **tired** all the **time**.	yer **täi**-yrrdäll the ty-**eem**.
3.	Bob and **Betty** are confused every **time**.	bäb'n **bed**dyer c'nfyuzd evry **ty**-eem.
4.	He's **ready** once a **week**.	heez **reddy** wəntsə **week**.
5.	It's not **sunny** all **day**.	itsnät**sənny** äll **day**.
6.	Are they hungry on a daily **basis**?	är they **həngry** änə day-lee **bay**-səs?
7.	She's on **time** every **Monday**.	sheezän ty mevry **mən**day.
8.	We're **worried** twice a **day**.	wir wrr-reed twy sə **day**.

9. **You** are **satisfied** every **morning**.   yer **sæd**əsfyd evry **morn**ing.

10. **Some** people are **focused** almost   səm peepler **foc**əst ähmost evry **day**.
   every **day**.

Before you take the Chapter 1 test, let's quickly review the verb map. You have learned a lot in a short time, and you can now see clearly where you are on the map. You have mastered the verb **to be** in the *simple present tense*.

在你做第一章的测试之前，让我们先快速复习一下动词地图。你在短时间内已经学了很多东西，现在你很清楚自己在地图上的哪个位置。你已经掌握了be动词在一般现在时中的用法。

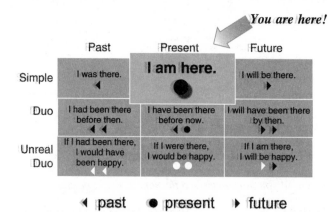

◄ past   ● present   ► future

Let's review everything you have learned in Chapter 1, including singular and plural nouns, pronouns, the present tense of the verb **to be**, time words, and word order. Make sure you get 100% on the test before going on to the next chapter. The Answer Key is on page 309.

我们来复习一下在第一章中学到的内容，其中包括名词的单复数、代词、be动词的一般现在时、时间副词、词序。记住：只有当你在测试中拿了满分以后，你才可以接着学习下一章。参考答案在第309页。

To test your grammar and accent skills at this point or later, call (001) 800-457-4255.

若想检验自己的英语语法和发音技能，在中国大陆请拨打001-800-457-4255，在美国本土请直接拨打800-457-4255。

Part 1: *Fill in the proper pronoun for the blue words.*

1. **The boy** is a student.   He

2. **That woman** is my friend.   She

3. **My parents** are very helpful.   They

Part 2: *Replace all nouns with pronouns.*

1. Bob and Bill are in the kitchen.   it

2. Sue and Jill are in a car.   are

                                                it

Part 3: *Fill in the proper verb:* **is**, **am**, **are**.

1. I   *am*   a student.

2. You   are   my friend.

3. We   are   having a good time.

4. They   are   at a party.

5. She   is   out of the office.

6. He **is** on his way.
7. It **is** raining hard.
8. I **am** in my pajamas. (in my PJs)
9. It **is** not in this room.
10. They **are** playing outside.

Part 4: *Change the sentence to the plural.*

1. This test is easy. — *These tests are easy*
2. There is a book. — *There are a book*
3. That man is hungry. — *Those men are hungry*
4. The tree is tall. — *These trees are tall*
5. My sister is a nurse. — *My sisters are nurses*

Part 5: *Put in the verb contraction.*

1. It is a good idea. — *It's*
2. That is old. — *That's*
3. We are here. — *We're*
4. You are there. — *You're*
5. I am in class. — *I'm*
6. She is late. — *She's*
7. He is funny. — *He's*

Part 6: *Change the positive statement to a negative. Do **not** use contractions or pronouns.*

1. Shelly is in Europe. — *isn't*
2. Paul and Larry are here. — *aren't*
3. The girls are tired. — *aren't*

Part 7: *Change the positive statement to a negative. **Use** contractions and pronouns.*

1. The boys are outside. — *aren't*
2. Charlie is happy. — *isn't*
3. My eyes are closed. — *aren't*

Part 8: *Change the statement to a question. Do **not** use pronouns.*

1. Your brother is in college. — *is*
2. His bike is in the shop. — *is*
3. My watch is fast. — *is*

Part 9: *Change the statement to a question. Change the nouns to pronouns.*

1. The car is in the garage. — *is it in it*
2. Her son is in the pool. — *is he in it*
3. My watch is in a box. — *is it in it*

Part 10: *Indicate where the blue words should go.*

1. He — is — rude — never
2. I — am — late — every day
3. We — are — confused — often
4. She — is — sleepy — in the morning
5. You — are — right — usually

Part 11: *Underline the words that should be stressed.*

1. Bob is my friend.
2. The boys are in the car.
3. The teacher is in the room.
4. The students are happy.
5. The dogs are in the yard.

Part 12: *Identify the sound in each of the following words.*

1. plan   ☑ æ   ☐ ä   ☐ ə
2. does   ☐ æ   ☐ ä   ☑ ə
3. lot   ☐ æ   ☑ ä   ☐ ə

Using what you have learned, write a five-sentence essay about your favorite subject in school. You can also write about yourself.

利用学过的知识，就你最喜欢的学科写一篇5句话的作文。你也可以写写自己。

You can handwrite your paragraph below or e-mail it to **para@grammar.bz** These paragraphs are not graded or reviewed, but simply by writing them, your English will improve. You can also request feedback and training at (001) 800-457-4255.

你可以在下面写这段话，也可以发邮件至para@grammar.bz。我们不会对这段话进行打分或点评，但只要你写了，你的英语水平就会提高。如果需要我们的反馈或指导，在中国大陆请拨打001-800-457-4255，在美国本土请直接拨打800-457-4255。

Student Paragraph	
Send Chat Attach Address Fonts Colors Save As Draft Photo Browser Show Stationery	
To:	para@grammar.bz
Cc:	
Bcc:	
Subject:	My favorite Subject in School

Signature: Corporate

My name is _____

My Favorite subject in school   is   _____ .
     Noun   Verb   Noun

_____ It _____   is   _____ .
                    Noun or Adjective

_____ It _____   is   not   _____ .
                    Noun or Adjective

_____ I _____   am   _____ .
                    Adjective/Noun

_____ This _____   is   _____ , isn't it!
                    Adjective

Chapter 2
第二章

Modified Nouns and Main Verbs
被修饰的名词和主动词

This chapter covers nouns, pronouns, prepositions of location, conjunctions, time words, and the present tense of main verbs and helping verbs.

本章涵盖了名词、代词、方位介词、连词、时间副词，以及主动词和助动词的一般现在时。

Listen carefully to the dictation and write the five sentences. Use standard spelling and make a note of important sounds, such as, **æ**, **ä**, and **ə**.

仔细听音频中的听写材料，并记下这五句话。写的时候要用标准的拼写方式，并标注一下重要的发音，如æ，ä和ə。

Exercise 2-1: Dictation   Track 043

Listen to the audio and write the exact transcription in the spaces below. Then check the Answer Key.

1. _____
2. _____
3. _____
4. _____
5. _____

STORY

This is a continuation of the story about Max. In Chapter 1, we worked with the nine-grid for stories, using only the verb **to be** in the present tense (*is, am, are*).

Max

这个故事还是关于Max的。在第一章，我们用九宫格写了个故事，并且只用了be动词的一般时态(is，am，are)。

Here, we are going to use the same format, but we add simple intro words such as **suddenly** and **fortunately**. We also use *main verbs* in addition to the verb **to be**. This is still in the present tense.

这次，我们还用同样的形式，但是增加了简单的介绍词汇，如suddenly和fortunately。另外，除了要使用be动词以外，我们还会用到主动词。不过，时态仍然是现在时。

Exercise 2-2: "The Incident in Venice"   Track 044

*Listen to the audio and repeat out loud five times. Focus on the intonation. The verbs are blue. Look up new vocabulary in the back of the book and write the definition above the word. Notice that each sentence has a **subject** in the beginning, a **verb** in the middle, and an **object** at the end.*

I'm a **body**builder. **One** day, I'm in Gold's **Gym** in Venice, **California**. After **training**, I go to the **parking** lot. **Suddenly**, I hear three **gun**shots. There are three **guys**. **One** of them has a **gun**. He shoots a man! I think that they're in a **gang**. It's really **dangerous**. I go **home**. **Fortunately**, I'm not **hurt**. My **girl**friend, **Eve**, is **careful**, but she's **used** to living in **Venice**.

Exercise 2-3: "The Incident in Venice" — Pronunciation   Track 045

Listen to the audio and repeat out loud five times. Focus on the pronunciation and the word connections.

ACCENT

Imə **bä**dybilder. **One** day, aimin Goldz **Gym** in Venəs, Cæləfornyə. æfter training, I go t' thə **pärking** lät. **Suddenly**, I hir three **gen**shots. Therər three **guyz**. Wənəvəm hazə **gen**. He **shoots** a mæn! I **think** thət thehr inə **gæng**. It's rilly **danjeres**. I go **home**. **Forch**ənətly, I'm nät **hrrt**. My **girl**friend, **Eve**, iz **care**fəl, bət sheez **ustə** living in **Venəs**.

An important part of telling a story is how well you reduce the high-frequency words. *The reduced sounds are the unstressed vowels. These lose their original pronunciation and sound like a schwa(ə).* Look at the story above, and notice all the schwa(ə) symbols. There are a couple dozen in just this short story!

要把故事讲好就要做到一点：弱读高频词。被弱读的音往往是非重读元音。这些音不再发它们本来的音，而是变得像非重读央元音ə。看看上面的故事，注意里面所有的非重读央元音符号(ə)。仅在这个小故事里，就有二十几个非重读央元音！

If you count all the words an American uses in a day, the number one word is **the**(thə). Make sure you have a clear, popping TH and a very reduced schwa, **uh**(ə).

如果你数一数美国人一天中用过的所有单词，就会发现用得最多的是the（thə）。念the的时候，请务必清晰地发出TH的音，但非重读央元音uh(ə)只要轻轻带过就可以了。

Exercise 2-4: Top 30 High-Frequency Words and Sounds   Track 046

Listen to the audio and repeat out loud five times. The high-frequency words are in blue. They are shown in context to help you pronounce them naturally.

1–5

the **car**	**one** of us	on and **on**	once a **week**	We plan to **go**.
thə car	wənəvəs	änənän	wəntsə week	We plan də go.

6–10

in it	Is he?	You **know**?	that I **said**	**Get** it!
innit	Izzy?	Y' know?	the dai sed	Geddit!

11–15

He says O**K**.	How was it?	It's for **you**.	I'm on it.	What are they **doing**?
hee sezoh K	How wəzzit?	its fr **you**	aimänit	whadder they doing?

16–20

as **big** as	with us	my **only**	They **like** it.	**Bob** and I
əz bigəz	withus	myonly	they ly kit	**bä**ban I

21–25

this time	There it is.	This or that?	She's here.	Can I have one?
this ty-eem	theridiz	thiser that?	sheez here.	Knai hæv w'n?

26–30

Did he do it?	We are here.	Let's get it.	How?	That's not it.
diddee do⁽ʷ⁾it?	Wir here.	lets geddit.	hæow?	That's nädit.

In Chapter 1, we learned that nouns are people, places, and things. We also learned that pronouns replace nouns (Joe=he).

在第一章中，我们学过名词是指人、地点和事物。我们也学过代词可以替代名词(Joe=he)。

We are going to start adding information to nouns. This added information is called a **modifier**.

我们将开始往名词上增加信息。这些被增加的信息叫做修饰语。

Then, we're going to work with **prepositions** to tell us where the noun is, and with **conjunctions** to link nouns and sentences together.

然后，我们学习介词，介词会告诉我们名词所处的位置；再学习连词，连词会把名词和句子连接起来。

Describing Nouns
描述名词

Now that we know what nouns are, we're going to start dressing them up a bit. If you say, **He has a car**, this leaves out a lot of information. You need to describe the noun: a new car, an old car, a black car, a red car, a big car, a small car, some cars, ten cars.

既然我们已经知道了名词是什么，我们就要开始稍微打扮打扮它们了。如果你说He has a car（他有汽车），那就把很多信息都给遗漏了。你需要描述一下这个名词：a new car（一辆新车），an old car（一辆旧车），a black car（一辆黑色的车），a red car（一辆红色的车），a big car（一辆大车），a small car（一辆小车），some cars（一些车），ten cars（十辆车）。

Let's talk about the **intonation** of nouns for a moment. When you introduce new information, you need to stress the noun: It's a new **car**.

让我们花点时间谈谈名词的声调。当你引入新信息的时候，你需要重读名词，如：It's a new **car**。

Exercise 2-5: New Information   **Track 047**

Listen and repeat five times, focusing on the intonation.

1. He has a blue **pen**.
2. She seems like a nice **person**.
3. You take long **walks**.
4. I like my red **coat**.
5. She plays two **instruments**.

You can also use contrast by stressing the modifier: It's a **new** car, not an **old** one.

你也可以重读修饰语来形成对比：It's a **new** car, not an **old** one.

Exercise 2-6: New Information and Contrast · Track 048

Listen and repeat five times, focusing on the intonation.

	New Information	**Contrast**
1.	He has a blue **pen**.	He has a **blue** pen, not a **black** one.
2.	She seems like a nice **person**.	She **seems** like a nice person, but she is **not**.
3.	You take long **walks**.	You take **long** walks, not **short** ones.
4.	I like my red **coat**.	I **like** my **red** coat, but I **love** my **blue** one.
5.	She plays two **instruments**.	She plays **two** instruments, not **three**.

In Max's story, you may have noticed words like **bodybuilder**, **girlfriend**, and **parking lot**. Two nouns are stuck together to form a new word, with a new meaning. This is called a compound noun. The stress goes on the first noun: **body**builder, **girl**friend, **parking** lot.

在Max的故事中，你可能已经注意到了诸如bodybuilder，girlfriend和parking lot这样的词。当两个名词结合在一起，它们形成了有全新意思的新词。这就是"复合名词"。这种情况下，要重读的是第一个名词：**body**builder，**girl**friend，**parking** lot。

Exercise 2-7: Descriptions · Track 049

Listen and repeat five times, placing the emphasis on the second word.

1.	It's a metal **clip**.		6.	It's a thick **book**.
2.	It's a good **book**.		7.	It's fresh **sauce**.
3.	It's a plastic **cup**.		8.	It's a bronze **pot**.
4.	He's a little **boy**.		9.	It's a paper **plane**.
5.	It's a rusty **can**.		10.	It's an expensive **grater**.

Exercise 2-8: Compound Nouns · Track 050

Listen and repeat five times, placing the emphasis on the first word.

1.	It's a **paper** clip.		6.	It's a **note**book.
2.	It's a **book**shelf.		7.	It's **hot** sauce.
3.	It's a **coffee** cup.		8.	It's a **tea**pot.
4.	He's a **cow**boy. 牛仔		9.	It's an **air**plane.
5.	It's a **trash**can.		10.	It's a **cheese** grater.

Exercise 2-9: Contrasting Descriptions and Compound Nouns · Track 051

Listen and repeat five times, focusing on the intonation.

	Descriptions	**Compounds**
1.	It's a metal **clip**.	It's a **paper** clip.
2.	It's a good **book**.	It's a **book**shelf.

3.   It's a plastic **cup**.   It's a **coffee** cup.
4.   He's a little **boy**.   He's a **cow**boy.
5.   It's a rusty **can**.   It's a **trash**can.
6.   It's a thick **book**.   It's a **note**book.
7.   It's fresh **sauce**.   It's **hot** sauce.
8.   It's a bronze **pot**.   It's a **tea**pot.
9.   It's a paper **plane**.   It's an **air**plane.
10. It's an expensive **grater**.   It's a **cheese** grater.

Exercise 2-10: Max Revisited   Track 052

Listen and repeat five times, focusing on the difference between descriptions and compounds.

I'm a **bodybuilder**. One day, I'm in Gold's **Gym** in Venice, **California**. After **training**, I go to the **parking** lot. Suddenly, I hear three **gun**shots. There are three **guys**. One of them has a gun. He shoots a man! I think that they're in a gang. It's really **dangerous**. I go home. Fortunately, I'm not hurt. My **girl**friend, Eve, is careful, but she's used to living in Venice.

Let's do a quick review of nouns and pronouns. With **he / she / it** add -s to the end of the main verb.

让我们迅速复习一下名词和代词。当主语是he/she/it时，主动词后面要加-s。

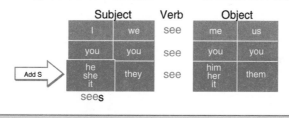

Exercise 2-11: Noun and Pronoun Review

Let's do a quick pronoun review. Notice the compound nouns and descriptions. Fill in the blanks with the appropriate pronoun. The emphasis is on the noun in the first set and on the verb in the second set. When you're done, check the Answer Key.

	Nouns		Nouns	Pronouns		Pronouns
	The **boy**	eats	an **apple**.	He	eats	one.
1.	**Susie**	studies	**French**.	She	studies	~~there~~ it
2.	The **employees**	need	long **breaks**.	They	need	long ones
3.	**Students**	ask	hard **questions**.	They	ask	hard ones
4.	The **child**	breaks	his favorite **toy**.	He	breaks	it
5.	Your **parents**	make	a **phone** call.	They	make	it
6.	The **CEO**	forgets	his latest **plan**.	He	forgets	it
7.	**Commuters**	take	the **bullet** train.	They	take	it
8.	My **sister**	wants	a new **car**.	She	wants	one
9.	Your **mom**	likes to cook	**pan**cakes.	She	likes to **cook**	them
10.	**The dogs**	need	warm **baths**.	they	need	ones

ACCENT

Now, let's see how that sounds. Listen to the audio and repeat five times.

Nouns	**Pronouns**
1. **Suzee** stədeez **French**.	She **stədee** zit.
2. Thee⁽ʸ⁾**employeez** need **breaks**.	They **need**'m.
3. **Students** æsk **kwesj'nz**.	They **æsk**'m.
4. The **child** breaks hiz **toy**.	He **break** sit.
5. Your **perents** may kə **phone** call.	They **may** kwən.
6. The **CEO** frgets hiz **plæn**.	He fr**get** sit.
7. **Cəmmyuderz** take **trains**.	They **take**'m.
8. My **s'strr** wantsə new **car**.	She **wänts** wən.
9. Yrrrr **mäm** likes t' cook **pæn**cakes.	She likes to **cook**'m.
10. The **dägz** need wōrm **bæthz**.	They **need** wōrm wənz.

Exercise 2-13: Replacing Nouns

Rewrite each sentence, replacing all nouns with pronouns. The stress moves from the nouns to the verbs.
Check the Answer Key when you're done.

Edward likes his **classes**.   He **likes** them.

1. Joe and **Frank** saw a **movie**.
2. **Tammy** plays **tennis**.
3. **Mary** and I took a **trip**.
4. **Dave** married **Susie**.
5. Our **friends** gave the **book** to **Ed** and me.

Things and Locations
事物和位置

in the house   **under the tree**

Prepositions tell you the **location** of a thing. Location includes **places**, **people**, and **time**.

介词告诉你事物的位置。对于位置的描述包括地点、人物、时间。

The classic definition is "What a plane can do to a cloud." *In* a cloud, *by* a cloud, *near* a cloud, etc.
关于位置的经典定义是："飞机能对云做什么"。在云里面、在云旁边、在云附近，等等。

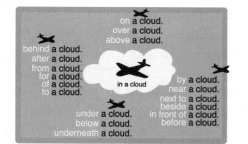

This explains where a plane can be in relation to a cloud. Of course, it can be much more than just **in** a cloud.

这解释了飞机和云的位置关系。不过，它们的关系可不仅限于 in a cloud(在云里面)。

For locations, you can use a single word (*above*) or a phrase (*on top of*).

要描述位置，你可以用单个的词(above)，也可以用短语(on top of)。

The **be-** words(below, behind, before, beside, beneath) are stressed on the second syllable and the first syllable is shortened (b'**low**, b'**hind**, b'**fore**, b'**side**, b'**neath**).

以 be-开头的单词(below, behind, before, beside, beneath)要把重音放在第二个音节上，并把第一个音节缩短(b'**low**, b'**hind**, b'**fore**, b'**side**, b'**neath**)。

Exercise 2-14: Prepositions of Location

Circle the appropriate location word. Then check the Answer Key.

1.	The little **boy** hides	on / under / over	the **table**.
2.	My **sister** jumped	over / of / after	the **bush**.
3.	I **always** go	after / beyond / through	the **tunnel**.
4.	My **dog** is always	for / beside / to	me.
5.	**Look**	before / behind / after	the **couch**.
6.	It is	underneath / for / behind	the **super**market.
7.	I always sit	for / next to / under	the **door**.
8.	I put it	under / to / for	the **door**mat.
9.	Is it	for / over / on	the **table**?
10.	She gets **letters**	in / above / from	her **sister**.
11.	I **put** that	on / after / in	a **box**.
12.	You say that	under / in front of / from	them this time.
13.	I have a **scar**	in / on	my **knee**.
14.	You are	on / in / by	a good **mood**.
15.	Is the little **box**	above / under / to	the **couch**?
16.	He is looking	below / for / behind	her.
17.	She only uses **English**	in / at / by	**class**.
18.	I am working	in / at / by	**home** today.
19.	The students live	in / at / by / on	the second **floor**.
20.	We live	in / at / on	**New** York.

There Is / There Are

As you have seen, patterns are important. Instead of learning thousands of words, you can learn a couple of patterns and then just mix and match. Let's go back to the verb **to be** for a moment. Now that we have prepositions of location, we can use **there** and the verb **to be** to indicate the existence and general location of things, as in **there is** and **there are**. Notice that, instead of individual words, we're now linking phrases. Look at the chart below. In the first column, we have **there + is / are**. In the noun column, we add modifiers. The last column is for the location. Learn the various phrases and then link them together in order: A-B-C.

正如你看到的那样，模式很重要。你不用忙着记住数以千计的单词，你可以先只学几个模式，然后对它们进行排列组合就可以了。让我们花点时间再讲讲be动词。既然我们学过了方位介词，我们就可以用单词there和be动词来表示事物的存在和一般位置了，如there is 和 there are。请注意：它们不再是单个的词，而变成短语了。请看下面的图表：在第一栏，我们有there + is/are；在名词一栏，我们增加了修饰语；最后一栏则描述了事物的位置。先学习以下不同的短语，再把它们按A-B-C的顺序组合起来。

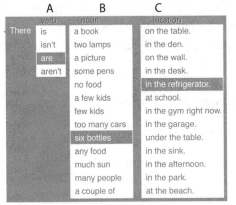

This exercise lets you start combining phrases, rather than single *words*.
这个练习让你开始学习把短语组合起来，而不只是组合单个的单词。

Exercise 2-15: *There Is* vs. *There Are*   Track 054

Listen to the audio and pay close attention to the intonation.

A	B	C	Pronunciation
	What / Who	**Where**	
There is	a **fly**	in my **soup**!	therzə **fly**in my **soop**. (*not theriza*)
There is	a **credit** card	in my **wallet**.	therzə **credit** card in my **wäll**et.
There are	**cars**	in the **garage**.	therer **cär**zin the gə**raj**.
There is	not enough **room**	in my **house**.	therz nädə nəff **room**in my **house**.
↻ There are	some **people**	at my **door**.	therer s'm **pee**pəlat my **dore**.
Are there	many **students**	at this **school**?	är ther meny **stud**entsat this **skool**?
There are	a couple of **dogs**	over there.	thererə couplə **däg** zover there.
There are	very many **words**	**here**.	therer very meny **wrrdz hir**.
There are	not many **people**	at the **party**.	therer nät meny **pee**pəlat thə **pär**dy.
↻ There are	too many **cooks**	in the **kitchen**!	therer too meny **cük**sin thə **kit**chen.
Is there	a good **restaurant**	near my **house**?	iz therə güd **res**tränt nir my **house**?
There are	a few **zebras**	in **California**.	ther arə few **ze**brəzin cælə **for**nyə.
There are	few **zebras**	in **Alaska**.	therer few **ze**brazinə **laes**kə.

Note: a few = some / few = not many

60

Linking Words, Phrases, and Sentences
把单词、短语、句子连接起来

Let's use **conjunctions** to link nouns, phrases, and sentences together.
让我们用连词把名词、短语、句子连接到一起。

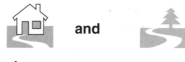

a house   **a tree**

The five primary conjunctions are **and**, **but**, **so**, **or**, and **because**.
五个最主要的连词分别是：and, but, so, or和because。

And is the same as a *plus sign*.	**A + B = C**
and 与加号的作用是一样的。	Bob and Betty are friends.
But indicates the *opposite* situation.	**A, but not B**
but 表示相反的情况。	Joe likes to drive, but not to fly.
So means *for that reason*.	**A, so B**
so 意为因为某个原因。	It's cold, so we put on a sweater.
Or indicates a *choice*.	**A or B**
or 表示选择。	Apples or oranges
Because indicates a *reason*.	**A because B**
because 表示原因。	He cries because he is sad.

It can sound childish to use short sentences. As your language skills develop, you will use conjunctions to take many short thoughts and create a single, longer sentence. Notice how the following goes from five sentences to just one. (**Oranges** is pronounced **ornj'z**.)

使用短句显得比较幼稚。随着你的语言技能的提升，你要用连词把很多小想法连接起来，组成一个较长的句子。注意下列五个句子是如何变成一个的。（Oranges读作ornj'z。）

Ed bought some apples. He bought some pears.
He bought some oranges. He did not buy any bananas.
He did not buy any grapes.

Ed bought apples, pears, **and** oranges,
but **no** bananas **or** grapes.

You are listing several items, so notice the phrasing.
因为你列举了好几个项目，所以请注意语调的变化。

Ed bought apples, ⤴ pears, ⤴ **and** oranges, ⤴
but **no** bananas **or** grapes. ⤵

Exercise 2-16: Conjunctions — *And, But, So, Or, Because*

*Fill in the appropriate conjunction, using **and**, **but**, **so**, **or**, and **because**. Then check the Answer Key.*

She knows how to drive	but	she prefers to ride her bike.
1. We can't swim,	so	we don't go to the pool.

2. Everyone eats *and* drinks at weddings.

3. We don't have a map, *so* we get lost.

4. We get lost **☺* we don't have a map.

5. The workers are tired, *so* they take a break.

6. We are tired, *but* we go to work anyway.

7. The tourists go to Italy *and* France.

8. The tourists go to Italy *but* not France.

9. They want to speak French, *so* they go to France.

10. The kids ride bikes *and* fly kites.

VERBS

In Chapter 1, we used the verb **to be** and its forms *am*, *is*, and *are*.
在第一章中，我们使用了be动词以及由它衍生出来的am, is和are。

Now, we are going to work with *main verbs* in the present tense. These are action words, such as **run**, **go**, and **work**. We will also begin using *helping verbs* to make questions, negatives, and the emphatic form.

现在，我们要学习主动词在现在时态下的用法。它们是表示行动的词，如run, go和work。另外，我们还要学会用助动词来造出疑问句、否定句，以及强调句。

Main Verb: *Do*
主动词: *Do*

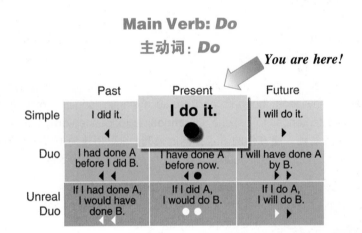

We'll be using the same patterns and pronouns as before. Nouns and pronouns are both important, but pronouns are much more common.

我们会使用与前面一样的模式和代词。名词和代词都很重要，但代词更常用。

Remember: The stress falls on the *nouns*. When pronouns are used instead of nouns, the stress falls on the *verb*.

请记住：要重读名词。当代词替换了名词以后，则要重读动词。

Tom sees Bob.
He him.

Täm seez Bäb.
He him.

Also remember that the letter **O** sounds like **ah**, **S** sounds like **Z**, and the **H** fades away.

还要记住：字母O听起来像ah，字母S听起来像Z，而H基本不发音。

The 16 Most Common Verbs

to be	to do	to have	to come
to see	to seem	to give	to take
to make	to put	to send	to say
to go	to keep	to get	to let

These are the most commonly used *verbs*.
这些动词是使用频率最高的。

62

It's also important to know opposite verb pairs. Make sure that you know the meaning of each set.

知道相互对立的动词也很重要。确定你知道每组的含义。

Some words have more than one opposite, such as **play** / **work** and **play** / **fight**.

有些词的对立词不止一个，如play / work和play / fight。

Common Verb Opposites			
to ask	to tell	to win	to lose
to bring	to take	to play	to work
to come	to go	to play	to fight
to forget	to remember	to push	to pull
to give	to take	to put	to remove
to get	to give	to put on	to take off
to hope	to wish	to read	to write
to like	to not like	to talk	to listen
to look for	to find	to walk	to ride
to find	to lose	to walk	to drive

Main verbs change from person to person, normally by adding an -s to the third-person form. This is called **conjugating** the verb.

主动词会根据不同的人称而变化，一般情况下要在第三人称单数的后面加上-s。这就叫做动词的词形变化。

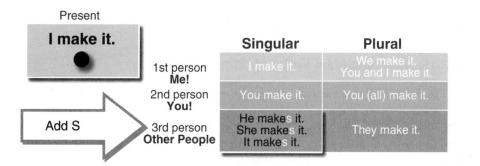

Exercise 2-17: Changing Main Verbs (Regular)

Circle the proper form. Then read the sentences out loud, stressing the nouns. When you're done, check the Answer Key.

	Lou		**sells**	used **cars**.
1.	**Bob**	speak	speaks	**English**.
2.	**Betty** (**beddy**)	live in	lives in	**America**.
3.	**People**	need	needs	**money**.
4.	**The book**	seem	seems	**easy**.
5.	**Teachers**	give	gives	**tests**.
6.	**That person**	want	wants	a **car**.
7.	Bob and **Betty**	make	makes	a lot of **mistakes**.
8.	Your **boss**	send	sends	an **e-mail**.
9.	Your **friend**	get	gets	a **job**.
10.	The **class**	take	takes	a **break**.

Just as you saw with plurals in Chapter 1, third-person verbs ending in **O**, **X**, **Z**, **SS**, **SH**, and **CH** add **-es** at the end, instead of just **-s**, to make the plural form.

就像你在第一章介绍复数时看到的那样，以O、X、Z、SS、SH和CH结尾的动词，在与第三人称连用时，要在动词的末尾加上-es，而不是-s。

A little girl came home from school and said, "Mommy, we learned how to make babies today!" The mother was quite surprised and said, "Um, what do you mean?" The little girl replied, "Well, you just drop the Y and add IES! "

Exercise 2-18: Changing Main Verbs (Adding -es)

Add -es to the verb. Then check the Answer Key.

	She	wash**es**	her hair every day.	wash
1.	**Elsie**		to the **store**.	go
2.	The **manager**		a lot of **work**.	do
3.	**Joe**		at the **gym**.	box
4.	My **alarm** clock		at 6:00 **am**.	buzz
5.	The **mother**		the **baby**.	kiss
6.	The **boy**		the **ball**.	catch
7.	The **child**		the **swings**.	push

Exercise 2-19: Changing Main Verbs (Adding -ies)

Change the -y to -ies. This does not include -oy, -ay, or -ey. When you're done, check the Answer Key.

	The student	rel**ies**	on the teacher.	rely
1.	The class		the lessons.	study
2.	The baby		all night.	cry
3.	She		very hard.	try
4.	The bird		south for the winter.	fly
5.	The cook		eggs for breakfast.	fry
6.	He		doing it.	deny

Exercise 2-20: Changing Main Verbs (Go)

Complete the sentence, using either go or goes. Then check the Answer Key.

1.	He		to the movies.
2.	I		up the stairs.
3.	We		to the mall and shop.
4.	She		out with her boyfriend.
5.	They		hiking.

Exercise 2-21: Changing Main Verbs (Do)

Complete the sentence, using either do or does. Then check the Answer Key.

1.	You		not care about good **grades**.
2.	We		enjoy that **restaurant**.
3.	She		dance really **well**.
4.	It		make a **difference**.
5.	I		need to **help** him.

Exercise 2-22: Changing Main Verbs (*Have*)

*Complete the sentence, using either **have** or **has**. Then check the Answer Key.*

1. She   a long **name**.
2. You   the best **ideas**!
3. We   an excellent **plan**.
4. They   a **really** nice **house**.
5. It   four **doors**.

> There is an ancient invention that allows people to see through walls.
> It's called a "window."

Changing and Unchanging Verbs
变化和非变化动词

The next few pages are very important. Do not go further until you understand them perfectly. You will use these concepts every time you speak English.

接下来的这几页非常重要。等你完全理解了这些内容以后，再接着往后学。因为每次说英语的时候，你都会用上这些概念。

Main verbs tell the action. Every sentence has a main verb （or the verb **to be**). The main verb has two forms: the *changing* form (**see / sees**) and the *unchanging* form (**see**).

主动词表示动作。每个句子都有一个主动词(或be动词)。主动词有两种形式：变化形式(see / sees)和原形(see)。

The unchanging form is the action part of the main verb: **see**, **do**, **go**, **make**. This is also called the *simple* form. You cannot add -s to the simple form.

原形表示主动词的动作，如：see, do, go, make。这种形式也叫做一般式。你不能在一般式的后面加-s。

Helping verbs are a *changing* form. They always go together with the *simple* form of the main verb. The helping verb takes over the job of the main verb.

助动词是变化形式。它们总要与主动词的一般式一起搭配使用。助动词接替了主动词的工作。

Let's add a *helping* verb to make a regular statement *emphatic*. This shows a stronger opinion. In a regular statement, you skip over the spot for the *helping* verb.

让我们给一个常规陈述句加上一个助动词，把它变成强调句。这使得观点更加有力。在常规陈述句中，你只是没有把助动词的位置填上东西罢了。

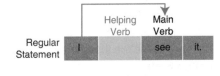

He sees it.
He **does** see it!

With **he / she / it**, the helping verb changes from **do** to **does**. The main verb stays in the simple form. The emphatic form is not high frequency, but it will help you make negative statements and questions.

当主语是he / she / it的时候，助动词从do变成了does，而主动词仍保留一般式。强调句式并不常用，但它会帮助你学习否定句和疑问句。

Exercise 2-23: Adding *Do* for Emphasis（I, You, We, They）

Add ***do*** *to make the statement stronger. Use the unchanging form of the main verb. Then check the Answer Key.*

Main Verb	**Helping Verb + Unchanging Form**
The boys **eat** apples.	The boys **do eat** apples!
1. The **kids** play at the **park**.	
2. The **dogs** get **dirty**.	
3. You **forget** many **things**.	
4. These re**ports** need **work**.	
5. I **work** too **hard**.	

The *simple* unchanging form stays the same. The *helping verb* changes for **he / she / it**.
动词的一般式保持不变。he / she / it的助动词要注意变化。

Exercise 2-24: Adding *Does* for Emphasis（He / She / It）

Add ***does*** *to make the statement stronger. Use the unchanging form of the main verb（simple form）. Then check the Answer Key.*

Main Verb	**Helping Verb + Unchanging Form**
The boy **eats** apples.	The boy **does eat** apples.
1. My **bus** comes **late**.	
2. My **boss** needs this **done**.	
3. The **clock** costs a **lot**.	
4. **Tom** makes **mistakes**.	
5. The **car** runs **well**.	

The One-S Rule
一个-S原则

With the third person singular(he, she, it), notice that there is only one S at a time, either on the subject noun or on the verb, but **not on both**.

当出现第三人称单数(he, she, it)时，请注意：一个句子只加一个S，要么加在作主语的名词上，要么加在动词上，两者不能同时加。

> The boy eat**s** the apple.
>
> The boy doe**s** eat the apple.
>
> The boy**s** eat the apple.
>
> The boy**s** do eat the apple.

Exercise 2-25: Adding *Do* or *Does* for Emphasis

*Add **do** or **does** to make the statement stronger. Use the simple unchanging form for the main verb. Then check the Answer Key.*

Main Verb	**Helping Verb + Unchanging Form**
Sam **eats** apples.	Sam **does eat** apples.

1. The **kids** play at the **park**.
2. My **bus** comes **late**.
3. The **dogs** get **dirty**.
4. My **boss** needs this **done**.
5. You **forget** many **things**.
6. The **clock** costs a **lot**.
7. **Tom** makes **mistakes**.
8. These re**ports** need **work**.
9. I **work** too **hard**.
10. The **car** runs **well**.

Exercise 2-26: Adding *Can*

*Add **can** to indicate ability. Use the unchanging form for the main verb. Then check the Answer Key.*

Main Verb	**Can + Simple Form**
Sam **eats** apples.	Sam **can eat** apples.

1. The **kids** play at the **park**.
2. My **bus** comes **late**.
3. The **dogs** get **dirty**.
4. My **boss** gets things **done**.
5. You **forget** many **things**.
6. The **clock** costs a **lot**.
7. **Tom** makes **mistakes**.
8. These re**ports** change **every day**.
9. I **work** too **hard**.
10. The **car** runs **well**.

Positive	Negative	Extra Positive	Extra Negative
I can do it.	I can't do it.	I can do it.	I can't do it.
I c'n do it.	I cæn't do it.	I cææn do it.	I cææn 't do it.

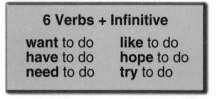

6 Verbs + Infinitive

want to do **like** to do
have to do **hope** to do
need to do **try** to do

The infinitive is **to** + *simple form*, such as **to be**, **to do**, or **to go**. It is used like a noun. You can say **I eat pizza**, **I want pizza**, or **I want to eat pizza**.

不定式就是"to＋一般式"，如：to be, to do或to go。它的用法跟名词差不多。你可以说 I eat pizza, I want pizza 或 I want to eat pizza。

Exercise 2-27: Adding a Verb + To

Add one of the six verbs in the box above to each sentence. Use the unchanging form for the main verb. Notice that the meanings are more positive with these words. When you're done, check the Answer Key.

Main Verbs

Sam **eats** apples.

Verb + To + Simple Form

Sam **likes** to eat apples.

1. The **kids** play at the **park**.
2. My **friend** comes **early**.
3. The **dogs** get **a bone**.
4. My **boss** has this **done**.
5. You **remember** many **things**.
6. The **girl** dances a **lot**.
7. **Tom** makes **money**.
8. These **guys** find **work**.
9. I **work hard**.
10. **Sam** runs **fast**.

	Past	Negative Present	Future
Simple	I didn't do it.	I don't do it.	I won't do it.
Real Duo	I hadn't done A until I did B	I haven't ever done it.	I won't have done A before I do B.
Unreal Duo	If I hadn't done A, I wouldn't have done B.	If I didn't do A, I wouldn't do B.	If I don't do A, I won't do B.

Negatives
否定式

Negatives follow the same pattern as the emphatic form. The remaining spot is filled with **not**. It goes between the helping verb and the unchanging form of the main verb. As usual, the helping verb **do** changes to **does** with **he**, **she**, and **it**. The negative of **can** is **cannot**.

否定式与强调式的模式是一样的。下表中间那个空填上not就可以了。not被放在助动词和主动词原形的中间。同样，当主语是he, she, it时，助动词从do变成does。can的否定式是cannot。

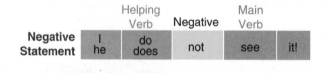

	Helping Verb	Negative	Main Verb	
Negative Statement	I he	do does	not	see	it!

Exercise 2-28: Adding *Not*

*Add **not** between the helping verb and the main verb. Use the unchanging form of the main verb. Then check the Answer Key.*

Sam does eat apples.

Sam does **not** eat apples.

1. The kids **do** play at the park.
2. My bus **does** come late.
3. The **dogs** can get **dirty**.
4. My boss **does** need this done.
5. You **do** forget many things.
6. The clock **does** cost a lot.
7. **Tom** can make mis**takes**.
8. These reports **do** need work.
9. I **do** work too hard.
10. The **car** can run **well**.
11. My sister **does** want to help him.
12. I **do** have to study.
13. We **do** need to practice.
14. They **do** like to dance together.
15. He **does** want to take the test.

Contractions
缩略式

Full Form	Contraction
I do not do it.	I don't do it.
You do not do it.	You don't do it.
He does not do it. She does not do it. It does not do it.	He doesn't do it. She doesn't do it. It doesn't do it.

Full Form	Contraction
We do not do it.	We don't do it.
You do not do it.	You don't do it.
They do not do it.	They don't do it.

Exercise 2-29: Changing to a Contraction

*Replace the o in **not** with an apostrophe. Make it into a single word. Then check the Answer Key.*

Sam **does not** eat apples.

Sam doesn't eat apples.

1. The **kids** do not play at the **park**.
2. My **bus** does not come **late**.
3. The **dogs** do not get **dirty**.
4. My **boss** does not need this **done**.
5. You do not for**get** many **things**.
6. The **clock** does not **cost** a lot.
7. **Tom** does not make **mistakes**.
8. These re**ports** do not need **work**.
9. I do not **work** too hard.
10. The **car** does not **run** well.
11. My **sister** does not want to **help** him.
12. I do not have to **study**.
13. We do not need to **practice**.

14. They do not like to **dance** together.
15. He does not want to take the **test**.

Questions
疑问句

Let's work with questions now. You will be using the same helping verbs, **do** and **does**, but they will change position with the subject. This is called the *Question Flip*.

现在我们来学习疑问句。你会用到同样的助动词，即do 和 does，但它们要和主语交换位置。这就是疑问句词序颠倒。

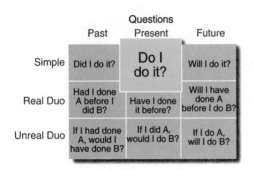

As usual, you will use the unchanging form of the main verb (called the *simple form*).
同样，你会用到主动词的原形（又叫做一般式）。

Rule: The Question Flip ↻ + Simple Unchanging Form
规则：疑问句词序颠倒 ↻ + 不变化的一般式

To make a question from an emphatic statement, you just need to flip the first two words.
要把强调性的陈述句变成疑问句，你只需要颠倒前两个单词的位置。

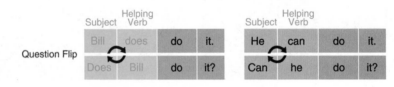

Exercise 2-30: Making a Question from an Emphatic Statement ↻

*Reverse the noun and the helping verb to form a question. Use the **unchanging** form of the main verb (simple form). Then check the Answer Key.*

Sam and Ed **do** eat apples.	**Do** Sam and Ed eat apples?
Sam **does** eat apples.	**Does** Sam eat apples?
Betty **can** play the piano.	**Can** Betty play the piano?

1. The kids **do** play at the park!
2. My bus **does** come late!
3. The dogs **can** get dirty!
4. My boss **does** need this done!
5. You **do** forget many things!
6. The clock **does** cost a lot!
7. Tom **can** make mistakes!
8. These reports **do** need work!
9. I **do** work too hard!
10. The car **does** run well!

11. My sister **can** help him!
12. I **do** have to study!
13. We **do** need to practice!
14. They **do** like to dance together!
15. He **does** hope to pass the test!

The next exercise is very similar to the previous one, but you will start with a regular statement, instead of an emphatic one.

以下练习与上一个练习很相似，但下面你要练的是把常规的陈述句转换成疑问句，而不是把强调句转换成疑问句。

Exercise 2-31: Making a Question from a Regular Statement ↻

*Add **do**, **does**, or **can** to the beginning of each statement to form a question. Use the unchanging form of the main verb. Remember, there is no -s with the simple form. When you're done, check the Answer Key.*

The boy **eats** apples.   **Does** the boy **eat** apples?
The boys **eat** apples.   **Do** the boys **eat** apples?
The boys **can eat** apples.   **Can** the boys **eat** apples?

1. The **kids** play at the **park**.
2. My **bus** comes **late**.
3. The **dogs** can get **dirty**.
4. My **boss** needs this **done**.
5. You for**get** many **things**.
6. The **clock** costs a **lot**.
7. **Tom** can make **mistakes**.
8. These re**ports** need **work**.
9. I **work** too **hard**.
10. The **car** runs **well**.
11. My **sister** can **help** him.
12. I have to **study**.
13. We need to **practice**.
14. They like to **dance** together.
15. He **hopes** to pass the **test**.

Exercise 2-32: Making a Question with Pronouns ↻

*Add **do**, **does**, or **can** to the beginning of each statement to form a question. Change the nouns to pronouns. The stress moves to the verb. When you're done, check the Answer Key.*

The **boy** eats apples.   Does **he** eat them?
The **boys** eat apples.   Do **they** eat them?
The **boys** can eat apples.   Can **they** eat them?

1. The kids **play** there.
2. My **bus** comes **late**.
3. The **dogs** can get **dirty**.
4. My **boss** needs this **done**.

5. You for**get** many **things**.
6. The **clock** costs a **lot**.
7. **Tom** can make **mistakes**.
8. These re**ports** need **work**.
9. **Bob** works too **hard**.
10. The **car** runs **well**.
11. My **sister** wants to **help** our **friend**.
12. I have to study the **lesson**.
13. We need to practice the **guitar**.
14. The **family** likes to **dance** together.
15. Sam hopes to pass the **test**.

Exercise 2-33: Making a Question with Pronouns—Pronunciation　　　Track 055

*Now, let's see how that sounds. Listen to the audio and repeat five times. Notice that the **Hs** and the **THs** get dropped. Trust the phonetics. Looks weird, sounds great!*

Duzz Sæm eedapplz?

1. Do the kidz **play** there?
2. Duzz my **bəs** kəm **late**?
3. C'n the **dägz** get **dirdy**?
4. Duzz my **bäss** need this **dən**?
5. Do you for**get** many **things**?
6. Duzz the **cläck** cäst a **lät**?
7. C'n **Täm** make **mistakes**?
8. Do theez re**ports** need **work**?
9. Duzz **Bäb** work too **hard**?
10. Duzz the **cär** run **well**?
11. C'n my **sister help**im?
12. Dwäi hæf tə stədy the **lessən**?
13. Dwee need tə præctice the **guitar**?
14. Duzz thə **fæmlee** like tə **dæns** təgether?
15. Duzz **Sæm** hope tə pæss thə **test**?

Duzzy eedem?

Do they **play** there?
Duzzit kəm **late**?
C'n they get **dirdy**?
Duzzy need it **dən**?
D'you fer**ge**dem?
Duzzit **cäst** a lät?
Canny **may** kem?
Do they **need**it?
Duzzy **wrrrrk** too hard?
Duzzit **run** well?
C'n she **help**im?
Dwäi hæf tə **stədy** it?
Dwee need tə **præc**tice it?
D'they like tə **dæns** təgether?
Duzzy hope tə **pæss** it?

Exercise 2-34: Making a Tag Question

*Reverse the order and the polarity to form a tag question. If the verb is positive, the tag is negative. If the verb is negative, the tag is positive. The last five are a review of the verb **to be**. When you're done, check the Answer Key.*

Sam eats apples,	**doesn't he?**	duzzanee
1. The **kids** don't play at the **park**,		doo they
2. My **bus** comes **late**,		duzzanit
3. The **dogs** can get **dirty**,		cant they
4. My **boss** needs this **done**,		duzzanee

5.	You **forget** many **things**,	donchyoo
6.	The **clock** costs a **lot**,	duzzanit
7.	**Tom** can make **mistakes**,	cantee
8.	These **reports** need **work**,	doan they
9.	I **work** too **hard**,	doanai
10.	The **car** doesn't run **well**,	duzzit
11.	**Bob** is **late**,	izzanee
12.	Your **mom** isn't **worried**,	iz she
13.	The **papers** are **torn**,	arnt they
14.	I'm **here**,	*aren't I*	ar nai
15.	I'm not **here**,	amai

Using the same pattern, change your tone to make an assertion.

运用同样的模式，但改变你的音调，以表达肯定的语气。

Exercise 2-35: Making a Tag Assertion ⟳

Reverse the order and the polarity to form a tag assertion. If the verb is positive, the tag is negative. If the verb is negative, the tag is positive. The last five are a review of the verb to be. When you're done, check the Answer Key.

	Sam eats **apples**,	**doesn't** he!	**duzz**anee!
	Sam doesn't eat **apples**,	**does** he!	**duzz**ee!
1.	The **kids** don't play at the **park**,		**doo** they!
2.	My **bus** comes **late**,		**duzz**anit!
3.	The **dogs** can get **dirty**,		**cant** they!
4.	My **boss** needs this **done**,		**duzz**anee!
5.	You **forget** many **things**,		**donch**yoo!
6.	The **clock** costs a **lot**,		**duzz**anit!
7.	**Tom** can make **mistakes**,		**can**dy!
8.	These **reports** need **work**,		**doan** they!
9.	I **work** too **hard**,		**doa**nai!
10.	The **car** doesn't run **well**,		**duzz**it!
11.	**Bob** is **late**,		**izz**anee!
12.	Your **mom** isn't **worried**,		**iz** she!
13.	The **papers** are **torn**,		**arnt** they!
14.	I'm **here**,		**ar** nai!
15.	I'm not **here**,		**am**ai!

Remember: The inflection on a tag question is **up**, **up**. The inflection on a tag assertion is **down**, **down**.

记住：反意疑问句的音调变化是升调，再升调。反意断言句的音调变化是降调，再降调。

Exercise 2-36: Identifying Intent   Track 056

Listen to the audio and identify if each item is a question or an assertion. Put in either a question mark (?) or an exclamation point (!). Then check the Answer Key.

1. I see him, don't I _____
2. They don't like it, do they _____
3. She wasn't there, was she _____
4. Bob had to leave, didn't he _____
5. You need one, don't you _____
6. You like it, don't you _____
7. He doesn't know, does he _____
8. We can work on it, can't we _____
9. They think so, don't they _____
10. It is good, isn't it _____

Exercise 2-37: Contractions, Negatives, and Questions

*Complete the grid for the verb **to do**. Then check the Answer Key.*

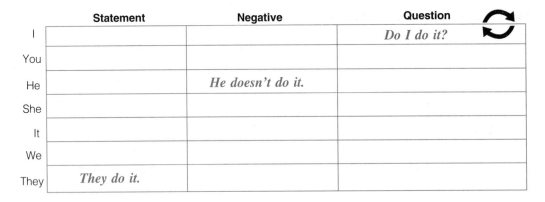

	Statement	Negative	Question
I			*Do I do it?*
You			
He		*He doesn't do it.*	
She			
It			
We			
They	*They do it.*		

Commands and Suggestions
命令句和建议句

Commands are easy in English. All you need is the simple form of either the verb **to be** or the *main verb*. Colloquially, a command can start with **go**. Formal commands use the present tense of the verb **to be**. You can make a suggestion with **let's**. Commands can be either positive or negative.

用英语下命令很容易，因为你只要用be动词或主动词的一般式即可。在口语中，你可以用go来开始命令句。而正式的命令句要用be动词的现在时。提建议时，你可以用let's。命令既可以是肯定的，也可以是否定的。

Positive	Negative
Be good!	Don't be bad!
Stop it! Go away!	Don't stop! Don't go!
Go get me a hammer.	Don't go and forget about it!
Let's go!	Let's not do it.
You are to be here by 5:00.	You are never to speak of this again.

Exercise 2-38: Commands

Change the positive commands to the negative. Then check the Answer Key.

Get lost!	**Don't** get lost!
Let's try it again!	Let's **not** try it again!
You are to finish by tomorrow.	You are **not** to finish by tomorrow.

1. Give up!
2. They are to be informed!
3. Try again!
4. Let's think about it!
5. Bring it back!

TEST

Let's review everything you have learned in Chapter 2, including nouns, main verbs, helping verbs, commands, prepositions of location, conjunctions, and tag endings. Check your work using the Answer Key.

让我们复习一下你在第二章中所学的全部内容，其中包括：名词、主动词、助动词、命令句、方位介词、连词、反意疑问/断言句。做完测试题后请核对答案。

Part 1: *Replace all nouns with pronouns.*

1. Edgar buys a new yacht. — He / one
2. Sam and Charlie fly the kite. — They / it
3. Moira plans her classes. — She / them
4. The book tells a good story. — It / one
5. The dogs bark at the mailman. — They / him

Part 2: *Select the appropriate preposition, based on the picture.*

1. The gray ball is **on** the table.
2. The red ball is **under** the table.
3. The plant is **in** the pot.
4. The plant is **besides** the table.
5. The table is **under** the gray ball.

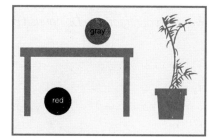

Part 3: *Select the appropriate conjunction.*

1. They speak French **and** Italian.
2. We eat the cheese, **but** not the crackers.
3. It is late, **but so** we are in a hurry.
4. I don't speak French **and or** Italian.
5. He is tired **because** he works hard.

Part 4: *Circle the proper verb form.*

1.	Susie	speak	speaks	French.
2.	Fred and John	eat	eats	dinner.
3.	Ella	go to	goes to	school.
4.	Edward	like	likes	his classes.
5.	The dogs	bark at	barks at	the cat.
6.	The zookeeper	feed	feeds	the animals.
7.	Our family	have	has	a good time there.
8.	Joe and Ellie	tell	tells	funny jokes.
9.	The gardener	doesn't	don't speak	English.
10.	Summer	is	are	hot.

Part 5: *Add **do** or **does** for emphasis.*

1. They see him every day.
2. He tells the truth.
3. We have fun.

Part 6: *Add the helping verb **can**.*

1. The boy sees the toys.
2. The girl speaks well.
3. This book is helpful.

Part 7: *Make the sentence negative. Do not use pronouns or contractions.*

1. Lou knows Ed.
2. It works well.
3. The cars go fast.
4. The well is dry.
5. The boys are in the house.

Part 8: *Make the sentence negative using contractions. Do not use pronouns.*

1. George works in Las Vegas.
2. Sandy sells seashells.
3. The team members play every day.
4. Big cities are often crowded.
5. It's really hot today.

Part 9: *Change the statement to a question.* ↻

1. It rains every day.
2. He calls us all of the time.
3. You like it.
4. They are very kind.
5. He is in trouble.

76

Part 10: *Indicate the proper tag ending.* ↻

1. He likes it,   ?
2. She is a teacher,   ?
3. They want one,   ?
4. They are here,   ?

Part 11: *Identify the story order, by putting 1, 2, and 3 in the boxes in the proper order.*

☐ He is happy.
☐ He buys one.
☐ Bob wants a car.

Using what you have learned, write a paragraph about yourself. Next, write a paragraph about how many keys are on your keychain, and what they are for.

用你学过的知识写一段关于你的文章。接下来，再写一段话谈谈你的钥匙链上有几把钥匙，都是用来干什么的。

You can handwrite your paragraphs below or e-mail them to **para@grammar.bz** to be stored. These paragraphs are not graded or reviewed, but simply by writing them, your English will improve. Use the SVO format — **Subject-Verb-Object** (or **Noun-Verb-Noun**).

你可以把作文写在下方，也可以把它们发送到邮箱 para@grammar.bz 以存档。我们不会对你的作文进行打分或点评，但只要你写了，你的英语水平就会提高。请使用SVO模式，即主语—动词—宾语（或名词—动词—名词）。

◉◯◯   Student Paragraph

✈   ◯   📎   ▭   *Aa*   ⬭   ▭   ▭   ▯▯
Send   Chat   Attach   Address   Fonts   Colors   Save As Draft   Photo Browser   Show Stationery

To:	para@grammar.bz
Cc:	
Bcc:	
Subject:	About Me

Signature: Corporate ↕

My name is _____

_____ _____ _____ and/but/or/so/because _____ _____ _____ .
    S   V   O   S   V   O

_____ _____ _____ conjunction _____ _____ _____ .
    S   V   O   S   V   O

_____ _____ _____ conjunction _____ _____ _____ .
    S   V   O   S   V   O

_____ _____ _____ conjunction _____ _____ _____ .
    S   V   O   S   V   O

_____ _____ _____ conjunction _____ _____ _____ .
    S   V   O   S   V   O

When you have finished, look at **every** noun and make sure it is one of these:
写完以后，逐个检查一下名词，确保它们符合下列情况之一：

1. Modified with **a**, **the**, **this**, **many**, **my**, etc.
   前面有a，the，this，many，my等词修饰。

2. Plural
   复数

3. A pronoun
   代词

   Look at every verb and make sure it is one of these:
   逐个检查一下动词，确保它们符合下列情况之一：

1. Verb **to be** — is / am / are
   be动词——is / am / are

2. Main **verb** — he / she / it + S
   主动词——he / she / it + S

Chapter 3

Comparisons and the Past
比较级和过去时

DICTATION

You are now moving toward the end of the beginning level. In this chapter, you will review articles and modifiers, and you will learn comparisons, prepositions of direction, time words, tag endings, and the phrasal verb **get**. With the past tense, you are no longer limited to **now**: You can talk about things that happened **before**, including negatives and questions.

学完这一章，基础部分就学完了。在本章，你要复习冠词和修饰语，你还要学习比较级、方向介词、时间副词、反意疑问/断言句，以及由get组成的动词短语。你还要学习过去时，学会以后你就不会仅局限于描述现在了：你可以谈论以前发生的事情，包括运用否定句和疑问句。

Exercise 3-1: Dictation   Track 057

Listen to the audio and write the exact transcription in the spaces below. Then check the Answer Key.

1. _____

2. _____

3. _____

4. _____

5. _____

Max's Diet

STORY

When I **competed**, people were **surprised** by my **diet**. I ate a **lot**. I **needed** to take in **6,000** calories every **day**. The **average** American man eats **2,000** or **2,500** calories every day. Before a big **tournament**, I needed **10,000** calories every day. It was pretty **expensive**. For **example**, for **breakfast**, I had a dozen **eggs**. **Yes**, I ate **12** eggs for **break**fast every **morning**. I had **omelettes**, scrambled **eggs**, **fried** eggs, **hard**-boiled eggs, and **poached** eggs. As a matter of **fact**, I ate them **every** way but **raw**. My doctor checked my **cholesterol** level every **month**. He **also** checked my **liver**. Many **body**builders have **trouble** with their **livers**, but **I** don't. I'm a **miracle** of modern **science**, **aren't** I?

Exercise 3-2: Story Pronunciation   Track 058

Listen to the audio and repeat, focusing on intonation and pronunciation.

When I **c'mpeeded**, peepəl wrr **sprized** by my **diet**. I aydə **lät**. I **need**əd to take in **6,000** cæləreez evry **day**. The **ævrage** əmerəcan **man** eats **two** thouzənd or **twe**nny five **hendrəd** cæləreez evry day. Bəforə big **tərnəmənt**, I needəd **10,000** cæləreez evry day. It wəz priddy **ekss-pens've**. Fregg **zæm**pəl, fər **brekfəst**, I hædə dəzə **neggz**. **Yes**, I⁽ʸ⁾ate **twel veggz** fər **brek**fəst evry **morning**. I had **ämlettes**, scræmble **deggz**, **fry** deggz, **härd** boil deggz, and **poach** deggz. Aza mæddərə **fæct**, I ay dem **evry** way but **rah**. My däktr chekt my **kəlesteräl** level evry **mənth**. He **älso** chekt my **liver**. Many **bädy**bildərz hæv **trəbəl** with their **liverz**, bədäi don't. I'mə **mirəkəl** əv mädern **science**, **är** nai!

Exercise 3-3: Squeezed Out Syllables   Track 059

Listen and repeat.

	Spelling	Pronunciation			Spelling	Pronunciation
1.	asp**i**rin	asprin		11.	fam**i**ly	famlee
2.	av**e**rage	avr'j		12.	fin**a**lly	fynlee
3.	basic**a**lly	basiclee		13.	gen**e**ral	genr'l
4.	bus**i**ness	bizness		14.	hist**o**ry	hisstree
5.	choc**o**late	choclate		15.	int**e**rest	intrest
6.	comf**or**table	comft'bl		16.	nat**u**ral	nachrul
7.	conf**e**rence	confrence		17.	om**e**lette	omlet
8.	corp**o**rate	corpr't		18.	prob**a**bly	problee
9.	diff**e**rent	diffrent		19.	sev**e**ral	sevral
10.	ev**e**ry	evry		20.	sep**a**rate	seprate

This section covers an important aspect of nouns: how to tell if they are new info or not. It also shows you how to **compare**. Comparison words are another form of modifier. With the superlative, you need a double modifier, such as **the best**, **the only**, **the first**.

这部分会讲述有关名词的一个重要方面：如何辨别信息是不是新的。还会告诉你如何进行比较。单词的比较级是另一种修饰形式。当你用最高级时，你需要两个修饰语，如：the best, the only, the first。

In Chapter 2, we looked at prepositions of location. Now, we are going to use prepositions of **direction**, which show movement.

在第二章中，我们讲到过方位介词。现在，我们要讲讲方向介词的用法，方向介词是用来指示运动的。

Count Us
数一数我们

We're general. 我们是泛指的。
We're single or multiple. 我们要么是单个的，要么是多个的。

Single	Multiple
a water drop	**some** water drops
	a couple of water drops
	several water drops
	most water drops
	all water drops
an airplane	**both** airplanes
	three airplanes
	a few airplanes
	a lot of airplanes
a chair	**many** chairs
	so many chairs
	too many chairs
	not many chairs

Exercise 3-4: *A* or *Some*

*Fill in the blank with **a** or **some**. Then check the Answer Key.*

I have _____ bike.		**I have a bike.**
I have _____ bikes.		**I have some bikes.**

1. There are _____ stars in the sky at night.
2. We need _____ details about that.
3. There was _____ hurricane in Florida.
4. You put _____ cup of salt in the potatoes!
5. Give me _____ minute to finish.
6. We have _____ things to do!
7. May I have _____ cup of tea, please?
8. He drank _____ glasses of water.
9. She needs _____ more time.
10. Where is _____ public telephone?

Don't Count Us
不要数我们

We're single or multiple.
我们要么是单个的，要么是多个的。
But now... we're specific, **we're** known.
但是现在……我们是具体的，我们是已知的。

A and **the** are important signals in front of a noun. They tell you three things about the noun:
a和the是位于名词前的重要标志。它们可以告诉你有关名词的三件事：

Is it **general** or **specific**?

它是泛指的还是具体的?

Is it **new** information or **known** information?

它是新信息还是已知信息?

Is there **one** or **more than one**?

它是单个的还是多个的?

Let's take a look at this sentence with two nouns: The **sun** is a **star**.

让我们看看这个有两个名词的句子: The **sun** is a **star**.(太阳是一颗恒星。)

We say **the sun** because
there is only *one* sun.

我们说the sun, 因为太阳只有一个。

We say **a star** because
there are *many* stars.

我们说a star, 因为恒星有很多。

When the word is known and specific, use **the**.

当某个词是已知的且表示特指时, 要用the。

Exercise 3-5: *A / An* or *The*

*Fill in the blank with **a / an** or **the**. Then check the Answer Key.*

I have a job.   I have **the** best job in the world.

1. This is ~~the~~ best coffee!
2. Wait _a_ minute, please.
3. It's _a_ long way to Texas from here.
4. It's ~~the~~ wrong way to do it. Please do it ~~the~~ right way.
5. I have _the_ longest name in the **Phone** book.
6. That's _a_ great idea!
7. I need _a_ new zip drive.
8. I need _the_ new zip drive that I bought today.
9. This is ~~the~~ only time I need it.
10. Please give me _a_ quarter. (korder)
11. Please pass ~~the~~ salt.
12. Are you going away next week? No, ~~the~~ week after next.
13. My friends live in ~~the~~ *an* old house in ~~the~~ small town. There is _a_ beautiful garden behind ~~the~~ house. I would like to have ~~the~~ garden like that.
14. I would like to have _the_ same garden.
15. I would like to have _a_ similar garden.
16. The kids are playing in ~~the~~ yard.
17. Cats can see in ~~the~~ dark.
18. What's ~~the~~ next step?
19. I have to wait _a_ year for them to send me ~~the~~ documents.
20. ~~The~~ first step is to find _a_ lawyer.

21. In _the_ beginning, we worked on it all of _the_ time.
22. Did you listen to _the_ news on _the_ radio?
23. Does he usually follow _the_ rules?
24. *Casablanca* is _a_ classic movie.
25. We hope to see them over _the_ holidays.
26. Do you know what _the_ answer is?
27. They went in one at _the_ time. They went in one by one.
28. Do you remember _the_ time we were three hours late?
29. Don't forget to lock _the_ door on your way out.
30. I have to go to _the_ **bath**room. Is there _a_ **bath**room in this building?
31. I had _a_ good time. It was _the_ best time of all.
32. What's that under _the_ desk?
33. An office usually has _a_ desk.
34. _An_ apple _a_ day keeps _the_ doctor away.
35. It's _a_ fast car, but definitely not _the_ fastest.

There are two terms for comparing things. These are the *comparative* and the *superlative*. When you have two items, use the comparative. When you have three items or more, use the superlative. With the superlative, you need a double modifier, such as the **first**, the **best**, or the **only**.

事物之间进行比较时有两种形式，即比较级和最高级。对两个事物进行比较时，要用比较级。对三个或三个以上的事物进行比较时，要用最高级。 在使用最高级时，还需要双重修饰语，如：the first，the best或the only。

The **absolute** is the term for a regular adjective.
描述形容词原形的术语是原级。

Big, **Bigger**, **The Biggest**

This key is big. This key is bigger. This key is the biggest.

This key is smaller than that key. This key is bigger than that key.

This key is **as big as** that key.
These keys are the same size.
These keys are equally large.

With short words, add **-er** to compare and **-est** for the superlative. If the word ends in **-y**, drop the **Y** and add **-ier** or **-iest**. For example, **pretty** becomes **prettier / prettiest**.

对于较短的形容词来说，加上-er就构成比较级，加上-est就构成最高级。如果某词是以-y结尾，那就要去掉Y再加-ier或-iest。例如：pretty变成prettier / prettiest。

When the word ends in a consonant, add **-er** or **-est**. For some words, you may need to double the final consonant—for example, **bigger / biggest**, **hotter / hottest**, etc.

当单词以辅音字母结尾时，加上-er或-est。对于有些词来说，你需要双写词尾的辅音字母——例如：bigger / biggest，hotter / hottest等。

Short Words
短单词

Big	Bigger	Biggest
tall	taller	the tallest
short	shorter	the shortest
smart	smarter	the smartest
hot	hotter	the hottest
cold	colder	the coldest
rich	richer	the richest
hard	harder	the hardest
easy	easier	the easiest
funny	funnier	the funniest
happy	happier	the happiest
pretty	prettier	the prettiest

Absolute Adjective	Comparative (-er)	Superlative (-est)
as ____ as + noun	**____-er than + noun**	**the ____-est + preposition**
as big as a house	*bigger than a house*	*the biggest in the world*
as ____ as + adjective	**____-er than + pronoun**	**the ____-est + ever**
as good as new	*bigger than yours*	*the biggest ever*
	____-er than + time word	**the ____-est + phrase**
	bigger than before	*the biggest I've ever seen*
	____-er than + phrase	
	bigger than I thought	

These five are irregular, so you need to memorize them. Remember that you need to use **the** with **superlatives**. With **comparatives**, you need to use **than**.

下列五个单词是不规则形容词，所以你要记住它们。记住：最高级要用the，比较级要用than。

Absolute	Comparative	Superlative
good	better	the best
bad	worse	the worst
some	more	the most
little	less	the least
far	farther	the farthest
	further	the furthest

Exercise 3-6: Short Comparison Words

Fill in the blank with the appropriate form. Then check the Answer Key.

	The sun is	**the closest**	star.	close / closer / **the closest**
1.	This idea is		in the whole world.	good / better / the best
2.	Those cars are		than the new ones.	cheap / cheaper / the cheapest
3.	An F is		grade on a test.	bad / worse / the worst
4.	I needed a long,		shower.	hot / hotter / the hottest
5.	Einstein was		than most people.	smart / smarter / the smartest
6.	Lola isn't		on her team.	tall / taller / the tallest
7.	Alaska isn't very		in the winter.	warm / warmer / the warmest
8.	Alaska is much		than Florida.	cold / colder / the coldest
9.	This is even		than before.	good / better / the best
10.	Spanish is		than Chinese.	easy / easier / the easiest
11.	He is		man in the world.	old / older / the oldest
12.	I am		to be here.	happy / happier / the happiest
13.	Diamonds are		than glass.	hard / harder / the hardest
14.	My house is as		as your house.	nice / nicer / nicest
15.	This is twice as		as the other one.	big / bigger / the biggest
16.	↻ Which is		, a fly or a bee?	fast / faster / the fastest
17.	↻ Which is		, rice, bread, or pasta?	good / better / the best
18.	↻ Who has		money, Ed or Sam?	some / more / the most
19.	↻ Who is		, Ed or Sam?	rich / richer / the richest
20.	↻ Is L.A. or New York		from Bangkok?	far / farther / the farthest

What five-letter word becomes shorter when you add two letters to it?
哪个五个字母的单词加上两个字母后会变得更短？

Answer 答案
The word is **short**. Add -er, and it becomes **shorter**.
这个词是short（短的）。给它加上-er，它就变成了shorter（更短的）。

With long words, add **more** before the word to compare and **the most** before the word for the superlative.

对于较长的单词来说，要在前面加上more构成比较级，加上the most构成最高级。

Long Words
长单词

Beautiful	More Beautiful	The Most Beautiful
expensive	more expensive	the most expensive
important	more important	the most important
interesting	more interesting	the most interesting
wonderful	more wonderful	the most wonderful
delicious	more delicious	the most delicious
terrible	more terrible	the most terrible
exciting	more exciting	the most exciting
pathetic	more pathetic	the most pathetic
irritating	more irritating	the most irritating
playful	more playful	the most playful

Exercise 3-7: Long Comparison Words

*Fill in the blank with the appropriate form, including **more** and **the most** where necessary. Then check the Answer Key.*

	He is	the most intelligent	one in the class.	intelligent
1.	That is		story I heard today.	interesting
2.	That was		pear!	delicious
3.	That child becomes		every day.	obedient
4.	This is really		for me.	difficult
5.	These shoes are		than we expected.	expensive
6.	Did you have a		time at the wedding?	wonderful
7.	That excuse was		you have ever used.	unusual
8.	Were those exercises		than before?	complicated
9.	That final detail was		item on our list.	important
10.	The seal pup is		animal.	wonderful

Exercise 3-8: Long and Short Comparison Words

*Fill in the blank with the appropriate form, including -er, -est, **more**, or **the most**, where necessary. Then check the Answer Key.*

	They have	better	shoes than we do.	good
	She is	more reliable	than the others.	reliable
1.	Peace is		than war.	effective
2.	Donuts are		by the dozen.	cheap

3. That situation is ⬜ than you realize.   dangerous
4. This is ⬜ issue of our time.   important
5. Bill Gates is ⬜ than most people.   rich
6. My grammar is ⬜ than my pronunciation.   good
7. Snakes are ⬜ than spiders.   scary
8. The Mississippi is ⬜ river in America.   long
9. 8:00 a.m. is ⬜ than 9:00 a.m.   early
10. Is Saturn ⬜ planet?   close

Things and Directions
事物和方向

into the house

along the path

In Chapter 2, we saw that prepositions tell you the *location* of a thing—*What a plane can do to a cloud.* Examples are **in** *a cloud*, **by** *a cloud*, **near** *a cloud*, and so on.

从第二章我们知道介词可以指示事物的位置——What a plane can do to a cloud.（飞机可以对云做什么？）例子是in a cloud（在云的中间），by a cloud（在云的旁边），near a cloud（在云的附近）等。

The ✈ goes **through** the cloud.

Now we're going to work with direction. This time, you'll be using prepositions to indicate movement. **To** is the most common preposition in English. It is pronounced **tə** or **də**.

现在我们要学习的是方向。这里你将要用介词来指示运动。to是英语中最常见的介词，它读作tə或də。

Exercise 3-9: Prepositions of Direction   **Track 060**

Listen and repeat.

1. The **boy** ran   away from   the **bully**.
2. The **man** jumped   out of   the **window**.
3. The **cat** fell   into   the **box**.
4. My **sister** spoke   to   her **friend**.
5. I was **walking**   toward   the **door**.
6. We **ran**   through   the **tunnel**.
7. They **walked**   up to   the **desk**.
8. It's a **quarter**   past   **five**. (5:15)
9. The **smoke** spread   throughout   the **house**.
10. His **actions** were   beyond   **belief**.
11. The girls were talking   to   the **teacher**.
12. The boys are yelling   at   each **other**.

13. The dog is barking	**at**	the **mailman**.
14. She threw the ball	**to**	the **catcher**.
15. She threw the ball	**at**	the **catcher**.

Common Prepositions
常用介词

The numbers indicate the Top 10 most common prepositions.
用数字标出的是最常用的10个介词。

about [10]	at [7]	beyond	into	outside	under
above	away from	by	near	over	underneath
across	before	during	next to	past	until
after	behind	except	of [2]	since	up to
against	below	for [4]	off	through	with [5]
along	beneath	from [9]	on [6]	throughout	within
among	beside	in [3]	onto	to [1] (tə or də)	without
around	between	inside	out [8]	toward	

As you saw in Chapter 2, the infinitive uses **to**, as in **I have to be there**, **He wants to do that**, or **She plans to go there**. This, plus the **to** of direction, makes **to** the most commonly used preposition.

正如你在第二章学到的那样，不定式要用to，如：I have to be there, He wants to do that或She plans to go there。这一用法加上to指示方向的用法，使to成了使用频率最高的介词。

With prepositions, you can add a **noun** (*to the store*) or **-ing** (*without taking*). With the infinitive, use the simple form.

to作介词时，后面可以加名词（to the store）或动词的-ing形式（without taking）。to作不定式时，后面加动词原形。

Exercise 3-10: *To* as a Preposition   Track 061

*Listen and repeat. Remember that **to** is pronounced tə or də.*

1.	We plan to **do** it.	We plændə do [w] it.
2.	Give it to the **clerk**.	G'v't t' the clerk.
3.	Everyone wanted to **practice** more.	Evrywən wändəd də præct's more.
4.	They hope to **see** you again.	They hope tə see you [w] əgen.
5.	I'm looking forward to **seeing** you again.	I'm lüking forw'rd də seeing you [w] again.
6.	She asked me to **help**.	She [y] æskt me də help.
7.	Let's go to the **movies**.	Let's go də the moveez.
8.	You don't need to **do** that.	You don't need də do that.
9.	A **customer** walked up to the **counter**.	ə customer wähkt up tə the counter.
10.	Our **dog** likes to bark at the **mailman**.	är däg likes tə bärk at the mailman.

You don't need **to** in phrases like He told him, He called him, He paid him.
在有些说法中不需要用to，如：He told him, He called him, He paid him等。

Exercise 3-11: Top 10 Prepositions   **Track 062**

*Listen and repeat the top ten prepositions of **direction**, **location**, and the **infinitive**.*

1.	She went to **school** every **day**.	She went tə **school** every **day**.
2.	It was in Chapter **20**.	It wəzin Chæpter **twenny**.
3.	It was on page **8**.	It wəzän pay **jate**.
4.	Please **come** with me.	Pleez **cəme** with me.
5.	My **car's** in front of my **house**.	My **cärz** in front of my **house**.
6.	Call me at **5**:00.	**Cäll** me at **5**:00.
7.	He **did** it for **us**. He did it **for** us.	He **did**it frəs. He didit **for** əs.
8.	Where are you **from**?	Where are you **frəm**?
9.	Send it to the **boss**.	Send it tə the **boss**.
10.	We hope to **see** him in three **days**.	We hope tə **see** him in three **days**.
11.	What do you hope to find **out**?	Wəddə you hope tə find**out**?
12.	We can't **work** with him.	We cænt **wrrk** withim.
13.	It's the best of **all**.	It's the best əv**äll**.
14.	What are you **talking** about?	Wədder you **tähking** əbout?
15.	Thank you for under**stand**ing.	Thænk you fr ənder**stænd**ing.
16.	They learned to do it them**selves**.	They lrrnd də do ⁽ʷ⁾it them**selves**.
17.	She ran out of the **house**.	She ræn oudəv the **house**.
18.	When do you plan on **telling** them?	When d' you plæn än **telling** 'em?
19.	He said it without **thinking**.	He sɛdit without **thinking**.
20.	At **first**, we didn't under**stand**.	At **first**, we didn't ənder**stænd**.
21.	Let's keep him from finding **out**.	Let's keepim frəm finding **out**.
22.	He fell in the **water**.	He fellin the **wäder**.
23.	He landed on his **back**.	He landəd äniz **back**.
24.	He's about **six** feet **tall**.	Heezə bout **six** feet **tall**.
25.	I'm on my **way**.	I män my **way**.

Verbs	In Chapters 1 and 2, we looked at verbs in the present tense: 在第一章和第二章中，我们学习了动词的现在时：

is, am, are, do, does

Now, we are going to work with the past. In addition to **was** and **were** for the verb **to be** we will learn about main verbs in the past. The pattern and intonation stay the same as the present tense, but the verb changes.

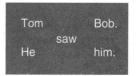

现在，我们要学习过去时。除了要学习be动词的过去式was和were，我们还要学习主动词的过去式。句子的模式和语调都跟现在时是一样的，但动词发生变化了。

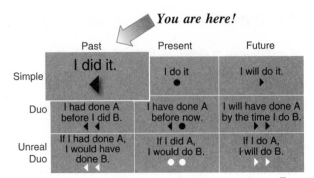

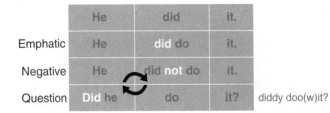

The past tense follows the same patterns as the present tense. For example, alone, the main verb **to do** changes to **did** in the past: **I did it**. When you have a helping verb, you must also use the unchanging form of the main verb: **I did do it**. The word **not** falls in the same position between the helping verb and the main verb: **I did not do it**. Questions have the same subject/verb flip: **Did I do it**?

过去时与现在时的模式是一样的。例如，在过去时中，只要把主动词do变成did即可：I did it。当句子中有助动词时，你也必须使用主动词的原形：I did do it。not仍然要放在助动词和主动词之间：I did not do it。疑问句也同样要颠倒主语和动词：Did I do it?

	He	did	it.
Emphatic	He	**did** do	it.
Negative	He	did **not** do	it.
Question	**Did** he	do	it?

diddy doo(w)it?

Good news! For questions, and negative and emphatic statements, the past tense of **do** only uses one form, **did**. There is no conjugating.

好消息！在疑问句、否定句和强调陈述句中，do的过去式只有一种形式，即did。它没有更多的词形变化了。

There are about 50 irregular verbs, however, and you just have to learn them.

不过，大约有50个动词的变化形式是不规则的，所以你必须记住它们。

Verb Form
动词形式

For regular verbs, add -**ed** to make the past tense.
对于规则动词来说，在词尾加上-ed就构成了过去式。

If the verb ends in **y**, change it to -**ied** (study > studied).
如果动词以y结尾，那就要把y变成-ied以构成过去式（study > studied）。

Pronunciation
发音

Notice that when the final consonant is *unvoiced* (P, K, S, SH, CH), the -**ed** ending sounds like a **T**.
注意：当词尾辅音是清辅音(P, K, S, SH, CH)时，尾音-ed听起来像T音。

Regular Verbs		
Infinitive	Past	Pronunciation
to work	**work**ed	wrrkt
to jump	**jump**ed	jumpt
to pull	**pull**ed	pulld
to need	**need**ed	needed
to pin	**pin**ned	pind
to change	**chang**ed	chanjd
to study	**stud**ied	studeed

hoped / hopt

washed / washt

watched / watcht

When the final consonant is *voiced* (B, G, Z, ZH, J) or a *vowel*, the **-ed** ending sounds like a **D**. For a final T or D, the ending sounds like -**ə**d.

当词尾辅音是浊辅音（B，G，Z，ZH，J）或元音时，尾音-ed听起来像D音。如果词尾是T或D，尾音听起来就像-əd。

50 Main Irregular Verbs

to be	**was / were**	to know	**knew**
to become	**became**	to leave	**left**
to begin	**began**	to lose	**lost**
to break	**broke**	to make	**made**
to bring	**brought**	to mean	**meant**
to catch	**caught**	to meet	**met**
to choose	**chose**	to put	**put**
to come	**came**	to read	**read**
to do	**did**	to ride	**rode**
to drink	**drank**	to run	**ran**
to drive	**drove**	to say	**said**
to eat	**ate**	to see	**saw**
to fall	**fell**	to sell	**sold**
to feel	**felt**	to send	**sent**
to fight	**fought**	to sit	**sat**
to find	**found**	to speak	**spoke**
to fly	**flew**	to stand	**stood**
to forget	**forgot**	to take	**took**
to give	**gave**	to teach	**taught**
to get	**got**	to tell	**told**
to go	**went**	to think	**thought**
to grow	**grew**	to throw	**threw**
to have	**had**	to understand	**understood**
to hear	**heard**	to win	**won**
to hold	**held**	to write	**wrote**

Pronunciation
发音

äh

saw / caught / brought / taught / lost / thought / got / forgot / fought

ü

took / put / looked

stood / understood

z

was / chose

eh

said = sɛd

meant = mɛnt

read = rɛd

T sounds like D

Italy / Idaly

water / wader

better / bedder

Exercise 3-12: Change to the Past

Change the verb from the present tense to the past tense.（The emphasis stays on the nouns.）When you're done, check the Answer Key.

Sam eats apples.   Sam **ate apples.**

1. The **teachers** write on the **black**board.
2. **Larry** rides his **bike** everywhere.
3. Your **cousin** flies first **class**.
4. The **managers** arrange **meetings**.
5. I give many **presents**.
6. We **think** about it all of the **time**.
7. They throw it **away** every **day**.
8. **Virginia** has long **hair**.

9. **Happy** people have good **luck**.
10. Her **sister** says **hello**.
11. The **kids** want to ride their **bikes**.
12. **Students** try to pass **tests**.
13. **Ed** likes to go to the **gym**.
14. The **class** hopes to have a **party**.
15. **Every**one needs to have more **fun**.

Exercise 3-13: Change to the Emphatic

*Add **did** between the helping verb and the main verb. (The S disappears from the main verb.) Then check the Answer Key.*

Sam ate apples.   Sam **did eat** apples!

1. The teachers wrote on the blackboard.
2. Larry rode his bike everywhere.
3. Your cousin flew first class.
4. The managers arranged meetings.
5. I gave many presents.
6. We thought about it all of the time.
7. They threw it away every day.
8. Virginia had long hair.
9. Happy people had good luck.
10. Her sister said hello.
11. The kids wanted to ride their bikes.
12. The students tried to pass the tests.
13. Ed liked to go to the gym.
14. The class hoped to have a party.
15. Everyone needed to have more fun.

Exercise 3-14: Change to the Negative

*Add **not** between the helping verb and the unchanging form of the main verb. (There's no S on the main verb.) Check the Answer Key when you're done.*

Sam did eat apples.   Sam did **not** eat apples.

1. The teachers did write on the blackboard.
2. Larry did ride his bike everywhere.
3. Your cousin did fly first class.
4. The managers did arrange meetings.
5. I did give many presents.
6. We did think about it all of the time.
7. They did throw it away every day.
8. Virginia did have long hair.

9. Happy people did have good luck.
10. Her sister did say hello.
11. The kids did want to ride their bikes.
12. The students did try to pass the tests.
13. Ed did like to go to the gym.
14. The class did hope to have a party.
15. Everyone did need to have more fun.

Exercise 3-15: Change to Negative Contractions

*Change **did not** to a contraction.* （*There's no S on the main verb.*）*Check the Answer Key when you're done.*

Sam did not eat apples.	Sam did**n't** eat apples.

1. The teachers did not write on the blackboard.
2. Larry did not ride his bike everywhere.
3. Your cousin did not fly first class.
4. The managers did not arrange meetings.
5. I did not give many presents.
6. We did not think about it all of the time.
7. They did not throw it away every day.
8. Virginia did not have long hair.
9. Happy people did not have good luck.
10. Her sister did not say hello.
11. The kids did not want to ride their bikes.
12. Students did not try to pass tests.
13. Ed did not like to go to the gym.
14. The class did not hope to have a party.
15. Everyone did not need to have more fun.

Exercise 3-16: Change the Positive to Negative Contractions

Let's review. Change the positive to a negative contraction, using pronouns. Then check the Answer Key.

Sam ate apples.	He **didn't eat** them.

1. The teachers wrote on the blackboard.
2. Larry rode his bike everywhere.
3. Your cousin flew first class.
4. The managers arranged meetings.
5. I gave many presents.
6. We thought about it all of the time.
7. They threw it away every day.
8. Virginia had long hair.
9. Happy people had good luck.

10. Her sister said hello.

11. The kids wanted to ride their bikes.

12. Students tried to pass tests.

13. Ed liked to go to the gym.

14. The class hoped to have a party.

15. Everyone needed to have more fun.

Exercise 3-17: Change the Emphatic to a Question ↻

Flip the subject and the helping verb. Then check the Answer Key.

| Sam did eat **apples.** | **Did Sam** eat apples? |
| Sam can eat **apples.** | **Can Sam** eat apples? |

1. The teachers did write on the blackboard.

2. Larry did ride his bike everywhere.

3. Your cousin can fly first class.

4. The managers did arrange meetings.

5. I can give many presents.

6. We did think about it all of the time.

7. They did throw it away every day.

8. Virginia did have long hair.

9. Happy people can have good luck.

10. Her sister did say hello.

11. The kids did want to ride their bikes.

12. Students did try to pass tests.

13. Ed did like to go to the gym.

14. The class did hope to have a party.

15. Everyone did need to have more fun.

The next exercise is very similar to the previous exercise, but this time, instead of starting with the emphatic form, you will make the question directly from a regular statement.

以下练习与上一个练习很相似，但下面你要练的是把常规的陈述句转换成疑问句，而不是把强调句转换成疑问句。

Exercise 3-18: Change a Regular Statement to a Question ↻

*Add one of the four helping verbs **did**, **didn't**, **could**, or **couldn't** and use the unchanging form of the main verb. Remember that the helping verb shows the past: **He went.** > **Did he go?** You can't say, **Did he went?** Check the Answer Key when you're done.*

Sam ate **apples.**	**Did Sam** eat apples?
Sam ate **apples.**	**Didn't Sam** eat apples?
Sam ate **apples.**	**Could Sam** eat apples?
Sam ate **apples.**	**Couldn't Sam** eat apples?

1. The teachers wrote on the blackboard.
2. Larry rode his bike everywhere.
3. Your cousin flew first class.
4. The managers arranged meetings.
5. I gave many presents.
6. We thought about it all of the time.
7. They threw it away every day.
8. Virginia had long hair.
9. Happy people had good luck.
10. Her sister said hello.
11. The kids wanted to ride their bikes.
12. Students tried to pass tests.
13. Ed liked to go to the gym.
14. The class hoped to have a party.
15. Everyone needed to have more fun.

Exercise 3-19: Change to Pronouns ⟳

Replace all nouns with pronouns. Put the stress on the verb. Then check the Answer Key.

Did Sam eat apples?　　　　　　　　　　**Did he eat them?**

1. Did the teachers write on the blackboard?
2. Did Larry ride his bike everywhere?
3. Did your cousin fly first class?
4. Can the managers arrange meetings?
5. Did I give many presents?
6. Did Bob think about Betty all of the time?
7. Can Will throw the trash away every day?
8. Did Virginia have long hair?
9. Did happy people have good luck?
10. Can her sister say hello?
11. Did the kids want to ride their bikes?
12. Can the students try to pass tests?
13. Did Ed like to go to the gym?
14. Did the class hope to have a party?
15. Did everyone need to do the dishes?

Exercise 3-20: Change a Regular Statement to a Question ⟳

*Add an appropriate helping verb to the **unchanging** form of the main verb. Pay attention to the tense. Change nouns to pronouns. The stress goes on the verb. Check the Answer Key when you're done.*

Sam ate apples.　　　　　　　　　　**Did he eat them?**

1. The teachers write on the blackboard.
2. Larry rode his bike everywhere.

3. Your **cousin** flies first **class**.

4. The **managers** arranged **meetings**.

5. I gave many **presents**.

6. We **think** about it all of the **time**.

7. They threw it **away** every **day**.

8. **Virginia** has long **hair**.

9. **Happy** people had good **luck**.

10. Her **sister** says **hello**.

11. The kids wanted to ride their bikes.

12. Students try to pass tests.

13. Ed liked to go to the gym.

14. The class hopes to have a party.

15. Everyone needed to do the dishes.

16. The **dogs** jumped over the **hedge**. (hej)

17. My **sister** likes **ice** cream.

18. My **brother** wants an **ice** cream cone.

19. **Joe** always loses **patience** with **Will**.

20. The **sailors** got in **trouble** again.

21. The **cook** burned the **meal**.

22. **Soft**ware gets **viruses**.

23. The **senator** dropped out of the **race**.

24. The **kids** fell in the **mud**.

25. **Teachers** give **tests**.

26. The **police** found the **criminals**.

27. The hot **coffee** burned your **mouth**.

28. Your **team** lost the **race**.

29. The **president** forgot to get his **schedule**.

30. My **boss** changed her **mind**.

Exercise 3-21: Change to a Tag Question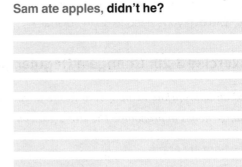

Add a tag question to the end of the statement. Check the Answer Key when you're done.

Sam ate **apples**.   **Sam ate apples, didn't he?**

1. The teachers wrote on the blackboard,

2. Larry rode his bike everywhere,

3. Your cousin flew first class,

4. The managers arranged meetings,

5. I gave many presents,

6. We thought about it all of the time,

7. They threw it away every day,

8. Virginia had long hair,

9. Happy people had good luck,

10. Her sister said hello,
11. The kids wanted to ride their bikes,
12. Students tried to pass tests,
13. Ed liked to go to the gym,
14. The class hoped to have a party,
15. Everyone needed to do the dishes,

Exercise 3-22: Change to a Tag Question — All Verbs ↻

Add a tag question to the end of the statement. Change positive verbs to negative and vice versa. Then check the Answer Key.

1. I drive too fast,
2. You like it,
3. You liked it,
4. You don't like it,
5. You didn't like it,
6. We made some mistakes,
7. They can plan well,
8. She is on the phone,
9. I'm sure,
10. She told the truth,
11. They aren't ready,
12. I'm not sure,
13. There were some problems,
14. There was some trouble,
15. There wasn't any trouble,

Exercise 3-23: Past Tense Review

Fill in the proper past tense form. Check the Answer Key when you're done.

When **Edison** first _thought_ (**think**) of the **lightbulb**, it _was_ (**be**) because of a personal **need**. He _was_ (**be**) afraid of the **dark**, so he _wanted_ (**want**) to **create** something to deal with the **night**. He _tried_ (**try**) a **thousand** different **ways** to **do** it, but **none** of them _worked_ (**work**). **Finally**, as we all **know**, he _invented_ (**invent**) the electric **lightbulb**. **Once**, when he _was_ (**be**) **asked** how he _handled_ (**handle**) the **failure** of his many **attempts**, he _replied_ (**reply**) that **none** of them _were_ (**be**) failures. Each one _teached_ _taught_ (**teach**) him **one** more **way not** to make a **lightbulb**.

Exercise 3-24: Past Tense — Pronunciation   **Track 063**

Listen to the audio, focusing on past tense pronunciation and intonation.

When **Edəson** frrrrst thähd'v the **light** bəlb, it wəz bəkəzəvə prrrrrsonal **need**. He wəzzə fray dəv the **därk**, so he wän'ed to **create** səmething to deal with the **night**. He try də **thouzend** diffrent

wayz to **do** it, but **nən**əvəm wrrkt. **Fyn-lee**, az we äll **know**, he inven'd thee⁽ʸ⁾ əlectric **light** bəlb. **Once**, whennee wəzæskt howeee hændld the **fay**-yəl-yr əviz many **əttempts**, he rəplyd that **nən**əvəm wrr fay-yəl-yrz. Each one tädim **one** more **way nät** to make a **light** bəlb.

The letter I in the **unstressed** position is a schwa. The letter T before or after a schwa is a D. S before a schwa sounds like Z.

非重读的字母I是非重读央元音。当字母T的前面或后面有非重读央元音时，要读作D。当字母S后面跟有非重读央元音时，要读作Z。

Exercise 3-25: Middle "I" Track 064

Listen to the audio and repeat. Read from the blue columns.

ability	abilədy	Florida	Florəda	physical	phyzəcal
accident	aksədent	foreigner	forəner	positive	päzəd'v
activity	activədy	gravity	gravədy	possibility	pässəbilədy
America	əmerəcə	hepatitis	hepətidəs	possible	pässəble
animal	anəmal	identity	idendədy	president	prezədent
article	ardəcle	imitation	imətation	principle	princəple
availability	availabilədy	immigration	imməgration	priority	priorədy
beautiful	byoodəful	invisible	invizəble	qualify	qualəfy
California	Caləfornia	janitor	janədor	quality	qualədy
chemical	chemacal	Jennifer	Jennəfer	quantity	quandədy
chemistry	chemastry	liability	liabilədy	resident	rezədent
clarity	clarədy	Maryland	Merəland	security	secyurədy
communication	comyunəcation	medicine	medəs'n	seminar	semənar
confident	cänfədent	majority	majorədy	similar	simələr
critical	cridəcal	maximum	maxəmum	technical	technəcal
difficult	diffəcult	Michigan	Mishəgan	typical	tipəcal
Edison	Edəson	minimum	minəmum	uniform	unəform
engineer	engəneer	minority	minorədy	unity	yunədy
evidence	evədence	modify	mädəfy	university	yunəversədy
facility	facilədy	monitor	mänədor	visitor	vizədor

Get

The word **get** is in the top 20 of high-frequency words. It is used in its basic meaning of **to receive** or **to acquire**, but in combination with other words, it takes on many other meanings. Here are some common combinations.

单词get位于使用频率最高的20个单词之首。它的基本义是to receive（收到）或to acquire（获得），但当它与其他单词连用时，又产生了很多其他的意思。以下是一些常见的组合。

get up	arise	get back	return from a place
get down	descend	get back	receive again
get on (a bus)	enter	get annoyed	become irritated
get off (a bus)	leave	get along	have good relations
get in (a car)	enter	get confused	become mixed up
get out of (a car)	leave	get worried	become concerned
get away	escape	get ahead	make progress
get tired	become fatigued	get behind	fall behind
get tired of	lose enjoyment of	get in an accident	be in a car crash
get started	begin	get in an argument	have a fight
get used to	become accustomed to	get upset	become sad or angry
get impatient	lose patience	get dressed	put one's clothes on
get done	be finished	get undressed	take one's clothes off
get excited	develop strong feelings	get married	enter in a civil union
get lost	lose one's way	get divorced	break the civil union
get sick	become ill	get rid of something	give or throw away
get better	improve	get even	take revenge
get worse	become less good	get in trouble	have problems
get well	regain health	get together	meet
get somewhere	arrive	get bored	lose interest
get there	arrive somewhere	get by	have the minimum
get fired	lose one's job	get drunk	drink too much alcohol
get hired	become employed	get hungry	need food

Exercise 3-26: *Get*

*Add the proper **get** phrase. Then check the Answer Key.*

1. They don't get ____ any more. | have good relations
2. When did you get ____ from vacation? | return
3. He got ____ because he was always late. | lost his job
4. When I lived in Ohio, I never got ____ to the cold winters. | accustomed to
5. If you don't take care of yourself, you could get ____. | become ill
6. You'd better get ____ from that tree! | descend
7. Hey, would you like to get ____ some time? | meet
8. Don't get mad, get ____! | take revenge
9. Don't get ____ just because you missed one question. | become sad or angry
10. If you want to get ____ in life, you must work hard. | make progress
11. They got very ____ about winning the lottery. | develop strong feelings
12. I tend to get ____ with repetitive tasks. | lose interest
13. Are you getting ____ the bus at the next stop? | leave
14. What a wonderful holiday I have planned to get ____. | escape
15. You married the wrong guy so you need to get ____. | break the civil union
16. It's too early to get ____. | become fatigued

17. Let's get ____ for a cup of coffee.	meet
18. You get ____ so easily!	lose patience
19. Bring a map or you will get ____.	lose one's way
20. We're late because it took you so long to get ____.	put one's clothes on
21. With this promotion I can finally get ____!	make progress
22. You get ____ over the smallest things!	become concerned
23. When are you going to get ____ from Africa?	return
24. Get ____ the car or I'm leaving without you.	enter
25. I get ____ working all day.	lose enjoyment of
26. You need insurance in case you get ____.	be in a car crash
27. You can get ____ in the dressing room.	take one's clothes off
28. My aunt needs to get ____ her extra clothes.	give or throw away
29. Be good or you will get ____!	have problems
30. Study hard and your grades will get ____.	improve
31. I need to get ____ early.	arrive
32. Farmer John gets ____ at 5 a.m. to milk the cows.	arise
33. I get ____ on long drives.	lose interest
34. That boy had better get ____ from that tree!	descend
35. Keep it up if you want to get ____ with me.	have a fight
36. Some people go along to get ____.	have good relations
37. Her boss could not believe that it could get ____.	become less good
38. Let's get ____ with this meeting.	begin
39. If you want to get ____ that sweater, give it to me!	give or throw away
40. I tried to get my money ____, but I couldn't.	receive again
41. Don't get ____ and drive!	drink too much alcohol
42. He hopes to get ____ for the new job.	become employed
43. Eat lunch before you get too ____ and cranky.	need food

Time Words: End of the Sentence
放在句尾的时间副词

When we worked with time words in Chapter 1, they came either *before* the adjective （I am **always** late）or *after* the adjective （I am late **every day**.）Now, let's look at time phrases with *main verbs*.

我们在第一章讲述时间副词时提到，它们要么出现在形容词前（I am **always** late），要么出现在形容词后（I am late **every day**）。现在，让我们看看时间副词短语与主动词连用的情况。

				Time Words
Main Verb	I	buy	bread	every day.

Exercise 3-27: Ending Time Phrases with Main Verbs   Track 065

Listen to the audio and repeat.

	Main Verb		Time Phrases
1. I	buy	bread	almost every day.
2. You	brush	your teeth	all the time.
3. Jeff	makes	money	on a daily basis.
4. He	reacts	badly	every time.
5. It doesn't	rain	hard	all day.
6. Do they	stop	by	once a week?
7. She	thinks about	it	every Monday.
8. We	call	him	twice a year.
9. You all	exercise		every morning.
10. Some people	appreciate	life	every day.
11. They	don't buy	bread	any more.

With **to be**, *time words* come in the middle of the sentence after the verb.

当句子里有be动词时，时间副词要放在句子的中间，即动词之后。

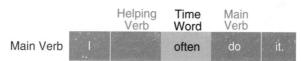

You can see that the time words are in the same position with main verbs, but the helping verb box is empty.

当句子里有主动词时，时间副词的位置与前面的情况是相同的，不过助动词那格是空的。

	Helping Verb	Time Word	Main Verb
Main Verb	I		often	do	it.

Let's review time words with both the verb **to be** and *main verbs*.

让我们来复习一下时间副词的用法，包括句中动词是be动词和主动词的情况。

Exercise 3-28: Time Words with the Verb *To Be* and Main Verbs   Track 066

Listen to the audio and repeat until you have mastered the sounds and concepts.

1. I am always late.	I always buy bread.
2. You are almost always tired.	You almost always brush your teeth.
3. They are generally confused.	They generally make money.
4. He is usually ready.	He usually reacts badly.
5. It is often sunny.	It often rains hard.

Let's review everything you have learned in Chapter 3, including the past tense, negatives, questions, prepositions of direction, the verb **get**, and comparisons. Make sure you get 100% on the test before going on to the next chapter. Check your answers using the Answer Key.

我们来复习一下在第三章中学过的全部内容，其中包括过去时、否定句、疑问句、方向介词、动词get，以及比较级。只有当你在测试中获得满分以后，你才能接着学习下一章。请参照答案检查正误。

Part 1: *Select the proper form.*

1. That plan is   of all.   good
2. My new apartment is   than my old one.   big
3. Your friend is very   .   nice
4. This blanket is   of all of them.   warm
5. That assignment is   than the others.   interesting

Part 2: *Select the proper word, based on the picture.*

1. The white plane is flying   the cloud.
2. The black plane is flying   the cloud.

Part 3: *Change the sentences to the past.*

1. Sam lives in Chicago.
2. We think about it.
3. We see him at the gym.
4. You find many good opportunities.
5. I know the answer.
6. She says anything!
7. Charlie does not make mistakes.
8. Does Laura get in trouble?
9. We have enough time.
10. It takes too long!
11. I am hungry.
12. You are right.
13. He is over there.
14. We are not on the committee.
15. She is going to the party.

Part 4: *Change to the negative. Do **not** use pronouns.*

1. Morgan heard the news.
2. Gordon followed the rules.
3. The girl was confused.
4. The boys were late again.

Part 5: *Change to the negative. **Use** contractions and pronouns.*

1. Ed bought a car.
2. The girl went with her father.
3. The woman was on her bike.
4. The men were in the lake.

102

Part 6: *Change to a question. Do **not** use pronouns.*

1. James drove to New York.
2. Susie is in black.
3. Andrea said hello.
4. Fred and Jim were outside.
5. I like pie.

Part 7: *Rewrite the sentences, with the time and frequency words in the proper place.*

1. Edgar buys groceries.   (all the time)

2. Sam and Charlie fly the kite.   (never)

3. Moira organized her schedule.   (every once in a while)

4. The book tells a good story.   (often)

5. The dogs barked at passers-by.   (all day)

Part 8: *Fill in the proper tag ending.*

1. He was funny,
2. You're coming,
3. They were happy,
4. I am here,
5. It's over,
6. They thought about it,
7. You like it,
8. They tried it,
9. I know him,
10. She didn't say it,

Part 9: *Fill in the blank with either **a, some,** or **the**. Use — if no modifier is needed.*

1. We saw _a_ good movie last night.
2. It was _a_ comedy.
3. That movie was _the_ best this year.
4. I ordered _Some_ popcorn and _a_ soda.
   _a_   _Some_

Part 10: *Fill in the blank with the appropriate **get** phrase.*

1. We worked so hard that we got really ____. (fatigued)
2. It's hard to get ____ living in another country. (accustomed to)
3. What time did you get ____ last night? (finished)
4. Let's get ____ for coffee next week. (meet)
5. Use a map or you might get ____. (lose your way)

 **ESSAY**

Using what you have learned, write two paragraphs on the following:
利用你学过的知识写两段话，话题如下：

1. What is your strongest memory from childhood?
   你童年时期印象最深的是什么？

2. What was your first job?
   你的第一份工作是什么？

Try joining your sentences with the conjunctions you have studied. After writing each paragraph, check for SVO structure and proper modifiers on each noun.

试着用你学过的连词把句子连接起来。在写完每段话后，请检查一下句子的SVO结构是否正确，以及名词前的修饰语是否恰当。

You can handwrite your paragraphs below or e-mail them to **para@grammar.bz** to be stored. These paragraphs are not graded or reviewed, but simply by writing them, your English will improve.

你可以把作文写在下方，也可以把它们发送到邮箱 para@grammar.bz 以存档。我们不会对你的作文进行打分或点评，但只要你写了，你的英语水平就会提高。

● ○ ○			Student Paragraph				
Send	Chat	Attach	Address	Fonts	Colors	Save As Draft	Photo Browser	Show Stationery

To: para@grammar.bz

Cc:

Bcc:

Subject: Chapter 3

Signature: Corporate

My name is _____.

_____ _____ _____ and _____ _____ _____
  S   V   O   but   S   V   O
                      or
                      so
                      because

_____ _____ _____ conjunction _____ _____ _____
  S   V   O   S   V   O

_____ _____ _____ conjunction _____ _____ _____
  S   V   O   S   V   O

_____ _____ _____ conjunction _____ _____ _____
  S   V   O   S   V   O

_____ _____ _____ conjunction _____ _____ _____
  S   V   O   S   V   O

Chapter 4
第四章

Noun Countability and Continuous Verb Forms
名词的可数性和动词的进行时形式

DICTATION

In earlier chapters, we learned about nouns and modifiers. Here, we are going to review them, and also look at *countable* and *uncountable* nouns, *prepositions* of time and manner, and the *5 W Words*. For verbs, we will study the continuous form of both the present and past tense(**is doing** and **was doing**), with a review of **get**, **do / doing**, and **have / having**.

在前几章，我们学习了名词和修饰语。本章我们要复习一下学过的内容，同时也要学习可数名词、不可数名词、时间介词、方式介词，以及5个以W开头的词。我们还要学习动词在现在时态和过去时态下的进行时形式(is doing和was doing)，同时复习一下get, do / doing，以及have / having的用法。

Exercise 4-1: Dictation   Track 067

Listen to the audio and write the exact transcription in the spaces below. Then check the Answer Key.

1. _____
2. _____
3. _____
4. _____
5. _____

STORY

In this chapter of the story, Max has a wild series of continuing actions. Notice the various -**ing** forms in the story, including **was doing**, **started doing**, and **kept doing**.

在本章的故事中，Max有一连串正在进行的疯狂举动。注意故事中的各种-ing形式，包括was doing, started doing和kept doing。

Exercise 4-2: "The Windshield Incident"   Track 068

*Listen to the audio and repeat out loud five times. Focus on the intonation. Lincoln Boulevard is a main street in Venice, California. Jeep is a kind of car. The **continuous** has been highlighted in blue.*

One day, I was driving along in **Venice**. It was a beautiful **day**. I was cruising along Lincoln **Boulevard** in my **Jeep**. **Suddenly**, a **car** cut me **off**. It was very **dangerous**. A young **girl** was driving a **Ford** Mustang **convertible**. I got really **mad** because she was driving so **badly**. I caught **up** to her and cut her **off**. She made a rude **gesture** with her **hand** and drove **away**. I smacked the **wind**shield. It **shattered**. Then I was **really** angry. I drove **fast** and I caught **up** to her again. I started **yell**ing at her. I said that she was a terrible **driver**. She kept **laugh**ing, so I yelled **again**. She looked **over** and **saw** me. Her **eyes** got **big**. She was **scared**. **Remember**, I'm Mr. **World**. I'm 6′4″ and I weigh **300 pounds** (almost 2 meters tall / 136 kilos). She stepped on the **gas**, ran a red **light**, and disappeared in **traffic**. I just kept **driving**, but I was **laughing**.

Exercise 4-3: Story Pronunciation   Track 069

Listen to the audio and repeat out loud five times. Focus on pronunciation and word connections.

One day, I wəz driving aläng in **Venice**. I(t) wəzzə byoodəful **day**. I wəz croozing əläng Ling-k'n **Bül**əvärd in my **Jeep**. **Səddenly**, ə **cär** cət me^(y)**äff**. It wəz very **dangerəs**. ə yəng **grrrrrrrəl** wəz drivingə **Ford** Məstæng **c'nvrrdəble**. I gät rilly **mæd** bicəz she wəz driving so **bædly**. I **cäh dəp** too^(w)er and **cədder äff**. She maydə rude **jesjer** with her **hænd** and drovə **way**. I smæckt the **wind**shield. It **shædderd**. **Then**, I wəz **rilly** æŋgry. I drove **fæst** and I **cähdəp** too^(w)er əgen. I stärdəd **yell**ing ædder. I sed thət she **wəzza** terrəble **driver**. She kept **læffing**, so I yell dəgen. She lük **dover** and **säh** me. Her **ayz** gät **big**. She wəz **scerd**. **R'member**, I'm Mr. **Wrr-rəld**. I'm six **forrrr** and I way **300 pæonz**. She step dän thə **gæs**, rænə red **light**, and disəppir din **træffic**. I jəst kept **driving**, bədäi wəz **læffing**.

Exercise 4-4: Reduced Vowels   Track 070

We have worked with the most reduced vowel, which is the schwa(ə), but now we're going to look at three others, **ih**, **eh**, and **ü**. These are called *lax vowels* because your mouth is relaxed while you are pronouncing them. When you have a word like list, it's almost like the vowel is gone. You don't want to say **least**, which would be a tense vowel.

我们已经学过了最弱的元音，即非重读央元音(ə)，但现在我们要学习另外三个：ih, eh和ü。这几个叫做松元音，因为你发这些音的时候嘴巴是很放松的。当你读诸如list这样的单词时，元音几乎消失了。你可不能把它念成least，因为后者含有紧元音。

i	eh	ə	ü		ee
big	beg	bug	put		beet
pick	peck	puck	book		peek
chip	check	chuck	could		cheap
ship	shed	shut	should		sheep
whip	wet	what	would		we
lip	let	luck	look		leap
rid	red	run	rook		real

Let's focus on **ü** for a moment. It's what we call the chicken sound. As you know, chickens don't have lips. In order to make an **ooh** sound, you need to round your lips to say **soon** or **choose**. Chickens can only say **bük, bük, bük**! This sound is used in **book, took, good, look, could, would,** and **should**. These are all very high-frequency words. The secret to saying the following sentence is to put on a wide smile for the entire thing. Do not round your lips. Smile!

让我们先重点看一下 ü，这个音就是我们所说的鸡喙音。众所周知，鸡没有嘴唇。为了发出ooh 音，你需要把嘴巴张圆才能说出soon或choose。但鸡只能发出bük, bük, bük！ 这个音出现在book，took，good, look, could, would和should中。这几个都是使用频率非常高的词。念下面这句话的秘诀就是：在说整句话的时候都面带大大的微笑。不要张圆嘴巴，要笑！

The cook took a good look at the cookbook and said,
"By hook or by crook, I should cook! "

Sometimes, people have trouble with the difference between **ah** and **uh**. Let's practice that.
有时候，人们弄不清楚ah和uh的区别。让我们来练一练。

äh	**ə**
saw	some
dock	duck
chalk	chuck
lost	luck
wrong	rung

How much wood would a woodchuck chuck, if a woodchuck could chuck wood?
How məch wüd wüd ə wüdchəck chəck, if ə wüdchəck cüd chəck wüd?

NOUNS

This section covers an important aspect of nouns—if they are *countable* or not. We'll also review plurals and modifiers.
本部分要讲有关名词的一个重要方面——名词是可数还是不可数。我们也会复习一下名词的复数形式和修饰语。

Countable nouns: **one chair / two chairs**
可数名词：one chair / two chairs

Uncountable nouns: **furniture / some furniture**
不可数名词：furniture / some furniture

Countable and Uncountable Nouns
可数名词和不可数名词

Let's compare **things** and **stuff**. Things are individual. Stuff is a collection of **things**. You can count **things**. You can't count **stuff**.
我们来比较一下things和stuff。things是一个个分开的事物，stuff则是很多事物的集合。你可以数things，但你不能数stuff。

	A Thing	**Some Stuff**
	a water drop	some water
	an airplane	some air
	a chair	some furniture

Uncountable Noun Rule
不可数名词的规则

1) Anything that can be sliced, scooped, or poured (separated from a **lump** or a **mass** of stuff). Things like bread, ice cream, and liquids can't be counted: Bread is sliced. Ice cream is scooped. Water is poured. These are all *uncountable* nouns.
不可数名词包括任何可以用刀切、用勺子舀、能倒出来的东西（可从一大块或大量事物中分离出来的东西）。诸如面包、冰激凌、液体之类的东西是不能数的：面包可以用刀切；冰激凌可以用勺子舀；水可以倒出来。这些都是不可数名词。

2) A collection of items. Furniture is a collection of individual items, such as chairs, couches, dressers, and lamps.
不可数名词还包括事物的集合。家具是单个物品的集合，如：椅子、沙发、梳妆台、电灯等。

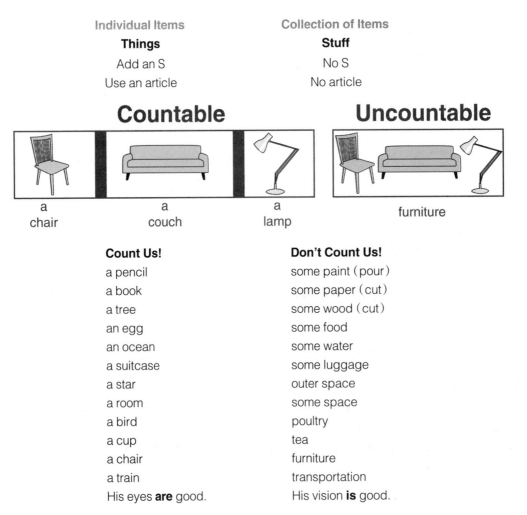

Individual Items	**Collection of Items**
Things	**Stuff**
Add an S	No S
Use an article	No article

Count Us!	**Don't Count Us!**
a pencil	some paint (pour)
a book	some paper (cut)
a tree	some wood (cut)
an egg	some food
an ocean	some water
a suitcase	some luggage
a star	outer space
a room	some space
a bird	poultry
a cup	tea
a chair	furniture
a train	transportation
His eyes **are** good.	His vision **is** good.

No modifier is needed with uncountable nouns, although you can use **some**. Remember: No naked nouns are allowed, but you may have an invisible **some** or **all**. **Would you like coffee?** and **Would you like some coffee?** have basically the same meaning.

不可数名词不需要加修饰语，尽管你可以用some。记住：世界上没有不加修饰语的名词，但可以有隐形的some或all。所以，Would you like coffee? 和 Would you like some coffee? 的意思基本上是相同的。

Exercise 4-5: Countable and Uncountable Nouns (*A /* 一)

*Fill in the blanks with **a** or* 一*. Use the* 一 *when no words are needed.(**Some or all** are optional.) Then check the Answer Key.*

I need ___ car.　　　　　　　　　　　I need **a** car.

I need ___ transportation.　　　　　I need(**some**) transportation.

1. ___ sugar is sweet.
2. Our veins are filled with ___ blood.
3. ___ lead is heavy.
4. We put ___ paint on the walls.
5. Sam had ___ sandwich for lunch.
6. Joe brought ___ good food to the party.
7. Those guys are always ready for ___ good time.
8. Museums are filled with ___ art.
9. My cell phone is made of ___ plastic.
10. Let's work on ___ new project!

Exercise 4-6: Countable and Uncountable Nouns (*A / An / Some /* 一)

*Fill in the blank with **a**, **an**, **some**, or* 一*. Then check the Answer Key.*

Would you like ___ coffee?　　　　Would you like **some** (a, 一) coffee?

1. Could you give me ___ pencil?
2. I need ___ cream for my coffee.
3. The rocket flew into ___ outer space.
4. We need ___ information about it.
5. Buy ___ suitcase for your trip.
6. Here is ___ ice cube for your drink.
7. Do you put ___ ice in ___ tea?
8. I have ___ headache.
9. ___ bottle is made of ___ glass.
10. Would you like ___ glass of ___ water?

When you **limit** an uncountable noun, you can count the **segments**.
当你对不可数名词的数量进行限定以后，就可以按照部分来数它们了。

Don't Count Us!	Now Count Us!
paint	**a drop of** paint
paper	**a piece of** paper
wood	**a chunk of** wood
food	**a mouthful of** food
cheese	**a slice of** cheese
lead	**a pencil** lead
water	**a splash of** water
luggage / baggage	**a piece of** luggage / baggage
tea / coffee	**a cup of** tea / coffee
furniture	**a set of** furniture
transportation	**a means of** transportation
communication	**a mode of** communication

When you want to indicate large quantities, use **much** or **many**. **Much** is used with uncountable nouns (*much time*), and **many** is used with countable nouns (*many times*).

当你想表示数量很大的时候，请使用much或many。 much用来修饰不可数名词(much time)，many用来修饰可数名词(many times)。

Quick Rule: If you see an **S**, choose **many**.
快捷规则：如果你看见了S，就用many。

Exercise 4-7: *Much* or *Many*

*Select **much** or **many**. Then check the Answer Key.*

I have so ___ to do!
1. I drank too ___ glasses of water.
2. I put too ___ water in the glass.
3. The kids have so ___ to do.
4. The kids have so ___ things to do.
5. There aren't very ___ people in Nome.
6. There isn't very ___ time to work on this.
7. We ordered too ___ furniture for the house.
8. We ordered too ___ chairs for the house.
9. There aren't ___ opportunities.
10. There isn't ___ chance of that!

I have so **much** to do!

Some old prepositional phrases have been worn down by use and dropped **the**: to bed / to school / to work / to town. Some others have even dropped **to**: home / downtown / back / somewhere.

有些年代久远的介词短语随着使用慢慢简化，省略了the：to bed / to school / to work / to town。有些甚至把to都省略了：home / downtown / back / somewhere。

Exercise 4-8: Phrases with No *The*   **Track 071**

Listen and repeat the following phrases. The intonation is marked for you.

1. He went **home**.
2. We're going to **town**.
3. He went to **bed**.
4. I'm on my way to **work**.

5. They went down**town**.
6. When are you coming **back**?
7. They want to **go** somewhere.
8. When did you **get** there?

Exercise 4-9: Prepositions of Time

Circle the appropriate time preposition. Then check the Answer Key.

1. He visits   in / on   **January**.
2. He visits   in / on   January **10**th.
3. They always call us   in / on   **Sunday**.
4. They always call us   in / on   the **morning**.
5. They always call us   in / on   Sunday **morning**.
6. Let's go skiing   in / on   the winter.
7. I saw him   in / at   night.
8. I saw him   in / at   the evening.
9. Let's leave   on / at   5:00.
10. Let's leave   on / in / at fifteen minutes.

Exercise 4-10: Prepositions of Manner

Circle the appropriate preposition of manner, which tells you how something was done. Then check the Answer Key.

1. She said it   by / in / with   English.
2. *Hamlet* was written   by / for   Shakespeare.
3. I wrote it   in / by / of   ink.
4. I saw it   in / by / at   the newspaper.
5. They said it   in / by / with   French.
6. They wrote it   by / with / of   hand.
7. He got there   by / with / of   car.
8. He came   on / with / of   foot.
9. I did it   for / of   you.
10. I came here   to / for   learn.
11. The gardener takes care of / by / with   the yard.

Exercise 4-11: "Jack and the Beanstalk"

*Fill in the blanks with **a**, **an**, **the**, **some**, **any**, or — (if another word isn't necessary). Then check the Answer Key.*

Once upon ___ time, there was ___ poor widow and her son Jack. One day, ___ widow said, "Jack, we don't have ___ food. Take ___ cow to ___ town and sell her so that we can have ___ money for ___ food." Jack said OK and went to ___ town, leading ___ cow behind him. Very soon, he came back all alone. "See what I got for our cow, Mother," he said happily. "I sold her to ___ man for ___ three magic beans." When Jack's mother heard that he traded ___ cow for three beans, she was very angry. "Jack!" she yelled. "Three beans can't keep us from starving!" She threw ___ beans out of ___ window. Jack went to ___ bed.

___ next morning, they saw ___ huge vine. ___ vine rose above ___ house and disappeared into ___ clouds. Jack climbed up ___ vine and soon disappeared into ___ clouds, too. At ___ top of ___ vine, Jack saw ___ huge castle. ___ door was ten times his size. He called out, "Excuse me, do you have ___ food for ___ hungry boy?" ___ door opened, and Jack saw ___ woman who was as tall as ___ tree. She picked him up by his shirt and put him on ___ table. "So, you're hungry? Well, I'll give you ___ bite to eat. But watch out for my husband!" She handed Jack ___ slice of bread as big as ___ mattress, and ___ piece of ___ cheese high enough to sit on. But before Jack could eat, he heard ___ giant-sized footsteps and ___ voice said, "Wife, where's my dinner?" Jack hid out of sight in ___ shadows. Then he heard ___ giant say, "Fee, fie, fo, fum, I smell the blood of an Englishman!"

...

___ giant didn't want Jack to take ___ goose that laid golden eggs. One thing led to another, and there was ___ huge fight between Jack and ___ giant. Jack grabbed the goose and ran. ___ giant ended up chasing Jack down ___ beanstalk. Fortunately, Jack got to ___ bottom first, grabbed ___ ax, and chopped it down. ___ giant fell to his death and Jack and his mother lived happily ever after with the goose.

Exercise 4-12: "Jack and the Beanstalk" — Pronunciation   Track 072

Listen to the audio and repeat five times.

ACCENT

Wensa pənnə **time**, ther wəzzə poor **widow** anner sən **Jæck**. **One** day, the widow **sed**, "**Jæck**, we don't have any **food**. Take the **cow** tə **town** and **sell**er so thət we cən have səm **money** for **food**." Jæck sed **OK** and went tə **town**, **leeding** the cow be**hind**im. **Very** soon, he came **bæck** allə **lone**. "**See** whədai **got** for our **cow**, Məther," he sed **hæppəly**. "I **sold**er to⁽ʷ⁾ə **mæn** fr **three** mægic **beanz**." When Jæck's məther **hrrd** the dee **traded** the cow frr three **beenz**, she wəz very **angry**. "Jack!" she yelld. "Three **beans** cæn't keepəs frəm **starving**!" She **threw** the beans outtə the **window**. **Jæck** went tə **bed**.

The next **morning**, they sah-a hyooj **vine**. The **vine** rozə bəv the **house** and **disəppird** into the **clouds**. **Jack** climb dəp the **vine** and soon **disappeared** into the **clouds**, **too**. At the **tapa** the vine, **Jack** sah-a huge **cæssəl**. The **door** wəz ten **tymz** hiz **size**. He call **dout**, "Eks-**kyooz** me, do you have any **food** frə həngry **boy**?" The door **opend**, and Jack **säh**-ə **wümən** who wəzzəz **tall**əzə **tree**. She **pick** diməp by his **shirt** and **püdimän** the **table**. "So, yer **həngry**? **Well**, I'll give you⁽ʷ⁾ə **bite** tə **eat**. Bət **watch**out fr my **hezbənd**!" She **hænded** Jæckə sly s'v **bread** əz **big**əzə **mætt**ress, annə peesə **cheez high** enuf to **sid**dän. But be**fore** Jæck **cüd**eat, he herd **jiant**-sized **füt**steps annə

voice sed, "**Wife**, wherz my **d'nner**?" **Jæck** hid owddə sight in the **shædowz**. Thenee **herd** the giant **say**, "**Fee**, fie, fo, **fum**, **I** smell the **bləd** əvə **ninglish**man!"

...

The jiant didn't want Jack tə take the goose thət laid goldən eggz. **One** thing led to⁽ʷ⁾ **ənəther**, and there wəzza hyooj **fight** b'tween **Jæck** and the **jiant**. Jæck græbbd the goos and ræn. The jiant endədəp **chasing** Jæck down the **bean**stalk. **For**chənatly, **Jæck** gät t' the **bäddəm frrrrst**, **grab** dənæx and chäp dit **down**. The jiant fell to⁽ʷ⁾iz **death** and **Jæck** and his **mother** livd **hæppəly** ever **æfter** with the goos.

Exercise 4-13: Noun vs. Verb Intonation   Track 073

Listen to the audio and repeat five times.

Noun		Verb	
accent	**æc**cent	ac**cent**	ac**cent**
conflict	**cän**flict	con**flict**	c'n**flict**
contract	**cän**tract	con**tract**	c'n**tract**
convert	**cän**vert	con**vert**	c'n**vert**
default	**de**fault	de**fault**	d'**fault**
envelope	**än**velope	en**vel**op	en**vel**op
insult	**in**sult	in**sult**	in**sult**
perfect	**per**fect	per**fect**	per**fect**
permit	**per**mit	per**mit**	per**mit**
present	**pres**ent	pre**sent**	pr'**zent**
produce	**pro**duce	pro**duce**	pr'**duce**
progress	**prä**gress	pro**gress**	pr'**gress**
project	**prä**ject	pro**ject**	pr'**ject**
subject	**sub**ject	sub**ject**	s'**bject**

Exercise 4-14: Reading Comprehension

Read the following passage and answer the questions. Then check the Answer Key.

Sign Language

Most languages convey **information** with spoken **words**. **Sign** language uses **visual** signals. **Hearing**-impaired people use hand and **arm** gestures, **body** language, and **facial** expressions to convey **meaning**. **Sign** languages develop in deaf **communities**, which can include **interpreters** and **friends** and **families** of **deaf** people, as well as **people** who are **deaf** or hard of **hearing themselves**.

Wherever communities of **deaf** people **exist**, **sign** languages **develop**. In **fact**, their complex **grammars** are very **different** from **spoken** languages. There are **hundreds** of **sign** languages in use around the **world**.

Several sign languages are used in **stage** performances, such as **sign**-language **poetry**. Many of the poetic **mechanisms** available to **signing** poets are **not** available to **speaking** poets.

Like **other** languages, **sign** languages are **different** in **different** countries. In **spite** of this, **hearing**-impaired people from different **countries** seem to under**stand** each other **better** than **hearing** people.

Many people who can **hear** **also** want to learn to **sign**. For **example**, **scuba divers use sign language because they can't talk underwater.** **Fire**fighters and **police** officers sometimes sign to each **other** in order to communicate **silently**, while **dog**-trainers can use it to train **dogs**.

Answer the questions based on this text.

Give two synonyms for the word **deaf**.
1. _____   2. _____

Answer each question with **True** or **False**.
1.   Sign language conveys sound patterns.
2.   There are sign languages in every community of deaf people.
3.   There are almost a hundred different sign languages.
4.   The grammar of sign language and spoken language are the same.
5.   Sign language is the same in every country.
6.   Only deaf people use sign language.

How do most languages convey information?
What does sign language use?

List three reasons why people who can hear might also need to learn sign language.
1. _____
2. _____
3. _____

"Tee Aitch"
（Th的发音）

Th is a very important sound. After the schwa (ə), it's the highest-frequency sound in English. You will hear it in **the, this, that, these, those, they, them, there, their, they're,** and **then**.

　　Th是一个很重要的音。在英语中，它是除了非重读央元音(ə)之外使用频率最高的音。在如下单词中你都可以听到这个音：the，this，that，these，those，they，them，there，their，they're和then。

　　In terms of pronunciation, you need to distinguish between **Th** and **D** for two reasons. The first reason is clarity and comprehension, so **the** doesn't sound like **duh**. The second is because it sounds uneducated to say **Dese are da tings dat we tought about**.

　　就语音方面，你需要把Th和D区分开来，原因有两个：第一是为了听着清晰、便于理解，这样the听起来就不会像duh。第二是因为如果你说Dese are da tings dat we tought about.，听着就像没有受过教

If you ask an American how to pronounce **Th**, you will hear that you put the tip of your tongue between your teeth and blow the air out. This is not accurate when you are using **Th** in actual speech.

如果问美国人该怎么发Th这个音，你会听到这样的答案：先把舌尖放在牙齿中间，然后把气吹出来。不过在实际说话的时候，用这个方法发Th音并不准确。

The **Th** is actually very similar to the D, but the tongue position is about an inch forward in the mouth. For the D, put the tip of your tongue on the bumps behind your top teeth. Say, da, da, da. Now, press the tip of your tongue against the back of the top teeth, and let the air pop out, **the**.

Th和D其实很相像，但是舌头的位置不一样，发Th的时候舌头大约要多往前伸一英寸。发D的音时，要把舌尖放在上门牙牙龈的后面。念：da, da, da。现在，把舌尖抵在上门牙的后面，让气吹出来，发出the。

Exercise 4-15: Tee Aitch   Track 074

These are the things that we thought about.

Th	D	Th	D
they	day	these	D's
the	duh	though	dough
then	den	those	doze
there	dare	they'll	dale

There are actually two **Th** sounds. One of them is *voiced* (this, that, these, those) and the other is *unvoiced* (thing, think, thank, three, thought).

英语中实际上有两个Th音，一个是浊辅音(this, that, these, those)，另一个则是清辅音(thing, think, thank, three, thought)。

Exercise 4-16   Track 075

I think I need to thank them for three things.

Th	T	Th	T	Th	T
thank	tank	three	tree	thought	taught

Intonation and Meaning
语调和意思

With the same sentence and the same words, you can completely change the meaning by moving the intonation around.

同样的句子和同样的词，你可以通过改变声调而把意思完全改变。

Exercise 4-17: Intonation   Track 076

Listen and repeat.

1. **He** didn't say he needed my help. Someone **else** said that.
2. He **didn't** say he needed my help. **That's** not **true**.
3. He didn't **say** he needed my help, but he **indicated** it with his **body** language.
4. He didn't say **he** needed my help. I thought he meant someone **else**.
5. He didn't say he **needed** my help. He just seemed like he **wanted** it.
6. He didn't say he needed **my** help. It seemed like **anyone** could help him.
7. He didn't say he needed my **help**. Maybe he just wanted **advice**.

Note: With acronyms, always stress the final letter: C**D**, L**A**, ASA**P**.
注意：首字母缩略语的重音永远在最后一个字母上：C**D**，L**A**，ASA**P**。

VERBS

Now, you will change verbs in the simple present and the simple past to their continuous forms. The continuous form uses the helping verb **to be** plus a **main verb** and -**ing**.

现在，你要把一般现在时和一般过去时的动词改成进行时形式。构成进行时要用助动词 be，外加主动词和-ing。

go > is going / are going

went > was going / were going

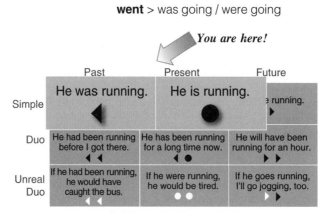

There are certain words that go with the continuous, such as **right now**.
有些词要与进行时搭配，比如：right now（马上）。

I am going to the store right now.

Present	Present Continuous	Past	Past Continuous
I go.	I am going.	I went.	I was going.
You go.	You are going.	You went.	You were going.
He goes.	He is going.	He went.	He was going.
She goes.	She is going.	She went.	She was going.
It goes.	It is going.	It went.	It was going.
We go.	We are going.	We went.	We were going.
They go.	They are going.	They went.	They were going.

The continuous form is used:
动词的进行时被用来：

1. To indicate that something is taking place right now.
   表示某事正在发生。

   The kids are playing outside right now.

2. To indicate that something is not permanent.
   表示某事只是暂时的。

   He doesn't drink coffee. (permanent situation)
   He isn't drinking coffee these days. (temporary situation)

3. To indicate that something is specific, not general.
   表示某事是特指的，而非泛指的。

   I take a shower every day. (general)
   I'm taking a shower now. (specific)

4. When something continues as compared to something that doesn't continue. You have the ongoing action and then another event.
   把某个持续性的事件与另一个非持续性的事件进行对比。这样的句子中既包含某个进行中的动作，又包含另外一个事件。

   He was cleaning his room when the power went out.

Note: Some -ing forms are actually nouns. **I like swimming. Skiing is fun.**
注意： 一些-ing形式实际上就是名词，如：I like swimming.(我喜欢游泳。) Skiing is fun. (滑雪很好玩。)

Exercise 4-18: Present Continuous

Rewrite the sentences using the present continuous form. Then check the Answer Key.

	I practice a lot.	**I'm practicing a lot these days.**
1.	I have **lunch** every day.	right now
2.	Bob gets sick.	right now
3.	It rains in California.	today
4.	It doesn't rain in California.	right now
5.	He works hard.	for a change
6.	She dances well.	this week
7.	He thinks about it.	at the moment (right now)
8.	He doesn't think about it.	for the moment (for now)

9. She makes cookies.

tonight

10. They don't drink coffee.

these days

Exercise 4-19: Past Continuous

Rewrite the sentences using the past continuous form. Then check the Answer Key.

I spoke Italian.   **I was speaking** Italian when they walked in.

1. The teachers wrote on the blackboard.

when the **bell** rang

2. Larry rode his bike.

when it started **raining**

3. Your cousin flew first class.

until he ran out of **money**

4. The managers still arranged the meetings.

before the **conference**

5. I didn't work hard.

last **year**, but I am **now**

6. We thought about it.

before the **situation** changed

7. They threw it away.

until they realized its **value**

8. Virginia didn't sell her car.

until she won the **lottery**

9. The candles burned steadily.

even though it was **windy**

10. Her sister said hello.

when he rudely **interrupted**

As you learned before, there are two ways to make contractions with pronouns and the verb **to be**. Use them in the next exercise.

正如你所学的，代词和be动词有两种缩写方式。请在下面的练习中运用这两种方式。

Exercise 4-20: Continuous Negative Contractions

Change to a negative contraction. Change all nouns to pronouns. Move the intonation to the verb. Check the Answer Key when you're done.

Sam is speaking Italian.

He **isn't** speaking it.   He**'s not** speaking it.

1. The teachers are writing on the blackboard.

2. Larry is riding his bike.

3. Your cousin is flying first class.

4. The managers are arranging the meetings.

5. I am giving many presents.

6. We are thinking about the play.

7. They are throwing the trash away.

8. Virginia is selling her car.

9. The candles are burning steadily.

10. Her sister was saying hello.

Exercise 4-21: Continuous Questions ↻

Change the statements to questions. Change all nouns to pronouns. Move the stress to the verb. Check the Answer Key when you're done.

Edward's speaking Italian.   **Is he** speaking it? Izzy speekingit?

1. The teachers are writing on the blackboard.

2. Larry and Joe are riding their bikes.

3. Your cousin is flying first class.

4. The managers are arranging the meetings.

5. I am giving many presents.

6. We were thinking about it.

7. Elwin and Martha were throwing the trash away.

8. Virginia was selling her car.

9. The candles are burning steadily.

10. Her sister was saying hello.

Note: The words **writing** and **riding** sound exactly the same.

注意：writing和riding这两个词读起来一模一样。

Contrasting the Simple Present and the Continuous Present
对比一般现在时和现在进行时

The *simple present* is used for a broader, more general present.

一般现在时描述的是更加宽泛、更加普遍的现在。

The *continuous present* is more immediate and continuing in the moment.

现在进行时描述的是更加贴近当下并且此刻正在进行的事情。

The ***past continuous*** can indicate an intention that has changed.

过去进行时可以表示某个已经发生改变的意图。

He was going to do it, but he changed his mind.

Exercise 4-22: Simple Present vs. Continuous Present

Listen and repeat.

Simple Present (in general)	Continuous (right now)
I do the **dishes** every day.	I'm doing the **dishes** now.
I have a **book**.	I'm reading a **book** right now.
He has a **head**ache.	He is getting a **head**ache.
We need a **break**.	We're taking a **break** now.
I always take a **taxi** to work.	I'm not taking a **taxi** this morning.
Call me **later**.	Are you **calling** me?
It's already **open**.	Look, it's finally **opening**.
It's too **far**.	He's going too **far** again.
That's a good **idea**.	He's being **good** for a change.
We **always** enjoy your **parties**.	We're enjoying your **party** this evening.
He can spell "**potato**."	He's spelling it **wrong** again.
You always forget to **call**.	Aren't you forgetting to **call**?
We almost **always** play **ball**.	Aren't you ever playing **ball** again?

Exercise 4-23: Simple Present vs. Continuous Present

Fill in the blank with either the simple present or the continuous form. Then check the Answer Key.

	She **dances well**, in general.	She **is dancing really well** today.	
1.	They	to the **gym** every **day**.	go
2.	They	to the **gym** right now.	go
3.	He	a **hat** on.	have
4.	He	a **hat**.	wearing

120

5.	He		**curry** for **lunch** today.	have
6.	He		**curry** for lunch every day.	have
7.	She		her **boy**friend.	like
8.	Elsa		to move to **Texas**.	want
9.	You and I		about it very often.	think
10.	Everyone else		about it right now.	think
11.	I		**hungry**.	be
12.	She		**pretty**.	be
13.	He		**ridiculous** about the situation.	be
14.	The **victim**		admitted to the **hospital** right now.	be
15.	↻ Who		**pan**cakes right now?	make
16.	↻ Why	___ you ___	**pan**cakes every **morning**?	make
17.	↻ Why	___ you ___	**pan**cakes again today?	make
18.	↻	___ you ___	for me?	wait
19.	↻	___ you ___	for me every **day**?	wait
20.	**Florida**		a major **heat** wave this **month**.	have
21.	**Florida**		**heat** waves every **year**.	have
22.	We		a great **time**! (right now)	have
23.	They		an awful **time**, so they left **early**.	have
24.	She		a **baby** next month.	have
25.	She		a **baby** last month.	have
26.	He		second **thoughts** about it now.	have
27.	Our **friends**		a **party** this **week**end!	have
28.	Our **friends**		a party **every** weekend!	have
29.	Her **boss**		**angry** because everyone is **late**.	get
30.	I		two **aspirin** for my **heart** every day.	take
31.	I		two **aspirin** because I just got a **head**ache.	take
32.	He		big **cars** all the time.	buy
33.	He		a big car to **impress** people.	buy
34.	She		that old **house** this **week**end.	sell
35.	She		**real** estate for a living.	sell
36.	That old **man**		**slowly** because he hurt his **foot**.	walk
37.	That old **man**		**slowly** when he goes to the **store**.	walk
38.	The **dancer**		so **well**!	dance
39.	The **dancer**		in the **ballet** tonight.	dance
40.	The **janitor**		really **hard** every **day**!	work
41.	The **janitor**		**hard** to get that **floor** clean.	work
42.	**So** many **people**		**lunch** right now.	eat
43.	**So** many **people**		**lunch** at **noon**.	eat
44.	**Laura**		**basket**ball on **Mondays**.	play
45.	**Laura**		**basket**ball right now.	play
46.	My **son**		a long **letter** to his **father** now.	write
47.	My **son**		really **well** for a **six**-year-old.	write

48.	The **guard**		that **report** every day.	do
49.	The **guard**		that **report** right now.	do
50.	The **apple**		n't fall **far** from the **tree**.	do

Get: Review with the Continuous
Get: 与进行时一起复习

As we saw in Chapter 3, **get** has many meanings. It's often used in the continuous form. Let's review.

如我们在第三章学到的，get有很多种意思。它还经常以进行时的形式出现。让我们来复习一下。

Exercise 4-24: Getting It Right

*Add the proper **get** phrase. Then check the Answer Key.*

We tried to get out of doing it. (**escape**)

1. They aren't getting ___, so I think they're getting ___. (have good relations; separated)
2. I get ___ to go to work. (arise)
3. The old lady is getting ___ the bus slowly. (enter)
4. My lucky coworker is getting ___ from it all in Hawaii. (escape from)
5. My mom is finally getting ___ to my loud music. (become accustomed to)
6. The **sales** staff is getting ___ about the new **product** line! (develop strong feelings)
7. After **studying** hard, the student's **grades** are getting ___. (improve)
8. We are getting ___ all the extra junk. (throwing away)
9. My coworker is getting ___ from Hawaii soon. (return)
10. The **tiger** is getting ___ because you are throwing **rocks** at him. (become irritated)
11. My **nephew** is getting ___ by all his **math** homework. (become mixed up)
12. I am getting ___ on all my **credit** card payments! (fall behind)
13. Don't tell me you're just getting ___ now?! (put one's clothes on)
14. The Wicked Witch is getting ___ with Snow White. (take revenge)
15. The diplomats are getting ___ to end the fighting. (meet)

Get is also used a great deal with emotions. Oddly, it tends to be used in a negative sense.

get还经常与表示情感的单词连用。奇怪的是，它更倾向于表达消极的意思。

Exercise 4-25: Getting Emotional   Track 077

Listen to the audio and repeat five times.

1. The **bankers** were getting **worried** about the **loans**.
2. The **kids** were getting really **excited** about the **trip**.
3. We were getting **tired**, so we stopped **working**.
4. She was getting **annoyed** at him.
5. **None** of the **patients** were getting any **better**.

6. The **fourth** graders were getting **bored** in the **assembly**.
7. I was getting really **confused** by his complicated **explanation**.
8. Getting **nervous** is a part of **stage** fright.
9. There's no point in getting up**set**. **That** won't **help**.
10. The **researcher** was getting increasingly **impatient** with the difficult **subject**.
11. **Every**one was getting **frustrated** by the long **delays**.
12. We're still getting **used** to the new **situation**.
13. The **students** were getting **happier** as they got **closer** to finishing their **home**work.
14. His **dad** was getting **madder** by the **minute** when **Joey** didn't make his **curfew**.
15. She was getting **angry** about the lack of **planning**.

Who is it? What is it?

Up to now, we've learned a certain type of question. You may have noticed that these questions can all be answered **yes** or **no**. Let's replace the subject with **who** or **what**, as we did in Chapter 1.

到目前为止，我们已经学习了某一类型的疑问句。你可能已经注意到了，这些疑问句都可以用yes或no来回答。让我们像在第一章里那样，把主语替换成who或what吧。

This is a quick and easy lesson, and you will use it a lot.
这个很容易学，你很快就能学会，而且以后经常会用到。

Verb **To Be**
Main Verbs

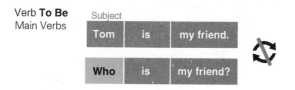

Who and **what** questions about the **subject** don't do the question flip.
以who和what开头的提问主语的疑问句不存在词序颠倒的问题。

The verb is singular (**is** or **was**).
动词为单数形式（is或was）。

Who?	
The boy is a student.	**Who** is a student?
The kids are at the park.	**Who** is at the park?
The teacher is gone.	**Who** is gone?
The workers are hungry.	**Who** is hungry?
My friends are excited.	**Who** is excited?
Movie stars are exciting.	**Who** is exciting?
The students were reading.	**Who** was reading?

What?	
The sun is a star.	**What** is a star?
The bikes are in the garage.	**What** is in the garage?
The dogs are gone.	**What** is gone?
The painting is beautiful.	**What** is beautiful?
The electrons are excited.	**What** is excited?

The movie is exciting.	**What** is exciting?
The phone was ringing.	**What** was ringing?
The car is parked outside.	**What** is parked outside?
The money is missing.	**What** is missing?

Exercise 4-26: *Who* and *What* — *To Be* Subject

*Replace the subject with **who** or **what**. For the word order, remember that there is no question flip. Then check the Answer Key. Remember, the verb becomes singular.*

The babies are crying.	**Who** is crying?
The cars are on fire.	**What** is on fire?

1. Our **parents** are **worried**.
2. That **watch** was **expensive**.
3. Those **forms** were filled **in**.
4. The **fire**men were on **duty**.
5. The **music** is **playing**.

    As usual, after the verb **to be**, we go on to *main verbs*. Again, because **who** and **what** replace the subject, there is no question flip. Use the same word order as you would for a statement.

    与之前一样，讲完be动词之后，我们接着讲主动词。再次说明一下，因为是用who和what替换主语，所以不需要颠倒词序，而是使用与陈述句一样的语序。

Bob likes Betty.	**Who** likes Betty?
Cars go fast.	**What** goes fast?

Exercise 4-27: *Who* and *What* — Main Verbs Subject

*Replace the subject with **who** or **what**. Use either nouns or pronouns in your answer. If you use pronouns, the emphasis is on the verb. For the word order, remember that there is no question flip. Check the Answer Key when you're done.*

The girls wrote the letter.	**Who** wrote it?
The noise scared the children.	**What** scared them?

1. **Janice** told Lou.
2. **The store** closed early.
3. **My parents** left early.
4. **The train** left the station.
5. **The bell** rang loudly.

124

In Exercises 4-26 and 4-27, where **who** and **what** replace the subject, the question flip is not used. These are questions, but they use the **statement** word order.

在练习4-26和4-27中，每当用 who 和 what 替代主语时，就不需要颠倒词序。它们虽然是疑问句，但要使用陈述句的语序。

In Exercises 4-28 and 4-29, we review **yes / no questions**. These do use the question flip.

在练习4-28和4-29中，我们会复习用yes / no来回答的疑问句。它们确实要颠倒词序。

Exercise 4-28: Yes / No Question Review — *To Be* Subject

Let's do a quick review. Convert each statement to a yes / no question. Then check the Answer Key.

The kids **are** in the pool.   **Are** the kids in the pool?
1. She is **excited** about the **party**.
2. The **party** is very **exciting**.
3. We weren't **invited**.
4. He isn't **ready** yet.
5. **Bob** is sick.

Exercise 4-29: Yes / No Question Review — Main Verbs Subject

Convert each statement to a yes / no question. Then check the Answer Key.

Boris understands.   **Does** Boris understand?
1. They like to **swim**.
2. He can tell you the **answer**.
3. You didn't eat **break**fast.
4. Bob has a **head**ache.
5. Ella doesn't **want** one.

Let's review what we know so far about statements and questions about the *subject*.

让我们复习一下到目前为止学到的有关陈述句以及就主语提问的疑问句的内容吧。

Kind	Order	Verb To Be	Main Verb
Statement		**He** is there.	**He** likes it.
Who Question		**Who** is there?	**Who** likes it?
What Question		**What** is there?	**What** likes it?
Yes/No Question		**Is he** there?	**Does he** like it?

What **is** it? What **does** it do?

Up to now, we've only been working with questions about the *subject*. Now, let's look at the *object*, using all *5 W* words. You can see that there is a relationship between these words because most of them have similar spellings.

到目前为止，我们只学过就主语提问的疑问句。现在，让我们来就宾语进行提问，并且用上全部5个以W开头的疑问词。你可以看到这几个词之间是有联系的，因为它们的拼写都很相似。

Who? He.
What? That.
Where? There.
When? Then.
Why? Because.

The next step is to take the *object* and replace it with one of the *5 Ws*. Use the question flip. ↻

下一步就是用这5个词中的任意一个替换宾语。请颠倒疑问句的词序。↻

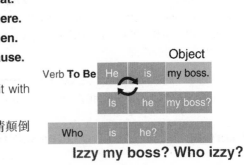

Izzy my boss? Who izzy?

Exercise 4-30: *5 W* Questions — *To Be* Object

Convert each statement to a question. Then check the Answer Key.

The kids are in the pool.   **Where** are the kids?

1.	He is jumping on **the couch**.	What?
2.	The book is **on the shelf**.	Where?
3.	He was here **at 3:00 p.m.**	When?
4.	He was here **at 3:00 p.m.**	What time?
5.	He isn't tired **because he doesn't work hard**.	Why?

Now that you understand the format for the verb **to be**, let's take a look at *main verbs*.

既然你已经理解了be动词的用法，就让我们来接着学主动词吧。

Duzzy like'm? What duzzy like?

Exercise 4-31: *5 W* Questions — Main Verbs Object ↻

Convert each statement to a 5 W question. Then check the Answer Key.

The kids like the pool.   **What** do they like?

1.	She shops at the **mall**.	Where?
2.	Janice told **Lou**.	Who?
3.	He started work **at 3:00 p.m.**	When?
4.	He stopped **because he was tired**.	Why?
5.	He wants to move **to another apartment**.	Where?

How is it?

Here, **how** tells the *quality* or *condition* of something.
这里，how告诉我们事物的质量或状况。

Is it **good**? Is it **bad**? **Old**? **New**?
它好吗？它坏吗？旧吗？新吗？

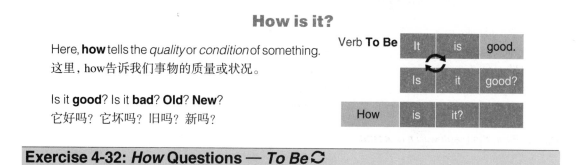

Exercise 4-32: *How* Questions — *To Be* ↻

*Convert each statement to a **how** question. Change the nouns to pronouns. Then check the Answer Key.*

I am fine.   **How** are you?

1. The boys were **excited**.
2. My sister isn't **happy**.
3. The books were in bad **condition**.
4. The food is **burned**.
5. Our vacation will be too **long**.

How also tells the *degree* of a quality or condition.
how 还告诉我们质量或状况的程度。

Is it **very** good? Is it **really** bad? A **little** old? **Kind** of new?

它非常好吗？它真的很坏吗？是有点旧吗？是有点新吗？

Exercise 4-33: *How* Questions — *To Be* ↻

*Convert each statement to a **how** question. （**How** replaces the adverb.） Change the nouns to pronouns. Check the Answer Key when you're done.*

They are very happy.   **How happy** are they?

1. The boys were really excited.
2. My sister is wonderfully happy.
3. The books were in very bad condition.
4. The food is really burned.
5. Our car is quite old.

Let's review everything you have learned in Chapter 4. Make sure you get 100% on the test before going on to the next chapter. Check your work using the Answer Key.

我们来复习一下在第四章中学过的全部内容。只有当你在测试中获得满分以后，你才能接着学习下一章。请参照答案检查正误。

Part 1: *Fill in the blank with* **a** *or* **an**.

1. Would you like _____ after-dinner mint?
2. Would you like _____ mint?
3. I'd like _____ apple, please.
4. He's _____ honest man.
5. It's _____ history book.

Part 2: *Fill in the blank with* **a** *or* **some**.

1. There was _____ water on the floor.
2. He took _____ bath last night.
3. Please take _____ more time if you need it.
4. We had _____ great time.
5. They put _____ butter on their toast.

Part 3: *Fill in the blank with* **a** *or* **the**.

1. Would you like _____ bite of my apple?
2. Please pass _____ salt.
3. We had _____ best time!
4. What _____ surprise!
5. It's _____ only way we can do it.

Part 4: *Fill in the blank with* **a** *or* — (*if another word isn't needed*).

1. They poured _____ water on the plants.
2. Did you bring _____ water bottle?
3. There is _____ mud on your shoes.
4. Would you like _____ more coffee?
5. Don't rush him. He needs _____ time to finish.

Part 5: *Fill in the blank with the appropriate* **preposition** *of* **time** *or* **manner**.

1. Call me ___ Wednesday ___ 3:00.
2. We went to the party ___ meet friends.

Part 6: *Fill in the blank with* **much** *or* **many**.

1. How _____ did it cost?
2. How _____ of them did you buy?
3. He called so _____ times!
4. Did you have _____ trouble?
5. Did you have _____ problems?

Part 7: Change from the simple present or past to the appropriate continuous form.

1. He is silly!
2. They work hard.
3. You chose one.
4. He lost the race.
5. I wrote to him.

Part 8: Select the simple present or past tense, or the appropriate continuous form.

1. He _____ right now.   sleep
2. He _____ hard every day.   work
3. He _____ about going out when she called.   think
4. He _____ in the pool.   be
5. He _____ admitted to the hospital right now.   be

Part 9: Change the positive statement to a negative.

1. Lou knows Ed.
2. The cars go fast.

Part 10: Change the statement to a question.

1. It rains every day.
2. It's raining.
3. You like it.
4. You're in charge.

Part 11: Complete each sentence based on the meaning of the changing intonation.

1. **My** brother doesn't like dogs,
2. My **brother** doesn't like dogs,
3. My brother **doesn't** like dogs;
4. My brother doesn't **like** dogs,
5. My brother doesn't like **dogs**,

Part 12: Make a question and change the subject to **who** or **what**.

1. The basketball players are starting the game now.
2. The boxes fell off the shelf.

Part 13: Convert each statement to a question.

1. They are sitting on the floor.   Where
2. We left at noon.   When
3. She looked at the book.   What
4. He laughed because it was funny.   Why

ESSAY

Using what you have learned, write two paragraphs on the following:
利用你学过的知识写两段话，话题如下：

1. What type of movie do you like?
你喜欢什么类型的电影？

2. Are you a dog person or a cat person?
你喜欢狗还是喜欢猫？

You can handwrite your paragraphs below or e-mail them to **para@grammar.bz** to be stored. These paragraphs are not graded or reviewed, but simply by writing them, your English will improve.

你可以把作文写在下方，也可以把它们发送到邮箱 para@grammar.bz 以存档。我们不会对你的作文进行打分或点评，但只要你写了，你的英语水平就会提高。

◉ ○ ○	Student Paragraph

Send Chat Attach Address Fonts Colors Save As Draft   Photo Browser   Show Stationery

To: para@grammar.bz

Cc:

Bcc:

Subject: Chapter 4

Signature: Corporate ⬍

≡ ▼

My name is _____

130

Chapter 5
第五章

Future Tense, Comparisons and Modifiers
将来时、比较级和修饰语

We studied comparisons in Chapter 3. Now, we will look at more comparisons, modifiers, articles, descriptions, compound nouns, word order, and more conjunctions, as well as **how much / how many.**

我们在第三章学习了比较级。本章我们要继续学习比较级、修饰语、冠词、描述语、复合名词、词序和连词，以及how much / how many的用法。

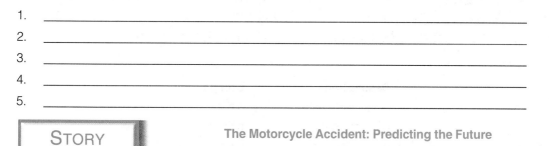

DICTATION

For verbs, we will work with the real and unreal futures, with both **will** and **going to**. We'll learn some idiomatic expressions with **use, do / make,** and **stand**. Look for the "Grammar in a Nutshell" section in this chapter.

动词方面，我们要学习用will和going to来表示的真实将来时和非真实将来时。我们还要学几个由use，do / make和 stand构成的习惯用语。请参看本章中的"语法小结"板块。

Exercise 5-1: Dictation   Track 078

Listen to the audio and write in the exact transcription in the spaces below. Then check the Answer Key.

1. _____

2. _____

3. _____

4. _____

5. _____

STORY

The Motorcycle Accident: Predicting the Future

In eight **years, three** days after I win Mr. **Europe,** I will be riding a **motor**cycle on a main **street** in Milan, **Italy**. I will be going about 80 miles an **hour**. All of a **sudden,** a **car** will pull in **front** of me. I'll **hit** the car and fly about 10 **yards**. My **leg** will break in three **places**. I will be **in** and out of the **hospital** for seven **months**. The **doctor** will put me in **traction** for the first **month** without a **cast**. After my **leg** is a little better, he will put a **cast** on. He will give me a lot of **antibiotics. Every**one will be very **worried** about me. The **news**papers and TV will report **every**thing that **happens**. It will take me **seven** months to **recover,** and it will be a **year** before I **compete** again.

131

I will **still** have a **scar** on my **shin**, and my **right** calf won't be as developed as the **other** one is. I'll be **lucky** to be **alive**, though.

Exercise 5-2: Story Pronunciation

Listen to the audio and repeat, focusing on intonation and pronunciation.

The Modercycəl Aksədent

Innate **yirz**, **three** day zæafter I win Missder **Yerup**, I'll be ridingə **moder**cycle ännə main **street** in M'lan, **Idəly**. I'll be goingə bout **aye**-dee mile zə **now**er. allEvə **sudden**, a **car'll** päullin **frənna** me. I'll **hit** the car and flyə bout ten **yardz**. My **leg'll** bray kin three **placez**. I'll be(y)inə noudə the **häspidl** fr seven **mənts**. The **däctor'll** put me in **træction** fr the first **mənth** withoudə **cæst**. After my **leg**izə liddle bedder, heel püda **cæst** än. He'll give me ə lät əv **andee-biodics**. **Every**one'll be very **wrrr-reed** about me. The **news**paperz and **TV'll** report **every**thing th't **hæppenz**. Id'll take me **seven** munts tə **recover**, and id'll be(y)ə **yir** b'fore I **compeedə** gen. I'll **still** havə **scär** än my **shin**, and my **right** cæf won bee(y)ə z d'velopt az thee(y)**other** oneiz. I'll be **lucky** to be **alive**, tho.

NOUNS
This section shows you how to compare, explains the difference between two types of nouns, and discusses word order and more conjunctions.
本部分会教你如何进行比较，如何解释两类名词之间的差异，还会讲解词序问题以及更多的连词。

ACCENT
We first looked at descriptions and compound nouns in Chapter 2. To review, a description is an adjective and a noun, and the stress goes on the noun. A compound noun is two nouns together, and the stress goes on the first noun. A compound noun is a set phrase, where you have a whole idea in one phrase. It can either be two words, two words with a hyphen, or a single word.

我们先来复习一下在第二章中讲到的描述语和复合名词。描述语由一个形容词和一个名词构成，且重音放在名词上。复合名词由两个名词组成，且重音放在第一个名词上。复合名词是固定短语，整个短语表达一个完整的意思。它既可以是两个单词，或者中间加了连字符的两个单词，也可以只是一个单词。

Descriptions	Compounds
a chocolate **cake**	a **pan**cake
a bright **light**	a **light**bulb
a nice **day**	my **birth**day
a new **guitar**	a **guitar** case

Exercise 5-3: Noun Intonation

Circle the word that should be stressed. Then check the Answer Key.

1. a nice time
2. a timeline

11. a big truck
12. a truck stop

21. a fried egg
22. an egg yolk

3. long hair	13. a hot tub (Jacuzzi)	23. a butter knife
4. a haircut	14. a hot coffee	24. a sharp knife
5. a hot dog (food)	15. a wedding cake	25. paper towels
6. a big deal	16. a delicious cake	26. clean towels
7. a cell phone	17. a house key	27. a housekeeper
8. a good plan	18. a small key	28. a messy house
9. a notebook	19. a hairbrush	29. a baseball
10. a long walk	20. a yellow brush	30. an orange ball

Here's an interesting tip: All soups are descriptions and all sauces are compound nouns. Although they may have similar ingredients, they follow different intonation patterns.

这里有一个有趣的小提示：所有的汤都是描述语，所有的调味酱都是复合名词。尽管它们可能包含相似的成分，但是要遵循不同的声调模式。

Soup	Sauce
tomato **soup**	**tomato** sauce
vegetable **soup**	**hot** sauce
lentil **soup**	**pasta** sauce
split pea **soup**	**barbeque** sauce
chicken noodle **soup**	**white** sauce
minestrone **soup**	**soy** sauce
alphabet **soup**	**Tabasco** sauce

Here is a list of general rules.
下面列出了基本规则。

	Rules	Examples
Emphasis on the **First Word** 重音落在第一个词上	Compound nouns 复合名词	**potato** chips, a **break**down, the **White** House
	Streets 街道名	**Elm** Street
	Co. or Corp. 公司名	**Xerox** Corporation
	Nationalities 国籍	a **Chinese** guy
	Food nationalities 食物国别	**French** food
Emphasis on the **Second Word** 重音落在第二个词上	Descriptions 描述语	a nice **time**, a white **house**
	Adverb + adjective 副词+形容词	really **nice**, chocolate **cake**
	Names 人名	Joe **Jones**
	Titles 头衔	Assistant **Manager**
	Road names 道路名	Fifth **Avenue**

Place names 地点名	Los **Angeles**, Las **Vegas**, New **York**
Acronyms 缩写	I**D**, IB**M**
Money 钱	two **dollars**
Phrasal verbs 短语动词	to break **down**

Exercise 5-4: Noun Intonation

In each of the blue phrases, underline the word that should be stressed. Then check the Answer Key.

1. They took a **shortcut** down a **dark alley** to the **supermarket**.
2. Are you taking an **airplane** to **Los Angeles**?
3. The **school bus** parked at the **amusement park** for **three hours** in the **hot sun**.
4. The **Vice President** doesn't live at the **White House** in Washington, **D.C.**
5. The **math students** went to a **bookstore** to buy their **textbooks**.
6. Did the **swim team** meet **every day last summer**?
7. There are many **secret recipes** for **junk food**.
8. Her **boyfriend** gave her a **diamond ring** for her **birthday**.
9. The **little dog** gave them a **sad look** from the **front porch** on that **cold day**.
10. There was a **breakdown** in communications, so the system **broke down**.

Word order follows certain patterns. No matter how big the circle, words like **my**, **your**, and **our** will always be on the outer ring, or at the beginning of the phrase.

词序遵循着一定的模式。无论圆环有多大，像my，your，our等词总会出现在最外面那一圈，即位于短语的起始位置。

**My five big, old, blue
American racecars**

Word Order List 词序列表

1.	Owner / Article 所有者 / 冠词
2.	Number 数字
3.	Size 尺寸
4.	Type 类型
5.	Color 颜色
6.	Material 材料
7.	Nationality 国籍
8.	Compound Noun 复合名词
9.	Noun 名词

134

Stacking Adjectives
堆叠形容词

Stacking adjectives is an important aspect of communicating in English. Beginning-level students tend to repeat nouns because they are making short sentences. For example: **I have five cars. The cars are red. My cars are American. They are really old. My cars are big. They are racecars.**

学会堆叠形容词是实现用英语交流的一个重要方面。初学者常常会重复名词，因为他们说的是短句。例如：I have five cars.（我有五辆车。）The cars are red.（车是红色的。）My cars are American.（我的车是美国产的。）They are really old.（它们真的很旧了。）My cars are big.（我的车很大。）They are racecars.（它们是赛车。）

This sounds clunky（not smooth）and immature（childish）in both spoken and written English. The goal is to learn how to **stack adjectives**. This will allow you to communicate a large amount of information in just a few words. Americans prefer to use fewer words whenever possible.

不论是在口语还是书面语中，这样做都会让你显得笨拙且幼稚。所以，我们要学习堆叠形容词。学会以后，你就能用几个词传达大量的信息了。无论什么时候，美国人总喜欢用尽量少的词表达相同的意思。

To figure out the word order, start with the outside edges. Find either the article or the owner for the first word, and then find the main noun for the last word. If the main noun is plural, there may not be an article or owner.

为了弄清楚词序，我们先从最外面那圈开始着手。先找到放在最前面的冠词或物主代词，再找到放在最后面的核心名词。如果核心名词是复数，可能就不需要冠词或物主代词了。

Exercise 5-5: Word Order

Rewrite the sentence with all of the blue words in the proper order. Then check the Answer Key.

1. _____ were very expensive.   **Chinese, rugs, his, three**

2. The dogs jumped onto _____.   **couch, my, red, big, leather**

3. He was taking notes in _____.   **French, a, notebook, tiny**

4. We replaced _____.   **wooden, the, bookshelf, old, brown**

5. She put _____ in the kitchen drawer.   **black, Thai, ten, chopsticks**

Exercise 5-6: Word Order

Rewrite the sentence with all of the blue words in the proper order. For the last two, create your own phrase. Then check the Answer Key.

1. **Japanese saw the students young three I English**

2. **China long only the Italian in on train black We're**

3. **tabletops ten Tunisian tin Todd's tiny are Where**

4. Article Number Color Compound Noun

5. Owner Size Color Material Compound Noun

For the next exercise, think back to Chapter 2, where we studied the five conjunctions: **and**, **but**, **so**, **or**, **because**.

在做下面的练习时，回想一下在第二章中学过的五个连词：and，but，so，or，because。

Exercise 5-7: Conjunctions   Track 080

Listen to the audio and repeat five times.

	He was happy _____ he lived in Beijing.
when	**At the time** that he lived in Beijing, he was happy.
whenever	**Every time** that he lived in Beijing, he was happy.
before	**Prior to living** in Beijing, he was happy.
until	**Up to the point** that he lived in Beijing, he was happy, then he wasn't.
because	Living in Beijing made him happy. (cause)
even though	**In spite of living** in Beijing, he was happy (contrary to expectations).
but	Living in Beijing is unusual for happy people.
but then	He used to be happy, but **the change** made him unhappy.
after	Upon moving away from Beijing, he was happy.
while	He was happy **during his stay** in Beijing.
as soon as	**The moment** he moved into his Beijing apartment, he was happy.
unless	Living in Beijing made him unhappy.
so	Happy people move to Beijing.
and	His mood and location were **unrelated events**.

Exercise 5-8: Conjunctions

Select the proper answer. Then check the Answer Key.

	They waited	until	the last moment.	☐ by ☑ until
1.	We won't rest		we find the answer.	☐ although ☐ until

136

2. They dropped the subject   it was boring.
☐ because
☐ so

3. We planned on going,   we cancelled.
☐ since
☐ but then

4. The old man fainted   he heard the news.
☐ until
☐ as soon as

5. The roof leaked   it rained.
☐ but
☐ whenever

6. I can't help you   you cooperate.
☐ unless
☐ so

7. They kept going   they were exhausted.
☐ as soon as
☐ even though

8. He called me   the earthquake.
☐ right after
☐ until

9. They've been busy   they got here.
☐ ever since
☐ until

10. The dancing started   dark.
☐ after
☐ until

How Many? So Many! Too Many!

In Chapter 4, we worked with **how** in the meaning of *in what way?*
在第四章中，我们学习了how的一种意思，即"以什么方式？"

It is good.   He works well.
Is it good?   Does he work well?
How is it?   How does he work?
           How well does he work?

Now, let's look at *to what extent?* We can express this by adding an adjective or an adverb. Let's also review countable and uncountable nouns.

现在，我们来学习它的另外一种意思，即"到什么程度？"只要加上一个形容词或副词，我们就可以表达这种意思了。同时，也让我们一起复习一下可数名词和不可数名词吧。

So is an intensifier.
We had so much fun.
There were so many people there!

Too is excessive.
He ate too much.
There were too many people there.

Uncountable
So Much / Too Much
Did you buy sugar?
Yes, I bought **so much** sugar!
I bought **too much** sugar!

Countable
So Many / Too Many
Did you buy bananas?
Yes, I bought **so many** bananas!
I bought **too many** bananas!

		How Much			How Many	

How Much
How much sugar did you buy?
How much did **it** cost?

How Many
How many banana**s** did you buy?
How much did **they** cost?

Single
How often do you buy **it**?
How long does **it** last?

Plural
How often do you buy **them**?
How long do **they** last?

Count Me!

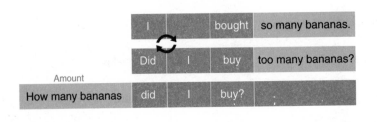

I		bought	so many bananas.
Did	I	buy	too many bananas?

Amount

How many bananas	did	I	buy?	.

Exercise 5-9: *How + Many* ↻

*Convert each statement to a **how** question, using either the verb **to be** or a main verb. Then check the Answer Key.*

There are **five** people in my family.   How many people are there in your family?
He has **two** uncles.   How many uncles does he have?

1. There were many cars on the road.
2. We had so many problems.
3. She wanted several alternatives.
4. They made a lot of mistakes.
5. He put two sugars in his coffee.
6. This car has two doors.
7. My aunt has forty pairs of shoes.
8. That boy has six dogs.
9. I only have five minutes to finish this.
10. The student is taking eighteen units.

Don't Count Me!

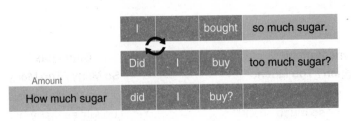

I		bought	so much sugar.
Did	I	buy	too much sugar?

Amount

How much sugar	did	I	buy?	

Exercise 5-10: *How + Much* ○

*Convert each statement to a **how** question, using either the verb **to be** or a main verb. Then check the Answer Key.*

There is not much time. **How much** time is there?
He does not have much time. **How much** time does he have?

1. I have too much ink.
2. This ink costs too much.
3. They cost $10 this year.
4. It costs $10 this year.
5. They cost $10 last year.
6. It cost $10 last year.
7. She doesn't have much energy.
8. There wasn't much rice left over.
9. It was a lot of fun.
10. There is a lot smoke in the air.

[handwritten:]
~~How~~ much rice was ~~there~~ left over
How much fun ~~does~~ was it
How much smoke is in the air

Exercise 5-11: *How Much / How Many* ○

*Convert each statement to a **how** question, using either the verb **to be** or a main verb. Then check the Answer Key.*

There's not much water. **How much** water is there?
There's a drop of water. **How many** drops of water are there?

1. There's too much noise out here!
2. There are so many singers.
3. There's enough cloth for that dress.
4. You are making three dresses.
5. I don't have enough gas in the car.
6. There are two gas stations there.
7. I don't have much hair.
8. I found several hairs in my sink.
9. You didn't learn much today.
10. You went to four classes today.

How Often?

Let's use the question flip with **how often**.
在用how often进行提问的时候，要颠倒疑问句的语序。

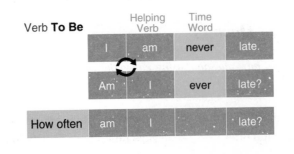

Verb **To Be**		Helping Verb	Time Word	
	I	am	never	late.
	Am	I	ever	late?
How often	am	I		late?

Exercise 5-12: *How + Often — To Be* ↻

*Convert each statement to a **how** question, using the verb **to be**. Pay attention to the verb tenses. You can use either nouns or pronouns in your answers. Check the Answer Key when you're done.*

The grass is watered **every day**.	**How often** is the grass watered?
The grass is **never** cut.	**How often** is the grass cut?

1. They are almost always in trouble.
2. The weather is almost always nice.
3. The staff is frequently out of the office.
4. Our dogs are often dirty.
5. His comments were generally ignored.
6. She is usually on the road.
7. Swans are sometimes vicious.
8. History is hardly ever repeated.
9. We are almost never confused.
10. He's never in L.A.

Main Verb		Helping Verb	Time Word	Main Verb	
	I		never	call	him.
	Do	I	ever	call	him?
How often	do	I		call	him?

Exercise 5-13: *How + Often — Main Verbs* ↻

*Convert each statement to a **how** question, using main verbs. Then check the Answer Key.*

You **frequently** go to the gym.	**How often** do you go to the gym?
You go to the gym **every day**.	**How often** do you go to the gym?

1. We always plan for the future.
2. She almost always had a Plan B.
3. I almost never eat donuts.
4. Ants frequently get into the kitchen.
5. Commuters sometimes take shortcuts.

6. I always do the right thing.
7. She's usually pretty direct.
8. It's often cold in Alaska.
9. This car is generally reliable.
10. He never changes his mind.

Two Bees or Not Two Bees
是或者不是两只小蜜蜂

There are several words and phrases for comparing and contrasting two items.
要对两个事物进行比较和对比，有若干单词和短语可供选择。

Both, **each**, **either**, **so**, and **too** are positive. **Neither** is negative.

both，each，either，so 和too用来表达肯定的意思，neither则表达否定的意思。

Either can be used for questions or as a response to a negative statement: **I don't do it. I don't either.**

either 可以用于疑问句，也可以用于对否定陈述句的回答：I don't do it.（我没有做。）I don't either.（我也没有。）

Exercise 5-14: *Two* Terminology   Track 081

Listen to the audio and repeat the phrases relating to the picture.

1. There are **two** bugs.
2. These are **both** insects.
3. They **both** have six legs. **Neither** of them has eight legs like a spider.
4. They **each** have a way of communicating.
5. **One of them** can fly, but **the other** can't.
6. Can **either** of them talk? No, **neither** of them can talk, but **both** of them can sting.
7. One of them **stung** me. It was **either** the ant **or** the bee. **Neither** of them stung you.
8. **The one on the left** is an ant. **The one on the right** is a bee.
9. The bee is small, and the ant is, **too**. The bee is small and **so** is the ant.
10. **Both** of them are small.

Exercise 5-15: *Two* Terminology — Fill in the Blanks

Fill in the blanks, using information about a horse and a zebra. Then check the Answer Key.

1. There are **two** ____.
2. These are **both** ____.
3. They **both** ____. **Neither** of them ____.

4. They **each** ____.

5. **One of them** ____, but **the other** ____.

6. Can **either** of them ____? No, **neither** of them can ____, but **both** of them can ____.

7. **One of them** ____. It is **either** the horse **or** the zebra. **Neither** of them ____.

8. **The one on the left** is a ____. **The one on the right** is a ____.

9. The horse is ____, and the zebra is, **too**. The horse is ____ and **so** is the zebra.

10. The ____ runs fast, and the ____ does, **too**. The ____ runs fast and **so** ____ the zebra.

Exercise 5-16: *Two* Terminology — Make Up Your Own Sentences

Make your own sentences using information about a mobile home and a cabin. Then check the Answer Key.

1. two
2. both
3. both / neither
4. each
5. one of them / the other
6. either / neither / both
7. one of them / either / neither
8. the one on the left / right
9. too / so (is)
10. too / so (main verb)
11. both

Use

Use has several meanings. The most basic is **to utilize** or **to employ**.
use有好几个意思。最基本的意思是"利用"或"使用"。

Used to is for a repeated past action.
used to可以用来表示过去的重复性动作。

To be used to doing something is to be accustomed to doing something.（habit + verb）
to be used to doing something的意思是"习惯做某事"。（习惯+动词）

To be used to something is to be accustomed to something.（habit + noun）
to be used to something 的意思是"习惯某事"。（习惯+名词）

Exercise 5-17: *Use*

Fill in the blank with the proper form of use, to be used, to be used to, or used to. Then check the Answer Key.

1. When I eat, I _____ a fork.   utilize, employ
2. I _____ walking to work.   accustomed to, habit
3. They _____ live in San Francisco.   previously
4. We _____ an oven for baking. (əvən)   utilize, employ
5. An oven _____ for baking.   is utilized, is employed
6. When he eats Chinese food, he _____ chopsticks.   utilize, employ
7. They _____ working hard.   accustomed to
8. She _____ work hard, but she doesn't anymore.   previously
9. Everyone _____ English in class.   utilize, employ
10. English _____ in class.   is utilized, is employed

Exercise 5-18: *Use* — Pronunciation   **Track 082**

Listen to the audio and repeat five times.

1. When I eat, I **yuze** a fork.
2. I'm **usta** walking to work.
3. They **usta** live in San Francisco.
4. We **yuze** an oven for baking. (əvən)
5. An oven **iz yuzd** for baking.
6. When he eats Chinese food, he **yuzez** chopsticks.
7. They're **usta** working hard.
8. She **usta** work hard, but she doesn't anymore.
9. Everyone **yuzez** English in class.
10. English **iz yuzd** in class.

Countable and Uncountable Collections
可数和不可数集合名词

We have worked with countable and uncountable nouns before. Now, we'll see how individual, countable items (left) form **collections** (right).

我们之前已经学过可数和不可数名词了。现在，我们来看看单个的、可数的事物(左边)是如何形成集合名词(右边)的。

Count Items	Don't Count Collections
a painting	art
a statue	
a photograph	
a storm	weather
a sunny day	
a heat wave	
a report	information
a data set	

a phone call	communication
a letter	
a memo	
an e-mail	
a conversation	
a novel	literature
a story	
a poem	

Exercise 5-19: *Much* or *Many* with Countables and Uncountables

Select **much** *or* **many**. *Then check the Answer Key.*

The dealer bought so _____ painting**s**.

The dealer bought so _____ art.

The dealer bought so **many** painting**s**.

The dealer bought so **much** art.

1. You gave me too _____ information.
2. You gave me too _____ facts.
3. There was not _____ communication.
4. There were not _____ e-mails.
5. She didn't eat _____ dessert.
6. She ate too _____ pies.
7. There's not _____ water in the glass.
8. There're _____ drops of water on the table.
9. How _____ traffic is there?
10. How _____ cars are there?

Notice the verb change between the singular and the plural.

1. Half **of the lakes** are **frozen**.
2. Both halves **of the book** are **useful**.
3. Some **of the loaves** are **stale**.
4. Not all **of the teas in China** are **green**.
5. Half **of the team members** are **late**.
6. **Ten percent of the people I know** are **away**.
7. There are **two** more **hours** to go.
8. There are **$10 bills** in my wallet.
9. There are **five** more **miles** until the end.
10. There are **two weeks** until graduation.

Half **of the water** is **frozen**.

The first half **of the book** is **useful**.

Some **of the bread** is **stale**.

All **of the tea in China** is **excellent**.

Two-thirds **of the team** is **late**.

Ten percent of the population is **away**.

Two hours is a long time.

Ten dollars is not enough.

Five miles is too far.

Two weeks isn't enough time.

Exercise 5-20: Half Is... Half Are...

Select the proper verb. Then check the Answer Key.

There are ten miles more to go.

Ten miles is a long way.

1. Half of the oranges ____ packed in boxes.　　　　　is / are
2. Most of the orange juice ____ in cartons.　　　　　is / are
3. ____ any of the family coming?　　　　　　　　　is / are
4. ____ any of your brothers or sisters coming?　　　is / are
5. The first half of the movie ____ fantastic.　　　　was / were
6. Half of the room ____ filled with balloons.　　　　was / were
7. Half of the rooms ____ damaged in the fire.　　　　was / were
8. Both halves of the amulet ____ quite valuable.　　　was / were
9. We think that 25% ____ a fair commission.　　　has been / have been
10. We think that 25% of them ____ ready to go.　　　has been / have been

This next topic is not very common, but it's important for passing tests. Some nouns can be both countable and uncountable, depending how you look at them. For example, the word **experience** can be countable, as there may be **a good experience** or **a bad experience**. In this meaning, it's an **event**.

下一个主题并不常见，但它对于通过考试很重要。一些名词既可以是可数的，也可以是不可数的，关键在于你怎么看。例如，experience这个词可以是可数的，因为你可以说a good experience（一次好的经历）或a bad experience（一次不好的经历）。这时，它代表的是一个事件。

However, it can also be a collection of events to mean a person's "background." For example, a person's schoolwork and previous jobs form a collection called **experience**. In this way, you can have both **He had many interesting experiences**（countable）and **He didn't have much experience**（uncountable）.

然而，它也可以是很多事件的集合，表示一个人的"背景"。例如，某人的学业状况和工作经历可以构成一个集合，叫作experience（履历）。这样一来，你既可以说He had many interesting experiences（可数名词），也可以说He didn't have much experience（不可数名词）。

An adjective can also make an uncountable noun countable. For example, **life** is uncountable, but you can say **He has a good life**.

形容词也可以把一个不可数名词变成可数名词。例如，life是不可数的，但你可以说He has a good life（他过得很好）。

Exercise 5-21: *Much* or *Many* with Countables and Uncountables

*Select **much** or **many**. Then check the Answer Key.*

He didn't have ____ experiences.　　　　He didn't have **many** experience**s**.

He didn't have ____ experience.　　　　　He didn't have **much** experience.

1. I need so ____ space for my stuff.
2. I need so ____ spaces for the cars.
3. There were too ____ noises outside.
4. There was too ____ noise outside.

5. There was ____ discussion about it.
6. There were ____ discussions about it.
7. There is too ____ light in here!
8. There are too ____ lights in here!
9. We ate so ____ ice cream. (in a bowl)
10. We ate so ____ ice creams. (on a stick)
11. He didn't have too ____ success there.
12. He didn't have too ____ successes with it.
13. He doesn't have ____ memory left.
14. He doesn't have ____ good memories.

Exercise 5-22: Eureka!

*Fill in the blank with **a**, **an**, **the**, or — (if another word isn't needed). Then check the Answer Key.*

Here is ____ famous **experiment**; ____ **king** buys ____ new **crown** from ____ **crafts**man. ____ **crafts**man says that ____ **crown** is ____ pure **gold**, but ____ King thinks that ____ cheaper, lighter metal like ____ **silver** is **in** it, **too**. He **asks** his **friend**, **Archimedes**, to **find** out if ____ **crafts**man is **telling** ____ **truth**. ____ **silver** is **lighter** than ____ **gold**, so you **need** more than **one** cup of **silver** to **weigh** ____ **same** as **one** cup of **gold**. If he mixes **silver** into ____ **crown**, there will be **more** cups of ____ **metal** in it than in ____ **same** weight of pure **gold**. **Archimedes** says, "I **have** to figure **out** if there are **more** cups of **metal** in ____ **crown** than in ____ **same** weight of pure **gold**. But, if I **melt** ____ crown to find **out**, it **won't** be ____ **crown** anymore. ____ **king** will be **angry**. How can I find **out** how many **cups** there are without **melting** ____ **crown**?"

Archimedes decides to **take** ____ **bath**. He **steps** into his **tub** and ____ **over**flowing **water** gives him ____ **idea**. He **fills** ____ **bucket** with **water**. He puts ____ **pound** of gold in ____ **bucket**. ____ **cup**ful of **water** spills **out**. **Then** he puts ____ pound of **silver** in ____ bucket. **Two** cupfuls of water **spill** out! **This** is because **silver** weighs **less** than **gold, so** ____ **pound** of it (weight) takes up **more room** (volume) than ____ **pound** of gold and **pushes** out **more water**. ____ King's **crown** weighs ____ **pound**. **Archimedes** puts it into ____ full **bucket**. If **one** cupful of water spills **out**, there is ____ **pound** of gold in ____ **crown**. If **more** than **one** cupful of water spills **out**, it **can't be** pure **gold**. **This** way, he **doesn't** have to melt ____ **crown**. **All** he has to do is **measure** ____ **water** that spills **out**. It's ____ **great** idea! **Archimedes** gets so **excited** that he **jumps** out of ____ **tub**, and runs **naked down** ____ **street** shouting "**Eureka!** " In **Greek**, this means, "I **found** it! "

When **Archimedes** does ____ **experiment**, he **finds** that ____ **crown** pushes out **more** water than ____ **equal** weight of **gold** does. **That** means that the **gold** is mixed with **silver**. ____ **crafts**man is **cheating** ____ **King**.

ü	u
put	truth
push	you
pull	two
full	room
cupful	to(w)a

Exercise 5-23: Yer-reekə!   **Track 083**

Listen and repeat.

ACCENT

Hir zə faməs **eksperam'nt;** ə **king** by zə new **crown** frəmə **crafts**m'n. Thə **crafts**man sez thət thə **crown**iz pyoor **gold,** bət thə king thinks thada cheaper, lyder medəl like silver iz**in**it, **too.** He **asks** his **frend,** **Arkəmeedeez,** to **fyn** dout if the **crafts**m'n iz **telling** thə **truth. Silver** iz **lyder** thən **gold,** so you **need** more thən **one** cuppa **silver** tə **way** the **same** əz **one** cuppa **gold.** Iffee mixəz **silver** into the **crown,** there'll be **more** cupsa **medəl** init thənin the **same** way dov pyoor **gold. Arkəmeedeez** sez, "I **haf**ta figyer **out** if there are **more** cupsa **medəl** in the **crown** thenin the **same** waydov pyoor **gold.** Bədify **melt** the crown tə fyn **dout,** it **won't** be[y]ə **crown** nanymore. The **king**'ll be [y]**angry.** How c'nai fyn **dout** how many **cups** there are without **melting** the **crown?**"

Arkəmeedeez d'cidz tə **tay** kə**bath.** He **step** sinto hiz **tub** and thee[y]**over**flowing **wäder** give zima ny **deə.** He **fill** zə **bucket** with **wäder.** He pütsə **poundə gold** in the **bucket.** A **cup**füll **wäder** spill **z**out. Thenee pütsə poundə **silver** in the bucket. **Two** cupfulzə wader **spill**out! **This** iz b'cuz **silver** wayz **less** thən **gold, so**[w]ə **pound**əvit take səp **more room** thanə **poundə gold** and **pushəz**out **more wäder.** The kingz **crown** wayzə **pound. Arkameedeez** putsidinto[w]ə full **bucket.** If **one** cupfullə wader spill **zout,** therzə**poundə gold**in the **crown.** If **more** thən **one** cupfullə wader spill **zout,** it **cæn't** be pyoor **gold. This** way, he **dəznt** haftə **melt** the **crown. Allee** has tə do[w]iz **mezher** the **wäder** that spill **zout.** Itsə **gray** dydeə! **Arkəmeedeez** getsso[w]**excidəd** the dee **jump** soudə the **tub,** and runz **naked down** th' **street** shouding **yer-reekə!** In **Greek,** this meenz, I **foun** dit!

When **Arkəmeedeez** dəz thee[y]**eksperəm'nt,** he **findz** thət the **crown** pushəzout **more** wäder thanən**eekwəl** way dəv **gold** dəzz. **That** meenz thət the **gold**iz mixt with **silver.** The **cræfts**man iz **cheading** the **king.**

crown	**clown**
æ	æo
craftsman	crown
angry	pound
asks	down
bath	shout
have to	found
can't	around

VERBS

In this section, you will learn both the real and unreal futures, with **will** and **going to.**

在这部分中，我们要学习用will和going to表示的真实将来时和非真实将来时。

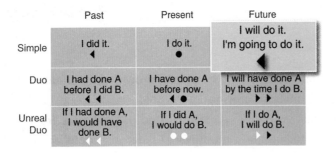

	Past	Present	Future
Simple	I did it. ◀	I do it. ●	I will do it. I'm going to do it. ◀
Duo	I had done A before I did B. ◀◀	I have done A before now. ◀●	I will have done A by the time I do B. ▶▶
Unreal Duo	If I had done A, I would have done B. ◀◀	If I did A, I would do B. ●●	If I do A, I will do B. ▶▶

The helping verb **will** is used with both the verb **to be**—I **will be there**—and main verbs—I **will do it**. With **going to**, you will hear native speakers use a very colloquial pronuciation: aimana. This will make **I'm going to try it** sound like: Aimana try it. Trust the phonetics.

辅助动词will既可以和be动词连用——I will be there，也可以和主动词连用——I will do it。以英语为母语的人在说going to的时候，发音是非常口语化的：aimana。这样一来，I'm going to try it听起来就会像Aimana try it。请相信语音学。

Exercise 5-24: Simple Future

Put the sentences in the future. Remember to use the unchanging form of the main verb. Then check the Answer Key.

I speak Italian.   **I will speak** Italian.

1. The teachers write on the blackboard.
2. Larry rides his bike everywhere.
3. Your cousin flew first class.
4. The managers arrange meetings.
5. I gave many presents.
6. We think about it.
7. They threw it away.
8. Virginia sold her car.
9. The candles burn steadily.
10. Her sister said hello.

> The *simple present* can be used to indicate the *near future*.
> 一般现在时也可以用来表示很近的将来。
>
> I have a doctor's appointment at one o'clock tomorrow.
> His plane arrives on Sunday night.
> There's a party next week.

Exercise 5-25: Negatives

Change the positive to a negative. Then check the Answer Key.

He will make money.   He **will not** make money.

1. The teachers will write on the blackboard.
2. Larry will ride his bike everywhere.

3.   Your cousin will fly first class.
4.   The managers will arrange meetings.
5.   I will give many presents.
6.   We will think about it.
7.   They will throw it away.
8.   Virginia will sell her car.
9.   The candles will burn steadily.
10. Her sister will say hello.

Exercise 5-26: Negative Contractions

Change the positive to a negative contraction. Then check the Answer Key.

He will look at it.   He **won't** look at it.

1.   The teachers will write on the blackboard.
2.   Larry will ride his bike everywhere.
3.   Your cousin will fly first class.
4.   The managers will arrange meetings.
5.   I will give many presents.
6.   We will think about it.
7.   They will throw it away.
8.   Virginia will sell her car.
9.   The candles will burn steadily.
10. Her sister will say hello.

Exercise 5-27: Negative Contractions

Change to the other form of the contraction with the negative present of **to be**. *Check the Answer Key when you're done.*

He isn't looking at it.   He**'s not** looking at it.

1.   They aren't writing on it.
2.   He isn't riding it.
3.   She isn't flying in one.
4.   They aren't arranging them.
5.   He isn't giving them.
6.   We aren't thinking about it.
7.   They aren't throwing it away.
8.   Virginia isn't selling it.
9.   They aren't burning steadily.
10. She isn't saying hello.

Contrasting *Will Do* and *Going To Do*
对比Will Do 和 Going To Do

Will do and **going to do** are largely interchangeable, but **will** is a bit more formal.

在很大程度上，will do 和 going to do是可以互换的，但will要显得稍微正式一点。

Exercise 5-28: Two Futures   Track 084

Listen and repeat.

Will Do	**Going To Do（prior plan）**
I'll call you later.	I'm going to have to call you later.（aimana hafta）
He'll **think** about it.	He's going to **think** about it.
We'll let you know **later**.	We're going to let you know **later**.
It'll **happen** before **long**.	It's going to **happen** before **long**.
You'll have a good time.	You're going to have a good time.

Exercise 5-29: Changing Future Forms

*Change the **will** form to the **going to** form. Use contractions and change nouns to pronouns. Then check the Answer Key.*

He'll go.   **He's going to go.**

1. We'll think about it.
2. They'll throw it away.
3. Virginia will sell her car.
4. The candles will burn steadily.
5. Her sister will say hello.

Exercise 5-30: Questions ⟳

Change the statements to questions. Then check the Answer Key.

Jane will dance well.   **Will Jane dance well?**

1. The teachers will write on the blackboard.
2. Larry will ride his bike everywhere.
3. Your cousin will fly first class.
4. The managers will arrange meetings.
5. I will give many presents.
6. We will think about it.
7. They will throw it away.
8. Virginia will sell her car.
9. The candles will burn steadily.
10. Her sister will say hello.

Exercise 5-31: Questions with Pronouns⟳

Change the statements to questions. Change all nouns to pronouns.（*Duzzy, Izzy, Willy?*）*Check the Answer Key when you're done.*

Joe will drink his coffee.   **Will he drink it?**

1. The teachers will write on the blackboard.
2. Larry will ride his bike everywhere.
3. Your cousin will fly in a jet.
4. The managers will arrange meetings.
5. I will give many presents.
6. Bob will think about his classes.
7. Jenny and Norbert will throw it away.
8. Virginia will sell her car.
9. The boys will sit in a row.
10. Her sister will say hello.

"Only One Will"

"只用一个will"

The **simple future** is used with
until, before, after, when, even if, unless, etc.
一般将来时可以与until，before，after，when，even if，unless等词连用。

I **will call** you when I **get** there.
We **won't rest** until we find out what **is** going on.

Exercise 5-32: Present Tense to Indicate the Future

Rewrite the sentences using the simple present or the continuous form. Then check the Answer Key.

He will get a job after he graduates.   He's getting a job after he graduates.

1. She **will make** the decision **when** she **is** here.
2. I **won't tell** you **until** she **gets** here.
3. We**'ll leave when** it's **over**.
4. He won't get **up until** it's time to **go**.
5. Everyone **will work until** the bell **rings**.
6. They**'ll go** home **after** the stores **close**.
7. I**'ll take** a walk **even if** it**'s** raining.
8. We**'ll go** to bed **when** the sun **sets**.
9. She **was** very rude to me. I **refuse** to speak to her again **until** she **apologizes**.
10. I**'ll start after** I **get** organized.
11. We'll do something **soon, before** it's too **late**.
12. I won't **call** him **unless** I **need** to.

13. We'll go **shopping** even if it's **snowing**.

14. I will be a **nurse** when I pass the **exam**.

15. I won't **tell** you until after we finish **class**.

Exercise 5-33: Present Tense to Indicate the Future   Track 085

Listen to the motorcycle story again, but this time focus on the use of the present tense to indicate the future. These five instances are indicated in blue.

In eight years, three days **after I win** Mr. Europe, I will be riding a motorcycle on a main street in Milan, Italy. I will be going about 80 miles an hour. All of a sudden, a car will pull in front of me. I'll hit the car and fly about 10 yards. My leg will break in three places. I will be in and out of the hospital for seven months. The doctor will put me in traction for the first month without a cast. **After my leg is a little better,** he will put a cast on. He will give me a lot of antibiotics. Everyone will be very worried about me. The newspapers and TV will report everything that **happens**. It will take me seven months to recover, and it will be a year **before I compete** again. I will still have a scar on my shin, and my right calf won't be as developed as the other one **is**. I'll be lucky to be alive, though.

If ...

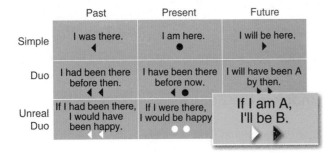

The **simple future** can be used with the **simple present** to indicate an **unreal situation**. Notice that both verbs are represented by the symbol for the future, ▶, but now the first triangle is white. This is because it represents something that hasn't happened or won't happen. The **white** symbols are **unreal**. The **black** symbols indicate things that **will happen** if certain conditions are met.

　一般将来时可以和一般现在时连用以表示非真实的情况。请注意：两个动词都是用将来时符号▶表示的，但第一个三角形是白色的。这是因为它代表某事还没有发生或者不会发生。白色的符号表示非真实。黑色的符号则表示只要满足特定条件，某事就会发生。

If + To Be

This looks like the present(**If I am A**), but when you ask the question, **Will I be A?**, you can see that it is the future. With the statement **If I am there, I'll be available**, you can ask, **Am I there?** The answer is, "Maybe, maybe not." The same is true with the second half, **Will I be available?** Again, "Maybe, maybe not." We don't know yet, and we won't know until the if condition is met.

　这句话看起来像现在时(If I am A)，但如果你问"Will I be A?"，你就明白它是将来时了。面对陈述句If I am there, I'll be available，你可以问"Am I there?"，答案是"可能会在，也可能不在"。对后半句进行提问也是一样的，如果问"Will I be available?"，答案是"可能有空，也可能没空"。我们现在还不能确定，因为我们还不知道if的条件能不能得到满足。

Exercise 5-34: The Unreal — *To Be*

*Fill in the blank with the proper form of the unreal, using the verb **to be**. Then check the Answer Key.*

Current fact	**Conjecture about the future**
The store is open. I am inside.	If the store is open, I'll be inside.

1. The **boxes** are **full**. They are **heavy**.
2. The boxes are **empty**. They are not **heavy**.
3. It's **raining**. You are **cold**.
4. He's **lying**. He is in **trouble**.
5. He is **sorry**. His friends are **understanding**.
6. They are on **time**. They are **satisfied**.
7. The **wheel** is **loose**. The **driver** is **scared**.
8. He is **here**. He is **helpful**.
9. He isn't **here**. He isn't **helpful**.
10. They are **tired**. They stay **home**.

Main Verbs
主动词

Just as with the verb **to be**, with **main verbs** you will always use the **simple present** form after **if**.

和be动词一样，if后面的主动词也总要用一般现在时。

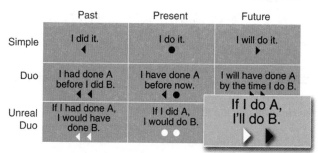

Exercise 5-35: The Unreal — Main Verbs

Fill in the blank with the proper form of the unreal, using main verbs. Use the unchanging form of the main verb for the second half of the sentence. Check the Answer Key when you're done.

Current fact	**Conjecture about the future**
He goes. He has fun.	If he goes, he'll have fun.

1. He has **time**. He goes to the **party**.
2. She runs a red **light**. She gets a **ticket**.
3. She knows all the **answers**. She passes the **test**.
4. He tries **hard**. He **succeeds**.
5. You tell the **truth**. He **appreciates** it.
6. They get to work **late**. They get **fired**.
7. She drives too **fast**. She has an **accident**.

8. He forgets to **pay**. He gets in **trouble**.

9. I lose the ring. He is up**set**.

10. We are **hungry**. We stop for **lunch**.

Exercise 5-36: Future Tags

All three forms of the future use tags in the same way we have learned. Fill in the correct tag. Then
check the Answer Key.

He'll be there,	**won't he?**
He's going to do it,	**isn't he?**
If he is there, he'll help us,	**won't he?**

1. She'll think about it,

2. You're going to try,

3. If they like it, they'll get one,

4. Everyone will take the day off,

5. Nobody's going to worry,

Grammar in a Nutshell
语法小结

So far, we have studied the simple present, the past, and two forms of the future, as well as the
continuous. Let's review all of this in Grammar in a Nutshell.

到目前为止，我们已经学习了一般现在时、过去时、将来时的两种形式，以及进行时。让我们在
"语法小结"这部分把它们都复习一遍吧。

Exercise 5-37: Grammar in a Nutshell   Track 086

Listen to the audio and repeat, reading from the right-hand column.

	Grammar	Pronunciation
1.	**Dogs** eat **bones**.	**däg z**eet **bounz**
2.	The **dogs** eat the **bones**.	the **däg** zeet the **bounz**
3.	The **dogs** are eating the **bones**.	the **däg** zr reeding the **bounz**
4.	The **dogs** ate the **bones**.	the **däg** zate the **bounz**
5.	The **dogs**'ll eat the **bones**.	the **däg** zə leet the **bounz**
6.	The **dogs** are going to eat the **bones**.	the **däg** zer g'nna eat the **bounz**

Notice how similar the following pairs sound.
请注意下面各组词的发音有多相似。

Similar sounds: are eating / are reading

相似的发音：are eating / are reading

Note: Don't ever write **gonna** or **wanna**.

注意：在书面语中千万不要写gonna 或wanna。

Exercise 5-38: Grammar in a Negative Nutshell   **Track 087**

Listen to the audio and repeat, reading from the right-hand column.

	Grammar	Pronunciation
1.	**Dogs** don't eat **bones**.	**dägz** doe neet **bounz**
2.	The **dogs** don't eat the **bones**.	thə **dägz** doe neet thə **bounz**
3.	The **dogs** aren't eating the **bones**.	thə **däg** zär needing thə **bounz**
4.	The **dogs** weren't eating the **bones**.	thə **dägz** wrrn deeding thə **bounz**
5.	The **dogs** won't be eating the **bones**.	thə **dägz** wont be⁽ʸ⁾eeding thə **bounz**
6.	The **dogs** didn't eat the **bones**.	thə **dägz** didn neet thə **bounz**
7.	The **dogs** won't eat the **bones**.	thə **däg** zwoa neet thə **bounz**
8.	The **dogs** aren't going to eat the **bones**.	thə **däg** zärnt g'nna eat thə **bounz**

> ### Similar Sounds
> The dogs don't eat the bones. The dogs don't need the bones.
> The dogs are going to eat the bones. The dogs aren't going to eat the bones.

Exercise 5-39: Grammar in a Nutshell? ↻   **Track 088**

Listen to the audio and repeat, reading from the right-hand column.

	Grammar	Pronunciation
1.	Do **dogs** eat **bones**?	D' **däg** zeet **bounz**?
2.	Do the **dogs** eat the **bones**?	D'thə **däg** zeet the **bounz**?
3.	Did the **dogs** eat the **bones**?	Did thə **däg** zeet the **bounz**?
4.	Are the **dogs** eating the **bones**?	Är thə **däg** zeeding the **bounz**?
5.	Were the **dogs** eating the **bones**?	Wrr thə **däg** zeeding the **bounz**?
6.	Will the **dogs** eat the **bones**?	Will thə **däg** zeet the **bounz**?
7.	Are the **dogs** going to eat the **bones**?	Är thə **dägz** g'nna eat the **bounz**?
8.	Were the **dogs** going to eat the **bones**?	Wrr thə **dägz** g'nna eat the **bounz**?
9.	What eats the **bones**?	W'deets the **bounz**?
10.	What ate the **bones**?	W'date the **bounz**?
11.	What will **eat** the **bones**?	Whədə **leet** the **bounz**?
12.	What do the **dogs** eat?	W'd' thə **däg** zeet?
13.	What did the **dogs** eat?	W'd'd thə **däg** zeet?
14.	What will the **dogs** eat?	Wədəll thə **däg** zeet?
15.	Where do the **dogs** eat the **bones**?	Where də thə **däg** eat the **bounz**?
16.	Where did the **dogs** eat the **bones**?	Where d'd thə **däg** eat the **bounz**?
17.	Where will the **dogs** eat the **bones**?	Wherəll thə **däg** zeet the **bounz**?
18.	When do the **dogs** eat the **bones**?	When d' th' **däg** zeet the **bounz**?
19.	When did the **dogs** eat the **bones**?	When d'd th' **däg** zeet the **bounz**?
20.	When will the **dogs** eat the **bones**?	Whenəll the dag zeet the **bounz**?

21.	Why do the **dogs** eat the **bones**?	Why d' th' **däg** zeet the **bounz**?
22.	Why did the **dogs** eat the **bones**?	Why d'd th' **däg** zeet the **bounz**?
23.	Why will the **dogs** eat the **bones**?	While the **däg** zeet the **bounz**?
24.	How do the **dogs** eat the **bones**?	How d' th' **däg** zeet the **bounz**?
25.	How did the **dogs** eat the **bones**?	How d'd th' **däg** zeet the **bounz**?
26.	How will the **dogs** eat the **bones**?	Hal thə **däg** zeet the **bounz**?
27.	**Who** gives the **bones** to the **dogs**?	**Who** gives the **bounz** t'th' **dägz**?
28.	**Who** gave the **bones** to the **dogs**?	**Who** gave the **bounz** t'th' **dägz**?
29.	**Who** will give the **bones** to the **dogs**?	**Hool** give the **bounz** t' th' **dägz**?
30.	**Who** let the **dogs** out?	**Who** let the **dägz** out?

Exercise 5-40: Grammar in a Nutshell— Pronouns   Track 089

Listen to the audio and repeat, reading from the right-hand column.

	Grammar	Pronunciation
1.	They **eat** them.	they **eed**'m
2.	They're **eating** them.	ther **reed**ing'm
3.	They were **eating** them.	they wrr **reed**ing'm
4.	They'll **eat** them.	thell **leed**em
5.	They're going to **eat** them.	ther g'nna **eed**'m

Similar Sounds

They're eating them. / They're reading them.

Exercise 5-41: Grammar in a Negative Nutshell — Pronouns   Track 090

Listen to the audio and repeat, reading from the right-hand column.

	Grammar	Pronunciation
1.	They don't **eat** them.	they doe **need**'m
2.	They aren't **eating** them.	they är **need**ing'm
3.	They weren't **eating** them.	they wrr **need**ing'm
4.	They won't **eat** them.	they woe **need**'em
5.	They aren't going to **eat** them.	they ärn g'nna **eed**'m
6.	They weren't going to **eat** them.	they wrnt g'nna **eed**'m

Exercise 5-42: Grammar in a Nutshell — Pronouns ↻   Track 091

Listen to the audio and repeat, reading from the right-hand column.

	Grammar	Pronunciation
1.	Do they **eat** them?	d'they **eed**'m?
2.	Did they **eat** them?	d'd they **eed**'m?

3.	Are they **eating** them?	är they **eed**ing'm?
4.	Were they **eating** them?	wrr they **eed**ing'm?
5.	Will they **eat** them?	will they **eed**'m?
6.	Are they going to **eat** them?	är they g'nna **eed**'m?
7.	Were they going to **eat** them?	wrr they g'nna **eed**'m?
8.	What **eats** them?	w'**deet** s'm?
9.	What **ate** them?	w'**day** d'm?
10.	What will **eat** them?	wədə**lee** d'm?
11.	What do they **eat**?	whadda they **eat**?
12.	What did they **eat**?	whadd'd they **eat**?
13.	What will they **eat**?	whaddəll they⁽ʸ⁾**eat**?
14.	Where do they **eat** them?	where d'they **eed**'m?
15.	Where did they **eat** them?	wherd they **eed**'m?
16.	Where will they **eat** them?	wherəll they **eed**'m?
17.	When do they **eat** them?	when d'they **eed**'m?
18.	When did they **eat** them?	when d'd they **eed**'m?
19.	When will they **eat** them?	whenəll they **eed**'m?
20.	Why do they **eat** them?	why d'they **eed**'m?
21.	Why did they **eat** them?	wide they **eed**'m?
22.	Why will they **eat** them?	while they **eed**'m?
23.	How do they **eat** them?	how d'they **eed**'m?
24.	How did they **eat** them?	howd they **eed**'m?
25.	How will they **eat** them?	howəll they **eed**'m?
26.	Who **gives** them to them?	who **giv** zem to⁽ʷ⁾'m?
27.	Who **gave** them to them?	who **gav**'em to⁽ʷ⁾'m?
28.	Who will **give** them to them?	whoəll **giv**'em to⁽ʷ⁾'m?
29.	Who let them **out**?	who leddem **out**?

Similar Sounds

Were they going to eat them? / Where are they going to eat them?

Do and Make

These are many useful idiomatic expressions with the verbs **do** and **make**. Just learn them the way they are, as there are no rules for this form.

动词do和make有很多习惯表达。请把它们死记硬背下来，因为它们没有规律可循。

Do the dishes	**Make** a mistake
Do the laundry	**Make** an appointment
Do the shopping	**Make** a promise
Do homework	**Make** the bed
Do your best	**Make** dinner

Do a favor	**Make** time for
Do a good job	**Make** trouble
Do something over	**Make** a mess
Do the right thing	**Make** a noise
Do something the right way	**Make** money
	Make arrangements

Exercise 5-43: *Do* or *Make*

Fill in the blank with the proper form of **do** *or* **make**. *Then check the Answer Key.*

Do the dishes.   **Make** the bed.

1. They _____ the shopping together every week.
2. They _____ a lot of mistakes.
3. He didn't _____ his homework on time.
4. She _____ a huge mess yesterday.
5. How _____ you do? It's a pleasure to meet you.
6. You and I _____ our best.
7. He needs to _____ an appointment.
8. Why don't you _____ the right thing?
9. Why don't you _____ more money?
10. _____ the travel arrangements soon!

Stand

Stand is another verb with a wide range of meanings, including **represent**, **defy**, **loiter**, **excel**, **replace**, and **tolerate**.

动词stand也有很多不同的意思，包括"代表"、"抵抗"、"徘徊"、"优于"、"替代"、"忍受"等。

Einstein was outstanding in his field.
This man is outstanding in his field.

stand up (arise)
stand in for someone (take someone's place)
stand pain (tolerate pain)
stand trial (be tried for a crime)
stand guard (protect)
stand on (rest, plant, repose)
stand one's ground (hold a position)
stand on one's own two feet (be independent)
stand by (wait)
stand aside (get out of the way)
stand still (not to move)

be standoffish（be reserved）

stand out（be noticeable）

be outstanding（be exceptional）

stand to reason（be logical）

can't stand someone or something（dislike intensely）

stand a chance（have any opportunity for success）

stand for something（tolerate）

stand for something（represent）

stand up for someone（take someone's side）

stand up to someone（defy someone）

from my standpoint（view or perspective）

Exercise 5-44: *Stand*

*Fill in the blank with the proper form of **stand**. The synonym is on the right. Then check the Answer Key.*

1. The old manager was lenient, but the new one won't stand ____ any
   infractions of the rules at all.   tolerate

2. The situation reached a head when one of the clerks stood ____ him   defy
   and demanded a union meeting to rewrite the regulations.

3. He realized the depth of feeling in the department when all the   took her side
   employees stood ____ her.

4. Without his support, though, the issue didn't stand ____ with   have any hope for
   management.   success

5. The typist stood her ____ and eventually an amicable solution was   held her position
   worked out.

> In the calendar, some months have 30 days and some months have
> 31 days. How many months have 28 days?
> 在日历中，有些月份有30天，有些月份有31天。有几个月份有28天呢？
> **Answer:** All of them.
> 答案：所有月份。

| TEST | Let's review everything you have learned in Chapter 5. Make sure you get 100% on the test before going on to the next chapter. Check your work using the Answer Key. |

我们来复习一下在第五章中学过的全部内容。只有当你在测试中获得满分以后，你才能接着学习下一章。请参照答案检查正误。

Part 1: *Underline the word that should be stressed.*

1. They took a **long walk**.
2. May I borrow your **laptop**?
3. I ran out of **paper clips**.
4. It was a really **hot day**.

5. They live in a **beautiful house**.
6. Do they have a **fax machine**?
7. Is that a **new shirt**?
8. He has a **broken leg**.
9. What's the **expiration date**?
10. I really like your new **sunglasses**!

Part 2: *Fill in the appropriate conjunction.*

1. He changed his mind   considering the options.   ☑ after ☐ because
2. We won't go   we have your support.   ☐ but ☑ unless
3. He jumped in the pool   he got there.   ☑ as soon as ☐ while

Part 3: *Fill in the proper article (**a**, **the**, **some**, or **none**).*

We were walking down _a_ dark street. _The_ moon wasn't out, so we couldn't see ~~some~~ _a_ thing. _The_ sidewalk was uneven, and I almost took _a_ fall. We were lost, so we figured that _the_ best thing would be to go back _the_ way we had come. _none_ of us knew where we were, so it took quite _some_ time to get back home.

Part 4: *Change past or present to future, using **will**.*

1. Charlie went to France.

2. Sam gives a speech.

3. John is reading a book.

4. Marcus did not order shoes from Italy.

5. Did Larry fix my computer?

Part 5: *Change the positive statement to a negative contraction.*

1. Timmy will answer your questions.

2. Lea will be dancing in Fresno.

3. Jill is going to facilitate the file transfer.

4. The clown will joke with the crowd.

5. Twenty trees will crash to the ground in the storm.

6.   The secretary is going to file the forms.

Part 6: *Change the statement to a question.*

1.   Shorty will eat his dog food.

2.   The cell phone will need to be charged.

3.   Nate is going to make a big announcement.

Part 7: *Fill in the blank with **do** or **make**.*

1.   Could you   me a favor, please?
2.   Try not to   any more mistakes.
3.   We need to   a final decision.
4.   Lucy forgot to   her homework.
5.   Josie promised to   her best.

Part 8: *Fill in the blank with **up**, **still**, **for**, **out**, or **on**.*

1.   People stand   when the President enters the room.
2.   What does ASAP stand   ?
3.   The actors were standing   the stage.
4.   Stop wiggling!   Stand   !
5.   That red text really stands   on the black background.

Using what you have learned, write two paragraphs on the following topics:

利用你学过的知识写两段话，话题如下：

1. What is your favorite season, and why?
   你最喜欢哪个季节？为什么？
2. What is your most prized possession?
   你所拥有的最有价值的东西是什么？

You can handwrite your paragraphs below or e-mail them to **para@grammar.bz** to be stored. These paragraphs are not graded or reviewed, but simply by writing them, your English will improve.

你可以把作文写在下方，也可以把它们发送到邮箱 para@grammar.bz 以存档。我们不会对你的作文进行打分或点评，但只要你写了，你的英语水平就会提高。

```
 ○○○                           Student Paragraph
 ✉        ⬤      📎      ▢      Aa      ⬤        ▢                    ▭              ▯▯
Send    Chat   Attach Address  Fonts  Colors  Save As Draft        Photo Browser   Show Stationery

         To:  para@grammar.bz
         Cc:
        Bcc:
    Subject:  Chapter 5
 ☰ ▾                                                      Signature:  Corporate ⬍

    My name is _____


```

Let's review everything you have learned in Chapters 1 through 5. Make sure you get 100% on this test before going on to the next chapter. Check your work using the Answer Key.

MIDTERM

我们来复习一下从第一章到第五章的全部内容。只有当你在测试中获得满分以后，你才能接着学习下一章。请参照答案检查正误。

Part 1: *Underline the words that should be* **stressed***.*

1.   The dogs were playing in the yard.
2.   The taxi driver put my suitcase in the trunk.
3.   There was a big earthquake in San Francisco last week.

Part 2: *Identify the sound in each of the following words.*

1. chance   ☐ æ   ☐ ä   ☐ ə
2. done   ☐ æ   ☐ ä   ☐ ə
3. saw   ☐ æ   ☐ ä   ☐ ə

Part 3: *Fill in the rest of each sentence based on the changing intonation.*

1.   **I** didn't hear him say that,
2.   **I didn't** hear him say that,

3. I didn't **hear** him say that,

4. I didn't hear **him** say that,

5. I didn't hear him **say** that,

6. I didn't hear him say **that**,

Part 4: *Make a question and change the subject to* **who** *or* **what**.

1. My family came to visit.

2. The cars were painted again.

Part 5: *Convert each statement to a question.*

1. She was dancing in the park.   Where

2. He graduated in 2009.   When

3. They ordered sushi.   What

4. We cried because it was so sad.   Who

Part 6: *Replace all* **nouns** *with* **pronouns**.

1. The meetings were cancelled because of the earthquake.

2. My mother is going to visit my brother and me.

Part 7: *Change each sentence to the* **plural**.

1. This building was poorly built.

2. Can the child have some more?

3. That person was not ready.

Part 8: *Fill in the proper* **article** (*a, an, the*).

1. Do you have ____ moment?

2. That was ____ second time he tried it.

3. It was ____ awkward situation.

4. I know ____ really good Italian restaurant.

5. I know ____ best Italian restaurant.

Part 9: *Fill in the appropriate* **conjunction**, *using* **and**, **so**, **but**, *or* **or**.

1. Would you prefer coffee ____ tea?

2. It was late, ____ we went home.

3. We couldn't figure it out, ____ we kept trying in spite of the difficulty.

4. I'd like to travel ____ see the world.

Part 10: *Fill in the appropriate* **preposition** *of* **location** *or* **direction**.

1. Please sit next ____ me at the movies tomorrow.
2. He put the pencils ____ the drawer.
3. Leave the report ____ my desk, please.
4. Do you want to come ____ us?
5. I think he wrote his report ____ hand, not ____ the computer.

Part 11: *Fill in the proper* **comparison** *word*.

1. That's the ____ idea!	**good**
2. The problems were ____ than we thought.	**big**
3. She's much ____ than she used to be.	**happy**
4. I think he earns ____ than we do, but more than he did before.	**little**
5. OMG! He's the ____ dancer! LOL!	**bad**

Part 12: *Fill in the blank with* **much** *or* **many**.

1. He caused so ____ trouble!
2. He had so ____ problems.
3. How ____ time will it take?
4. How ____ times did you take the test?

Part 13: *Rewrite the sentences, with the* **time words** *in the proper place*.

1. We used to go to the beach.   (all the time)

2. They talk about it.   (always)

3. Let's do it.   (today)

Part 14: *Change the sentences to the* **past**.

1. I drive fast.
2. She thinks about it every day.

Part 15: *Change the sentences to the* **continuous**.

1. She laughed.
2. He won't help us this time.
3. She dances and sings well.

Part 16: *Change the sentences to the* **future**.

1. He works on it all the time.
2. They need more time.

Part 17: *Select the* **simple present** *or* **past** *tense, or the appropriate* **continuous** *form.*

1. They _____ the new system yesterday.   **start**
2. She _____ lunch at the same restaurant every day.   **eat**
3. They _____ TV when the phone rang.   **watch**
4. He _____ here tomorrow.   **be**

Part 18: *Change the* **positive** *statement to a* **negative**.

1. He knows how to do it.
2. She understood.
3. They will try it again.
4. She is ready.

Part 19: *Change the statement to a* **question.** ↻

1. They were ready.
2. She bought one.

Part 20: *Put in the* **verb contraction**.

1. She will not tell you.
2. They cannot get here in time.
3. He is not coming.

Part 21: *Fill in the proper* **tag ending**.

1. You won't tell them,   ?
2. He was late again,   ?
3. She likes it,   ?

Part 22: *Fill in the blank with* **do** *or* **make**.

1. Try not to _____ any mistakes.
2. Nobody wanted to _____ the dishes or _____ their beds.
3. Let's _____ an appointment for next week.

Part 23: *Identify the story order, by putting 1, 2, 3 in the boxes in the proper order.*

☐ He bought a ticket and moved to Marina del Rey.
☐ He will always remember his exciting adventures as a California bodybuilder.
☐ Max wanted to live in America.

Chapter 6
第六章

Indirect Speech and the Unreal Duo
间接引语和非真实双重时态

In this chapter we will look at intro clauses and indirect speech, **so / such**, and other joiners beyond conjunctions, such as **that**, **when**, and **if**.

本章我们将学习引入语、间接引语、so / such，以及其他非连词连接词，如that，when和if。

For verbs, we will be working with the present unreal duo, opinion words, **do / to do / doing**, the difference between **take / have**, **say / tell**, and **speak / talk**, verbs of probability and obligation, and verbs of perception.

动词方面，我们要学习一般非真实双重时态，观点词，动词do / to do / doing，动词take / have，say / tell，speak / talk之间的差异，表示可能性和义务的动词，以及感官动词。

Before we start Chapter 6, let's take a moment to think about applying what you have learned so far. Using the vocabulary, grammar, and pronunciation from Chapters 1 through 5, you can communicate clearly and accurately. Early on, you learned two important patterns in English:

在开始学习第六章之前，我们先来想一想要如何运用已经学到的东西。运用好从第一章到第五章学到的词汇、语法和发音等方面的知识，你就能清楚并准确地与人交流了。之前，你学了英语中两个很重要的模式：

SVO and modifier + noun
SVO和"修饰语+名词"

It is important to force yourself to use these simple patterns. It's very tempting to try to learn the advanced forms, but if you don't have a solid foundation, there is no point in doing that. Students may have several reactions at this point.

强迫自己使用这些简单的模式很重要。学习更加高级的模式当然非常诱人，但如果基础没有打牢的话，学习高级模式也就没有意义了。学生对此可能反应不一。

"But in my language..."
"但在我的母语中……"

Many people feel that their language is "right," and they are correct. Every language is right. However, people shouldn't try to apply their own rules to English. In some languages, you can change the word order around, you can leave words out or add in different words, you don't conjugate the verb, you always have the verb at the end, and so on. This is fine for your language, but for English, you need to force yourself to use the SVO order. Later, you will gain more flexibility, but you have to have a solid foundation first.

很多人都觉得自己的母语是"对的"，自己是正确的。每种语言都是对的。但是，人们不应该把自己母语里的规则强加到英语中去。一些语言或可以颠倒词序，或可以省略词语或加入不同的词，或者不需要对动词进行词形变化，或者动词始终放在句尾，等等。你的母语可以这样，但是英语不能，你需要强迫自己使用SVO语序。以后，你可以运用得更加灵活，但首先你要把基础打扎实。

"We don't have that sound/structure/concept in my language."
"我的母语里没有那种声音／结构／概念。"

Well, learn it.

好吧，但是你还得学。

"When I'm talking, I don't have time to think about it."
"我在说话的时候，没有时间去想。"

Yes, you do. Think first, then speak. Instead of just jumping in and saying whatever comes to mind, pause, plan, and then speak. When in doubt, SVO. If you're not sure, SVO. What to do? SVO.

不，你有时间。请先思考，然后再说。不要开口就说，不要脑子里想到什么就说什么，请先停顿一下，计划一下，然后再说。当你犹豫时，用SVO结构。当你不确定时，用SVO结构。当你不知道怎么办时，用SVO结构。

Then, when you are **not** in a conversation with someone, think about the rules and practice applying them. Take your time and think about it. Practice enough that it happens automatically, and you don't have to think about the rules. Repetition, repetition, repetition.

另外，当你不和别人说话时，想想这些规则并试着运用它们。慢慢想，好好想。只要练习得够多，自然就能脱口而出，并且不用边说边想规则。请重复，重复，再重复。

"I think in my language, and then translate to English."
"我会先用母语思考，然后再翻译成英语。"

Well, don't. Practice in English. Think in English. Write in English. Count in English. Daydream in English. Repetition, repetition, repetition.

请不要这么做。请用英语练习，用英语思考，用英语写作，用英语数数，用英语做白日梦。请重复，重复，再重复。

"SVO?"

Subject	Verb	Object

Learn it. Own it. Use it.

学习它。掌握它。运用它。

From this point on, you will be working at the intermediate level, and you need to have mastered the basics before continuing.

从现在起，你就要步入中级英语水平了，在开始学习新东西之前，你需要完全掌握前面的基础知识。

Listen to the audio and write the exact transcription in the spaces below. Then check the Answer Key.

1. _____
2. _____
3. _____
4. _____
5. _____

The Italian Incidents

STORY

One day, I was wa**l**king in Marina del **Rey**. I heard some people **talking**. They were **speaking** Italian. They were **talking** about me. They **said** that I was so **big**. They started **saying** some rude **things** about me. They **said**, "**Look** at that guy! He's so **big**! If you stuck a **pin** in him, he would **pop** like a **balloon**! " I **said**, "Hey, I **speak** Italian! " They were really **embarrassed**. They **said** that they were **sorry**. I **told** them that I didn't **care** and I **told** them to go **away**.

Another day, I overheard some **other** people **speaking Italian**. They thought I was **American**, so they started **talking about** me. Before they could **say** anything, I **said**, "Excuse me, but I **speak** Italian." They **said** hello and we **talked about** living in America. They **told** me that they were from Milan. One of them **spoke** English very well. After we **talked** for a while, we **said** good**bye**.

Listen to the audio and repeat, focusing on intonation and pronunciation.

One day, I wəz w**äh**king in M'reena Del **Ray**. I hrrrrrd s'm peeple **tähking**. They wrr speekinga **tælian**. They wrrr **täking** əbout me. They sed thə dai wəz so **big**. They starded **saying** s'm rude **thing** zəbout me. They sed, "**Lük**ət that guy! Heez so **big**! Ifyu stəckə **pin** innim, heed **päp** lykə **bəlloon**!" I **sed**, "Hey, I **speak**ə tælian!" They wrr rilly **emberrast**. They **sed** thət they wrr **särry**. I **told** them thə dai didn't **care** and I **told** 'em tə go⁽ʷ⁾**away**.

Another day, I overhrrd s'm**əther** peepəl **speaking ə**tælian. They thädai wəzza **merək**'n, so they starded **talking** əbout me. B'for they cüd **say** anything, I sed, "Eks-kyoozzzz me, bədäi **speek**ə tælian." They **sed** hello and we **tähkt** about living in əmerəca. They **told** me thət they were fr'm Milan. wənəvəm spok **Kinglish** very well. æfter we **tähkt** frə while, we sed güd**by**.

NOUNS

This is an important section. You will review how to ask direct questions and learn how to ask questions *indirectly*. You will start by using intro phrases. There will be some word-order changes that are important to notice and master.

这部分的内容很重要。你要先复习如何进行直接提问，再学习如何进行间接提问。你会从使用引入语开始学起。你还要留心并掌握一些重要的词序变化问题。

Common and Useful Intro Phrases
常见的实用引入语

You can add a good deal of information with a simple intro phrase before your standard SVO. This can be a one-word adverb, such as **suddenly**, **fortunately**, **actually**, **originally**, **naturally**, **surprisingly**, and so on. See how different the following sentences are:

只要在标准的SVO结构前加上一个简单的引入语，你就可以大大提高句子的信息含量。引入语可以是单个的副词，如suddenly，fortunately，actually，originally，naturally，surprisingly等。请看下面的句子是多么地不同：

> **Suddenly,** he stopped the car.
> **Fortunately,** he stopped the car.
> **Actually,** he stopped the car.

The same can be done with *phrases*:

引入语也可以是短语，效果也是一样的：

> **As usual,** he stopped the car.
> **As a matter of fact,** he stopped the car.
> **All of a sudden,** he stopped the car.
> **By the way,** he stopped the car.
> **On the other hand,** he stopped the car.
> **Now that you mention it,** he did stop the car.
> **First,** he stopped the car, next he got out.
> **At first,** he stopped the car, but then he kept going.

Joiners
连接词

In Chapter 2, we studied the five conjunctions **and**, **but**, **so**, **or**, and **because**. In the broader sense of a conjunction—let's call it a *joiner*—you can link sentences with **that**.

在第二章中，我们学习了5个连词：and，but，so，or和because。如果从更宽泛的角度去理解连词——让我们叫它连接词——你可以用that把句子连接起来。

Exercise 6-3: Joining Phrases and Sentences with *That*

*Join the two statements using **that**. Then check the Answer Key.*

It's obvious. He's not ready.   It's obvious **that** he's not ready.

1.   They are happy. They won the lottery.

2.   You are concerned. They are working too hard.

3. The farmers were happy. It was finally raining.

4. It's not clear. They're telling the truth.

5. We aren't worried. Things aren't going well.

Indirect Speech
间接引语

With indirect speech, you combine two statements, and they both have the same SVO order.
You can replace the **subject** or the **object**:

间接引语就是把两个陈述句连接起来，并且它们都是SVO结构。其中，主语和宾语可以被替换：

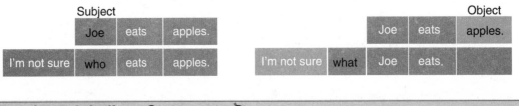

Exercise 6-4: Indirect Statements

*Change the statement to an indirect statement. The word order is the same; there is no flip. Change the blue text to one of the 5 Ws and **how**. Check the Answer Key when you're done.*

They bought a car.   **I'm not sure what they bought.**

1. They saw **their friends**.

    I'm not sure

2. She did **her homework**.

    They are confused about

3. They went **to the park**.

    It's not clear

4. They did it **on Wednesday**.

    Please confirm

5. They were in trouble **because of all the mistakes**.

    It's clear

6. They got there **by bus**.

    Let us know

7. She didn't ask him **because she didn't want to know the answer**.

    It isn't obvious

8. They thought about **changing the situation**.

    The note didn't indicate

9. Rigel is located **on Orion's belt**.

    In your astronomy class, you learned

10. Jane gave her coat to **her sister**.

We don't want to know

11. The post office closes **at five**.

It's not posted

12. I put my keys **on the table**.

Tell me

13. She moved to France **in 2007**.

Ask her

14. They bought **some expensive suits**.

Show me the record of

15. We never watch TV **because we don't have time**.

You know

Indirect Questions
间接疑问句

With indirect questions, the word order for the main sentence doesn't do the question flip. Why? **Because the flip occurs in the introduction**.

在间接疑问句中，主句不需要颠倒词序。为什么？因为词序颠倒出现在句子的引入部分。

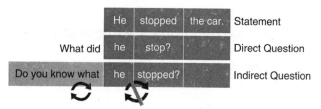

This is true for indirect questions about both the **subject** and the **object**.
这个规则同样适用于分别就主语和宾语进行提问的间接疑问句。

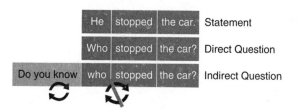

Once again, it's important to remember that with a **who** or **what** question about the **subject**: No flip. You just add the question directly onto the intro phrase without changing the word order.

再次重申，请务必记住这一条：由who或what引导的、就主语提问的疑问句，不需要颠倒词序。你只要直接在引入语后面加上问句就可以了，不需要改变词序。

Right	Wrong, Wrong, Wrong	
I don't know why he did it.	I don't know why did he do it?	X
Can you tell me where she is?	Can you tell me where is she?	X
Do you know where he went?	Do you know where did he went?	X
Do you know where he is?	Do you know where is he?	X

Exercise 6-5: Indirect Yes / No Questions — Subject ↻ ... ↻

*Change the statement to an indirect question by adding either **who** or **what** to the intro phrase provided.*
Then check the Answer Key.

The submarine is underwater.   **Do you know** what **is underwater?**
They told you.   **Does she know** who **told you?**

1.   **He** took the test.
Do you remember

2.   **It** happened.
Did they find out

3.   **Joe** saved him.
Does he know

4.   **The situation** is going on.
Do they understand

5.   **The entire basketball team** was there.
Did they realize

With ***object*** questions using the **5 Ws**, use the statement word order.
由5个以W开头的词引导的、就宾语进行提问的疑问句，也要用陈述句的词序。

Exercise 6-6: Indirect Yes / No Questions — Object ↻ ... ↻

Change the statement to an indirect question. （*There is no question flip in the main sentence.*）*Change*
*the object noun/pronoun to one of the **5 Ws** or **how**. Check the Answer Key when you're done.*

They bought a car.   **Do you know** what **they bought?**

1.   They saw **their friends**.
Do you remember

2.   She did **her homework**.
Can you tell me

3.   They went **to the park**.
Do you know

4.   They did it **on Wednesday**.
Does anyone know

5.   They were in trouble **because of all the mistakes**.
Is it clear

6.   They got there **by bus**.
Are we clear on

7.   She didn't ask him **because she didn't want to know the answer**.
Isn't it obvious

8.   They thought about **changing the situation**.
Did the note indicate

9.   Rigel is located **on Orion's belt**.
In your astronomy class, will you learn

10. Jane gave her coat to **her sister**.

    Will you confirm

11. The post office closes **at five**.

    Do you know

12. I put my keys **on the table**.

    Do you know

13. She moved to France **in 2007**.

    Will you be asking her

14. They bought **some expensive suits**.

    Do you have a record of

15. We never watch TV **because we don't have time**.

    Isn't it apparent

16. They lost **their luggage**.

    Will they be able to get back

17. He's **here**.

    Do you know

18. It was **there**.

    Did he explain

19. I got there **by bus**.

    Can you guess

20. You figured it out **with a good deal of hard work**.

    Did you tell them

Exercise 6-7: Subject and Object ○...○

*Change the statements to indirect questions using the phrase "Do you know..." (There is no question flip in the main sentence.) Change the subject or object noun/pronoun to one of the 5 Ws or **how**. Then check the Answer Key.*

Jane **saw Bill**.	**Do you know** who **saw Bill?** (subject)
Jane saw Bill.	**Do you know** whom * **she saw?** (object)

1. **The car** was in the garage.

2. The car was **in the garage**.

3. **The man** ran quickly to the pool.

4. The man ran **quickly** to the pool.

5. The man ran quickly to **the pool**.

6. **The boys** played baseball.

7.   The boys played **baseball**.

8.   **The book** cost $10.

9.   The book cost **$10**.

****Whom** replaces **who** when used as an object.
**用作宾语时，who要用whom来代替。

Question Review
复习疑问句

As you have seen, there are several types of questions. It's important know if you are asking about the subject or the object.

正如你看到的那样，疑问句有好几种类型。要弄清楚你是在就主语还是宾语提问，这一点很重要。

	Kind	Order	Verb To Be	Main Verb
Subject	**Statement**		**He** is there.	**He** likes it.
	Who?	↻	**Who** is there?	**Who** likes it?
	What?	↻	**What** is there?	**What** likes it?
	Yes or no?	↻	**Is he** there?	**Does he** like it?
Object	**Statement**		He is a doctor.	Joe saw **Bill and his dog.**
	Who?	↻	**Who** is a doctor?	**Who** did he see?
	What?	↻	**What** is he?	**What** did he see?
	Where?	↻		**Where** did he see them?
	When?	↻		**When** did he see them?
	Why?	↻		**Why** did he see them?
	How?	↻		**How** did he see them?
	Yes or no?	↻		**Did he** see them?

So and *Such*
So 和 Such

So + *adjective*   Such + *noun*

There are two similar words that can be used to intensify meaning. You can add **so** to an *adjective* and **such** to a *noun*.

英语中有两个相似的词可以用来强化意思。你可以在形容词前加so，在名词前加such。

174

Exercise 6-8: *So or Such?*

Fill in the blank with **so** *or* **such**. *Then check the Answer Key.*

1. That was _____ a great movie!
2. She is _____ worried today.
3. The staff is _____ busy these days.
4. I don't think it's _____ a good idea.
5. He is _____ a funny guy!
6. He is _____ funny!
7. It was _____ exciting!
8. He was in _____ trouble.
9. They are _____ liars!
10. They are _____ dishonest!
11. I am _____ lucky!
12. I have _____ good luck!
13. I am _____ a lucky person!
14. That is _____ an interesting story!
15. He is _____ cute!

It's Iffy
它是不确定的

VERBS

This section reviews the **present unreal duo**, clarifying the very important distinction between the **future** (what **will** happen), the **present** (what **does** happen), and the **unreal present** (what **would** happen if certain conditions were met). This ties in with **hope** and **wish**.

本部分会复习一下一般非真实双重时态，以阐明将来时（将来会发生什么）、现在时（发生什么）和非真实现在时（如果满足条件会发生什么）之间的重要区别。这就与hope和wish联系到了一起。

In Chapter 5, we studied the simple future and the future unreal duo. Now, we are ready to move on to the **present unreal duo**. As usual, let's start with the verb **to be**.

在第五章中，我们学习了一般将来时和将来非真实双重时态。现在，我们要接着学习现在非真实双重时态。像往常一样，我们先从be动词开始学。

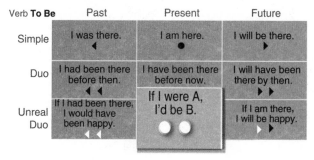

Looking at the verb map, you see three things: First, this is the **present** (even though the verb seems to be a past form); second, there are **two events**; third, the events **don't actually happen** (the symbols are white).

在动词地图上，你会看到三样东西：第一，这是现在时（虽然动词看起来是过去式）；第二，发生了两件事；第三，事情实际上并没有发生（符号是白色的）。

175

The nice thing is that this form doesn't need to be conjugated—it's **were** and **would** for everyone.

这个句型有一点很好：动词不需要变形——任何人称都用were和would。

| Fact | I **am** six feet tall. I **will** try out for the basketball team. |
| Unreal | If I **were** six feet tall, I **would** try out for the basketball team. |

But I'm not.

I am only five feet tall, so I'll stick to baseball.

| Fact | He **is** rich. He **lives** in a big mansion in Beverly Hills. |
| Unreal | If he **were** rich, he **would** live in a big mansion in Beverly Hills. |

But he's not.

He lives in a small but charming house in Elkhorn, Nebraska.

You can change either a ***present, present continuous,*** or ***future*** statement to the present unreal. Notice the relationship between **will** and **would**.

你可以把现在时、现在进行时、将来时的陈述句转换成一般非真实句。注意will和would之间的关系。

| Real | I **will** try it. | I **hope** you **will** try it. |
| Unreal | I **would** try it if I were you. | I **wish** you **would** try it. |

Exercise 6-9: Unreal Duo — Present / *To Be*

*Change the sentences to the present unreal, using **were** and **would**. Then check the Answer Key.*

I **am** six feet tall. I **will** try out for the basketball team.
If I **were** six feet tall, I **would** try out for the basketball team.

1. It's obvious. I understand it completely.

2. They are in good shape. They will win the competition.

3. We are prepared. She will hire us.

4. I am working on it. I will make the deadline.

5. She is honest. She will not lie.

6. You are not available. You won't offer to help.

7. He is running late. He will call us.

8. It's hot. We're sweating.

9. You are sincere. I trust you completely.

10. I'm sure about it. I recommend it to everyone.

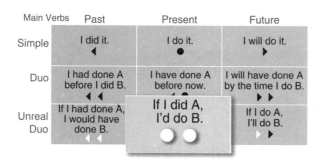

With main verbs, the **_present_** unreal uses a form that looks like the **_past_**. The way you can tell it's the present is by asking a question: **If I had time, I would go.**

在一般非真实时态中，主动词看上去用的是过去式。有一个方法可以判断它是不是现在时，即问一个问题：If I had time, I would go。

Do I have time?

You can see that the question identifies the time as the present.

看了这个句子，你就会明白为什么时间是"现在"了。

| **Fact** | He weighs 350 pounds. He will become a sumo wrestler in Japan. |
| Unreal | If he **weighed** 350 pounds, he **would** become a sumo wrestler in Japan. |

But he doesn't.

He's quite small, so he just wrestles with his conscience.

| **Fact** | They **know** all the answers. They **teach** the world. |
| Unreal | If they **knew** all the answers, they **would** teach the world. |

But they don't.

So, they just try to do what is right.

Exercise 6-10: Unreal Duo — Present / Main Verbs

*Combine the sentences starting with **if**. Use the present unreal duo. Then check the Answer Key.*

She **studies** hard. She **will** succeed.

If she **studied** hard, she **would** succeed.

1. You like to ski. You go as often as possible.

2. I will tell you. You won't remember.

3. We practice every day. We will get better.

4. He eats a lot. He is overweight.

5. I study every day. I speak English well.

6. They talk too much. They get in trouble.

7. It works well. We use it every day.

8. They pay attention. They understand.

9. Everyone knows how to do it. We don't need the instruction manual.

10. It makes us mad. We complain about it.

Intro Phrases with the Unreal Duo
非真实双重时态的引入语

Exercise 6-11: Intro Phrases

*Connect the phrases using **if**. Then check the Answer Key.*

> **It's not clear. They like it.**
> **It's not clear if they like it.**

1. I'm not sure. It works.

2. I'm not sure. It will work.

3. I'm not sure. It worked.

4. He doesn't know. He will be there.

5. I don't know. He was there.

6. I don't know. He is here.

Hope: Real (真实的)	Wish: Unreal (非真实的)
a possibility in the future	a desire that probably won't happen
将来有可能发生	很可能不会实现的愿望
hope + will	**wish + would**

Exercise 6-12: *Hope* or *Wish*?

*Fill in the blank with the proper form of **hope** or **wish**. Then check the Answer Key.*

1. I _____ you can help me.
2. I _____ you could help me.
3. They _____ it is true.
4. They _____ it were true.
5. They _____ it was true.

6. They   it had been true.
7. You   they would take care of it.
8. You   they will take care of it.
9. She   that he wouldn't argue so much. (but he will)
10. She   that he won't argue this time. (maybe he won't)
11. We   they stop fighting soon.
12. They   they would stop fighting soon.
13. I   you're happy.
14. I   you were happy.
15. She   she will win the lottery.

Opinion Words
观点词

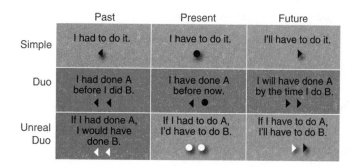

	Past	Present	Future
Simple	I had to do it.	I have to do it.	I'll have to do it.
Duo	I had done A before I did B.	I have done A before now.	I will have done A by the time I do B.
Unreal Duo	If I had done A, I would have done B.	If I had to do A, I'd have to do B.	If I have to do A, I'll have to do B.

The lighter areas indicate the tenses we've studied up through this chapter, using **have to**.
颜色浅的区域表示直到本章为止我们已经学过的时态，这里用了词组have to。

What Are the Odds? 可能性有多大？
Action(行动) vs. Non-Action(不行动)

Will	I will do it.	100% probability
Must	I must do it!	strong probability
May	I may do it.	50% possibility
Might	I might do it.	50% possibility
Could	I could do it.	slight possibility
Would...if	I would do it if I had time.	unreal
Won't	I won't do it.	0% probability

May and **might** have the same meaning.
may和might的意思一样。

Exercise 6-13: Probability

*Fill in the blank with the appropriate form of **will**, **must**, **may**, **might**, **could**, **would**, or **won't**. Then check the Answer Key.*

1. I ____ call you **tomorrow**.   100% probability
2. My **boss** says we ____ need to work **over**time.   0% probability
3. I'm not **sure**, but he ____ be **wrong**.   possibility
4. Be **careful**, or you ____ get **hurt**.   slight possibility
5. He ____ be **crazy**; he wants to **swim** across the **lake**!   strong probability
6. She ____ buy a **Mercedes**, if she had more **money**.   unreal
7. It was 20 **degrees** last night; you ____ have been **freezing**! strong probability
8. If you had **asked** me, I ____ have **told** you.   unreal
9. Don't jump to **conclusions**; he ____ have been at **work**.   slight possibility
10. The **weather** report said that it ____ **rain** this afternoon. possibility
11. I ____ not give any more **help** even if he **asked** me.   0% probability
12. She ____ wear a **power** suit if she wants to get that **job**!   strong probability
13. My **brother** says he ____ fix my **car**.   slight possibility
14. The **teacher** ____ give us **home**work today — it's **Friday**! 0% probability
15. You ____ **do** it if I **tell** you to.   100% probability

Duty Calls! Duty Calls!
职责所在！

have to	I have to do it.	strong obligation
must	I must do it.	strong obligation
had better	I had better do it.	obligation
had better	You had better!	warning
should	I should do it.	obligation
should	I should have done it.	past advice
ought to	I ought to do it.	obligation
may	You may do it.	permission
can	I can do it.	ability
could	Could you do it, please?	polite request

Exercise 6-14: Obligation

Fill in the blank with the appropriate form of **have to**, **must**, **had better**, **should**, **ought to**, **may**, **can**, *or* **could**. *Then check the Answer Key.*

1. We ____ **think** about it.   strong obligation
2. You ____ get **out** of here, or there'll be **trouble**!   warning
3. You ____ be **care**ful with that **knife**.   warning
4. ...and the little train said, "I **think** I ____."   ability
5. ...and the little train said, "I **thought** I ____."   past ability
6. You ____ n't have opened the **gate**; the **dog** got out!   past advice
7. Yes, you ____ **leave** now.   permission
8. I ____ jump **high**.   ability

180

9. ____ you **help** me with this, please? polite request
10. You ____ watch **out**! warning
11. She ____ drink **coffee** in the **morning**. strong obligation
12. **Americans** have that "____ do" **spirit**! ability
13. If you want to earn **money**, you ____ get a **job**. warning
14. Since you're **tired**, you ____ **rest**. obligation
15. **One** day, you ____ travel to **Europe**. possibility

Asking for Advice
征求意见

Dear Annie, What should I do?

Dear Annie,

I'd like to go away to college, but my parents think I should live at home. What should I do?

Sincerely,

Not A Kid Anymore

Ask Annie

Dear Not A Kid Anymore,

You may have to have a serious talk with them. If they're paying for your education, they should have a say in your living arrangements. If you're paying your own way, you may just have to make this grown-up decision on your own.

Best Regards,

Annie

Exercise 6-15: Three Verb Forms

*Fill in the blank with the proper form of the verb, using the simple form, the infinitive, or -ing (**do**, **to do**, **doing**). Remember that prepositions are followed by -ing. Check the Answer Key when you're done.*

I will _____ that. **I will do that.**
I want _____ that. **I want to do that.**
I enjoy _____ that. **I enjoy doing that.**

1. I want ____ that. do
2. We plan on ____ that. do
3. He refused ____ me what he was ____. tell / do
4. What do you hope ____? accomplish
5. I appreciate you ____ me with this. help
6. I anticipate your ____ with this. help
7. By not ____, you're guaranteeing a poor grade. study
8. He insisted on ____. pay
9. You have ____ the report by Friday. submit
10. The site recommends ____ online. register
11. We used ____ for long drives in the country. go
12. I've never heard of ____ it that way. use

13. He likes _____ fast.   drive
14. My boss won't let me _____ the week off.   take
15. The children promised _____ quietly.   play
16. I don't recall _____ that before.   see
17. Let's have him _____ in early tomorrow.   come
18. I needed _____ him _____ with me.   ask / work
19. We can't put off _____ him any longer!   tell
20. They tried _____ _____ her the bad news.   avoid / tell
21. We'd be interested in _____ your plan.   hear
22. Let's think about _____ it first class.   ship
23. You've got _____ a lot in order to succeed.   practice
24. There's no use _____ about it.   complain
25. There's no point in _____ about it.   worry
26. I prefer _____ it myself.   do
27. I would rather _____ it myself.   do
28. Would you mind _____ me with this?   help
29. Thank you for _____ me with this.   help
30. I _____ him run out of the house yesterday.   see
31. I _____ him to come back in last night.   tell
32. I _____ him go down the stairs at midnight.   hear
33. We hope _____ you again sometime.   see
34. They enjoyed _____ you again.   see
35. We are looking forward to _____ them later on.   meet
36. He asked if I would _____ ready.   be
37. "May I see that?" He asked _____ it.   see
38. "Ed, show me that." He asked Ed _____ it to him.   show
39. They stopped _____. (Their goal was to eat.)   eat
40. They stopped _____. (They were no longer eating.)   eat
41. We can read the reviews online before _____.   decide
42. I was waiting for him _____.   finish
43. We let them _____ outside.   go
44. We allowed them _____ outside.   go
45. We didn't make them _____ outside.   go
46. We had them _____ outside.   go
47. He helped us _____ the project.   do

Say, Tell, Speak, Talk

These verbs are all used to indicate communication. **Say** is the most common. **Tell** is more direction-oriented; you tell someone something. It is similar to **inform**. You also use **tell** with **tell the truth**, **tell a lie**, and **tell a story**. **Speak** is a more formal version of **talk,** and is used with languages, such as **I speak Spanish**. **Talk** is similar to converse. It is also used in short sentences such as, **What are you talking about**? or **Who were you talking to**?

182

这几个动词都是用来表示交流沟通的。say是最常用的一个词。tell的方向感较强，即你告诉某人某事。tell与inform(告诉，通知)类似。tell还可以这样用：tell the truth, tell a lie, tell a story。speak比talk更加正式，而且经常与某种语言连用，如：I speak Spanish.(我说西班牙语。)talk与converse(交谈)类似。talk也用在以下短句中，如：What are you talking about?(你在说什么呢？)或 Who were you talking to?(你在跟谁说话呢？)

Exercise 6-16: *Say, Tell, Speak, Talk*

*Fill in the blank with the proper form of **say**, **tell**, **speak**, or **talk**. Then check the Answer Key.*

What are you _____ about?   **What are you talking about?**

1. Don't   me that!
2. How do you   *sushi* in English?
3. Let's   this over, OK? Let's discuss this.
4. I'll   you a secret.
5. Don't   French during English class!
6. Don't   the boys about their surprise party.
7. I don't want to   about it anymore.
8. What did you   ? Who were you _____ to?
9. Did you   the truth? (Note: **Speak the truth** is not commonly used.)
10. Don't   him what happened.

Exercise 6-17: *Say, Tell, Speak, Talk*   **Track 094**

Now that you are familiar with the four verbs, listen to "The Italian Incidents" again.

One day, I was walking in Marina del Rey. I heard some people **talking**. They were **speaking** Italian. They were **talking** about me. They said that I was so **big**. They started **saying** some rude **things** about me. They said, "**Look** at that guy! He's so **big**! If you stuck a **pin** in him, he'll **pop** like a **balloon**! " I **said**, "Hey, I **speak** Italian! " They were really **embarrassed**. They **said** that they were **sorry**. I **told** them that I didn't **care** and I **told** them to go **away**.

Another day, I overheard some **other** people **speaking** Italian. They thought I was American, so they started **talking about** me. Before they could **say** anything, I said, "Excuse me, but I **speak** Italian." They **said** hello. And we **talked about** living in America. They **told** me that they were from Milan. One of them **spoke** English very well. After we **talked** for a while, we **said** goodbye.

Verbs of Perception
感官动词

Look, **see**, and **watch** are similar in that they are all about visual perception. However, there are two main differences. One is **intentionality**, as you intentionally **look** at something, but you just **see** whatever falls within your field of vision. The other difference is **movement**, as you **look at** something that is stationary, but you **watch** something that is moving.

look, see和watch有一点是相似的，即它们都是视觉感官动词。不过，它们之间有两大区别。第一大区别是意向性，因为你可以有意地去看(look at)某物，但你只看见(see)了在你视野范围内的东西，不管那东西是什么。第二大区别是移动性，因为你看（look at）的是静止的事物，但你观看（watch）的是移动的事物。

Exercise 6-18: *Look / See / Watch*

Fill in the blank with the proper form of **look**, **see**, *or* **watch**. *Then check the Answer Key.*

1. ____ at the sky; it's beautiful!
2. Let's ____ TV for a while.
3. How does this ____?
4. Could you ____ my kids for a minute, please? Keep an eye on them!
5. Cats can ____ in the dark.
6. Could you take a quick ____ at my paper?
7. Do you ____ what I'm saying?
8. We have to ____ our weight. We have to monitor our poundage.
9. Let's wait and ____ how it turns out.
10. We should ____ around for a better job.

Hear and **listen** are also distinguished by intentionality, as you intentionally **listen to** something, but you just **hear** whatever comes in hearing range.

hear和listen在意向性方面也有区别，因为你可以有意地听（listen to）某物，但你只听到（hear）了在你听觉范围内的东西，不管那东西是什么。

Exercise 6-19: *Hear / Listen*

Fill in the blank with the proper form of **hear** *or* **listen**. *Then check the Answer Key.*

1. What was that noise? I didn't ____ anything.
2. Would you please ____ when I'm talking to you!
3. Don't ____ to him; he's just talking nonsense.
4. Have you ____ the good news?
5. I'll let you know if I ____ anything about it.
6. ____, we need to re-think this!
7. Can you ____ me now?
8. Stop ____ to the radio and pay attention!
9. ____ carefully, you can ____ the ocean!
10. I've never ____ of such a thing!

Exercise 6-20: Verbs of Perception

Select the proper word. Then check the Answer Key.

1. He ____ like a nice guy.

    ☐ looks
    ☐ appears
    ☐ hears
    ☐ sounds

2. That ____ like a really good plan.

3. How do you _____ about that?

    ☐ feel
    ☐ appear

4. With my own eyes, I _____ him take it.

    ☐ looked
    ☐ saw

5. With my own ears, I _____ him say it.

    ☐ listened
    ☐ heard

6. They _____ to be very responsible.

    ☐ appear
    ☐ look

7. It's so cold; I can't _____ my fingers.

    ☐ feel
    ☐ touch

8. She _____ so young!

    ☐ looks
    ☐ appears

9. Don't _____ the stove; it's hot!

    ☐ feel
    ☐ touch

10. What are you _____ on your MP3 player?

    ☐ hearing
    ☐ listening to

Exercise 6-21: Linking Verbs of Perception

Select the proper verb of perception. Then check the Answer Key.

1. Now that he has gray hair, he _____ much older.

    ☐ looks
    ☐ sounds

2. Over the phone, you _____ very young.

    ☐ sound
    ☐ look

3. The committee _____ to be reconsidering its position.

    ☐ appears
    ☐ feels

4. These are so soft and silky... they _____ very smooth.

    ☐ sound
    ☐ feel

5. You are getting hoarse. You _____ like you're getting sick.

    ☐ look
    ☐ sound

Involuntary	**Voluntary**	**Perception or Opinion**
无意的	有意的	感知或意见
He hears a noise.	He listens to the radio.	It sounds good.
We see the colors.	We look at the painting.	They look beautiful.
She felt a shock.	She touched the wire.	She feels sad.
You smelled the coffee.		The coffee smelled good.
You tasted the candy.		The candy tasted good.

Exercise 6-22: Verbs of Perception

Select the proper option. Then check the Answer key.

1. Did you ____ about the accident?
   - ☐ hear
   - ☐ listen
   - ☐ sound

2. Cats can ____ in the dark.
   - ☐ see
   - ☐ look

3. The kids were ____ TV again.
   - ☐ seeing
   - ☐ looking
   - ☐ looking at
   - ☐ watching

4. They weren't ____ to the teacher.
   - ☐ hearing
   - ☐ listening
   - ☐ sounding

5. He ____ a little tired.
   - ☐ sees
   - ☐ looks

6. Don't ____ the sun during an eclipse.
   - ☐ look
   - ☐ look at

7. Great speech! That ____ terrific.
   - ☐ heard
   - ☐ sounded

8. You ____ warm; you might have a fever.
   - ☐ feel
   - ☐ touch

9. Don't ____ the wet paint!
   - ☐ feel
   - ☐ touch

10. He's trying to ____ his weight.
    - ☐ feel
    - ☐ look
    - ☐ look at
    - ☐ watch

Exercise 6-23: *Have* or *Take*?

Fill in the blank with the proper form of **take** *or* **have**. *Then check the Answer Key.*

1. What are we ____ for breakfast?
2. I think I'll ____ a nap now.
3. Will they ____ time to finish?
4. Let's ____ a five-minute break.
5. He ____ a shower last night.
6. We ____ dinner at midnight.
7. Let's ____ a trip to Rio.
8. ____ an aspirin if you ____ a headache.
9. We should ____ turns with this.
10. I think he's ____ piano lessons.

Take

Take is used in its basic meaning of **to lay hold of something**, **accept**, or **to remove**, but in combination with other words, it has many other meanings. Here are some common combinations.

take 的基本意思是"拿起某物""接受"或"拿走"，但当它与其他词组合起来，就会产生很多别的意思。以下是一些常用的组合。

take after	look like, resemble	take apart	take something to pieces
take aside	get someone alone to talk to him	take away	remove, deduct from
take advantage	benefit by	take advice	receive guidance
take advantage	exploit	take bribes	accept illegal money
take back	make someone nostalgic	take down	make notes or write down in full
take back	retract a statement, admit something was wrong	take down	remove from a high place
take in	absorb information	take it	accept something negative, like criticism
take in	make clothes smaller	take it upon yourself	take responsibility, often without consulting other people
take it out on	abuse someone because you're angry	take notes	write down what was said at a meeting
take off	make great progress	take on	employ
take off	reduce the price of an item	take on	assume responsibility
take off	when a plane departs or leaves the ground	take over	assume control of
take off	remove from an object	take up	fill or occupy time or space
take out	extract, remove, delete	take up	start a new hobby, pastime, etc.
take out	borrow, for instance a library book or a loan	take to	make a habit of something
take place	happen	take out	go out socially with someone, especially on a date
take time	need time	take out	remove from within
take up room	occupy space	take turns	alternate

Exercise 6-24: Take It Easy! Take Five!

*Fill in the blank with the proper form of **take** using the information at the end of the sentence. Then check the Answer Key.*

1. It would be great to have another computer, but unfortunately it would take ____ too much room. (**space**)
2. The prices will never be this low again, so it would be to our benefit to take ____ of them now. (**profit by**)
3. The salesman took ____ the secretary's kind nature to find out the company pricing policy. (**used, exploited**)
4. The dispatcher wasn't sure how much time it would ____ to get through the route so he allowed an extra hour. (**duration**)
5. The typist thought that she should hurry, but the manager told her to take her ____ to avoid making mistakes. (**go at her own pace**)
6. The chairman was sick, so the director took his ____ at the board meeting. (**replace, stand in for**)
7. The committee chairman requested that the secretary take ____ at the meeting. (**write down what was said**)
8. It is illegal not only to offer money for favors, but to take ____. (**accept money**)
9. If they had taken my ____, there wouldn't have been any trouble. (**if they had listened to me**)
10. Neither company could decide who should have responsibility for maintaining the premises, so they settled on taking ____. (**alternating**)

TEST	Let's review everything you have learned in Chapter 6. Make sure you get 100% on the test before going on to the next chapter. Check your work using the Answer Key.

我们来复习一下在第六章中学过的全部内容。只有当你在测试中获得满分以后，你才能接着学习下一章。请参照答案检查正误。

Part 1: *Fill in the blank to complete each response.*

1. Did he do it?   Yes,
2. Did he do it?   No,
3. Will they call you?   No,
4. Can they try it?   Yes,
5. Would she like that?   No,

Part 2: *Rewrite the sentences, replacing **Who** with **He** or **She**.*

1. Who did it?

2. Who should do it?

Part 3: *Start each sentence with **I don't know who**.*

1. He did it.

2. They like them.

Part 4: *Answer the question using **We can't figure out**.*

1. Do you know who did it?

2. Do you know who makes them?

Part 5: *Convert from a statement to a **What** question.*

1. He did it.

2. They will buy them.

Part 6: *Convert from a statement to a **Where** question.*

1. He did it there.

2. They will go to the park.

Part 7: *Convert from a statement to a **When** question.*

1. He did it then.

2. We dance on Wednesdays.

Part 8: *Convert from a statement to a **How** question.*

1. He did it quickly.

2. She paints beautifully.

Part 9: *Respond using **I'm not sure if**.*

1. Did he do it?

2. Do we need one?

3. Will he do it?

Part 10: *Answer the question using* **Because** *and your own words.*

1. Why do people drive so fast?

2. Why is the sky blue?

Part 11: *Fill in the blank with the proper form of* **say**, **tell**, **speak**, *or* **talk**.

1. What did you ____?
2. Could you ____ me who was there?
3. What are you ____ about?
4. Sam always ____ the truth.
5. Do you ____ any other languages?

Part 12: *Select the proper verb of* **obligation** *or* **probability**.

1. It's very late. You ____ tired!
   - ☐ will be
   - ☐ must be

2. He's making a lot of mistakes. He ____ a beginner.
   - ☐ will be
   - ☐ may be

3. There's a slight possibility that he ____ on time today.
   - ☐ will be
   - ☐ could be

4. I need to do this now. It ____ completed immediately.
   - ☐ will be
   - ☐ has to be

5. ____ I help you?
   - ☐ may
   - ☐ will

6. He is very smart. He ____ answer your questions.
   - ☐ can
   - ☐ may

7. I have a deadline. I ____ work faster.
   - ☐ should
   - ☐ will be

ESSAY   Using what you have learned, write two paragraphs on the following:
利用你学过的知识写两段话，话题如下：

1. If you could travel to any country, where would you go and what would you do?
   如果你可以去任何国家旅行，你会去哪里，会干什么？

2. If you could have one super power, what would it be?
   如果你有一种超能力，它会是什么呢？

190

You can handwrite your paragraphs below or e-mail them to **para@grammar.bz** to be stored. These paragraphs are not graded or reviewed, but simply by writing them, your English will improve.

你可以把作文写在下方，也可以把它们发送到邮箱 para@grammar.bz 以存档。我们不会对你的作文进行打分或点评，但只要你写了，你的英语水平就会提高。

	Student Paragraph	
Send Chat Attach Address Fonts Colors Save As Draft		Photo Browser Show Stationery

To: para@grammar.bz

Cc:

Bcc:

Subject: Chapter 6

Signature: Corporate

My name is _____

Chapter 7
第七章

Reverse Modifiers and Opinion Words
后置修饰语和观点词

This chapter covers a different form of *adjective*, a phrase that comes after the noun. Additionally, we will work with **something / nothing**, **else**, and **time words**. We will contrast **how**: **quality** vs. **degree**, as well as do a thorough review of **how + 5 W**s.

本章会讲到形容词的另一种形式,即位于名词后面的短句。另外,我们要学习something / nothing,else,以及时间词。我们还会比较how就质量和程度提问的情况,并会全面复习一下how和5个以W开头的词。

DICTATION

For verbs, we'll learn the present real duo, review all verbs we've studied to date using **there**, along with the phrasal verb **turn**, and go over the differences between **there is**, **it is**, and **it has**.

这里,我们要学习动词的真实双重现在时,并结合there复习到目前为止学过的所有动词,复习动词turn构成的短语,以及there is,it is和it has的区别。

Exercise 7-1: Dictation   Track 095

Listen to the audio and write the exact transcription in the spaces below. Then check the Answer Key.

1. _____
2. _____
3. _____
4. _____
5. _____

STORY

The Boy Who Cried Wolf

The **strangest** thing is happening. There's a **flight** attendant **who** keeps **calling** me and leaving **messages** on my **machine**. Six **months** ago, I flew from **Italy** to LA**X** on TW**A**. The attendant **knew** who I **was** and we **chatted** a little. After I had **been** here for a while, I started getting **phone** messages from her. I never called her **back**, but she started calling more and **more**. She would **say** things like she wanted to go **out** with me, and that she **loved** me!   My **girl**friend is **furious**. I **told** her that I hadn't **given** this woman my **phone** number. I **suppose** that she got it from the **computer** at the **air**line. My **girl**friend doesn't **trust** me, however. Because of my little **joke** with the **flowers** (I'll tell you about this soon!), she thinks that I want to chase other **women**. I **guess** it's just like the little **boy** who cried **wolf**. When he was **kidding**, everyone **believed** him, but he did it **once** too **often**, and then when the wolf really **came**, no one **believed** him. I **swear**, I don't know **who** this woman is or **why** she is calling me!

Exercise 7-2: Story Pronunciation   Track 096

Listen to the audio and repeat, focusing on intonation and pronunciation.

Thə **strangest** thingiz hæppəning. Therzə **fly**də tendənt who keeps **calling** me and leaving **mess'j'z** än my **m'sheen**. Six **mənts**a go, I flew fr'm **Idəly** to LA**X** än TW**A**. The(y) əttendənt **knew** who I **wəz** and we **chædd'd** a liddle. æfter I had **bin** hir frə while, I starded gedding **phone** mess'j'z fr'mmer. I never call der **bæck**, but she starded cälling more and **more**. Sheed **say** things like she wännəd to go **out** with me, and that she **ləvd** me! My **girl**frend iz **furiəs**. I **told**er that I hadn't **given** this wüm'n my **phone** number. I **s'poz** that she gäddit from the **c'mpuder** at the **air**line. My **girl**friend dəzznt **trəst** me, however. B'cuz of my liddle **joke** with the **flowers** (all tell you(w) about this soon), she thinks the dai wänt to chase əther **wimmen**. I **guess** it's just like the liddle **boy** who cried **wüf**. Whenee wəz **kidding**, everyone **believe** dim, bəddee did it **once** too(w) **offen**, and then when the wüf rilly **came**, no one **believe** dim. I **swear**, I don't know **who** this wüm'n iz or **why** sheez cälling me.

Exercise 7-3: *What, But, That*   Track 097

Listen to the audio and repeat, focusing on intonation and pronunciation.

	What	But	That
a	wədə	bədə	thədə
I	wədäi	bədäi	thədäi
I'm	wədäim	bədäim	thədäim
I've	wədäiv	bədäiv	thədäiv
if	wədif	bədif	thədif
it	wədit	bədit	thədit
it's	wədits	bədits	thədits
is	wədiz	bədiz	thədiz
isn't	wədizn'	bədizn'	thədizn'
are	wədr'	bədr	thədr
aren't	wədärn'	bədärn'	thədärn'
he	wədee	bədee	thədee
he's	wədeez	bədeez	thədeez
her	wədr	bədr	thədr
you	wəchew	bəchew	thəchew
you'll	wəchül	bəchül	thəchül
you've	wəchoov	bəchoov	thəchoov
you're	wəchr	bəchr	thəchr

Listen to the audio and repeat, focusing on intonation and pronunciation.

1. I don't know what it **means**.   I don⁽ⁱ⁾know wədit **meenz**
2. But it **looks** like what I **need**.   bədi⁽ⁱ⁾**lük** sly kwədäi **need**
3. But you **said** that you **wouldn't**.   bəchew **sed** thəchew **wüdnt**
4. I **know** what you **think**.   **I know** wəchew **think**
5. But I don't **think** that he **will**.   bədäi don⁽ⁱ⁾**think** thədee **will**
6. He said that if we can **do** it, he'll **help**. he sed the diff we k'n **do**⁽ʷ⁾it, hill **help**
7. But isn't it **easier** this **way**?   bədizni **dee**zier thi sway?
8. We **want** something that isn't **here**.   we **wänt** something thədizn¹ **here**
9. You'll **like** it, but you'll **regret** it **later**. yül **lye** kit, bəchül r'**gre** dit **laydr**
10. But he's not **right** for what **I want**.   bədeez nät **right** fr wədäi **wänt**
11. It's **amazing** what you've **accomplished**.   its a**ma**zing wəchoovəc**cäm**plisht
12. What if he **forgets**?   wədifee fr**gets**
13. **OK**, but aren't you **missing** something?   **O**K, bədärn¹ chew **miss**ing səmthing
14. **I** think that he's **OK** now.   I think thədeez **OK** næo
15. She **wanted** to, but her **car** broke down.   She **wä**nəd to, bədr **cär** broke dæon
16. We **think** that you're taking a **chance**.   **We** think thəchr taking a **chænce**
17. They don't know what it's **about**.   They don't know wədit sə**bæot**

This noun section covers *reverse modifiers*, **how** with *quality* and *degree*, a review of the *question* forms, **something**, **something else**, and *time words*.

这个名词板块要讲后置修饰语，要讲表示质量和程度的how，要复习疑问句，复习something, something else和时间词。

Reverse Modifiers: *That or Who*
后置修饰语：That或Who

As you know, adjectives come *before* the noun.
正如你所知道的，形容词要放在名词前。

> **Nice** people go far in life.
> The **helpful** assistant is not here today.
> I met a **really nice** girl.

Now, you can also put a modifier *after* the noun by using **who**.
现在，你也可以利用who把修饰语放在名词的后面。

> People **who are nice** go far in life.
> The assistant **who helped us** is not here today.
> I met a girl who was **really nice**.

This also works with **-ing** or **-ed** modifiers.

现在分词(-ing)或被过去分词(-ed)修饰语也同样适用于这种变化。

The **dancing** man is over there.
The man **who is dancing** is over there.

The **embarrassed** children hid their faces.
The children **who were embarrassed** hid their faces.
The children **who hid their faces** were embarrassed.

Exercise 7-5: Regular Adjective to Reverse Adjective

*Flip the adjective in each of the following sentences. If the subject is a person, use **who**. If the subject is not a person, use **that**. Check the Answer Key when you're done.*

Evil people get their just rewards.
People who are evil **get their just rewards.**

1. The **loudly ticking** bomb is about to go off.

2. The **well-known** facts are not in dispute.

3. The **recently admitted** audience clapped loudly.

4. A **two-year-old** child can't read.

5. The **downsized salesmen** protested loudly.

Exercise 7-6: Reverse Adjective to Regular Adjective

Flip the adjective in each of the following sentences. Then check the Answer Key.

A situation that is familiar **is often more comfortable.**
A familiar situation is often more comfortable.

1. A person **who is illiterate** can't work for the government.

2. An object **that was unidentified** flew over the city.

3. The car **that was recently purchased** runs really well.

4. The players **who were eliminated** cheered for the remaining contestants.

5. The detective **who retired** has written a book about his experiences.

You may be wondering why there are two similar but different ways to modify a noun (**nice people** and **people who are nice**). They are similar in that they both give information about the noun. They are different in several significant ways, however.

你可能在想：为什么可以用两种相似但不同的方法来修饰名词呢（nice people 和 people who are nice）？它们的相似之处在于：他们都给出了名词的相关信息。但是，他们又存在几大显著的区别。

Reverse modifiers are used for *emphasis* or *clarification*. However, there are many instances where you can't use a simple adjective because there is too much information in the reverse modifier, such as *The guy **who runs the donut shop** speaks Thai* or *The certificate **that I requested** hasn't arrived yet*. You can't say, *The donut shop running guy speaks Thai*. You can say, *The requested certificate hasn't arrived yet*, but then it's not clear who requested it.

后置修饰语用来强调或阐释。然而，在很多情况下，因为修饰语的信息太多，所以你不能把后置修饰语转换成前置修饰语，例如：The guy who runs the donut shop speaks Thai（开甜甜圈店的人说泰语）或者 The certificate that I requested hasn't arrived yet（我申请的执照还没有送到呢）。你不能说：The donut shop running guy speaks Thai。虽然你可以说：The requested certificate hasn't arrived yet，但是这样说就不能清晰地表明是谁申请的了。

When we talk, we can throw in as many words as we like in order to get our point across. In writing, however, being concise is better. In editing, you will often find yourself going back and forth between the two forms, in order to find the best way to present the information. Let's look at the various possibilities.

在口语中，为了能说明白，我们可以想用多少词就用多少词。但在写作中，要以简洁为佳。在修改文章的时候，为了找到呈现信息的最佳方式，你可能会经常在这两种形式之间摇摆。我们来看看各种可能性。

When the speaker is immediately familiar with the topic or it's an obvious characteristic, the adjective comes before the noun.

当说话者对话题非常熟悉或者某个特征很明显的时候，形容词要放在名词前。

It's a **green** car.
He's a **good** teacher.
It's a **good idea**.

The emphasis is on the noun.
重音要落在名词上。

The **reverse** adjective lets you start with the noun and then develop the description. You can use more complex phrases and more detailed verb tenses.

It's a car **that runs on water**.
He's a teacher **who thrives on challenges**.
It's a idea **whose time has come**.

后置形容词让你先说名词，然后再进行描述。你可以在其中使用更复杂的短语和更具体的动词时态。

The rhythm also lets you stress both the noun and the main word of the modifier.
韵律方面，你要重读名词和修饰语中的主词。

As you get into the higher levels of speaking, reading, and writing, you'll notice that these two forms are used together.

当你的英语听说读写水平变得更高时，你会注意到：这两种形式常常一起使用。

Constantly barking **dogs** that have been left home alone are often bored.
Densely populated **areas** that suffer from a lack of medical facilities are a breeding ground for disease.

Compacting Sentences: *That* or *Who*
压缩句：That 或 Who

Now that we've discussed reverse modifiers, let's look at another approach to the same thing. You can join two sentences by changing the subject of the second sentence into **that** or **who**. We'll call this *compacting*. **That** is for *things*, and **who** is for *people*. However, you will hear Americans using **that** for people, as well.

既然我们已经讨论了后置修饰语，那就再来看看有异曲同工之妙的另一种方法吧：通过把第二句话的主语变成that或who，你可以把两个句子合并成一句话。这就叫做压缩。that 用来指代事物，who 用来指代人。不过，你也会听到美国人用that指代人。

The man is nice. **He** is over there.
The man **who is nice** is over there.
The man **who is over there** is nice.

A book is well written. **It** may be out of print.
A book **that is well written** may be out of print.
A book **that is out of print** may be well written.

You'll notice that the meaning of the sentence changes with the position of the blue clause. In the first example, the focus is on the man's location, and the fact that he is nice is secondary (The man **who is nice** is over there). In the second example, his personality is primary and his location is secondary (The man **who is over there** is nice).

你可以看到：句子的意思会随着蓝色句子位置的改变而改变。在第一组例子中，第一个句子的重点是人的位置，而他的友好是第二位的（那个友好的人在那儿）。在第二个句子中，他的个性是第一位的，而位置是第二位的（那边那个人很友好）。

Exercise 7-7: Compacting Subjects

*Combine the two sentences, using **that** or **who** to replace the **subject** of the second sentence. Then check the Answer Key.*

My brother lives in California. **He** likes to surf.
My brother **who lives in California** likes to surf.
My brother, **who likes to surf,** lives in California.

1. **The kids** are playing on the swings. **They** are having a great time.

2. **The house** was painted blue. **It** is next door to us.

3.   **My sister** is married. **She** is very happy.

4.   **The teacher** gave us a test today. **She** will grade it later.

5.   **The dress** doesn't fit anymore. **It** would be better off given to someone else.

Note the punctuation difference between *My brother who lives in California likes to surf* and *My brother, who lives in California, likes to surf*. In the first sentence, I have more than one brother and the sentence distinguishes that brother from the one who lives somewhere else. In the second sentence, I only have one brother and I'm giving more information about him. **That** changes to **which** when you add commas: *The pen **that** I have in my pocket is blue* and *The pen, **which** I have in my pocket, is blue*. (Traditionally, these are called restrictive and non-restrictive clauses.)

注意下面两句话在标点符号上的区别：My brother who lives in California likes to surf（我那个住在加利福尼亚的哥哥喜欢冲浪）和 My brother, who lives in California, likes to surf（我的哥哥住在加利福尼亚，他喜欢冲浪）。在第一句中，我至少有两个哥哥，这句话把句中的哥哥和住在其他地方的哥哥区别了开来。在第二句中，我只有一个哥哥，而我提供了关于他的更多信息。加上逗号后，that要变成which：The pen that I have in my pocket is blue（放在我口袋里的钢笔是蓝色的）和The pen, which I have in my pocket, is blue（我的钢笔放在口袋里，它是蓝色的）。（在传统语法体系中，这些被称为限制性定语从句和非限制性定语从句。）

Now, we will compact **object-subject**. All you have to do is replace the second subject with **who** or **that**.

现在，我们来进行"宾语—主语"的压缩，你要做的就是用who或that代替第二个句子的主语。

	Object		Subject
That	I need a **car**.	**It**	should run really well.
	I need a **car**	that	runs really well.
Who	I see a **girl**.	**She**	is wearing a red dress.
	I see a **girl**	who	is wearing a red dress.

Exercise 7-8: Compacting Objects

*Combine the two sentences, using **that** or **who** to replace the **object** of the second sentence. Then check the Answer Key.*

She met **a guy**. **He** didn't know much.   She met a guy **who** didn't know much.
We saw **a movie**. **It** was hilarious.   We saw a movie **that** was hilarious.

1.   I met **a man**. **He** had nine kids.

2.   We heard a **rumor**. **It** wasn't true at all.

3.   I like **people**. **They** are nice.

4. There was a **mistake** in his report. **It** caused a lot of problems.

5. They will organize a **protest**. **It** will change everything.

In the following exercise, use **where** for *location*, **when** for *time*, and **whose** for *possession*.
在下面的练习中，请用where指代地点，when指代时间，whose指代所有权。

Exercise 7-9: It's All Relative

*Fill in the blanks with **who, whose, where, when,** or **that.** Then check the Answer Key.*

I'd like to **welcome** you to our **company**, **introduce** you to the people *Who* work here, and tell you about the **job** *What* you'll be **doing**. Mr. **Edwards** is the man *Who* **started** this company. **This** room is *When* we hold our weekly **meetings** at 8:00 am （ay day/ **yem** ）, although **morning** is usually *that* we make most of our **calls**. This is Mr. **Roberts**, *who* you'll be working with. **Finally**, here's the room *When* you will be working and the **ID** card *that* you'll need to carry at all times. This is the **best** company *what* I've ever **worked** for.

that

How Does It Work?
它运行得怎么样？

How tells the *manner* of something. It answers the question, "In what way?" We will use:
how告诉我们事情的方式。它回答了"以什么方式？"这个问题。我们可以使用：

1. Adverbs: **easily, quickly, fast, roughly** (words ending in **-ly** are adverbs)
2. Phrases: **in a hurry, by himself, all alone**
3. Supporting words: **by, with, like, as, the way**

The supporting words have rules:
辅助词的使用规则如下：

	Example	Structure
1.	He does it **like** a pro.	like + noun
2.	He does it **by** work**ing** hard.	by + ing
3.	He broke it **with** a hammer.	with + noun
4.	He does it **the way** he learned.	the way + phrase
5.	He does it **as** he was taught.	as + phrase

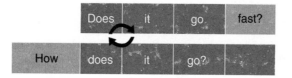

Exercise 7-10: How Questions of Manner ↻

*Convert each statement to a **how** question. Change any nouns to pronouns. Remember to use the unchanging form of the main verb. **How** replaces the **adverb**. Check the Answer Key when you're done.*

The cars go **fast**.   **How** do they go?

1.   It works **well**.
2.   She got rich **by working hard**.
3.   He drives **like a maniac**.
4.   We opened it **with a letter opener**.
5.   They found it **by searching online**.
6.   He did it **like I showed him**.
7.   He did it **the way he was taught**.
8.   He did it **as he was taught**.
9.   We traveled **by plane**.
10. He made friends **by being friendly**.

How also tells the *extent* of something. It answers the question, "How much?" or "To what extent?"
how也告诉我们事情的程度。它回答了如下问题："有多少？"或"在多大程度上？"

Exercise 7-11: *How* Questions of Extent
↻

*Convert each statement to a **how** question. Change the nouns to pronouns. Remember to use the unchanging form of the main verb. **How** replaces the **modifying adverb**. Check the Answer Key when you're done.*

The cars go **really** fast.   **How fast** do they go?

1.   It works **extremely well**.
2.   She got **really rich**.
3.   He drives **too fast**.
4.   We opened it **very slowly**.
5.   They found it **surprisingly late**.
6.   He was **SO dumb**!
7.   It was **mind-bogglingly ridiculous**.
8.   They were **blazingly furious**.
9.   Her house was **outlandishly modern**.
10. His hands were **bizarrely small**.

Exercise 7-12: 5 W Review
↻

*Convert each statement to a **how** question. Change the nouns to pronouns. Then check the Answer Key.*

The Pilgrims celebrated Thanksgiving in Massachusetts over 300 years ago by having a feast with the Indians because they were happy to be alive.

↻ **Who** celebrated it?

↻ **What** did they celebrate?

↻ **Where** did they celebrate it?

↻ **When** did they celebrate it?

↻ **Why** did they celebrate it?

↻ **How** did they celebrate it?

↻ **Did** they celebrate it? (Yes/No)

1. In 1969, with great courage and technical expertise, Neil Armstrong landed Apollo 11 on the moon in order to win the space race.

   ↻ Who

   ↻ What

   ↻ Where

   ↻ When

   ↻ Why

   ↻ How

   ↻ Y/N:

2. Over 500 years ago, Christopher Columbus sailed a ship across the Pacific, from Spain to America, with the goal of establishing a new trade route.

   ↻ Who

   ↻ What

   ↻ Where

   ↻ When

   ↻ Why

   ↻ How

   ↻ Y/N:

3. In 1863, Friedrich Miescher, a Swiss physician, first isolated DNA after discovering a microscopic substance on discarded surgical bandages as he was trying to isolate nuclein.

   ↻ Who

   ↻ What

   ↻ Where

   ↻ When

   ↻ Why

   ↻ How

   ↻ Y/N:

Let's review what we know so far about statements and questions about the *subject* and *object*.
让我们复习一下目前学过的陈述句和就主语和宾语提问的疑问句。

	Kind	Order	Verb *To Be*	Main Verb
Subject	**Statement**		**He** is there.	**He** likes it.
	Who?	⇵	**Who** is there?	**Who** likes it?
	What?	⇵	**What** is there?	**What** likes it?
	Yes or No?	↻	**Is he** there?	**Does he** like it?
Object*	**Statement**		He is a doctor.	He saw them with her.
	Who?	↻	**Who** is he?	**Who** did he see?
	What?	↻	**What** is he?	**What** did he see?
	Where?	↻	**Where** is he?	**Where** did he see it?
	When?	↻	**When** is lunch?	**When** did he see it?
	Why?	↻	**Why** is he there?	**Why** did he see them?
	How?	↻	**How** is he?	**How** did he see them?
				Who did he see with her?**
	Yes or No?	↻	**Is** he a doctor?	**Did** he see them?

*The term **object** is used here, but with the verb **to be**, it's technically a *complement*.
这里用的是object(宾语)这个词，但如果句中有了be动词，那么严格来讲，就应该叫做表语。

****Whom** is the grammatically correct term, but it's not often heard in conversation. **With whom did he see her?** would sound awkward and stilted in everyday speech.
从语法上来讲，whom才是正确的，但它在口语中不常用。如果平常跟人说"With whom did he see her?"，那听起来会很别扭、很僵硬。

Some or Any
Some 或 Any

Some is used in a positive sentence, and **any** is used with negatives, questions, or in a very broad sense.
some用于肯定句，any用于否定句、疑问句，或者用来表示非常宽泛的意思。

Thing	**Place**	**Person**	
anything	anywhere	anyone	
something	somewhere	someone	**+ else**
nothing	nowhere	no one	
everything	everywhere	everyone	
What else?	**Where else?**	**Who else?**	

Time	**Way**	**Reason**
When else?	**How else?**	**Why else?**

Something else = another thing

Somewhere else = another place

Someone else = another person

Exercise 7-13: Something Else

*Change the **bold words** to an **else** phrase. Then check the Answer Key.*

1. I saw **another person**.

2. There was **no other thing** there.

3. **At what other time** could we do it? (wennelse kwee du⁽ʷ⁾it?)

4. **What other person** will be there?

5. We need **all the other things**.

6. Let's go **to another place**.

7. **For what other reason** would he do it?

8. They can't go **to any other place**.

9. Do you know **all the other people**?

10. **In what other way** can we do it?

11. **Every other place** is full.

12. Give it to **another person**.

13. Will there be **any more things** needed?

14. I can't find it **in any other place**.

15. **Another person** must have taken it.

Time Words
时间词

	Before	Now	Later
	Ago	**For**	**In**
Hour	an **hour** ago	for an **hour**	in an **hour**
Day	yesterday	today	tomorrow
Week	last **week**	this **week**	next **week**
Month	last **month**	this **month**	next **month**
Year	last **year**	this **year**	next **year**
Time	**last** time	**this** time	**next** time

Exercise 7-14: *Ago / For / In*

*Fill in the blank with **ago**, **for**, or **in**. Then check the Answer Key.*

It's six o'clock now. I'll eat dinner ___in___ an hour, at seven o'clock. I was supposed to meet Tom an hour _ago_ at five o'clock, but he wasn't there. I waited _for_ fifteen minutes, (from 5:00 to 5:15) and then I had to leave without him. He'll probably call me ~~before~~ a couple of minutes, at 6:15.
_in_

During or *While*
During 或 While

During + Noun	**While + Phrase (-ing)**
We talked **during** lunch.	He talked **while** eating.
He thought of it **during** the meeting.	He talked **while** they were eating lunch.

Exercise 7-15: *During* or *While*

*Fill in the blank with **during** or **while**. Then check the Answer Key.*

1. The **phone** rang _____ I was in the **shower**.
2. We never **see** each other _____ the **week**, only on **week**ends.
3. _____ the **war**, there wasn't enough **food**.
4. I broke my **racket** _____ I was teaching my **friend** how to **serve**.
5. My **boss** got sick _____ **lunch** and had to go **home**.
6. It's not polite to **interrupt** _____ someone is **talking**.
7. What kind of places did you **visit** _____ you were in **Mexico**?
8. _____ the **discussion**, I realized that I didn't under**stand** him at **all**.
9. What do you **do** _____ the **day**?
10. It is easy to make **mistakes** _____ learning something **new**.
11. _____ you're at the **store**, could you get some bread and **milk**, please?
12. Most of the **damage** happened _____ the **storm**.
13. _____ my **first** year of **high** school, I read over forty **books**.

14. It was **good** ____ it **lasted**.
15. The **quarter**back was **tackled** ____ he was **running** for a **touch**down.
16. I can't **believe** you left ____ he was still **talking**!
17. Don't talk ____ the **micro**phone is on — the audience can **hear** you.
18. It started **raining** ____ I was walking **home** yesterday.
19. The **baby** never cries ____ the **night**.
20. You can't **talk** ____ a **test**.

Deadlines and Boundaries
截止时间和边界

I will work **until** 8:00 and then stop. (up to, but no later than)

I will be back **by** 6:00. (before, a time window)

I will be back **at** 6:00. (right at 6:00)

Exercise 7-16: *By / Until*

*Fill in the blank with **by** or **until**. Then check the Answer Key.*

1. I **waited** for him at the station ~~until~~ five **o'clock**.
2. I finished **reading** the re**port** ~~by~~ two **thirty**.
3. We **talked** ~~until~~ midnight.
4. The **work** was so **tiring** that we were **exhausted** ~~by~~ noon.
5. The job was **tiring**, but we kept **working** ~~until~~ five.
6. Will you be done ~~by~~ the time I get back?
7. The **teacher** kept **explaining** ~~until~~ everyone **understood**.
8. ~~By~~ the **time** we got to the **meeting**, everyone **else** was **gone**.
9. We kept looking ~~until~~ we found it.
10. ~~By~~ **Christmas**, I'll have saved **five** hundred **dollars**.
11. The **chairman** of the **meeting** spoke ~~by~~ he was **hoarse**. *until*
12. You can **think** about it, but I need to kno**w** ~~by~~ **Monday**, and no **later**.
13. We can **study** ~~until~~ **ten**, but **then** we have to go to **bed**.
14. We have to start **studying** ~~until six~~ ~~by~~ **six**.
15. She **waited** ~~until~~ she was the **last** person **there**, and then **she** went home, **too**.

For	Since
Time span, duration.	**A date, a time in the past.**
持续的一段时间	过去的一个日期、一个时间
for 10 minutes, for a year,	since 1965, since last year,
for the rest of my life	since I came to America

Exercise 7-17: *For or Since*

*Fill in the blank with **for** or **since**. Then check the Answer Key.*

1. I've been **waiting** _for_ half an **hour**, but no one has **helped** me.
2. **America** has been a **nation** _since_ 1776.
3. **America** has been a **nation** _for_ more than **200 years**.
4. He is a different **man** _since_ he got **married**.
5. My **friend** has been on a **diet** _for_ six **months**.
6. We've **known** each other _for_ two **years**.
7. He's been in France _for_ 10 **years** now.
8. He's **been** there ~~for~~ 1999. _Since_
9. I've wanted to **travel** _for_ a long **time**.
10. My **boss** has been **happy** ever _since_ his **promotion**.

Ago / Before	In / After / Later
Ago	**In**
a time + **ago**	**In** + a time in the future
a week **ago**, a minute **ago**	**In** a week, **in** a minute
Before	**After**
Before + time	After + time
Before 1972	After a week, after that
Before + 'ing	**Later** (**relative time**)
Before working	Time + later
Before + noun	A week later
Before work	

Exercise 7-18: *Ago / Before / In / After / Later*

*Fill in the blank with **ago**, **before**, **in**, **after**, or **later**. Then check the Answer Key.*

1. The **project** will be **completed** ~~in~~ ~~After~~ _in_ a **month**.
2. It was first **proposed** over a **year** _ago_.
3. The **staff analyzed** the **cost** _before_ **starting**. (They analyzed and then they started.)
4. _After_ a **week**, they **realized** that it would be really **expensive**.
5. She graduated in **May**, and a month _later_ in **June**, she got **married**.
6. The **day** _after_ **Wednesday** is **Thursday**.
7. The **day** _before_ **Tuesday** is **Monday**.
8. _Before_ accepting his **invitation**, she **asked** to meet his **family**.
9. _After_ being **promoted**, he worked **harder** than **ever**.
10. Personal **computers** were **introduced** several **years** _ago_.

Notice the **position** of the words in the chart below. Each one has either a positive or negative meaning.

注意下表左栏中粗体单词在句中的位置。每个单词的意思要么肯定，要么否定。

Yet Up to now, so far 到目前为止，迄今	**Yet** is used in negative statements and questions: yet用于表否定的陈述句和疑问句中： **He is not here yet.** 他还没到呢。 **Is he here yet?** 他到了吗？
Already Previous 以前	**Already** is used in positive statements and questions: already用于表肯定的陈述句和疑问句中： **He is already here.** 他已经到了。 **Is he already here?** 他到了吗？
Still Continuing 进行中	**Still** is used in both positive and negative statements, and questions: still用于表肯定和否定的陈述句中，还可以用于疑问句中： **He is still here.** 他还在呢。 **He still isn't here.** 他还没到呢。 **Is he still here?** 他还在吗？
Anymore Discontinued 不再继续	**Anymore** is used in negative statements: anymore用于表否定的陈述句中： **He isn't here anymore.** 他已经不在这里了。 **Anymore** is a single word in this case, but it can also be a two-word phrase: anymore在这种情况下是一个词，但它也可以拆成两个词当短语用： **I don't buy books anymore because I don't need any more books.** 我不会再买书了，因为我不需要更多的书了。
No longer Discontinued 不再继续	**No longer** is used in negative statements. no longer用于表否定的陈述句中： **He is no longer here.** 他已经不在这里了。 It usually comes in the middle of a sentence. 它通常出现在句子的中间。 **No longer** has the same meaning as **not anymore**, but it's more formal. no longer和not anymore的意思是一样的，但no longer要更正式。

Exercise 7-19: *Yet / Already / Still / Anymore*

*Fill in the blank with **yet**, **already**, **still**, or **anymore**. Then check the Answer Key.*

1. It isn't time to **go** ~~Yet~~.
2. Have you **finished** ~~already~~ ~~Yet~~
3. We've ~~still~~ ~~already~~ **seen** that movie.
4. I can't **talk** about it ~~anymore~~
5. It hasn't stopped **raining** ~~yet~~, has it? No, it's ~~Still~~ **raining**.
6. We have ~~already~~ **finished** the **test**.
7. **Polio** used to be **incurable**, but it **isn't** ~~yet~~ ~~any more~~
8. He's **only** had this **umbrella** for a **week**, and it's ~~already~~ **broken**.
9. I've studied **French** for ten **years**, but I ~~still~~ don't **speak** it well.
10. The **doctor** had **explained** about **lung** problems, but the **patient** ~~Still~~ **smoked**.

Exercise 7-20: *Yet / Already / Still / Anymore*

*Fill in the blank with **yet**, **already**, **still**, or **anymore**. Then check the Answer Key.*

The **Cubans** and the **Americans** haven't settled their **differences** ____. They are ____ arguing about **communism** and **capitalism**. They've ____ **discussed** it many **times**. Most **people** don't hope for a speedy **resolution** ____ because it has gone **on** for so **long**.

VERBS

The present real duo is used when something from the past connects with the present. This is either through a repeated action, or a continuation of a past action into the present. You can't use words like **later** or **yesterday** with this tense. Words like **ago** and **never** are frequently used, however.

当过去的事情与现在产生联系时，要使用现在真实双重时态。它是通过重复性的动作或过去某个延续性的动作和现在联系起来的。这个时态不能和later或yesterday等词连用，但像ago和never这类词的使用频率却很高。

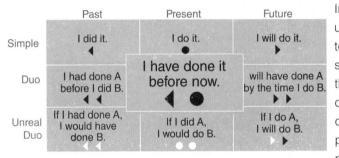

In English, time is important. Verbs tell us when something happened. Verb tenses are like a puzzle. It's important to see how all the pieces fit together, what their relationships are, and how they can change. With the present real duo—a combination of the past and the present—it's like you are pulling the past up into the present.

对英语来说，时间很重要。动词会告诉我们事情发生的时间，而动词时态就好比一个拼图。请务必弄明白这些板块是如何组合起来的，他们之间有什么关系，以及可以如何转化。对于现在真实双重时态来说——过去和现在的结合——就好像把过去搜到现在了一样。

If you say, **I did A. I also did B**, you should use the simple past. However, if you want to relate the past action of A to the present, as in, **I have done A many times before now**, you should use the *present* real *duo*.

如果你说I did A. I also did B，你就应该用一般过去时。但是，如果你想把过去的动作A与现在联系起来，你就应该用现在真实双重时态，就像这句：I have done A many times before now。

Simple Past 一般过去时	Present Real Duo 现在真实双重时态
Indicates that something is over. 表示某事已经结束。	Indicates that the situation is ongoing or there is still some relationship to the past. 表示某情形还在继续或者仍然和过去有联系。
You **lived** in L.A. for two years.	You **have lived** in L.A. for two years.
◀	◀●
You don't live in L.A. anymore.	You still live in L.A.

Today is February 28
今天是2月28日

The car was in the shop for three days.

The car has been in the shop for a week.

The car was in the shop for three days, three weeks **ago**. (2/1 to 2/3)
这辆车三周前在店里待了三天。

The car has been in the shop **for** a week now. (2/22 until now)
这辆车已经在店里待了七天了。

50 Irregular Verbs

be	was / were	**been**	know	knew	**known**
become	became	**become**	leave	left	**left**
begin	began	**begun**	lose	lost	**lost**
break	broke	**broken**	make	made	**made**
bring	brought	**brought**	mean	meant	**meant**
catch	caught	**caught**	meet	met	**met**
choose	chose	**chosen**	put	put	**put**
come	came	**come**	read	read	**read**
do	did	**done**	ride	rode	**ridden**
drink	drank	**drunk**	run	ran	**run**
drive	drove	**driven**	say	said	**said**
eat	ate	**eaten**	see	saw	**seen**
fall	fell	**fallen**	sell	sold	**sold**
feel	felt	**felt**	send	sent	**sent**
fight	fought	**fought**	sit	sat	**sat**
find	found	**found**	speak	spoke	**spoken**
fly	flew	**flown**	stand	stood	**stood**
forget	forgot	**forgotten**	take	took	**taken**
give	gave	**given**	teach	taught	**taught**
get	got	**gotten**	tell	told	**told**
go	went	**gone**	think	thought	**thought**
grow	grew	**grown**	throw	threw	**thrown**
have	had	**had**	understand	understood	**understood**
hear	heard	**heard**	win	won	**won**
hold	held	**held**	write	wrote	**written**

Exercise 7-21: "Have You Ever Been to Mexico?"

Fill in the blanks with the present duo. Then check the Answer Key.

I ~~have~~ been (be) to **Mexico** three **times** this year. My **brother** has never been (be) there. We ~~told~~ talked (talk) about it several **times**, but he has n't ever ~~found~~ (find) the **time** to go. He 还 has been waiting (be waiting) for a long **time**! We ~~make~~ have made (make) **plans** to go **later** this **year**, but he has n't decided (decide) **when**. When we **do** go, it'll be **great**.

Exercise 7-22: "A Has-Been or a Wannabe?"

Fill in the blanks with the present duo. Then check the Answer Key.

America is a good country, but it ____ (**be**) slowly crumbling ever since the Vietnam War. ____ we ____ (**learn**) the lessons of the past? Can we say that we ____ (**provide**) all of our children with a good education? We ____ (**devote**) far, far too much time, energy and money on the military. This country ____ (**arrive**) at a crossroads, and we can either survive and become stronger, or fall by the wayside in global significance.

Earlier in this chapter, you learned several *time words* that can be used with the present duo and the simple past. These key words—**since**, **yet**, **already**—will tell you which tense to use.

在本章的前半部分，你已经学习了几个时间词，这些词可以用于现在双重时态和一般过去时。这些重要的词——since，yet，already——会告诉你句子要用什么时态。

Exercise 7-23: Present Duo vs. Simple Past

Fill in the blanks with either the present duo or the simple past. Then check the Answer Key.

1. I ____ here since 1965.   **live**
2. I ____ here in 1965.   **move**
3. He ____ to get a better job.   **never try**
4. When he was 18, he ____ from L.A. to New York.   **drive**
5. Hey, someone ____ my spot!   **take**
6. It ____ three times today!   **happen**
7. They ____ working on your project, but they ____ yet.   **start / not finish**
8. When they ____, they went home.   **finish**
9. When they ____, they'll let you know.   **finish**
10. He ____ hard last week.   **work**
11. He ____ hard lately.   **be working**
12. It ____ yesterday.   **rain**
13. It ____ for a week.   **be raining**
14. ____ this movie yet?   (**you**) **see**
15. You ____ in that chair for three hours!   **sit**
16. You ____ down with a thud!   **sit**
17. You ____ that car for 10 years.   **drive**
18. You ____ like a maniac yesterday.   **drive**
19. You ____ so much in life in such a short time.   **see**
20. I ____ you take it.   **see**

Exercise 7-24: Present Duo vs. Simple Present

Fill in the blanks with either the present duo or the simple present. Then check the Answer Key.

1. You ____ that theater for years.   **like**
2. I ____ that movie.   **like**

3. When they _____, they'll let you know.   **finish**
4. They _____ on time because they are efficient.   **finish**
5. That lady _____ tomatoes.   **grow**
6. They _____ in her backyard for 60 years.   **grow**
7. You _____ this office well for a long time now.   **manage**
8. I _____ to cope with life.   **manage**
9. You _____ into such a lovely young lady.   **grow**
10. She _____ flowers.   **grow**

The V Sound
V这个音

People have trouble with the V sound. They either make it sound like a W or a B. The easiest way to get a good V is to start with F. Say **ffffffffffffffffffff**. Now, leave everything in exactly the same position—your upper teeth should be almost touching your lower lip—and put your finger on your throat. Make your throat vibrate and say **vvvvvvvvvvvvvvvv**.

人们发V这个音的时候有点困难。他们要么发得像W，要么发得像B。发V这个音有一个最简单的方法，那就是先从F开始。请念：ffffffffffffffffffff。现在，请保持口形不变——你的上牙应该几乎能接触到下嘴唇——然后把手指放在喉咙处。让你的喉咙振颤起来，然后发vvvvvvvvvvvvvv这个音。

Exercise 7-25: V as in Victory   **Track 099**

Listen to the audio and repeat five times.

	P	B	F	V	W
1.	Perry	berry	fairy	very	wary
2.	pat	bat	fat	vat	wax
3.	Paul	ball	fall	vault	wall
4.	pig	big	fig	vim	wig
5.	purr	burr	fur	verb	were

There Is or It Has
There Is 或 It Has

You have learned how to use **have** as well as **there is / there are**. We will now contrast the two forms. With **have**, we need an identified subject, such as **We have**, **They had**, or **I will have**. Frequently, though, the speaker just wants to point out the existence of something by indicating a subject. In this case, use **there + be**. Both forms are correct, but **there is** is more common and colloquial.

你已经学过该怎么用have以及there is / there are了。现在，我们来对比一下这两种用法。使用have时，我们需要一个明确的主语，比如we have，they had或者I will have。但很多时候，说话人只想指出某物的存在，而不想说明主语是什么。在这种情况下，就要用there + be。这两种用法都对，但there is更常用、更口语化。

There	Have
There is a car in the garage.	We have a car in the garage.
There are five people in my family.	I have five people in my family.
There isn't much time left.	We don't have much time left.
There aren't a lot of options for us this time.	We don't have a lot of options this time.
There was a war in 1812.	They had a war in 1812.
There was a big celebration last night.	Someone had a big celebration last night.
There wasn't enough food for everyone.	People didn't have enough food.
There weren't many people in the store.	The store didn't have many people in it.
There's going to be a party at my house.	We're going to have a party.
There won't be another opportunity.	We won't have another opportunity.
There can't be any noise during the play.	We can't have any noise during the play.

Exercise 7-26: *There* or *Have*

*Change each **have** sentence to a **there** sentence. Then check the Answer Key.*

I have a lot of books in my room. **There are** a lot of books in my room.

1. We don't have enough **time**.

2. We had a lot of exciting **stuff** to **do**.

3. You have no **need** to buy new **clothes.** (**kloz**)

4. They had no **reason** to arrange the **meeting**.

5. They had many **reasons** to arrange the **meeting**.

6. **Every**one had a lot of **trouble** with the **fax** machine. (**fakss m'sheen**)

7. We had many **hard**working **people** in the **office**.

8. You don't have to go to **work** today.

9. They had a lot of **seals** on the beach.

10. We will have **peace** someday.

11. We didn't have a **class** on **Friday**.

12. That **town** has a lot of **butter**flies.

13. They had a **shirt** on the floor.

14. We had no **need** to **do** that.

15. The **room** had a lot of **balloons**.

There Is or *It Is*
There Is 或 It Is

There + be is used to point out the existence or location of something. **It** is a pronoun, so it replaces a noun. With **it**, you always have to introduce the noun first. If you start out with, **It** was a _____. People will say or think, "**What** was a _____?" **It** is used with weather, time, color, and adjectives.

There + be常被用来指示某物的存在或者位置。it是一个代词，所以它代替的是名词。如果用it，那你就要先介绍相应的名词。如果你一开头就说：It was a _____。人们就会说或者想："What was a _____?"it经常和天气、时间、颜色，以及形容词连用。

Weather

It's sunny.	It's sprinkling.	It's drizzling.	It's raining.	It's pouring.
It's hot.	It's snowing.	It's cold.	It's stormy.	It's humid.
It's clear.	It's overcast.	It's windy.	It's cloudy.	It's muggy.
It's icy.	It's freezing.	It's beautiful.	It's foggy.	It's smoggy.

Time

It's noon.	It's midnight.	It's five o'clock.	It's early.	It's late.
It's Wednesday.	It's January.	It's winter.	It's 2009.	It's time to go.

Just because the topic is weather, however, you still need to follow the rules:

不过，正因为话题是天气，所以你仍然需要遵守以下规则：

There was a storm. It was stormy.

Exercise 7-27: *There* or *It*

*Fill in the blanks with either **there + be** or **it + be**. Then check the Answer Key.*

1. _____ a small **house** near us. _____ three **trees** in front.

2. _____ a **car**wash near here? Yes, _____ one on **Front** Street.

3. We **wanted** to go to the **beach**, but _____ not enough **time**.

4. _____ time to **go**? No, _____ still **early**.

5. _____ an **ocean** between the U.**S**. and **Europe**.

6. A few **days** ago, _____ a **storm**. _____ terrible. _____ a lot of **damage**. _____ a lot of **injuries**.

7. _____ **seven** colors in the **rain**bow.

8. Last **winter**, _____ very **cold**. _____ a lot of **snow**. _____ **snowy**.

9. After the **lecture** tomorrow, ____ an **opportunity** to ask **questions**.

10. ____ **no** need to get dressed **up**. We're **just** going to the **donut** shop.

11. They live on a busy **street**. ____ a lot of **noise** from the **traffic**.

12. ____ three **4**s in **twelve**.

13. ____ an **accident** in **Venice** yesterday, but ____n't **serious** and ____n't any **injuries**.

14. Where is the **car**? She said that ____ over **there**.

15. ____ many **people** there tomorrow.

16. We're **bored**. ____ nothing to **do** in this place. ____ **boring**.

17. I **hope** that ____ someone to meet me at the airport tomorrow.

18. I was **hoping** that ____ someone to meet me at the **air**port, but ____n't anyone **there**.

19. ____ too much **pressure** on us last year.

20. He doesn't **like** where he **lives** because ____ **better** to be **closer** to **work**.

21. ____ my **birth**day yesterday.

22. ____ a **museum** there, but it burned **down**. (**myoozim**)

23. I **wish** ____ n't **raining**. I **wish** ____ n't so much **rain** here. I **wish** ____ n't so **rainy** here in Seattle.

24. Do you think ____ a better **way** to **do** this?

25. Do you think ____ a long **way** from **Rome** to **Madrid**?

26. How far ____ from **Rome** to **Madrid**?

27. ____ **nice** to live in a **cabin** in the **mountains**.

28. ____ used to be a **theater** on **First** Street, but it closed a few **months** ago. (**munts**)

29. That **building** is now a **super**market. ____ used to be a **theater**.
    (It's the same building, converted to a supermarket.)

30. That **building** is a **super**market. ____ used to be a **theater** there.
    (It's a different building in the same location.)

31. I wanted to visit the **museum**, but ____ n't enough time.

32. ____ time to **leave**?

33. ____ anything on **TV** early in the **morning**.

34. ____ **trouble** at the **game** last night. They had to **cancel** it **because** of that.

35. The **room** was completely **empty**. ____ n't anything **there**.

36. Look in the desk **drawer**, ____ some **paper** clips there.

Verb Review
复习动词

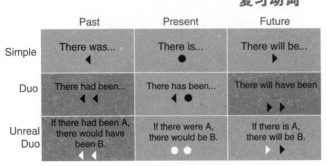

	Past	Present	Future
Simple	There was... ◀	There is... ●	There will be... ▶
Duo	There had been... ◀◀	There has been... ◀●	There will have been ... ▶▶
Unreal Duo	If there had been A, there would have been B. ◀◀	If there were A, there would be B. ●●	If there is A, there will be B. ▶▶

Here is a comprehensive review of various verb tenses, opinion words, and tag endings.

这里会全面地复习一下动词的各种时态、观点词，以及反意疑问句。

Facts

	There is / are	Present fact
100%	There was / were	Past fact
	There will be	Future fact
	There has / have been	Present fact
	There had been	Past fact
	There will have been	Future fact

Opinions and Obligations

	There had better be	Obligation or warning
90%	There must be, has to be	Strong probability, strong obligation
	There must have been	Strong probability
	There had to be	Strong probability
	There should be	Present probability, obligation, opinion, advice, suggestion
75%	There should have been	Past probability, obligation, opinion, advice, suggestion
50%	There may / might be	Present possibility
	There might have been	Past possibility
25%	There could be	Present slight possibility
	There could have been	Past slight possibility
	If there were, there would be...	Present unreal
0%	If there had been, there would have been...	Past unreal
	If there is, there will be...	Future unreal

Exercise 7-28: Verb Review

*Using the previous page as a guide, select the proper verb. Be mindful of the difference between **strong** and **weak** possibilities and **probabilities**. Fill in the blank with **is, was, were, will be, has been, have been, had been, may be, might be, should be, could be, must be, would be, will have been, may have been, must have been, should have been, would have been**, or **could have been**. Then check the Answer Key.*

1. There ____ a good **chance** that it will **rain** tomorrow.   Present fact
2. There ____ an **earth**quake in **Tokyo** yesterday.   Past fact
3. There ____ a lot of **problems** with the **fax** lately.   Present duo fact
4. The **news**paper says that there ____ a **storm** next week.   Future fact
5. They're not **sure**, but there ____ a **tornado**, too.   Present or future possibility
6. My **brother** thinks that there ____ a **soda** machine in every **class**room.   Opinion

7. **Otherwise**, there ____ some thirsty **people**.	Present or future slight possibility
8. There ____ a better **way** to lose **weight**!	Present strong opinion
9. There ____ more **time** if everyone **got** here **earlier**.	Present unreal
10. By **this** time next **year**, there ____ 25 **births**.	Future duo fact
11. The re**port** wasn't clear, but there ____ a **problem** with the **phone**.	Past possibility
12. Before we had **cars**, there ____ a lot of **horses**.	Past strong probability
13. My **parents** think that there ____ more **home**work last year.	Past opinion
14. If **Bob** hadn't forgotten the **map**, there wouldn't ____ any **problems**.	Past unreal
15. It was **dangerous** to **drive** so fast; there ____ an **accident**.	Past slight possibility
16. **Joe** didn't know that there ____ an **earth**quake.	Past duo
17. Sam's **letter** said that if there ____ any **trouble**, he'd come right **back**.	Reported speech
18. The **guests** ____ **chatting** prior to the **interruption**.	Past duo
19. The **president** ____ **persuasive**, since **everyone** agreed to **try** it.	Past strong probability
20. If **I** ____ you, there ____ an **investigation**.	Present unreal

Exercise 7-29: Change to the Past

Rewrite each sentence, changing the verb to the past tense. Then check the Answer Key.

I **should ask** him about his plans.   I **should have asked** him about his plans.

1. He must be able to think quickly. (probability)

2. He must be able to think quickly. (obligation)

3. It might be better to wait for them.

4. He says that they shouldn't go. (change both verbs)

5. If they take my car, they won't have to wait for the bus.

6. If they took my car, they wouldn't have to wait for the bus.

7. You can go home at five today. (ability)

8. He isn't supposed to take Jim's car without asking.

9. They say that they will be here until next week.

10. Al may use your car for the rest of the week. (possibility)

11. Al may use your car for the rest of the week. (permission)

12. I wish I knew what he wanted.

13. He knows what he's doing.

14. I forget why we did it.

Exercise 7-30: Tag Endings

Fill in the blank with the proper tag ending. Then check Answer Key.

1. The new clerk is very slow,   ?
2. But he can improve,   ?
3. She doesn't type very well,   ?
4. They lost their way,   ?
5. You don't think so,   ?
6. I don't think it's easy,   ?
7. I'm your friend,   ?
8. You won't be coming,   ?
9. He keeps the books,   ?
10. You couldn't tell,   ?
11. We have to close the office,   ?
12. We have closed the office,   ?
13. We had to close the office,   ?
14. We had the office closed,   ?
15. We had already closed the office,   ?
16. We'd better close the office,   ?
17. The office has closed,   ?
18. The office is closed,   ?
19. The office will be closed,   ?
20. The office has been closed,   ?
21. You'll be working late tonight,   ?
22. We've done our best,   ?
23. He should have been here by now,   ?

24. He should be promoted, _____ ?
25. I didn't send the fax, _____ ?
26. I won't get a raise this year, _____ ?
27. You use the computer, _____ ?
28. You're used to the computer, _____ ?
29. You used to use the computer, _____ ?
30. I can use the phone, _____ ?
31. We don't have to fill in all these forms, _____ ?
32. They have all kinds of trouble with their computer, _____ ?
33. He'd rather work overtime, _____ ?
34. You never used to work Saturdays, _____ ?
35. That wouldn't be possible, _____ ?
36. The police have never done that, _____ ?
37. I'd better get going, _____ ?
38. That's better, _____ ?
39. They didn't have to buy them all, _____ ?
40. They would reschedule, _____ ?

Remember: **Am I not** is not standard.
记住：Am I not 不是标准用法。

Turn

Turn usually indicates some kind of change.
Turn通常暗示着某种变化。

Verb	Meaning	Verb	Meaning
turn into something	change or become	turn up	increase the volume
turn out well	succeed	turn up	appear
turn out badly	fail	turn up	find or discover
turn out to be	be other than supposed	turn down	decrease the volume
turn over / turnover	flip / employee hiring cycle	turn down	refuse or reject
turn 25	become that age	a turning point	a directional change
		turn around	change directions 180°

Exercise 7-31: *Turn*

Fill in the blank with the appropriate preposition. Then check the Answer Key.

1. When the project was first introduced, no one had any idea that it would turn ____ so well. (**succeed**)

2. Although he wanted the promotion, he turned it ____ because it would have meant moving again. (**refused or rejected**)

3. During the hectic reorganization of the office, many files were mislaid and who knows when or where they'll turn ____ again. (**appear**)

4. At the time, everyone involved thought it would be a good idea, but it turned ____ to be a disaster. (**other than supposed**)

5. At first, the tracking system was more of a nuisance, but over the years, it turned ____ one of the wisest investments the company ever made. (**change or become**)

6. I love that song! Turn it ____! (**increase the volume**)

7. We all thought he was lazy but he turned ____ to be the hardest worker of us all. (**be other than supposed**)

8. I can't believe that my brother has turned ____. (**become the age of 30**)

9. It's a sign of bad management to have such high ____. (**employee hiring cycle**)

10. When you're finished with the test, turn your papers ____. (**flip**)

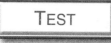

Let's review everything you have learned in Chapter 7. Check your work using the Answer Key. Make sure you get 100% on the test before going on to the next chapter.

我们来复习一下在第七章中学过的全部内容。只有当你在测试中获得满分以后，你才能接着学习下一章。请参照答案检查正误。

Part 1: *Select the proper form.*

1. He's the person *who* created the infrastructure. who/whose/that/what
2. That's the idea ~~which~~ *that* changed everyone's way of thinking. who/whose/that/what
3. I'm not sure *whose* idea that was. who/whose/that/what
4. This is not *what* I wanted! who/whose/that/what
5. I hope it *will* work out. will/is/was/were
6. I wish it *were* possible. will/is/was/were
7. If there *had been* time right now, we would take care of it. *were* is/were/had been
8. If there *is* time tomorrow, we will take care of it. is/were/had been
9. If there *were* time yesterday, we would have taken care of it. *had been* is/were/had been
10. You *should have been* there yesterday. should be/should have been
11. When I was young, I *could dance* well. could dance/could have danced
12. I'm sorry you had to walk. You *could have called* me. could call/could have called

Part 2: *Fill in the proper tag ending.*

1. We have to finish quickly, _____ ?
2. They had to redo it, _____ ?
3. She has been there before, _____ ?
4. They had never acted like that before, _____ ?
5. The school will be closed Thursday, _____ ?

6. She has good grades, ?
7. He had better think about it, ?
8. They'd rather play, ?

Part 3: *Select the proper form.*

1. He enlisted in the army two years *ago*.   for/ago/in
2. He's been in the army *for* two years now.   for/ago/in
3. He'll be getting out *in* a couple of days.   for/ago/in
4. They thought it over *during* the meeting.   during/while
5. We chatted amiably *during* the intermission.   during/while
6. *While* you're up, could you get me a glass of   during/while
   water?
7. What do you do *while* the day?   during/while
8. It's not safe to talk on the phone *during* driving.   during/while
9. We plan on working *until* 10:00.   by/until
10. We need to start *by* 7:00.   by/until
11. They have been here *for* ten years.   for/since
12. They have been here *since* 2001.   for/since
13. Let me call you back *after* couple of   in/after
    minutes, OK?
14. He had to take another call, but he called   in/after
    me back *in* a few minutes.
15. Have you finished *yet*?   yet/already/still/anymore
16. They have *already* finished.   yet/already/still/anymore
17. The others are *still* working on it. (continuing)   yet/already/still/anymore
18. We don't want to do this *anymore*   yet/already/still/anymore

Part 4: *Change from the simple present to the present duo.*

1. I watch TV.

2. They do the dishes.

3. People make mistakes.

4. Things fall in an earthquake.

5. The situation gets better.

6. The shredder tears the paper.

7. The children are well behaved.

220

8.   The competitors bring their own gear.

9.   The cats drink the milk.

10. Dennis broke his leg.

Part 5: *Change from the simple past to the present duo.*

1.   Everyone saw that movie.

2.   Joe stole the books.

3.   Louise took the test.

4.   The teacher chose the participants.

5.   The idea became more popular.

6.   The students learned the lessons.

7.   His parents were informed of the decision.

8.   The CEO was thinking about it.

9.   Many people forgot to answer.

10. The horses ate the hay.

Part 6: *Choose either the simple past or the present real duo.*

1.   He ____ about it many times before today.
     - ☐ thought
     - ☐ has thought

2.   Jennie ____ it two years ago.
     - ☐ bought
     - ☐ has bought

3.   We ____ to the mall this morning.
     - ☐ drove
     - ☐ have driven

4.   I ____ such a thing in my life.
     - ☐ never saw
     - ☐ have never seen

5.   Our friends ____ about it again last night.
     - ☐ talked
     - ☐ have talked

6.   Until now, ____ a good deal of discretion.
     - ☐ they always used
     - ☐ they've always used

7. Do you think he ____ his homework yet?
   ☐ did
   ☐ has done

8. The dogs ____ all day yesterday.
   ☐ barked
   ☐ have barked

9. Have you ever ____ to the races before?
   ☐ went
   ☐ gone

10. I think he ____ home.
    ☐ already went
    ☐ has already gone

11. He ____ about it all of the time.
    ☐ thinks
    ☐ has thought

12. He ____ about it for years.
    ☐ thinks
    ☐ has thought

13. We ____ to start studying now.
    ☐ need
    ☐ have needed

14. We ____ to start studying for quite some time now.
    ☐ need
    ☐ have needed

15. Jennie ____ there in 1968.
    ☐ lived
    ☐ has lived

16. Jennie ____ there since 1968.
    ☐ lived
    ☐ has lived

17. The janitor ____ in Fresno until December.
    ☐ worked
    ☐ has worked

18. The janitor ____ here for the past three months.
    ☐ worked
    ☐ has worked

ESSAY

Using what you have learned, write two paragraphs on the following topics:

利用你学过的知识写两段话，话题如下：

1. What one indulgence would you enjoy if there were no consequences?

   如果没有不良后果的话，你会放任自己去做哪件事？

2. If you could change one law, what would that be?

   如果你可以修改某条法律，你会修改哪条？

You can handwrite your paragraphs below or e'mail them to **para@grammar.bz** to be stored. These paragraphs are not graded or reviewed, but simply by writing them, your English will improve.

你可以把作文写在下方，也可以把它们发送到邮箱 *para@grammar.bz* 以存档。我们不会对你的作文进行打分或点评，但只要你写了，你的英语水平就会提高。

Student Paragraph

Send Chat Attach Address Fonts Colors Save As Draft Photo Browser Show Stationery

To: para@grammar.bz

Cc:

Bcc:

Subject: Chapter 7

Signature: Corporate

My name is _____

Chapter 8
第八章

Complex Intonation, the Past Unreal Duo, and the Causative
综合语调、过去非真实双重时态和使役动词

In this chapter we'll review common courtesy, as well as direct and indirect questions. We have worked with **how** （in terms of how many times）, and now we will look at it from the perspective of *extent* and *dimensions*. We have also worked with prepositions of location and direction, as well as with phrasal verbs. Here, we'll examine a variety of verbs with **to**, **for**, **of**, **about**, **on**, **with**, and **from**.

在本章，我们要复习一下常用的礼貌用语，以及直接疑问句和间接疑问句。我们已经学过how的一种用法（比如在how many times中的用法），现在我们要从程度和维度的角度来学习它。我们也已经学过方位介词、方向介词，以及动词短语。在本章，我们要学习一系列能与to, for, of, about, on, with和from等词搭配的动词。

For verbs, we will learn the *past unreal duo* and the *causative* （**let**, **have**, **get**, **make**, **force**, **allow**, **permit**, **persuade**, **convince**）.

动词方面，我们要学习过去非真实双重时态以及使役动词（let, have, get, make, force, allow, permit, persuade, convince）。

Exercise 8-1: Dictation   Track 100

Listen to the audio and write the exact transcription in the spaces below. Then check the Answer Key.

1. _____
2. _____
3. _____
4. _____
5. _____

The Flower Incident

My **girl**friend, **Eve**, sometimes gets **jealous**. I **tell** her that I'm too **busy** and too **tired** to be looking at other **women**, but she doesn't **trust** me. **One** time, as a **joke** to teach her a **lesson**, I ordered a **big** bouquet of **flowers** and had a girl **sign** them, "Love, **Sabrina**." I **had** them delivered to my house. When Eve came **home**, she **saw** them and **asked** me who had given me **flowers**. I just **shrugged**, so she

looked at the **card**. When she saw "**Sabrina**," she was really **mad**. I **laug**
apologize and **had** me give the flowers **away**. She didn't let me **near** her f
bit, she's gently forcing me to be a better **person** by not allowing that ki
trying to get me to **change** for a long **time**.

Exercise 8-2: Story Pronunciation

Listen to the audio and repeat, focusing on intonation and pronunciation.

My **girl**friend, **Eve**, səmtymz gets **jelləs**. I **tell**er the dime too **bizzy** and too **tired** t' be looking at other **wimmen**, bət she doesn't **trəst** me. **One** time, ezza **joke** t' teacher ə **lessən**, I order də **big** bokay əv **flowerz** and hadə girl **syn**em, "Luv, **S'breena**." I had them d'liverd to my house. Wheneev came **home**, she **säh** em and **askt** me who h'd given me **flowerz**. I jəst **shrugd**, so she lükt at the **cärd**. When she **säh** "**S'breena**," she wəz rilly **mæd**. I **læfft** ə lät, but she made me pälegize and had me give the flowers **away**. She didn't let me **near** her fr the restəv the **day**. Bit by **bit**, she's gently forcing me to be a better **person** by not allowing that kind of **behavior**. She's been trying to get me to **change** for a long **time**.

This is an important section because you will learn how to show appreciation, ask for a favor, apologize, and ask for an apology, as well as review how to ask questions, both *directly* and *indirectly*.

本部分的内容很重要，因为你会学到如何表达感谢，如何寻求帮助，如何道歉，如何要求别人道歉，还会复习如何直接地和间接地提问。

Common Courtesy
常用礼貌用语

The social graces are largely the same in every culture, but the terminology is quite specific to each language.

每种文化的社交礼仪基本上都差不多，但每种语言中的专门用语却都是各自独有的。

Appreciation
感谢

There are several ways to show appreciation, such as a direct **Thank you!** or **Thank you very much. Thanks!** is more casual, as is **Thanks a lot!** To be more specific, you can add **for -ing**, such as **Thank you for helping me with this.** You can add expressions such as **That was really nice of you, I really appreciate it, You've been very helpful, I appreciate your consideration / kindness / support / help / cooperation.** You can also use a short phrase such as **Thanks for the ride!** Sometimes people will show general appreciation with **Thank goodness!**

Acknowledging Appreciation
回应感谢

The most common acknowledgement is **You're welcome.** You'll also hear **Sure!**, **No problem, No prob, My pleasure, I was glad to help, That's OK,** or **Any time!** You can also say, **Thank *you*!** with the emphasis on **you.**

Giving Praise
称赞

When you want to let someone know that you are pleased with the effort, you can say **Excellent work!** or **Good job!** or **Nice report!**

Invitations
邀请

Would you like to get together for coffee?

Would you like to get together some time?

Would you like to come visit?

If you're ever in the neighborhood, feel free to drop by.

We're having a party on Saturday; would you like to come?

Would you like to be part of our study group?

Would you like to join us for lunch some time?

Phone Terminology
电话用语

If someone has mis-dialed, you say **I think you have the wrong number.** If you can't hear a person due to phone static, say **You're breaking up. Could you say that again?** Or, **Pardon me, I can't hear you.** If you hear another phone ring on their end, you can say, **Do you need to get that?**

Apologizing
道歉

Sad to say, the time comes when we all need to apologize. As soon as you realize that you have hurt someone's feelings, insulted someone, forgotten to do something, broken something, or committed some other social error, the best apology is direct and heartfelt. **I'd like to apologize for what happened the other day. I'm sorry I was so rude / so late. I shouldn't have done that / been late. There is no excuse for it and it won't happen again.** One thing you want to avoid is saying, **Sorry, but ...,** which is not a real apology.

There are lighter ways to express regret or to acknowledge a mistake, such as **Sorry I'm late!** or **Excuse me for stepping on your foot. Pardon me** is a bit more formal than **Excuse me** and is sometimes used ironically or sarcastically. It's also used to have someone repeat something. Of course, as we all know, the real apology is not doing it again.

Requesting an Apology
要求道歉

Ideally, we all learn manners by the age of six or seven, but there are times when someone has

Asking a Favor
寻求帮助

Could you do me a favor?

Would you please open the window?

Would you mind opening the window?

Would you mind if I opened the window?

May I open the window?

Could you help me with this, please?

It would mean so much to me if you could ____.

Could you give me a ride to ____?

Excuse me, can I get by?

Would it be possible to ____?

Excuse me, where's the restroom?

Could you lend me ____?

Could I borrow ____?

Could you help me out with ____?

Could you explain ____?

Could you let me know when ____?

Not Accepting an Apology
不接受道歉

There are times when the offender's behavior is so egregious or so often repeated that it is simply not in your best interest to accept the apology, no matter how it is offered. At this point, you can say **I'm sorry, but I simply can't forgive you for what you have done,** or **I'm sorry, I can't excuse this behavior yet again.** Or **I can't accept your apology. What you did was wrong and you should have known better.**

You can give yourself a little breathing room by saying something along the lines of **I have given this a great deal of thought, and discussed it with others. What you did was hurtful and I need to take some time to get some perspective on this.**

Accepting an Apology
接受道歉

Even if the apology is hollow or poorly delivered, you can graciously accept by

offended or insulted you, lied, cheated, stood you up, or broken something, and you need to let him or her know how you feel. You can say **I am upset that you said that. I'd like an apology.** Or **That was uncalled for. I think you should apologize,** or **I think you owe me an apology.**

saying, **Thank you, I appreciate your apology.** If the person seems sincerely contrite, you can say **Thank you, I accept your apology and we can put this behind us.**

Intonation and Attitude
语调和态度

There are certain sounds in any language that are considered nonsense syllables yet impart a large amount of information to the informed listener. Each language has a different set of these sounds, such as **eto ne** in Japanese, **em** in Spanish, **eu** in French, and **um** in English. These are the sounds that a native speaker makes when he is thinking out loud—holding the floor, but not yet committing to actually speaking.

每门语言中都有这样一些音，它们虽然被认为是无意义的音节，却给听话人传达了大量的信息。每种语言都有一套独特的音，如日语中的eto ne，西班牙语中的em，法语中的eu，以及英语中的um。人们在说母语的时候，如果还在思考问题，那他就会发出这种声音——他们先表明有话要说，但实际上还没有开始说。

Exercise 8-3: Intonation practice   **Track 102**

These are very common sounds. They can be nasalized or not, and said with the mouth open or closed. Intonation is the most important point. Listen and repeat.

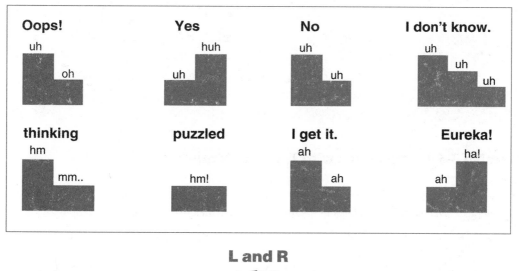

L and R
L 和 R

Let's start with L because it's easy, especially at the beginning of a word. Say **la-la-la**. Feel the tip of your tongue on the bumps behind your top teeth. The secret to the L is that you must always touch your tongue to these bumps. Where people run into trouble is at the end of a word, like **call** or **well**. They end up sounding like **caw** or **weo**. There are a couple of ways to deal with this. First, you can use word connections. For example, if you put a word starting with a vowel right after the final L, you can then make the L into the beginning letter of the second word. **Call Ann** becomes **cäh lænn**, instead of **caw æn**.

让我们先从L开始，因为它比较简单，尤其是位于词首的时候。请说la-la-la，并感觉用舌尖触碰你的上齿龈。说L的窍门是必须始终用舌尖触碰上齿龈。人们常遇到困难的是当L位于词尾的时候，如call或well。它们听起来就好像caw或weo。有几种方法可以处理这个尾音。第一种办法是你可以运用单词连读。例如，如果L后面跟的是以元音开头的单词，你就可以把L放到第二个单词的开头。call Ann变成了cäh lænn，而不是caw æn。

The second trick is to add a little schwa just before and after the L. Putting all of those words on a staircase will show just how many extra sounds you have to put in to make it "sound right." For example, if you were to pronounce **fail** as [fal], the sound is too abbreviated for the American ear— we need to hear the full [fayəl].

第二种办法是在L前和L后各加上一个非重读央元音。把所有这样的词放在台阶示意图上以后，你就会知道为了"发对音"，你需要额外加多少个音。例如，如果你把fail发成[fal]，对美国人来说这个音太过简略了——我们需要听到完整的[fayəl]。

Exercise 8-4: Final L with Schwas   Track 103

Listen and repeat. Do not round your lips for a final L.

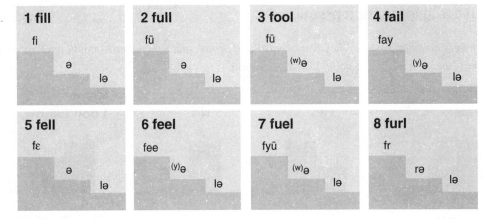

Exercise 8-5: Comparing L with T, D, and N Sounds

For this exercise, concentrate on the different ways in which the air comes out of the mouth when producing L, T, D, and N sounds. Look at the drawings to see the correct position of the tongue.

T/D
Plosive 爆破音
A puff of air comes out over the tip of the tongue. The tongue is somewhat tense.
一股气流从舌尖上冲出。舌头有点紧张。

228

N
Nasal 鼻音

Air comes out through the nose.
The tongue is completely relaxed.
气流从鼻子里出来。舌头完全放松。

L
Lateral 边音

Air flows around the sides of the tongue. The tongue is very tense.
The lips are *not* rounded!
气流在舌头两边流动。舌头非常紧张。
双唇不要张圆！

Exercise 8-6: L Combos   Track 104

Don't think about spelling. Listen and repeat.

	ərᵊl	äl	εl	il	ol	eel
1.	Earl	all	ell	ill	old	eel
2.	curl	call	kell	kill	cold	keel
3.	hurl	hall	hell	hill	hole	heel
4.	pearl	Paul	pell	pill	pole	peel
5.	world	wall	well	will		we're
6.	furl	fall	fell	fill	foal	fear
7.		shawl	shell	shill	shoal	shear
8.		tall	tell	till	told	tear
9.		stall	stellar	still	stole	steer

The Invisible R
隐形的R

The trouble with R is that you can't see it from the outside. With other sounds, such as B, P, or M, you can see when people put their lips together, but with R, everything takes place back down in the throat. It's hard to tell what the tongue is doing. It's especially important if you're used to making an R by touching your tongue to the ridge behind your teeth. So, what *should* your tongue be doing? To help you understand the correct tongue movements in pronouncing the R, use your hand.

发R这个音的难点在于你从外面看不到它。当人们发其他音的时候，比如B，P或M，你可以看到人们会把嘴唇碰到一起，但发R的时候，所有动作都是从喉咙发出的。我们很难说清楚舌头做了什么。如果你在发R这个音时习惯把舌头抵住牙齿后面的牙槽嵴，那这一点就更为重要了。那么，舌头应该做什么动作呢？为了帮你理解发R音时舌头的正确动作，要用一下你的手。

1. Hold your hand out flat, with the palm up, slightly dropping the back end of it. That's basically the position your tongue is in when you say **ah** [ä], so your flat hand will represent this sound.

   把你的手伸出来、放平，手掌向上，手腕稍微向下倾。基本上那就是你发ah[ä]时舌头的位置，所以这个手势就代表了这个音。

2. Now, to go from **ah** to **er**, take your fingers and curl them up slightly. Again, your tongue should follow that action. The sides of your tongue should come up a bit, too. When the air passes over that hollow in the middle of your tongue （look at the palm of your hand）, that's what creates the **er** sound.

   现在，我们要从ah音过渡到er音，这时要稍微弯曲一下手指。同样，你的舌头也要跟着做同样的动作。舌头的两侧也应该隆起来一点。当气流从你舌头中间的凹槽通过时（看着你的手掌），er这个音就发出来了。

Try it using both your hand and tongue simultaneously. Say **ah**, with your throat open （and your hand flat）, then curl your tongue up （and your fingers） and say **errr**. The tip of the tongue should be aimed at a middle position in the mouth, but never touching, and your throat should relax and expand. R, like L, has a slight schwa in it. This is what pulls the **er** down so far back in your throat.

请同时用你的手和舌头试试看。发ah的时候，把喉咙打开（手放平），然后把舌头卷起来（手指也一样）发errr音。舌尖应该指向口腔内的中间位置，但不要发生触碰，同时你的喉咙应该放松并延展。R和L一样，里面都有一个非重读央元音。这就是为什么发er这个音的时候，会被拉得很靠后。

| Exercise 8-7: R Combos | | | | | Track 105 |

Don't think about spelling. Listen and repeat.

	ər	är	ɛr	or	eer	æwr
1.	earn	art	air	or	ear	hour
2.	heard	hard	hair	horse	here	how're
3.	pert	part	pair	pour	peer	power
4.	word		where	war	we're	
5.	first	far	fair	four	fear	flower
6.	rather	cathartic	there	Thor	theory	11th hour
7.	sure	sharp	share	shore	shear	shower
8.	churn	char	chair	chore	cheer	chowder
9.	turn	tar	tear	tore	tear	tower
10.	stir	star	stair	store	steer	

Complex Intonation
综合语调

| Exercise 8-8: Descriptions and Compound Nouns | Track 106 |

To review, an adjective and noun make a description, and the second word is stressed. Two nouns make a compound noun, and the first word is stressed. Listen and repeat.

Description	Compound Noun
la **la**	**la** la
1. an old **house**	a **light**house
2. a famous **school**	a **dog** trainer
3. a good **game**	a **ball** game
4. a popular **show**	a **talk** show
5. a new **factory**	a **peanut** factory

Three-Word Phrases
三个词的短语

Exercise 8-9: Modifying Descriptions   Track 107

*When you modify a **descriptive phrase** by adding an adjective or adverb, keep the original intonation pattern and add another stress point. Listen and repeat.*

Description	Modified Description
la **la**	**la** la **la**
1. an old **house**	a **really** old **house**
2. a famous **school**	a **world**-famous **school**
3. a good **game**	a **pretty** good **game**
4. a popular **show**	a **wildly** popular **show**
5. a new **factory**	a **brand**-new **factory**

Exercise 8-10: Modifying Compounds   Track 108

*When you modify a **compound noun**, keep the same pattern, leaving the new adjective unstressed. Listen and repeat.*

Compound Noun	Modified Compound Noun
la la	la **la** la
1. a **light**house	an old **light**house
2. a **dog** trainer	a famous **dog** trainer
3. a **ball** game	a good **ball** game
4. a **talk** show	a popular **talk** show
5. a **peanut** factory	a new **peanut** factory

Exercise 8-11: Three-Word Compound Nouns   Track 109

*The next step is to combine **three things**:* Light + house + keeper. *Leave the stress on the first word:* **light**house keeper. *Although you are now using three words, they still mean **one new thing**. Listen and repeat.*

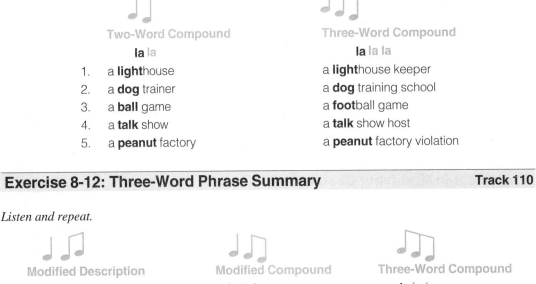

Two-Word Compound
la la

1. a **light**house
2. a **dog** trainer
3. a **ball** game
4. a **talk** show
5. a **peanut** factory

Three-Word Compound
la la la

a **light**house keeper
a **dog** training school
a **foot**ball game
a **talk** show host
a **peanut** factory violation

Exercise 8-12: Three-Word Phrase Summary   Track 110

Listen and repeat.

Modified Description
la la **la**

1. a **really** old **house**
2. a **world**-famous **school**
3. a **pretty** good **game**
4. a **wildly** popular **show**
5. a **brand**-new **factory**

Modified Compound
la **la** la

an old **light**house
a famous **dog** trainer
a good **ball** game
a popular **talk** show
a new **peanut** factory

Three-Word Compound
la la la

a **light**house keeper
a **dog** training school
a **foot**ball game
a **talk** show host
a **peanut** factory violation

Four-Word Phrases
四个词的短语

Exercise 8-13: Multiple Modifiers with Compound Nouns   Track 111

When you continue to modify a compound noun, keep the original intonation pattern and add another stress point. Listen and repeat.

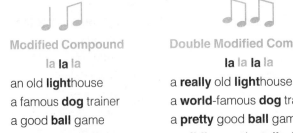

Modified Compound
la **la** la

1. an old **light**house
2. a famous **dog** trainer
3. a good **ball** game
4. a popular **talk** show
5. a new **peanut** factory

Double Modified Compound
la la **la** la

a **really** old **light**house
a **world**-famous **dog** trainer
a **pretty** good **ball** game
a **wildly** popular **talk** show
a **brand**-new **peanut** factory

Exercise 8-14: Modifying Three-Word Compound Nouns   Track 112

When you continue to modify a set phrase, you maintain the original intonation pattern and simply add an unstressed modifier.

| **Three-Word Compound** | **Modified Three-Word Compound** |
| **la la la** | **la la la la** |

1. a **light**house keeper   an old **light**house keeper
2. a **dog**-training school   a famous **dog**-training school
3. a **foot**ball game   a good **foot**ball game
4. a **talk** show host   a famous **talk** show host
5. a **peanut** factory violation a new **peanut** factory violation

Exercise 8-15: Building Up to Five-Word Phrases   Track 113

Listen and repeat.

1. It's a **pot**.   *noun*
2. It's **new**.   *adjective*
3. It's a new **pot**.   *description (noun)*
4. It's brand **new**.   *description (adjective)*
5. It's a **brand**-new **pot**.   *modified description*
6. It's a **tea**pot.   *two-word compound*
7. It's a new **tea**pot.   *modified compound*
8. It's a **brand**-new **tea**pot.   *modified compound*
9. It's a **tea**pot lid.   *three-word compound*
10. It's a new **tea**pot lid.   *modified three-word compound*
11. It's a **brand**-new **tea**pot lid.   *modified three-word compound*

1. It's a **house**.   It's a **school**.
2. It's **old**.   It's **famous**.
3. It's an old **house**.   It's a famous **school**.
4. It's really **old**.   It's world-**famous**.
5. It's a **really** old **house**.   It's a **world**-famous **school**.
6. It's a **light**house.   He's a **dog** trainer.
7. It's an old **light**house.   He's a famous **dog** trainer.
8. It's a **really** old **light**house.   He's a **world**-famous **dog** trainer.
9. He's a **light**house keeper.   It's a **dog**-training school.
10. He's an old **light**house keeper.   It's a famous **dog**-training school.
11. He's a **really** old **light**house keeper. It's a **world**-famous **dog**-training school.

1. It's a **game**.   It's a **show**.
2. It's **good**.   It's **popular**.

3. It's a good **game**.	It's a popular **show**.
4. It's really **good**.	It's really **popular**.
5. It's a **really** good **game**.	It's a **wildly** popular **show**.
6. It's a **ball** game.	It's a **talk** show.
7. It's a good **ball** game.	It's a popular **talk** show.
8. It's a **pretty** good **ball** game.	It's a **wildly** popular **talk** show.
9. It's a **foot**ball game.	She's a **talk** show host.
10. It's a good **foot**ball game.	She's a popular **talk** show host.
11. It's a **pretty** good **foot**ball game.	She's a **wildly** popular **talk** show host.

Exercise 8-16: Intonation of Numbers   Track 114

In short phrases （such as #1 and #2 below）, -teen can be thought of as a separate word in terms of intonation. In longer phrases, the number + -teen becomes one word. Listen and repeat.

1. How **old** is he?	2. How long has it **been**?	3. How **old** is he?
He's four**teen**. [for**téen**]	**Four**teen **years**.	He's **four**teen years **old**.
He's **for**ty. [**fór**dy]	Forty **years**.	He's **for**ty years **old**.

How Long, How Well, How Far, How Big

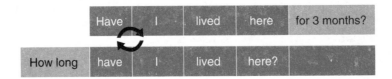

Let's use several **how** questions. They explain *extent*, *duration*, and *dimension*. Between **what** and **how** questions, there are some word-order changes that are important to notice and master.

　　我们来练习使用以how开头的疑问句。它们说明了事物的范围、持续时间，以及维度。在以what和how开头的疑问句之间有一些重要的词序变化需要注意并掌握。

What is the **distance**?	How **far** is it?
What is the **age**?	How **old** is it?
What is the **price**?	How **much** is it? How much does it cost?
What is the **frequency**?	How **often**? How frequently?
What is the **quantity**?（uncountable）	How **much**?
What is the **quantity**?（countable）	How **many**?
What is the **duration**?	How **long** is it? How long does it last?
What is the **length**?	How **long** is it?
What is the **width**?	How **wide** is it?
What is the **height**?	How **tall** is it?
What is the **thickness**?	How **thick** is it?

How? When? Where? How Often? How Much?

How do I do it?	**When** do I do it?	**How often** do I do it?
I do it **quickly**.	I do it **every day**.	I **always** do it.
I do it **rudely**.	I do it **all of the time**.	I **almost always** do it.
I do it **easily**.	I've **already** done it.	I **usually** do it.
I do it **suddenly**.	I'm doing it **right now**.	I **frequently** do it.
I do it **early**.	I'm doing it **at this time**.	I **generally** do it.
I do it **well**.	I'll do it **later**.	I **often** do it.
I do it **quite well**.	I'll do it **later today**.	I **don't often** do it.
I do it **extremely well**.	I'll do it **then**.	I **hardly ever** do it.
I do it **so well**.	I'll do it **right then**.	I **rarely** do it.
I do it **too well!**	I'll do it **again**.	I **never** do it.
I do it **well enough**.	I'll do it **first**.	I haven't **ever** done it.
I do **such** a good job.	I did it **last**.	I'm **not** doing it.
I do it **much better**.	I'll do it **next**.	I **don't** do it.
I do it **too much**.	I'm only doing it **once**.	
I do it **too many times**.	I haven't done it **lately**.	**How much** do I do it? (degree)
I do it **often**.	I've done it **recently**.	I **definitely** do it.
I do it **too often**.	I'll do it **when I can**.	I **obviously** do it.
I don't do it **often enough**.	I do it **every so often**.	I **absolutely** insist on doing it.
I do it **right**.	I do it **every once in a while**.	I **totally** forgot to do it.
I do it **just right**.	**Where** do I do it?	I **completely** understand how to do it.
I do it **perfectly**.	I do it **here**.	I don't **exactly** know how to do it.
I do it **alone**.	I do it **there**.	I'll **probably** do it.
I **just** do it.	I do it **everywhere**.	I **barely** do it.

Exercise 8-17: *How* + Adjective

*Convert each statement to a **how** question. Then check the Answer Key.*

	The book is 300 pages long.	How long is it?
1.	That tree is as wide as a building.	
2.	The car weighs two tons.	
3.	The notebook has 10 pages.	
4.	This chair is fairly old.	
5.	That painting is a million dollars.	
6.	I brush my hair every morning.	
7.	She ate three ice cream sandwiches.	
8.	She ate so much ice cream!	
9.	This building is 10 stories tall.	
10.	That meeting was four hours long.	

As you've seen, there is a relationship between certain adjectives and the noun form (How **long** is it? What is the **length**?). The next step is to include the verb form. You can do this by adding **-en** to the noun (**lengthen**).

正如你看到的那样，某些形容词和其名词形式之间是有关联的(How **long** is it? What is the **length**?)。下一步就是把动词形式也加进来。只要在名词后面加上-en，你就可以得到动词(lengthen)了。

Exercise 8-18: Nouns to Verbs

Convert each statement from the -en verb to **make** *and an* **adjective**. *Then check the Answer Key.*

We need to shorten this report.	**We need to make this report shorter.**
1. Lengthen this dress.	
2. It weakened the system.	
3. We need to strengthen our industries.	
4. Could you tighten this knot?	
5. I need to loosen my tie.	
6. It only deepened my love for them.	
7. It will heighten the suspense.	
8. We hope it will lessen the damage.	
9. Let's try to broaden its appeal.	
10. Try to widen the gap between them.	
11. You should thicken the sauce a little.	
12. This lamp will brighten the room.	
13. Use this to whiten your teeth.	
14. Could you darken the room, please?	
15. The farmer fattened the turkey.	

Let's review the relationships between nouns, verbs, and adjectives. As you know, a noun is a person, place, thing, or idea. Verbs are action words. Adjectives modify nouns. The adjective endings are -y, -ed, -able, -ible, -al, -ful, -ic, -ive, -less, -ous, -ent, -ant, etc.

我们来复习一下名词、动词和形容词之间的关系。正如你所知道的，名词可以表示人、地点、事物或想法。动词是表示动作的词。形容词用来修饰名词。形容词的结尾有-y, -ed, -able, -ible, -al, -ful, -ic, -ive, -less, -ous, -ent, -ant等等。

	Noun	Adjective	Verb
1.	It's a **cloud**.	It's **cloud**y.	It clouded our **judg**ment.
2.	It's an a**chiev**ement.	It's a**chiev**able.	We a**chie**ved it.
3.	It gave us a big **scare**.	It's **scary**.	It **scared** us.
4.	It has great **beauty**.	It's **beau**tiful.	She beautified the **garden**.
5.	It's an at**trac**tion.	It's at**trac**tive.	Honey at**tracts** flies.
6.	We took **care**.	He's **care**ful / **care**less.	We **cared** for them.
7.	He has a **book**.	He's **book**ish.	He **booked** a flight.
8.	We had no **in**terest in it.	It was **in**teresting.	The book **in**terested us.
9.	She has **con**fidence.	She is **con**fident.	She con**fid**ed in us.

236

10. We have **power**.	We are **power**ful.	The sun **powers** our lights.
11. There was con**fu**sion.	I'm con**fu**sed.	It con**fu**sed us.
12. It's an ani**ma**tion.	It was **an**imated.	Let's **an**imate this a little.
13. We were in **awe**.	It was **awe**some / **aw**ful!	I was awed by the **sight**.
14. It's absolute per**fec**tion.	It was **per**fect.	We want to per**fect** this.
15. It's an a**nal**ysis.	He is ana**ly**tic.	Let's **an**alyze this.
16. What's the **diff**erence?	How is it **diff**erent?	It **diff**ers from the others.
17. Do you have any ad**vice**?	It was ad**vi**sory.	We ad**vise** you not to do it.
18. He has no **wo**rries.	He was not **wo**rried.	It didn't **wo**rry him.
19. We did it with great **ease**.	It was **easy**.	He **eased** into it.
20. It's a bi**o**graphy.	It's bio**graph**ical.	I wrote a bi**o**graphy.
21. It was an an**noy**ance.	It was an**noy**ing.	He an**noy**ed us.
	He was an**noy**ed.	It an**noy**ed him.
22. It's an **im**age / **im**agery.	It's im**ag**inary.	I can't im**ag**ine such a thing.
He has no imagi**na**tion.	He's im**ag**inative.	

Prepositions
介词

To is the most commonly used preposition. It's usually pronounced **tə** or **də**.
To是使用得最为普遍的介词。它的发音通常是tə或də。

We first saw prepositions of *location* in Chapter 2, prepositions of *direction* in Chapter 3, and prepositions of ***manner*** and ***time*** in Chapter 4. We have seen phrasal verbs in every chapter, including **get**, **take**, **put**, **stand**, **give**, and **turn**. We have worked with the infinitive in the high-frequency phrases **want to do**, **like to do**, **have to do**, **need to do**, **try to do**, **hope to do**, and **plan to do**.

我们分别首次在第二章学习了方位介词，在第三章学习了方向介词，在第四章学习了方式和时间介词。在每一章我们还学习了短语动词，其中包括get、take、put、stand、give和turn。我们还学习了高频短语中的不定式，如want to do、like to do、have to do、need to do、try to do、hope to do和plan to do。

add to	Just **add** water **to** this mix!
adjust to	We can't **adjust to** daylight savings time.
agree to	They **agreed to** work on it a little more.
apologize to	Everyone **apologized to** the mayor.
be up to	I don't think he'**s up to** the job!
belong to	Does this glove **belong to** you?
get around to	I hope to **get around to** it before long.
get back to	It's time to **get back to** work.
get through to	We couldn't **get through to** him on his cell phone.
get used to	It was hard to **get used to** the cold weather.
happen to	Do you know what **happened to** the car?
introduce to	I'd like to **introduce** you **to** my cousin.
invite someone to	Let's **invite** Susie **to** the party.

lead to	I'm afraid that it will **lead to** more trouble.
listen to	I try not to **listen to** talk radio in the car.
look forward to	We **look forward to** hearing back from you.
object to	I think he **objected to** the general idea, not the specifics.
occur to	It didn't **occur to** him that the others would mind.
prefer A to B	Children generally **prefer** candy **to** vegetables.
refer to	What do you think he was **referring to**?
relate to	It's hard to **relate to** people who are so completely different.
stick to	He's trying to **stick to** his diet.
talk to	Who were you **talking to**?

Note: **I prefer** A **to** B is the same as **I like** A **better than** B, but it's a bit more formal.

注意：**I prefer** A **to** B和**I like** A **better than** B是一样的，但前者更加正式。

Exercise 8-19: *To*

Fill in the blanks with the words listed below. Then check the Answer Key.

I'd like to ~~talk~~ you to my cousin, and *invite* you to our company party. If you *agree* to do this, you'll be able to *introduce* to a lot of fun people. If you *happen* be busy that day, let me know. I'm having trouble *getting used* to your new schedule! Anyway, I *look forward* to seeing you there!

happen	invite	agree	~~talk~~
getting used	introduce	~~look forward~~	

For

For is also very commonly used in verb + preposition phrases. It's pronounced **fer**.

介词for 在"动词+介词"的短语中也很常用。它发fer的音。

apologize for	I'd like to **apologize for** my outburst.
apply for	He's **applying for** a new job today.
ask for	What did you **ask for**?
blame someone for	Why did they **blame** him **for** their mistake?
forgive someone for	We need to **forgive** him **for** being so rude.
have a reason for	Do you **have a good reason for** doing that?
keep for	Let's **keep** this **for** later.
listen for	I think they're **listening for** their cue.
look for	What are you **looking for**?
pay for	We have to **pay for** the new supplies one way or another.
prepare for	Nobody was **prepared for** the attack.
provide for	The contract **provides for** all services.
search for	They **searched for** hours, but couldn't find it.
send for	The president **sent for** the ambassador.
substitute for	Margarine is a good **substitute for** butter.

thank someone for	I'd like to **thank** you **for** your support.
vote for	Who did you **vote for**?
wait for	What are you **waiting for**?
wish for	Don't **wish for** the impossible.
work for	They **worked for** that company for 30 years.

Exercise 8-20: *For*

Fill in the blanks with the words listed below. Then check the Answer Key.

Could I ____ you for a favor? I ____ for the inconvenience, but I have a good ____ for asking. I'm ____ for a new apartment and I can't ____ for the real estate agent. I ____ for three apartments, but I wasn't able to get any of them. I wasn't ____ for this, and I'm starting a new job on Monday, so I really hope this ____ for me!

ask	looking	wait	applied
reason	works out	apologize	prepared

Of + About

accuse someone of	Are you **accusing** him **of** lying?
become of	Whatever **became of** Joe Smith?
consist of	The training **consists of** two main parts.
dream of	I **dream of** joining the Peace Corps.
get rid of	Let's **get rid of** these old magazines.
hear of	I've never **heard of** such a thing!
remind someone of	You really **remind** me **of** my sister.
suspect someone of	I **suspect** him **of** taking my notebook.
take advantage of	The bank **took advantage of** the farmer.
take care of	We **took care of** our mother for years.
think of	I can't **think of** anything else. Can you?
argue about	What are they **arguing about** this time?
complain about	Stop **complaining about** everything!
dream about	I **dream about** living in France.
forget about	Don't **forget about** the report that's due.
hear about	Have you **heard about** Bob's new job?
learn about	When did you **learn about** it?
see about	Well, let's **see about** that!
think about	I **think about** it all of the time.
wonder about	We **wonder about** his competence.
worry about	Actually, we **worry about** it a lot.

Of and **about** can be similar.
Remind someone **of** / remind someone **about**
Dream **of** / dream **about**

Hear **of** / hear **about**
Think **of** / think **about**
Learn **of** / learn **about**

Exercise 8-21: *Of* and *About*

Fill in the blanks with the words listed below. Then check the Answer Key.

1. Did you ____ about what happened last week?
2. They ____ your brother of taking someone's wallet!
3. They said he ____ of it, but kept the money. What was he ____ of?
4. It's all we can ____ about! I wonder what will ____ of him.

hear	**talk**	**got rid**
thinking	**accused**	**become**

On

agree on	Let's **agree on** one thing, OK?
blame something on	Don't try to **blame** that **on** me!
comment on	No one **commented on** the lack of documentation.
compliment someone on	He **complimented** her **on** her excellent work.
congratulate someone on	She **congratulated** him **on** his promotion.
concentrate on	It's hard to **concentrate on** this when it's so noisy.
decide on	We couldn't **decide on** the best way to do it.
depend on	I really **depend on** my support staff.
insist on	He **insisted on** doing it his way.
keep on	Let's **keep** the pressure **on** the competition.
rely on / depend on	Don't **rely on / depend on** him. He'll always let you down.
spend money on	Don't **spend money on** useless junk.
spend time on	You have **spent** a lot of **time on** that project.
waste money on	We **wasted** a lot of **money on** technical issues.
waste time on	It's a shame to **waste time on** meaningless things.

Exercise 8-22: *On*

Fill in the blanks with the words listed below. Then check the Answer Key.

I'd like to ____ you on your recent promotion. I hear that the bosses ____ on you for the position at the last meeting. As a matter of fact, the CEO ____ on your being selected, and said that future contracts depended on your continued involvement, and that you need to ____ on the big projects. They really ____ on you!

insisted   congratulate   decided   concentrate   rely

With

agree with someone	I couldn't **agree with** you more! I **agree with** you 100%.
argue with someone	Never **argue with** a crazy person.
catch up with	Try to **catch up with** the rest of the group, OK?
communicate with	I've tried, but I just can't **communicate with** him.
compare with	It's a great deal if you **compare** it **with** the others.
deal with	You'll just have to **deal with** it on your own.
get along with	He's very hard to **get along with**.
have patience with	Try to **have patience with** him.

Exercise 8-23: *With*

*Fill in the blanks with **communicating**, **get along**, **agree**, **patience**, **argue**, or **deal**. Then check the Answer Key.*

Have you noticed that the new chef doesn't ____ with the rest of the staff? I think he has a problem ____ with others. Whether you ____ with a person or not, you don't have to ____ with them. He needs to have more ____ with everyone and ____ with them as individuals.

From

borrow from	Could I **borrow** a dollar **from** you? Could you lend me a dollar?
come from	So, where do you **come from**, originally?
get back from	When did you **get back from** Scotland?
keep something from	We can't **keep** this **from** management any longer.
prevent from	You have to **prevent** him **from** making more mistakes.
protect from	You have to **protect** the lawn **from** the freezing weather.
recover from	It's hard to **recover from** such a disaster.
separate from	Let's consider this **separate from** the other issues.
stop from	**Stop** him **from** doing that again!
subtract from	**Subtract** that **from** the total, and add it to the balance.

Exercise 8-24: *From*

*Fill in the blanks with **get back**, **prevent**, **stop**, **recovered**, or **keeping**. Then check the Answer Key.*

So, when did you ____ from your vacation? I hear you had a pretty bad cold at the beginning. Have you ____ from it? It's hard to ____ yourself from getting sick, but it helps to wash your hands a lot. With children, you need to ____ them from touching their faces. Hey, are you still under the weather? Are you ____ something from me?

Exercise 8-25: Preposition Review

*Fill in the blank with **to**, **for**, **of**, **on**, **with**, **about**, **at**, **in**, **out**, **than**, **up**, or **from**. Then check the Answer Key.*

1. Let's agree _____ disagree.
2. You get what you pay _____ .
3. We just have to deal _____ this and move on.
4. He really needs to work _____ his presentation skills.
5. What are you talking _____ ?
6. Where did that come _____ ?
7. We should take care _____ that problem quickly.
8. It took a while to get used _____ his style.
9. Let's take advantage _____ the situation right away.
10. Could you ask the manager _____ a recommendation?
11. This saddle used to belong _____ Roy Rogers.
12. We've got to prepare _____ all possibilities.
13. We've got to get ready _____ he party.
14. We're looking forward _____ seeing how well he does.
15. Try comparing these results _____ the monthly ones.
16. What are you so worried _____ ?
17. In order to recover _____ the shock, she had to take a long walk.
18. It's not realistic to object _____ starting this project.
19. It's important to get along _____ one's colleagues and co-workers.
20. I happen _____ think that it wasn't an accident.
21. Don't try _____ prevent them from trying new things.
22. Let's think _____ it before making a decision.
23. They prefer actions _____ meetings.
24. I've been searching _____ this file for three days now.
25. You need to talk _____ your friends before making a decision.
26. Not many people agree _____ the last administration.
27. I think we should apply _____ a government grant.
28. It could happen _____ anyone!
29. Let's take care _____ this, once and for all.
30. It's natural to worry _____ the future.
31. I'm sorry to have been late _____ responding.
32. We can't rely _____ him any more.
33. We have to depend _____ them for information.
34. They had to start over due _____ his interference.
35. According _____ the news, the house burned to the ground.
36. Don't leave _____ the most important information!
37. I prefer _____ do it this way.
38. It's hard to deal _____ his mood swings.
39. What do you think _____ this?

242

40. Based   our calculations, we need to order more.
41. She simply didn't agree   his conclusions.
42. We hope to agree   the terms of the contract later this week.
43. He agreed   work harder.
44. Thank you so much   helping us with this.
45. Please take care   this immediately.
46. She forgot   lock the door again.
47. Do you believe   ghosts?
48. We have to get rid   all the old furniture.
49. They have been very kind   me.
50. I'm not good   fixing things.
51. Sugar is not good   you.
52. Look   the picture.
53. Look   the mirror.
54. We are very proud   how well you have done.
55. Are you scared   the dark?
56. A friend of mine called   invite me to the party.
57. I would like   invite you to my house for dinner.
58. The new one is different   the old one.
59. This one is better   the other one.
60. It is similar   the original version.
61. We have to fill   a lot of forms to see a doctor.
62. Please fill   this section of the form.
63. The room filled   quickly.
64. Have you ever heard   Michelangelo?
65. Have you heard   the accident?
66. I was   to leave.
67. We saw our friends   the concert.
68. They were   the front row.
69. We hope to see you   Saturday.
70. We hope to see you   5:00.
71. We hope to see you   the summer.
72. We hope to see you   June.
73. We hope to see you   Saturday afternoon.
74. We hope to see you   the afternoon.
75. We hope to see you   your birthday.
76. We hope to see you   your birthday party.
77. We hope to see you   the weekend.
78. We hope to see you   Los Angeles.
79. We met him   the way to the store.
80. We hope he doesn't get   the way this time.
81.   the way, they already know.
82. We wanted to go, but   the end, we decided to stay home.

83. The movie was good, but _____ the end, the dog died, so we were sad.
84. We decided _____ see it later.
85. We decided _____ the red one.
86. If you're upset, do something _____ it.
87. Come _____ lunch with us.
88. We just came _____ lunch.
89. I'm _____ my lunch break.
90. What are you having _____ lunch?
91. Come _____ us to lunch.
92. He pointed _____ each of the differences.
93. He pointed _____ the exit.
94. Give it _____ me!
95. We weren't sure he'd show _____ .
96. They were making fun _____ us.
97. If you don't know, look it _____ .
98. It's close _____ being done.
99. Make _____ your mind!
100. Could you drop me off _____ the corner?

Here, we will learn the *past unreal duo* and the *causative* (**let**, **have**, **get**, **make**, **force**, **allow**, **permit**, **persuade**, **convince**).

这里我们要学习过去非真实双重时态和使役动词（let、have、get、make、force、allow、permit、persuade、convince）。

Past Unreal Duo
过去非真实双重时态

	Past	Present	Future
Simple	I did it. ◄	I do it. ●	I will do it. ►
Duo	I had done A before I did B.	I have done A before now.	I will have done A by the time I do B.
Unreal Duo	If I had done A, I would have done B. ◄◄	If I did A, I would do B. ●●	If I do A, I will do B. ►►

Looking at the verb map, you see three things: First, this is the *past*; second, there are *two* events; third, the events *didn't actually happen* (the symbols are white).

看过动词地图后，你会发现三点：第一，这是过去时；第二，有两件事情；第三，事情实际上并没有发生（符号是白色的）。

Fact He weighed 350 pounds. He became a sumo wrestler in Japan.

Unreal If he **had weighed** 350 pounds, he **would have** become a sumo wrestler.

But he didn't.

He was quite small, so he just wrestled with his conscience.

244

Fact   They **knew** all the answers. They **taught** the world.

Unreal   If they **had known** all the answers, they **would have** taught the world.

But they didn't.

So, they just tried to do what was right.

Exercise 8-26: Past Unreal Duo — Main Verbs

Rewrite the sentences, changing from the real past to the past unreal duo. Then check the Answer Key.

She studied hard. She succeeded.

If she had studied hard, she would have succeeded.

1.   You liked to ski. You went as often as possible.

2.   I told you. You didn't remember.

3.   We practiced every day. We got better.

4.   He ate too much. He was overweight.

5.   I studied every day. I spoke English well.

6.   They talked too much. They got in trouble.

7.   It worked well. We used it every day.

8.   They paid attention. They understood.

9.   Everyone knew how to do it. We did not need the instruction manual.

10. It made us mad. We complained about it.

Exercise 8-27: Past Unreal Duo—Pronunciation   Track 115

Listen to the following and repeat five times.

1.   If yood lykt to ski, youdə gänə zäffə nəz pässəbəl.
2.   Ifyd tol joo, you wüdn nə r'membrd.
3.   If weed præctist evry day, weedə gättn bedder.
4.   Ifee deetn too much, heedə bin overweight.
5.   Ifyd stədied evry day, I wüdə spokən English well.
6.   If theyd talkt too much, they wüdə gättn in trouble.
7.   Ifid wrrkt well, weedə yooz dit every day.
8.   If theyd pay dəttention, they wüdə vənderstood.
9.   Ifevry one had known howdə do it, we wüdn needəd the instruction manual.
10. Ifid made us mad, we wüdəv complain da boudit.

Exercise 8-28: That's a Big If!

Select the proper form of the unreal duo — past, present, or future. Then check the Answer Key.

1. If he had had a bike, he _____ it.
   Did he have a bike? No.
   - ☐ will ride
   - ☐ would ride
   - ☐ would have ridden

2. If he has a bike, he _____ it.
   Will he have a bike? Maybe, maybe not.
   - ☐ will ride
   - ☐ would ride
   - ☐ would have ridden

3. If he had a bike, he _____ it.
   Does he have a bike? No.
   - ☐ will ride
   - ☐ would ride
   - ☐ would have ridden

4. If you _____ on time, we won't be late.
   - ☐ are ready
   - ☐ were ready
   - ☐ had been ready

5. If you _____ on time, we wouldn't be late.
   - ☐ are ready
   - ☐ were ready
   - ☐ had been ready

6. If you _____ on time, we wouldn't have been late.
   - ☐ are ready
   - ☐ were ready
   - ☐ had been ready

7. _____ if they got what they wanted.
   - ☐ They'll be happy
   - ☐ They'd be happy
   - ☐ They'd have been happy

8. _____ if they'd gotten what they wanted.
   - ☐ They'll be happy
   - ☐ They'd be happy
   - ☐ They'd have been happy

9. _____ if they get what they want.
   - ☐ They'll be happy
   - ☐ They'd be happy
   - ☐ They'd have been happy

10. If I _____ you, I'd think it over.
    - ☐ am
    - ☐ are
    - ☐ were
    - ☐ would be

Causative Verb Map
使役动词地图

	Past	Present	Future
Simple	I had him do it. ◄	I have him do it. ●	I will have him do it. ►
Duo	I'd had him do A before he did B. ◄ ◄	I've had him do it. ◄ ●	I'll have had him do A before he does B. ► ►
Unreal Duo	If I'd had him do A, I'd have had him do B. ◄ ◄	If I had him do A, I'd have had him do B. ● ●	If I have him do A, I'll have him do B. ► ►

246

A caused B to happen: A wants it to happen, but B doesn't necessarily want to do it.

A引起B的发生：A希望它可以发生，但B不一定想要它发生。

> The teacher **had** the students study.
>
> The teacher **made** the students study.
>
> The teacher **got** the students **to** study by promising them good grades.
>
> The teacher **forced** the students **to** study.
>
> The teacher **caused** the students **to** study.

A allowed B to happen: B wants to do it and A gives permission.

A许可B的发生：B希望它可以发生，而A给了B许可。

> The teacher **let** the students take a break.
>
> The teacher **allowed** the students **to** take a break.
>
> The teacher **permitted** the students **to** take a break.

Exercise 8-29: Giving Permission

*Change to **let**, **allow**, and **permit**. Then check the Answer Key.*

He wants to go to the beach. She says OK.

She lets	him go to the beach.
She allows	
She permits	

I would like to think about it. He says OK.

He lets	
He allows	
He permits	

We need to try again. They said OK.

They let	
They allow	
They permit	

Exercise 8-30: Causing an Action

*Change to **have**, **make**, and **get**. Then check the Answer Key.*

We want them to come back later.

We have	them come back later.
We make	
We get	

They wanted him to change the settings.

They had	
They made	
They got	

She needed us to work on it.

She had

She made

She got

Causative: Something Causes Something
使役：某事引起某事的发生

It has to do with:

它与下面两点有关：

1) Who **wants** something

2) Who is in **charge**

The causative is the intersection of power and desire.

使役是权力和欲望的交汇点。

Giving Permission

给予许可

let

permit ____ to do (formal)

allow ____ to do (formal)

give someone permission to do something

Causing an Action

引发行动

have (routine situation)

get ____ to do (persuasion)

talk someone into doing

persuade someone to do

convince someone to do

compel someone to

make (a little force)

force ____ to do (strong)

Let

Let's start with **let**. In this case, the boss is in charge and Ben wants to do something. Ben says to his boss, "Joe, can I leave early today?" The boss says, "Yes."

我们先从let开始讲。在这个例子中，老板是管事的，而Ben想做点事情。Ben对他的老板说："Joe，我今天可以早点下班吗？"老板说："可以。"

The boss **gives** Ben **permission to** leave early.

The boss **lets** Ben leave early.

The boss **allows** Ben **to** leave early.

The boss **permits** Ben **to** leave early.

Have

Ben's hair is too long and his car is dirty. He goes to the salon and says, "Pierre, please cut my hair." It is Pierre's job to cut people's hair. Pierre cuts Ben's hair. **Have** indicates a normal situation.

Ben的头发太长了，车太脏了。他去了美发店，然后说："Pierre，请给我剪一下头发。"Pierre的工作就是给人们剪头发。Pierre给Ben剪了头发。have表明这是个普通场景。

Ben **had** him cut his hair.

Ben took his car to the carwash to **have** them wash it.

Get

The next month, Ben went to the salon and Pierre was very, very busy. He said, "Sorry, Ben. There's no time for me to cut your hair today." Ben says, "I will give you an extra $10."

第二个月，Ben又去了美发店，但是Pierre特别忙。他说："对不起，Ben，我今天没有时间给你剪头发了。"Ben说："我可以多给你10美元。"

> Ben **gets** Pierre **to** cut his hair.
> Ben **talks** Pierre **into** cutting his hair.
> Ben **persuades** Pierre **to** cut his hair.
> Ben **convinces** Pierre **to** cut his hair.

Make

Ben's house was very dirty. His housekeeper was very lazy. Ben said, "Sam, clean the house now! " Sam said, "I'm tired. I don't want to clean the house." Ben said, "If you don't clean the house, you're fired."

Ben的房子很脏。他的管家很懒。Ben说："Sam，现在就打扫房间！"Sam说："我很累，我不想打扫房子。"Ben说："如果你不打扫房间，我就炒你鱿鱼。"

> Ben **made** Sam clean the house.

Make does not always indicate coercion. It can be used to intensify an action.
make并不总意味着强制，它也可用于强化动作。

The student **shortened** the report. The student **made** the report shorter.
The gardener **beautified** the garden. The gardener **made** the garden more beautiful.

Force

The prisoner didn't want to go back into his cell. The guards pushed him in.
犯人不愿意走回他的牢房。看守们把他推了进去。

> The guards **forced** the prisoner **to** go back into the cell.

Exercise 8-31: Causing an Action

*Change to the correct form of **let**, **have**, **make**, or **get**. Then check the Answer Key.*

Sam said to the teacher, "May I borrow this book?"
The teacher **let** Sam borrow the book.
Ed said to the barber, "Take a little off the sides, please."
Ed **had** the barber take a little off the sides.
The boss said, "Clean up this mess! "
The boss **made** us clean up the mess.

Betty said, "Bob, could you please help me with this? That would be great!"

Betty got Bob to help her.

1. Please meet us in Sacramento.

    We are ____ them meet us in Sacramento.

2. Take out the trash!

    I ____ him take out the trash.

3. I'd really appreciate it if you would take out the trash. I'll help you with your project!

    I ____ him to take out the trash.

4. Take out the trash, please.

    I ____ him take out the trash.

5. Please, please, please ask questions.

    I can't ____ you to ask questions.

6. Come in to work and I'll give you overtime pay.

    The boss tried to ____ the worker to come in to work.

7. Come in at 9:00.

    The boss ____ the worker come in at 9:00.

8. Come in at 9:00 or you're fired!

    The boss ____ the worker come in at 9:00.

9. Can I borrow this? Sure!

    My friend ____ me borrow it.

10. Go borrow some money from your parents, please.

    My friend ____ me borrow some money from my parents.

11. I'd really like it if you would make some delicious Thai curry.

    He ____ me to make Thai curry even though I was really busy.

12. Can we study on our own? No, you may not.

    The teacher didn't ____ us study on our own.

13. Empty your pockets!

    The police ____ us empty our pockets.

14. Do the dishes, please.

    My mom ____ me do the dishes.

15. I'd like everyone to sit down.

    Can I ____ everyone to sit down, please?

Let's review everything you have learned in Chapter 8. Make sure you get 100% on the test before going on to the next chapter. Check your work using the Answer Key.

我们来复习一下在第八章中学过的全部内容。只有当你在测试中获得满分以后，你才能接着学习下一章。请参照答案检查正误。

Part 1: *Fill in the appropriate preposition.*

1. We just can't get used ____ the time change this year.

2. Did they have a good reason ____ their actions?

3. What ever became ____ that box of old papers?
4. What on earth are they arguing ____?
5. Have you decided ____ a strategy?
6. Compared ____ the previous year, we are doing very well.
7. Where did this report come ____?
8. I hope you don't object ____ this schedule change.
9. We were simply not prepared ____ the demands of the job.
10. I'm not sure what you're referring ____.
11. I don't recall agreeing ____ those terms!
12. There is no substitute ____ good quality.
13. The new employee really reminds me ____ my cousin.
14. Well, we'll just have to see ____ that!
15. They insisted ____ doing it a particular way.
16. We just don't have time to deal ____ this right now!
17. I don't know if we'll ever recover ____ the shock.
18. Did you happen ____ find out who will be there?
19. We didn't think there was anything to apologize ____.
20. Many people prefer ____ skip breakfast.

Part 2: *Change each question to the standard* **how** *question.*

1. What is the **distance**?
2. What is the **age**?
3. What is the **price**?
4. What is the **frequency**?
5. What is the **quantity**? (uncountable)
6. What is the **quantity**? (countable)
7. What is the **duration**?
8. What is the **length**?
9. What is the **width**?
10. What is the **height**?
11. What is the **thickness**?

Part 3: *Fill in the proper form of the past, present, or future unreal duo.*

1. If he had thought of it, he ____ the e-mail.   **send**
2. If he thinks of it, he ____ the e-mail.   **send**
3. If he thought of it, he ____ the e-mail.   **send**
4. We would go to the beach if the weather ____ better. **be**
5. We would have gone to the beach if the weather ____ better. **be**
6. We will go to the beach if the weather ____ good.   **be**

Part 4: *Indicate if the following sentences are correct or not.*

1. This sentence is correct: **He has always permitted them to go.** ☐ True ☐ False
2. This sentence is correct: **He has usually let them to go.** ☐ True ☐ False

3. This sentence is correct: **He didn't want to make them to go.**   ☐ True ☐ False
4. This sentence is correct: **He has never allowed them to go.**   ☐ True ☐ False
5. This sentence is correct: **He can't force them to go.**   ☐ True ☐ False

Part 5: *Fill in the blank with the past real duo.*

1. He ____n't ____ the test before the bell rang.   **finish**
2. We ____n't ____ it was serious until the test results came back.   **think**
3. They ____ always ____ that cheaper was better.   **think**
4. She ____ always clearly ____ what the problem was.   **understand**
5. I ____n't ____ how much it meant to them.   **realize**

Part 6: *Rewrite the sentences, changing from the real past to the past unreal duo.*

1. You studied. You learned.

2. It was impossible. You stopped trying.

3. They showed me how to do it. It wasn't scary anymore.

Part 7: *Choose the proper verb form.*

1. Edward ____ to the bank yesterday.   **go**
2. Joe ____ English for three years now.   **speak**
3. The girls ____ English long before they came to the States.   **speak**
4. She ____ that she would support them in every way.   **always say**
5. We ____ about the problem for a month before it was officially reported.   **know**
6. They ____ really hard last year.   **study**

Part 8: *Convert each statement from the -en verb to **make** and an **adjective**.*

1. Could you shorten this essay?
2. Let's straighten this row.
3. She tried to loosen the knot.

ESSAY

Using what you have learned, write two paragraphs on the following topics:
利用你学过的知识写两段话，话题如下：

1. If you had to write a book, what would the subject be?
    如果你不得不写一本书，那你会写点什么？
2. Tell your favorite joke.
    讲一个你最喜欢的笑话。

You can handwrite your paragraphs below or e-mail them to **para@grammar.bz** to be stored. These paragraphs are not graded or reviewed, but simply by writing them, your English will improve.

你可以把作文写在下方，也可以把它们发送到邮箱 para@grammar.bz 以存档。我们不会对你的作文进行打分或点评，但只要你写了，你的英语水平就会提高。

	Student Paragraph		
Send Chat Attach Address Fonts Colors Save As Draft		Photo Browser	Show Stationery

To: para@grammar.bz

Cc:

Bcc:

Subject: Chapter 8

Signature: Corporate

My name is _____

Chapter 9
第九章

Comprehension and Reported Speech
理解和间接引语

DICTATION

In earlier chapters, we learned the various ways to use and modify nouns. This chapter presents a series of comprehension exercises, so you can make sure you understand rapid, natural speech. For verbs, we will be working with reported speech, the past unreal duo, and the phrasal verb **give**.

在前几章，我们学习了使用名词和修饰名词的多种方法。本章包含了一系列语言理解练习，这样你就可以确定自己能否理解语速快且自然的口语了。至于动词，我们要学习间接引语、过去非真实双重时态，以及与give相关的短语。

Exercise 9-1: Dictation
Track 116

Listen to the audio and write the exact transcription in the spaces below. Then check the Answer Key.

1. _____
2. _____
3. _____
4. _____
5. _____

The Bodyguard Incident

STORY

In **Italy**, in addition to being a **professional bodybuilder**, I'm also a **bodyguard**. I protect the president of a **famous car company** and an **international tennis star**, among others. One day, I was working in a **club** when a **fight** broke out on the floor. There were four or five **guys** involved, but **one** in particular was **very aggressive**. I think he was **high** on **coke**. He came into the office where I was and started **shouting** at me. He broke a **bottle** and **attacked** me; he **tried** to slash my **throat** with it. I wasn't about to **hit** him — he was **crazy** and he was holding **broken glass** — so I pulled out a **gun** and **shot** him. I'm a **good shot** because I was in the **Italian army** for two **years**. I shot him in the **leg**, not in the **body**, which would have **killed** him. That would have been a **big problem**. As it **was**, we had to go to **court**, which was a **big headache**.

Exercise 9-2: Story Pronunciation   **Track 117**

Listen to the audio and repeat, focusing on intonation and pronunciation.

In **Idəly**, in əddition tə being ə **pr'fessional bädybuilder**, I mälso ə **bädygärd**. I pr'tect the prezədent əvə **faym's cär cəmpəny** and an **innernæshənəl tennis star**, əməng əthrrz. One day, I wəz working innə **cleb** whenə **fight** broke out än the floor. There were four or five **guyz** invälvd, bət **one** in p'ticulər wəz **very aggressive**. I thinkee wəz **hi** (y)än **coke**. He came into thee (y)äffiss where I wəz and stärdəd **shæuding** at me. He brokə **bäddle** and **əttækt** me; he **tried** tə slæsh my **throat** with it. I wəznt əbout tə **hid dim** — he wəz **crazy** and he wəz holding **broken glæss** —so (w)I püll douda **gən** and **shäddim**. Im ə **güd shät** b'cuz I wəzzin thee (y)ətælyən **ärmy** fər two **yirz**. I shäddim in the **leg**, nät in the **bädy**, which wüdəv **kill** dim. Thæt wüda binna **big präbləm**. Az it **wəz**, we had tə godə **court**, which wəzzə **big hedake**.

> NOUNS

This section includes a general comprehension lesson, both with listening and reading. You will identify specific information, determine the gist, and draw conclusions.

本部分要讲的是普遍意义的语言理解，既有听力理解，也有阅读理解。在练习中，你需要确认具体信息，概括主旨，并得出结论。

Listening Comprehension
听力理解

Exercise 9-3: The Story of Human Language   **Track 118**

Listen to the audio and fill in the blanks. Then check the Answer Key.

"I _____ who is not interested in language," wrote the bestselling author and psychologist Steven Pinker. _____ that language fascinates us so. It not _____, placing us head and _____ the most proficient animal communicators, but it also beguiles us with its endless mysteries.

For example, _____? Why isn't there just one language? _____ change, _____, is that change _____ growth? _____ extinct? Consider how a single tongue spoken 150,000 years ago has evolved into the estimated 6,000 languages _____ _____.

Exercise 9-4: Polar Bears and Global Warming   **Track 119**

Select the appropriate response based on the audio. Then check the Answer Key.

1. Polar bears have been listed as an _____.

☐ dangerous species
■ endangered species

2. This will reduce the risk that they_____.
   - ☐ become extinct
   - ☐ become a stink

3. They will have new _____ under the Endangered Species Act.
   - ☐ protections
   - ☐ detections

4. The U.S. government cannot _____ the bears' existence.
   - ☐ check the eyes
   - ☐ jeopardize

5. The government could consider tougher _____ to clean up the air.
   - ☐ majors
   - ☐ measures

6. Scientists believe carbon _____ emissions cause global warming.
   - ☐ the oxide
   - ☐ dioxide

7. Unless global warming is _____, the bears will be extinct by 2100.
   - ☐ tamed
   - ☐ stemmed

8. There are about _____ polar bears worldwide.
   - ☐ 25,000
   - ☐ 2,500

9. There are about _____ polar bears in Alaska.
   - ☐ 4,700
   - ☐ 470

10. Polar bears tend to be _____ to blend in with the snow.
    - ☐ black
    - ☐ white

Exercise 9-5: Physics   Track 120

Listen to the audio and fill in the blanks. Then check the Answer Key.

"It doesn't ____ to understand modern physics," says Professor Richard Wolfson. ____ touch the very basis of physical reality, altering our commonsense notions of ____. Both have reputations for being bewilderingly complex. But the basic ideas behind relativity and quantum physics are, in fact, simple ____. The essence of relativity is summed up in a single, concise sentence: ____ uniform motion.

Exercise 9-6: The History of the English Language   Track 121

*Listen to the audio and select **True** or **False**. Then check the Answer Key.*

1. The origins of English are Germanic.
   ☐ True ☐ False
2. It has a 2,500-year history.
   ☐ True ☐ False
3. English is only spoken in America.
   ☐ True ☐ False
4. English is the international language of business and trade.
   ☐ True ☐ False
5. There are many literary and cultural achievements in English.
   ☐ True ☐ False

Exercise 9-7: Economics   Track 122

*Listen to the audio and check the box that best reflects the **gist** of the text. Then check the Answer Key.*

☐ Everyone is trained to be an economist, and we all save money based on our sophisticated understanding of the fundamentals of economics.

☐ Economic issues play a large part in our everyday lives, and it's important to have a deeper understanding of the fundamentals.

☐ It doesn't pay to be a good economist in working, buying, saving, investing, paying taxes, and voting.

Exercise 9-8: The Joy of Science   Track 123

*Listen to the audio and identify **specific facts**. Then check the Answer Key.*

People should be acquainted with the second ____ of thermodynamics. This law deals with the diffusion of ____ and has many ____ consequences. Also important are Newton's laws, the periodic table of elements, the double-helix ____ DNA, and scores of other masterpieces of ____.

Exercise 9-9: Drawing a Conclusion   Track 124

Read the text and listen to the audio. Then select the most logical conclusion. Check the Answer Key when you're done.

Question of Value

Our lives are filled with everyday questions of fact and finance. Which investment brings the highest return? What school district is the house in? What will this candidate actually do if elected? But the really fundamental questions of our lives are questions of neither fact nor finance. The really fundamental questions are questions of value. These are the deep questions that apply to every aspect of our lives. What is it that gives something genuine value? What things are really worth striving for? What is it that makes life worth living? Are there values that transcend cultural differences? Is all value subjective?

☐ Finances are the most fundamental question in our lives.

☐ The fundamental questions in our lives pertain to value.

☐ Values transcend all cultural differences.

Exercise 9-10: Listening for Specific Facts   Track 125

Listen to the audio and determine if each item is true or false. Then check the Answer Key.

1. Africa is the world's second-largest continent.   ☐ True ☐ False
2. It covers 16 percent of the Earth's total surface area.   ☐ True ☐ False
3. There are 406 countries in Africa, not including the island groups.   ☐ True ☐ False
4. The earliest hominids were discovered in Africa.   ☐ True ☐ False
5. There are no glaciers in Africa.   ☐ True ☐ False

Reading Comprehension
阅读理解

Exercise 9-11: John F. Kennedy

Read the selection and answer the questions. Then check the Answer Key.

John Fitzgerald Kennedy, who was often referred to by his initials, JFK, was the 35th president of the United States, serving from 1961 until his assassination in 1963. Kennedy was born in Massachusetts on May 29, 1917.

In the 1960 U.S. presidential election, Kennedy defeated Richard Nixon, in one of the closest races in American history. To date, he is the only practicing Roman Catholic to have been President. He was also the youngest man elected to the office, at the age of 43. JFK is the only president to have won a Pulitzer **Prize**. During his administration, events included the Bay of **Pigs** invasion, the Cuban **missile** crisis, the building of the Berlin **Wall**, the **space** race, the civil **rights** movement, and the early part of the Vietnam **War**.

Kennedy was assassinated on November 22, 1963, in Dallas, Texas. **Lee** Harvey **Oswald** was charged with the crime but was murdered **two** days **later** by Jack **Ruby**, before he could be put on trial. The **Warren** Commission concluded that Oswald was the assassin, but allowed for the probability of conspiracy. The event turned out to be an important moment in U.S. history because of how it profoundly affected the nation. Today, Kennedy continues to rank highly in public opinion ratings of former U.S. presidents.

1. What does JFK stand for?
2. Who were the two candidates in the 1960 election?
3. How old was Kennedy when he was elected?
4. What's another word for **murdered**?
5. Who killed JFK?
6. Was Lee Harvey Oswald the only gunman?
7. What happened to Oswald?
8. What's another word for **profoundly**?
9. How do people feel about Kennedy now?

Exercise 9-12: Rice

Read the selection and answer the questions. Then check the Answer Key.

Rice is a staple food for a large part of the world's population, providing more than one fifth of the calories consumed worldwide, making it the second-most-consumed cereal grain. The rice plant grows about 2 to 5 feet high and is a flowering plant.

Rice is composed of the grain and the husk. The grain is mainly used as food, but the vitamins, including B-complex, are found in the husk. Most people prefer to eat polished rice without the husk, but this can create a vitamin deficiency because polished rice doesn't have many vitamins.

Much of the rice that we eat comes from southeastern Asia and grows in all countries that have a warm and moist climate, including India, China, and Japan. The traditional method for cultivating rice is to flood the fields after planting the seedlings. This simple method requires planning and maintenance of the water supply, but reduces the growth of weeds and deters vermin. Flooding is not mandatory, but all other methods of irrigation require more effort in weed and pest control and different methods of fertilization.

What are the two edible parts of rice? _____

Rice grows in all the countries with climates that are:

A. ☐ cool and moist   C. ☐ warm and moist

B. ☐ warm and dry   D. ☐ cool and dry

What is another word for **consumed** in the first sentence? _____

Why is rice husk important?

A. ☐ because it tastes good   B. ☐ because it has many vitamins

Why do people who don't eat rice husk suffer from various deficiencies? Explain in one sentence.

_____

The following story has been in circulation on the Internet and the radio for the past 25 years. It's generally attributed to a church newsletter in Ohio, but this can't be verified. Take this with a grain of salt!

下面的故事已经在网络和电台上流传了25年了。笼统地来说，这要归功于俄亥俄州的一则教堂简讯，但是这种说法无法被证实。读这个故事的时候不用完全当真。

Exercise 9-13: Gin-Soaked Raisins

Read the following passage and answer the questions. The prepositions have been highlighted. Check the Answer Key when you're done.

Gin-Soaked Raisins Bring Relief to Arthritic Patient

When we heard this, we felt obligated **to** share it. It must be noted, however, that the claim is unsubstantiated, and is offered **to** you exactly as it is. Here is an unusual recipe **for** arthritic relief:

Empty one box **of** golden raisins **into** a large, shallow container. Pour **in** enough gin (the cheapest you can buy) **to** completely cover the raisins. Let it stand uncovered **until** all the liquid disappears (about seven days). Stirring occasionally helps the evaporation process. Then, put the raisins **in** a covered container and eat just nine raisins a day. If you don't like raisins, put them **on** your cereal or **in** a salad.

I began eating nine raisins a day **on** October 10. **By** November 10, my knees, which had sounded **like** castanets whenever I bent **over**, no longer clicked so loudly, and I was able **to** walk **up** and **down** those small steps **from** the sidewalk **to** the street **outside** our building **without** turning sideways **to** go one step **at** a time or hang **on to** a parked car. I could bend my head back to look **at** the stars **without** leaning **against** a tree or fence or holding the back of my neck **for** support. A couple weeks later, the swelling and pain were gone **from** my arthritic toes. By December, I could close my fingers **into** fists. **Before** October 10, a knife would slide **through** either hand. My whole body feels more limber; I can do exercises, including hugging my knees **to** my chest and rocking back and forth, **without** back pain. I can handle needles and pins **with** greater ease.

A friend **in** Massachusetts gave me this recipe last September. She had learned **about** it this past summer **from** her podiatrist, who had noticed her difficulty **in** getting **up to** leave his office. He learned **of** it **from** one **of** his patients, whose toes and knees were no longer swollen and who could stretch her hands flat **on** the table — all after just two months **of** eating nine raisins a day. **Before** her retirement, she was the assistant dean **of** a medical school. **On** a return trip **to** visit former colleagues, a friend told her that the school's specialist in rheumatology was prescribing this recipe **to** all his patients! (The podiatrist and his friends have been eating these raisins and have been playing their best golf **in** more than 30 years; they are **in** their 70's.)

Why does this recipe bring such fantastic results? As far back as early Biblical times, the people **of** India and Egypt discovered the healing properties **of** juniper berries. Gin is made **from** natural grains and juniper berries. Even if you are **on** medication that advises **against** alcohol, you can eat nine raisins a day. Most of the alcohol has evaporated and the small amount would be insignificant. That comes **from** my own physician.

In your own words, what is the main idea of the article?

_____

_____

What ingredient in gin helps healing and reduces swelling?

_____

_____

Exercise 9-14: Gin-Soaked Raisins — Pronunciation   Track 126

Listen and repeat.

Jin-Soakt Rayzinz Bring R'leef to Arthridic Paysh'nt

ACCENT   When we hrrd this, we felt äbləgadəd to share it. It məst be nodəd, however, thət thə claim iz ənsəbstænshee (y)adəd, and iz äfferd to you eggzækly əzidiz. Hirzən unuzhu (w)al rɛsəpee for ärthridic r'lief:

Empty one bäx of golden ray-zinz into a large shællow c'ntainer. Pour in ənəf jin (the cheapest you c'n buy) to c'mpleetly cəver the ray-zinz. Ledit stænd əncəverd until äll the likwid disəppirz (about 7 dayz). Stirring əccazhənəlly helps thee (y) əvæporashən præcess. Then, püt the ray-zinz in a cəverd cəntainer and eat jəst nine ray-zinz ə day. If you don't like ray-zinz, put them än your cire (y)əl or innə sæləd.

I b'gæn eeding 9 ray-zinz a day än äctober 10. By November 10, my kneez, which had soundəd like cæstənets whenever I bent over, no länger clickt so loudly and I wəz abəl to wälk up and down thoz smäll° steps from the sidewalk to the street outside är bilding without turning sidewayz to go one stepədə time or hæng on to a pärkt cär. I cüd bend my head bæck to lük at the stärz without leaning agenst a tree or fence or holding the bæck of my neck for s'pport. A cəpəl of weeks lader, the swelling and pain wr gän from my ärthridic toz. By D'cember, I cüd cloz my fingrz into fists. B'fore äctober 10, a nyf wüd slyd thru either hænd. My whole bädy feelz more limber; I c'n do exercizəz, including həgging my kneez to my chest and räcking bæckən forth, without bæck pain. I c'n hændle needəlz and pinz with greader eez.

A friend in Mæssə chussetts gave me this resəpee læst September. She had lrnd aboudit this pæst summer frommer p'dy⁽ʸ⁾ətrist, who had nodist her diffəcəlty in gedding əp to leeviz äffice. He Irrrndəvit frəm wənəviz patients, whooz toz and kneez were no länger swollen and who cüd stretch her hænds flædän the table — ällæf ter just 2 mənts əveeding 9 raisinz a day. B'fore her r'tirement, she wəz thee⁽ʸ⁾əssistant dean əvə medəcal school. ännə r'turn trip to vizit former cälleegz, a friend told her that the schoolz speshəlist in roomətäləgy wəz pr'scribing this resəpee to all his patients! (The p'dy⁽ʸ⁾ətrist and his frenz have been eeding theez ray-zinz and have been playing their best gälf in more th'n thirdee yirz — they are in their sevendeez.)

Why dəz this resəpee bring səch fæntæstic r'zəlts? Az fär bæck az erly bibləcəl timz, the people of India and Egypt d'scəverd the healing präperdeez ov junəper berreez. Jin is made from næchrəl grainz and junəper berreez. Even if you are än medəcation thət ədvizəz əgenst ælkəhäl, you c'n eat 9 ray-zinz a day. Most ov the ælkəhäl haz əvæporadəd and the small amount wüd be insignifəcənt. That cəmz frəm my own fəzishən.

Exercise 9-15: Review

Identify the appropriate word. Then check the Answer Key.

1. I can't get ____ how well he's dealing with this! ☐ up ☐ over
2. Don't put it ____ any longer. ☐ up ☐ off
3. Nobody can stand ____ his dictatorial ways. ☐ — ☐ up
4. That plane will take ____ at 9:15 a.m. ☐ up ☐ off
5. A tadpole turns ____ a frog. ☐ up to ☐ into
6. It's hard to get ____ jury duty. ☐ out of ☐ at
7. Keep trying! Don't give ____! ☐ up ☐ out
8. It certainly didn't turn ____ the way we expected! ☐ out ☐ up
9. Please put your coat ____ when you get home. ☐ off ☐ away
10. Could you turn ____ the radio, it's too loud. ☐ down ☐ away
11. What's his point? I'm not sure what he's getting ____. ☐ from ☐ at
12. That basketball player really stands ____ in a crowd. ☐ up ☐ out
13. It's time to ____ your homework. ☐ do ☐ make
14. Do it now! There's no point in putting it ____. ☐ away ☐ off
15. I'm sorry, we don't give ____ personal information. ☐ out ☐ up
16. What time do you get ____ work? ☐ off ☐ out
17. Because I was moving, I gave ____ all of my old CDs. ☐ away ☐ off
18. Don't worry, it'll turn ____ sooner or later. ☐ away ☐ up

19. It's important to stand ____ what you believe in. ☐ up to ☐ up for
20. I can't believe he turned ____ that job offer! ☐ down ☐ away
21. What time would you like to ____ lunch? ☐ take ☐ have
22. The children need to ____ a nap. ☐ have ☐ take
23. I hope they didn't ____ a mistake. ☐ make ☐ do
24. You need to ____ a shower after working out. ☐ have ☐ take
25. Did you ____ an appointment? ☐ make ☐ take
26. Did he ____ a promise? ☐ make ☐ do
27. Do you ____ good notes in class? ☐ take ☐ make
28. Their teacher didn't ____ them talk in class. ☐ let ☐ allow
29. They ____ us repaint the whole house. ☐ got ☐ had
30. We ____ him to change his mind. ☐ had ☐ got

VERBS

In this section, we'll learn about reported speech, the past real duo, and the phrasal verb **give**. This section also includes synopses of **would**, **had**, **be**, **to**, and **there**, as well as a comprehensive version of "Grammar in a Nutshell."

在这个部分中，我们要学习间接引语、过去真实双重时态，以及由give构成的动词短语。这部分还包含would，had，be，to和there之间的用法对照概览，以及综合性的"语法小结"板块。

He Said, She Said

The verb changes when speech is reported.

间接表达话语时，动词会发生变化。

Direct Speech	**Reported Speech**
"I **do** it."	I said that I **did** it.
"I **did** it."	I said that I **had done** it.
"I **will do** it."	I said that I **would do** it.

When you say something directly, you need to use quotation marks.

在书面语中，如果要写出说话人直接说的话，就需要用引号。

"I need to go," he said.

When you use reported speech, two things happen. The quotation marks disappear, and you push the verb tense back in order to match when the report is.

如果你使用了间接引语，那就会有两处变化。引号会消失，并且为了与说话时间一致，你还需要把动词的时态往前退。

He said that he needed to go.

Exercise 9-16: Reported or Indirect Speech

Change the direct statement to a reported statement using the provided phrase. Then check the Answer Key.

He doesn't like it.	**He said** that he **didn't** like it.

1. She does that every day.

I thought that

2. He will do it later.

He said that

3. They left early.

She believed that

4. Your friends left.

I thought that

5. He'll call you when he has time. (Hint: Both verbs change.)

He said that

6. You need to take a bath.

She believed that

7. She wants him to do his homework.

I thought that

8. These shoes are too small.

He said that

9. She looks great in that dress.

She believed that

10. The computer crashed.

I thought that

Past Unreal Duo
过去非真实双重时态

As you learned with the present unreal duo, you can link two events in time that are contrary to fact.
与现在非真实双重时态一样，你可以把两件与事实相反的事在时间上联系起来。

The **past unreal duo** clarifies the distinction between what actually took place and what hypothetically could have taken place.

过去非真实双重时态清楚地区分了过去实际发生的事与假设会在过去发生的事。

(Traditionally, this is known as the past subjunctive conditional.)
(在传统的语法体系中，这被称为表示过去的虚拟条件句。)

Exercise 9-17: Past Unreal Duo

Change from the past to the past unreal duo. Then check the Answer Key.

He studied hard. He did well.
If he had studied hard, he **would** have done well.
If he had studied hard, he **could** have done well.

1. She saved her money. She lived comfortably.

2. They considered all of the options. They were prepared.

3. We planted a garden. We have a lot of vegetables.

4. I didn't watch the road. I got in an accident.

5. We didn't do the laundry. We didn't have anything to wear.

Let's do a review of the verbs we've studied so far.
我们来复习一下目前学过的所有动词。

Exercise 9-18: Verb Tense Understanding

Fill in the blank with the proper verb form. Then check the Answer Key.

1. The accident ____ yesterday.
    - ☐ happens
    - ☑ happened

2. Nobody ____ what will happen tomorrow.
    - ☐ knows
    - ☐ will know

3. I ____ you in the morning.
    - ☐ call
    - ☐ will call

4. They ____ it many times over the years, but never succeeded.
    - ☐ try
    - ☐ have tried

5. There ____ a possibility for it later.
    - ☐ may be
    - ☐ has been

6. He ____ to England.
    - ☐ has never gone
    - ☐ has never went

7. You ____ that yesterday, right?
    - ☐ did
    - ☐ have done
    - ☐ had done

8. You ____ that before, right?
    - ☐ did
    - ☐ have done
    - ☐ had done

9. You ____ that before I met you, right?
    - ☐ did
    - ☐ have done
    - ☐ had done

10. He will ____ the water.
    - ☐ drink
    - ☐ drinks

11. I ____ going to the store yesterday.
    - ☐ was
    - ☐ will be

12. He ____ travel by train, but now he prefers his car.
    - ☐ used to
    - ☐ is used to

13. He ____ driving on the right side of the road.	☐ used to ☐ is used to
14. She ____ working really hard right now.	☐ was ☐ is
15. I ____ not born yesterday.	☐ was ☐ am
16. Do you think they ____ figure it out?	☐ will be able to ☐ are
17. She ____ survive the storm.	☐ didn't ☐ don't
18. He ____ off the roof this morning.	☐ fell ☐ falls
19. Don't ____ over spilled milk.	☐ cried ☐ cry
20. He ____ the house last year.	☐ paints ☐ painted

Three *Theres*

Exercise 9-19: Three *Theres*

Select the proper form. Then check the Answer Key.

There	They're	Their
There was a fire.	**They're** at the party.	It's **their** turn.

1. ____ will be an earthquake within the next 50 years.	☐ There ☐ They're ☐ Their
2. That's not ____ first time to work on this.	☐ there ☐ they're ☐ their
3. I think ____ not coming back.	☐ there ☐ they're ☐ their

Four *2s*

1 Preposition	3 Number
We went **to** the party.	I bought **two** hats.
2 Also	**4 Excess**
I have one, **too.**	There were **too** many people there.

Exercise 9-20: Four *2s*

Identify the proper form. Then check the Answer Key.

1. Don't eat ____ much!

    □ 1 □ 3
    □ 2 □ 4

2. We like it, ____.

    □ 1 □ 3
    □ 2 □ 4

3. They bought ____ of them.

    □ 1 □ 3
    □ 2 □ 4

4. Let's go ____ the beach!

    □ 1 □ 3
    □ 2 □ 4

Four *Hads*

1 Possession	3 Obligation
I **had** a bicycle.	I **had** to do it. I **had** better do it now.
2 Causative	4 Past Real Duo
I **had** him do it.	I **had** never done that before.

Exercise 9-21: Four *Hads*

*Identify which form of **had** is being used. Then check the Answer Key.*

1. I **had** to finish my homework before going out.

    □ 1 □ 3
    □ 2 □ 4

2. They **had** us wait at the office while they investigated the situation.

    □ 1 □ 3
    □ 2 □ 4

3. He **had** a ticket.

    □ 1 □ 3
    □ 2 □ 4

4. They **had** never had a pineapple before they went to Hawaii.

    □ 1 □ 3
    □ 2 □ 4

Four *Woulds*

1 Unreal Duo	3 Repeated Past
If I were you, I **would**n't do that.	When I was little, I **would** always play in the yard.
If I had been there, I **would** have done it.	
I wish he **would** do it.	
I **would** rather do it later.	
2 Polite	4 Reported Speech
Would you please help me with this?	"I will do it."
I **would** like a glass of water.	He said that he **would** do it.

266

Exercise 9-22: Four *Woulds*

Identify which form of **would** *is being used.* (*Remember:* **Would** *is always followed by the simple form of the main verb.*) *Check the Answer Key when you're done.*

1. I **would** like to try it again, please. □ 1 □ 3
    □ 2 □ 4

2. He told me that he **would** do it later. □ 1 □ 3
    □ 2 □ 4

3. When I lived in France, I **would** always speak French. □ 1 □ 3
    □ 2 □ 4

4. If you were sure, you **would**n't be nervous about it. □ 1 □ 3
    □ 2 □ 4

Seven Forms with *To Be*

1 -ing
He is runn**ing**.
It is excit**ing** (to me).
It is rain**ing**.
It's go**ing** to rain.

2 Adjective (quality, nationality, color, time, etc.)
He is **nice / happy / hungry / funny.**
He is **gone / back / available / ready.**
It is **wrong / right / stressful.**
He is **Italian.**
It is **blue.**
It is **Tuesday.**
It's **9:00.**
It's **January.**

3 -ed
It is clos**ed.**
He is excit**ed** (by it).
He is interest**ed** / confus**ed** / worri**ed.**
He is surpris**ed** / annoy**ed** / irritat**ed.**

4 Noun / Pronoun (person, place, thing, idea)
He is **a doctor.**
It's **mine.**

5 Preposition
He is **at** the park.
He is **like** the other people.

6 Passive
It was **written** by Shakespeare.
It was **stolen**.

7 Conjunction
It was **because** we wanted it that way.
It's **when** he quit that we started worrying.

Exercise 9-23: Seven *Bes*

*Identify the correct use of **be**. Look for the key word or form in the chart above. Hints for the first seven are in bold. Check the Answer Key when you're done.*

1.   He wasn't surpris**ed** by their offer.   ☐ 1 ☐ 3 ☐ 5
                                               ☐ 2 ☐ 4 ☐ 6
                                                          ☐ 7

2.   It isn't **available** right now.   ☐ 1 ☐ 3 ☐ 5
                                         ☐ 2 ☐ 4 ☐ 6
                                                    ☐ 7

3.   This is so excit**ing**!   ☐ 1 ☐ 3 ☐ 5
                                ☐ 2 ☐ 4 ☐ 6
                                           ☐ 7

4.   I think it's an automatic **response**. (noun)   ☐ 1 ☐ 3 ☐ 5
                                                      ☐ 2 ☐ 4 ☐ 6
                                                                 ☐ 7

5.   It was heard **by** over a million people. (A million people   ☐ 1 ☐ 3 ☐ 5
     heard it.)   ☐ 2 ☐ 4 ☐ 6
                                                                               ☐ 7

6.   I will be **in** L.A. for six weeks. (preposition)   ☐ 1 ☐ 3 ☐ 5
                                                          ☐ 2 ☐ 4 ☐ 6
                                                                     ☐ 7

7.   It's **why** we had to tell you.   ☐ 1 ☐ 3 ☐ 5
                                        ☐ 2 ☐ 4 ☐ 6
                                                   ☐ 7

8.   It's not like everything else.   ☐ 1 ☐ 3 ☐ 5
                                      ☐ 2 ☐ 4 ☐ 6
                                                 ☐ 7

9.   It's wrong.   ☐ 1 ☐ 3 ☐ 5
                   ☐ 2 ☐ 4 ☐ 6
                              ☐ 7

10. They are Indonesian.   ☐ 1 ☐ 3 ☐ 5
                            ☐ 2 ☐ 4 ☐ 6
                                       ☐ 7

11. That wasn't Wednesday; it was Tuesday.   ☐ 1 ☐ 3 ☐ 5
                                              ☐ 2 ☐ 4 ☐ 6
                                                         ☐ 7

12. It was a mistake.   ☐ 1 ☐ 3 ☐ 5
                         ☐ 2 ☐ 4 ☐ 6
                                    ☐ 7

13. We have been in the back office for three hours.   ☐ 1 ☐ 3 ☐ 5
                                                        ☐ 2 ☐ 4 ☐ 6
                                                                   ☐ 7

14. It's going to rain. ☐1 ☐3 ☐5 ☐2 ☐4 ☐6 ☐7

15. It's a little stressful. ☐1 ☐3 ☐5 ☐2 ☐4 ☐6 ☐7

16. It's not done yet. ☐1 ☐3 ☐5 ☐2 ☐4 ☐6 ☐7

17. They weren't very excited about it. ☐1 ☐3 ☐5 ☐2 ☐4 ☐6 ☐7

18. The kids were sunburned at the beach. ☐1 ☐3 ☐5 ☐2 ☐4 ☐6 ☐7

19. Oh, no! It's gone. ☐1 ☐3 ☐5 ☐2 ☐4 ☐6 ☐7

20. The website has been seen by millions. ☐1 ☐3 ☐5 ☐2 ☐4 ☐6 ☐7

Grammar in a Bigger Nutshell
语法扩展

All through this book, we have studied intonation. Here we will look at it in a single sentence with the various verb tenses.

语调的学习贯穿着整本书。现在，我们要看一下同一个句子在不同时态下的语调变化。

Subject		Object
The **show**		a **house**
The **talk** show		a **light**house
The **talk** show host		a **light**house keeper
The popular **talk** show host		an old **light**house keeper
The **wildly** popular **talk** show host	interviewed	a **really** old **light**house keeper

The **wildly** popular **talk** show host interviewed a **really** old **light**house keeper.

Thə **wildly** päpyəlrr **täk** show host dinnerview də **rilly** old **lyt** hæous keeper.

Exercise 9-24: Verb Tense Understanding   Track 127

Listen to the audio and repeat. No matter how complex the verb gets, remember to follow the basic Dogs eat bones intonation, where you stress the nouns. We will build up one complex noun for the subject, and another one for the object.

dinner viewz

1. The **wildly** popular **talk** show host interviews **really** old **light**house keepers all the time.

dizinner viewing

2. The **wildly** popular **talk** show host is interviewing a **really** old **light**house keeper right now.

dinner viewdə

3. The **wildly** popular **talk** show host interviewed a **really** old **light**house keeper last week.

də linner viewə

4. The **wildly** popular **talk** show host will interview a **really** old **light**house keeper next week.

də dinner viewə

5. The **wildly** popular **talk** show host would interview a **really** old **light**house keeper if she could **find** one.

dədə vinner viewdə

6. The **wildly** popular **talk** show host would have interviewed a **really** old **light**house keeper if she'd been able to **find** one.

thədə zinner viewdə

7. The **wildly** popular **talk** show host that has interviewed a **really** old **light**house keeper is living in France now.

də zinner viewdə

8. The **wildly** popular **talk** show host has interviewed a lot of **really** old **light**house keepers over the years.

də dinner viewdə

9. The **wildly** popular **talk** show host had interviewed a **really** old **light**house keeper before the huge storm in the Atlantic knocked over his lighthouse.

dələ vinner viewdə

10. The **wildly** popular **talk** show host will have interviewed a lot of **really** old **light**house keepers by the end of the season.

dädə inner viewə

11. The **wildly** popular **talk** show host ought to interview a **really** old **light**house keeper.

shü dinner viewə

12. The **wildly** popular **talk** show host should interview a **really** old **light**house keeper.

shüd·n ninner viewə

13. The **wildly** popular **talk** show host shouldn't interview **really** old **light**house keepers because it confuses the audience.

shüdə vinner viewdə

14. The **wildly** popular **talk** show host should've interviewed a **really** old **light**house keeper so an expert could have been heard.

shüd·nə vinner viewdə

15. The **wildly** popular **talk** show host shouldn't have interviewed a **really** old **light**house keeper because the audience was completely confused.

cü dinner viewə

16. The **wildly** popular **talk** show host could interview a **really** old **light**house keeper.

cüd·n ninner viewenny

17. The **wildly** popular **talk** show host couldn't interview any **really** old **light**house keepers because they were all on strike that month.

cüdə vinner viewdə

18. The **wildly** popular **talk** show host could've interviewed a **really** old **light**house keeper, but instead she went with a **very** attractive **lion** tamer.

cüd·nə vinner viewdə

19. The **wildly** popular **talk** show host couldn't have interviewed a **really** old **light**house keeper because none of them were in town last month.

my dinner viewə

20. The **wildly** popular **talk** show host might interview a **really** old **light**house keeper.

mydə vinner viewdə

21. The **wildly** popular **talk** show host might've interviewed a **really** old **light**house keeper, but we're not sure because the schedule was shredded earlier today.

məss dinner viewə

22. The **wildly** popular **talk** show host must interview a lot of **really** old **light**house keepers because she completely understands the issues. (probably)

məss də vinner viewdə

23. The **wildly** popular **talk** show host must've interviewed a lot of **really** old **light**house keepers because she completely understood the issues. (probably)

cə ninner viewə

24. The **wildly** popular **talk** show host can interview a **really** old **light**house keeper if she has time at the end of the show.

cæn dinner view

25. The **wildly** popular **talk** show host can't interview any **really** old **light**house keepers due to the union rules about discussing maritime issues with civilians.

Give

To give one's opinion	I'd like to give my opinion on that.
It is given that ...	It's given that the process needs to change.
To give up	They won't ever give up!
To give someone the benefit of the doubt	Let's give him the benefit of the doubt.
To give in	He held out for a while, but then gave in.
To give away	She gave away all of her worldly goods.
To give away	He gave away the end of the movie.
To give back	Let's hope they give us the money back.
To give off	The heater is giving off a strange odor.
To give out	Our old car finally gave out.

Exercise 9-25: *Give*

Select the proper option. Then check the Answer Key.

1. The boss insisted on paying, so we finally gave ____.
   - ☐ in
   - ☐ away

2. The director knew he was right, so he refused to give ____.
   - ☐ up
   - ☐ away

3. The junior execs were reluctant to give their ____.
   - ☐ opinion
   - ☐ benefit of the doubt

4. In government, ____ massive debt is a fact of life.
   - ☐ it's given that
   - ☐ it's given away

5. He protested so well that they gave him the ____.
   - ☐ opinion
   - ☐ benefit of the doubt

6. Don't give ____ the ending of the story!
   - ☐ back
   - ☐ away

7. Let's give ____ these old clothes and toys.
   - ☐ back
   - ☐ away

8. I'm sorry, we don't give ____ personal information.
   - ☐ out
   - ☐ off

9. We think you should give it ____ to him.
   - ☐ back
   - ☐ away

10. The fire is giving ____ a lot of smoke!
    - ☐ out
    - ☐ off

TEST

Let's review everything you have learned in Chapter 9. Make sure you get 100% on the test before going on to the next chapter. Check your work using the Answer Key.

　　我们来复习一下在第九章中学过的全部内容。只有当你在测试中获得满分以后，你才能接着学习下一章。请参照答案检查正误。

Part 1: *Fill in the proper word. Don't forget to capitalize the first letter.*

1. _____ he do it yesterday?
2. _____ he do it tomorrow?
3. _____ he doing it right now?
4. _____ he ever done it before?
5. _____ he do it if he had time?

Part 2: *Select the proper verb form.*

1. _____ you like it?
   - ☐ Do
   - ☐ Does
2. The director _____ the staff later.
   - ☐ inform
   - ☐ will inform
3. He _____ never figured it out.
   - ☐ has
   - ☐ hasn't
4. She _____ figured it out, if she had thought about it.
   - ☐ will
   - ☐ would
   - ☐ would've
5. She _____ figure it out, if she thought about it.
   - ☐ will
   - ☐ would
   - ☐ would've
6. She _____ figure it out when she thinks about it.
   - ☐ will
   - ☐ would
   - ☐ would've

Part 3: *Convert to a reported statement using **I said that** or **I thought that**.*

1. He does it.

2. She will buy one.

3. They have opened a new branch.

4. They designed a wonderful plaza.

5. We are trying our hardest.

Part 4: *Fill in the blank with the appropriate **give** phrase.*

1. I'm sorry, we can't give ____ that information.
2. Keep trying! Don't give ____!

Part 5: *Fill in the blank with the appropriate* **preposition**.

1.   That plane will take ____ at 9:15 a.m.
2.   It certainly didn't turn ____ the way we expected!

Part 6: *Change from the past to the past unreal duo.*

1.   He thought about it. He reconsidered.

2.   They brought their laptops. They got a little work done.

Part 7: *Fill in the blanks with* **their / they're / there**.

1.   ____ is a spot on my tie.
2.   I tried to borrow ____ car.
3.   She thinks ____ not really trying.

Part 8: *Fill in the blanks with* **to / too / two**.

1.   I have ____ go now.
2.   I have ____ hours to finish.
3.   I have ____ much to do.

Using what you have learned, write two essays on the following:
利用你学过的知识写两段话，话题如下：

1.   How many scars do you have and how did you get them?
     你有几个伤疤，它们是怎么留下的？

2.   Explain an aspect of American culture or habits that you find strange or
     confusing.
     阐述一下美国的文化习俗让你感觉奇怪或困惑的一面。

You can handwrite your paragraphs below or e-mail them to **para@grammar.bz** to be stored.
These paragraphs are not graded or reviewed, but simply by writing them, your English will improve.
　　你可以把作文写在下方，也可以把它们发送到邮箱 para@grammar.bz 以存档。我们不会对你的作文进行打分或点评，但只要你写了，你的英语水平就会提高。

```
○ ● ○                          Student Paragraph
  Send   Chat  Attach Address  Fonts  Colors  Save As Draft        Photo Browser   Show Stationery
```

To:	para@grammar.bz
Cc:	
Bcc:	
Subject:	Chapter 9

Signature: Corporate

My name is _____

Chapter 10
第十章

Comprehension and the Passive Voice
理解和被动语态

Here, we pull together all of the elements you have studied in comprehension exercises, along with word order, prefixes, synonyms, **doubt** vs. **question**, and **only**. For verbs, you will learn the passive voice, and the past and future real duo.

在这部分中，我们会把你在语言理解练习中学过的所有内容，连同词序、前缀、同义词、怀疑和疑问，以及only等内容都放在一起。对于动词来说，你要学习被动语态、过去真实双重时态和将来真实双重时态。

Exercise 10-1: Dictation   Track 128

Listen to the audio and write the exact transcription in the spaces below. Then check the Answer Key.

1. _____

2. _____

3. _____

4. _____

5. _____

6. _____

7. _____

8. _____
9. _____

10. _____

The Army Incident

What a Surprise ... Max Doesn't Think It Through

STORY

When I was **younger,** I was really **crazy**. I didn't **think** things **through** — I would just do **whatever I felt** like, no matter **what** the **consequences** would be. I felt **sorry** for whoever got in my **way,** because, **basically,** I just ran **over** them. When I was in the **army,** I wanted to go work **out** in the **gym,** but my commanding **officer** wanted me to do some **work.** I really needed to work **out** because I was getting **ready** for a **competition,** but the **officer** just wouldn't **listen** to me. He kept **yelling** at me to get **working,** so I grabbed a **machine gun** and started **firing.** The guy ran so **fast** and **jumped** behind a **wall.** If he hadn't been so **quick,** I'm sure I would have **shot** him. I **really** wasn't **thinking.** Of **course,** I got in **all** kinds of **trouble.** They put me in the **brig** for a couple of **days** and they wanted to **court** martial me. **Fortunately,** my **father,** who is a **doctor** and famous **bicyclist,** was able to get me **out** and to get the **charges** dropped. He was **so mad** at me that he didn't **speak** to me for a **year.** I **really** didn't think that one **through.**

Exercise 10-2: Story Pronunciation   Track 129

Listen to the audio and repeat, focusing on intonation and pronunciation.

ACCENT

When I wuz **younger,** I wuz rilly **crazy.** I didn't **think** thingz **thru** — I wüd just do **whadever I felt** like, no mædder **what** the **cänsequences** wüd be. I felt **särry** for whoever gät in my **way,** b'cuz, **basaklee,** I just ran **over** them. When I was in the **army,** I wänted to go work **out** in the **gym,** but my commanding **äfficer** wänted me t' do some **work.** I rilly needed to work **out** because I was gedding **reddy** for a **cämpetition,** but the **äfficer** just wüdn **lissen** to me. He kept **yelling** at me t' get **working,** so I græbbed a **m'cheen** gun and stärded **firing.** The guy ræn so **fast** and **jumpt** b'hind a **wall.** If he hædn't been so **quick,** I'm sure I wüda **shät** him. I **rilly** wuzn't **thinking.** Of **corss,** I gät in **äll** kindza **trubble.** They püt me in the **brig** for a coupla **dayz** and they wänted t' **court** märtial me. **Forchunately,** my **fäther,** who izza **däctor** and famous **bicyclist,** wuzable to get me **out** and t' get the **chärges** dräpt. He wuz **so mad** at me that he didn't **speak** t' me fora **yir.** I **rilly** didn't think that one **thru.**

M, N, Ng

Let's work on the three nasal consonants—M, N, and the NG combination. These sounds come out through the nose. For each one, the air is blocked in the mouth in one of three locations.

我们来学习一下三个鼻辅音——M，N，以及NG这个组合。这几个音都是从鼻腔发出来的，但对它们每一个来说，气流停留在口腔里的位置各不相同。

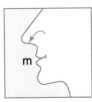 **M** is the easiest and most obvious. Like **B**, the lips come together, and the air can't get out, so it has to come out through the nose.

　　M的发音方式最简单，也最显而易见。就像发B这个音的时候一样，因为嘴唇并在一起，气流出不来，所以它不得不从鼻腔出来。

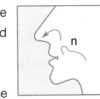 **N** is similar to **T**, but it is more relaxed. It fills the mouth, touching the insides of all the teeth, leaving no room for the air to escape, except through the nose.

　　N与T的发音方式相似，但是它要更加放松。气流充斥了整个口腔，触碰到所有牙齿的内壁，让气流无处可逃，最后只能从鼻腔出来。

 **NG** is back in the throat with [g]. The back of the tongue presses back, and again, the air comes out through the nose.

　　因为NG中有[g]这个音，所以整个音很靠后。舌头的根部先往后压，然后气流同样从鼻腔出来。

Exercise 10-3: Nasal Consonants　　　　　　　　　　Track 130

Let's contrast nasal and non-nasal consonants. Listen and repeat.

	Initial		Middle		Final	
m/b	my	by	grammar	grabber	rim	rib
n/d	no	dough	bunny	buddy	Ben	bed
ng/g	wrong answer	green	finger	digger	wrong	log

Exercise 10-4: Ending Nasal Consonants　　　　　　Track 131

Here we'll focus on the final sounds. Listen and repeat.

M	N	ND	NG
rumə	runə	round	rungə
some	son	sound	sung
dumb	torn	found	tongue
palm	pond	pound	song

The Held T
被抑制的T音

When you have an **N** immediately after a **T**, don't pop the **T**. Leave the tongue in the **T** position and hum. (There is no T and no ə.) Another point to remember is that you need a sharp upward sliding intonation up to the "held T," then a quick drop for the N.

278

当T后面直接跟着N时，念T的时候就不需要爆破，而是要把舌头放在发T音的位置，然后轻声哼一下。（这时没有T和E的音。）另外还要记住一点：在发这个"被抑制的T音"时，音调需要急速上滑，然后发N音时再把音调快速降下来。

written	sentence
gotten	certain
forgotten	mountain
important	button
eaten	rotten

Exercise 10-5: "Held T" Before N   **Track 132**

Read the following sentences out loud. Remember, there is no "uh" sound before the N.

1. He'd **forgotten** the **rotten written sentence.**
2. She wasn't **certain** who had **written** it.
3. They **certainly** haven't **gotten** a new **mountain** bike.
4. It's **important** not to be **frightened.**
5. The **kitten** has **eaten** the **button.**

NOUNS

In this section, we focus on word order, prefixes, synonyms, colloquial expressions such as **doubt** vs. **question**, and the position of **only** in a sentence.

在这个部分，我们要重点讲解词序、前缀、同义词、doubt和question等口语表达，以及only在句子中的位置。

Word Order
词序

One of the most important elements in both written and spoken English is proper word order. The main form that you use is SVO, but here is a synopsis of the three most common instances where the word order changes.

在英语中，不管是书面语还是口语，有一个因素都非常重要，那就是正确的词序。虽然你使用的主要形式是SVO，但还是有词序变化的情况，下面就概述了三种最常见的。

The Question Flip ↻
疑问句中的词序颠倒 ↻

When you change from a sentence to a question, the word order reverses.
当你把一个句子变成疑问句的时候，词序要颠倒。

He is here.
Is he here?

This also shows up with tag endings.

在反意疑问句中也是如此。

He is here.
He is here, isn't he?

Reverse Modifiers

后置修饰语

With noun descriptions, you can either use a standard adjective before the noun or a clause after it.

修饰名词的时候，你既可以在名词前加上标准的形容词，也可以在名词后加上一个从句。

nice people
people who are nice

Active and Passive

主动和被动

When you change from the active voice to the passive, you reverse the position of the subject and the object.

当你把主动语态转换成被动语态时，需要颠倒主语和宾语的位置。

Dogs eat bones.
Bones are eaten by dogs.

Only

The word **only** has several meanings, including **just, one, simply, merely,** and **but**, and this is determined by the word order. It tends to modify the word that is right next to it.

only这个词有好几种意思，包括just，one，simply，merely和but，但具体取哪个意思还是要看词序。only修饰的常常是紧挨着它的那个词。

Exercise 10-6: *Only*	Track 133

Listen to the audio and repeat, focusing on intonation and meaning.

Only my brother told the truth (No one else did).
My **only** brother told the truth. (I only have one brother.)
My brother **only** told the truth. (He didn't say anything else.)
My brother told **only** the truth. (He never lied.)
My brother told the **only** truth. (There is only one truth.)
My brother told the truth **only** if people wanted to hear it. (In the case that)
My brother told the truth, **only** to find that no one wanted to hear it. (negative result)
My brother told the truth, **only** this time, everyone was glad to hear it. (But this time)

Exercise 10-7: *Only*

Check the box with the appropriate response. Then check the Answer Key.

1. This information is for your eyes only.
   - ☐ It's for your viewing.
   - ☐ It's not for your ears.

2. He's an only child.
   - ☐ He doesn't have any siblings.
   - ☐ He is very young.

3. He's only a child.
   - ☐ He doesn't have any siblings.
   - ☐ He is very young.

4. Only we call on Wednesdays.
   - ☐ No one else calls.
   - ☐ That's the only day we call.

5. We only call on Wednesdays.
   - ☐ No one else calls.
   - ☐ That's the only day we call.

Doubt and *Question*
怀疑和疑问

Both **doubt** and **question** indicate a lack. **Doubt** is a feeling of uncertainty or a lack of conviction, whereas a **question** is used to gain information.

doubt和question都表示缺点东西。doubt表达出一种不确定感或者信念的缺乏，而question则是用来获取信息的。

Exercise 10-8: *Doubt / Question*

Select the appropriate response. Then check the Answer Key.

1. I have to say that I ____ that he'll be there.
   - ☐ doubt
   - ☐ question

2. He had a ____ about the lesson.
   - ☐ doubt
   - ☐ question

3. It was simply a ____ of time. (not if, but when)
   - ☐ doubt
   - ☐ question

4. Without a ____, he'll arrange it.
   - ☐ doubt
   - ☐ question

5. I don't ____ it for a moment.
   - ☐ doubt
   - ☐ question

6. The widow ____ the banker's rosy promises.
   - ☐ doubted
   - ☐ questioned

7. The detective ____ the suspect about where he had been.
   - ☐ doubted
   - ☐ questioned

8. We have our ____ about him.
   - ☐ doubts
   - ☐ questions

9. The students had a lot of ____ for the teacher about the test.
   - ☐ doubts
   - ☐ questions

10. I'd like to ask a ____.
    - ☐ doubt
    - ☐ question

Prefixes
前缀

It's useful to know the basic prefixes, as you can then guess the meaning of a word that you aren't familiar with. There are common changes, such as -**pel** to -**ulsion**（propel / propulsion）; -**vert** to -**version**（convert / conversion）; -**tend** to -**tention**（attend / attention）. The unstressed syllable is neutral（con**vert** / cən**vert**, re**duce** /rəd**uce**）. There is an intonation change between the noun (**pro**duce) and the verb (pro**duce**).

　　了解基本的前缀很有用，因为这样一来，当你碰到不熟悉的单词，你就可以猜它们的意思了。有一些很常见的变化，比如把-pel变成-ulsion（propel/propulsion）；把-vert变成-version（convert/conversion）；把-tend变成-tention（attend/attention）等。非重读的音节就是中性音节（convert/cənvərt，reduce/rəduce）。名词（produce）和动词（produce）之间存在音调变化。

Exercise 10-9: Vocabulary exercise — Prefixes and Suffixes   Track 134

Listen and repeat. The intonation is marked for you.

	-vert	-tend	-pel	-tract	-port	-duce/duct
a-	a**vert**	at**tend**	ap**pel**late	at**tract**	ap**por**tion	ad**duce**
con/com-	convert	con**tend**	com**pel**	contract	com**port**	conduct
di/dis/de-	di**vert**	dis**tend**	dis**pel**	dis**tract**	de**port**	de**duct**
e/ex-	e**vert**	ex**tend**	ex**pel**	extract	export	**ed**ucate
in/im-	in**vert**	intend	im**pel**	in**tract**able	import	in**duce**
pro/pre/per-	pervert	pre**tend**	pro**pel**	pro**tract**	pro**por**tion	produce
re-	re**vert**	retain	re**pel**	re**tract**	report	re**duce**

The following is a portion of President Barack Obama's inaugural speech, given on January 21, 2009. The first section is the standard text, with the intonation marked for you. The second section is the phonetic transcription. The third section is a simplified version of the speech.

　　下文节选自美国总统巴拉克·奥巴马于2009年1月21日发表的就职演讲。第一部分（灰色的）是标注了音调的标准版，第二部分（黑色的）是用音标写的语音版，第三部分（蓝色的）是演讲稿的简化版。

Exercise 10-10: Vocabulary, Comprehension, Pronunciation   Track 135

Listen and repeat.

My fellow citizens, I **stand** here **today humbled** by the task **before us**, **grateful** for the **trust** you have **bestowed, mindful** of the **sacrifices borne** by our **ancestors**. I thank President **Bush** for his **service** to our **nation**, as well as the **generosity** and **cooperation** he has shown through**out** this **transition**.

My fellow cidəzənz, I stænd hir təday həmbəld by the tæsk bəforəs, gratfəl fr thə trəst yoov bəstowd, mindfəl əv thə sæcrəfysəz born by är æncestrrz. I thænk Prezədent Büsh for hiz srrvəs to⁽ʷ⁾är nation, az welləz thə genəräsədy and co⁽ʷ⁾äperation he yəz shown thru⁽ʷ⁾out this trænzition.

Americans, I am here today with great respect for the job ahead of us. I thank you for the trust you have given to me. I know how much the previous generations have given up and done without. I thank President Bush for his hard work for our country, and for the help he has given me during the transition.

Forty-four **Americans** have now **taken** the presidential **oath**. The **words** have been **spoken** during **rising** tides of **prosperity** and the **still** waters of **peace**. **Yet, every** so **often** the oath is **taken** amidst gathering **clouds** and raging **storms**. At these moments, America has carried on **not simply** because of the **skill** or **vision** of **those** in high **office**, but because **We** the **People** have remained **faithful** to the **ideals** of our **forebearers**, and **true** to our founding **documents**. So it has **been**. So it must **be** with **this** generation of **Americans**.

Fordy-for əmerəcənz həv now takən the prezədenshəloath. Thə wrrdzəv bin spokən dyuring rizing tyd zəv präsperədy and thə still wäder zəv pees. Yet, evry so⁽ʷ⁾äffen theᵉ⁽ʸ⁾oathiz takən əmidst gæthering clæodz and raging stormz. ət theez moments, əmerəcə həz kerry dän nät simply bəcəzəv thə skill or vizhən əv thozin high⁽ʸ⁾äffəs, bət bəcəz We thə Peepəl həv rəmaind faithfəl tə theeᵉ⁽ʸ⁾ideeᵉ⁽ʸ⁾əlz əv our forbearerz, and tru to⁽ʷ⁾är founding däcyəmənts. So⁽ʷ⁾it haz bin. So⁽ʷ⁾it must be with this genaration'v əmerəcənz.

Up to now, forty-four Americans have made this statement to be president. They have said these words while our country was rich and peaceful. But, sometimes, they said them while we were poor or at war. At these times, America has continued, not only because of elected people who work hard or understand what needs to be done, but because Americans have stayed with the best ideas of the previous generations and hàve followed the Constitution. This is how it has been. This is how it has to be with us.

That we are in the **midst** of **crisis** is now well under**stood.** Our **nation** is at **war**, against a **far-**reaching **net**work of **violence** and **hatred**. Our **economy** is badly **weakened**, a **consequence** of **greed** and **irresponsibility** on the part of **some**, but **also** our collective **failure** to make hard **choices** and **prepare** the **nation** for a new **age**. **Homes** have been **lost; jobs shed; businesses shuttered.** Our **health** care is too **costly**; our **schools** fail too **many**; and **each** day brings further **evidence** that the ways we use **energy strengthen** our **adversaries** and **threaten** our **planet**.

That we are in the midst of crisis is now well understüd. Är nashən izzət war, əgenst ə fär-reaching netwrrk əv violence and hatred. Är ecänomy iz bædly weekənd, ə cänsəquents əv greed and irrespänsibility än thə pärdəv səm, bədälso är cəllectəv fay-yəlyer tə make härd choisəz and prəpar thə nation frə new age. Homzəv bin läst; jäbs shed; biznessəz shədderd. Är helth care iz too cästly; är schoolz fail too many; and each day bringz further evədents thət thə wayz we yuz energy strengthən är ædversereez and threat'n är plænət.

People now understand that we are in the middle of a huge problem. Our country is at war against a wide system of fighting and hate. Our economy is weak. This is a result of some greedy, irresponsible people. It is also the result of our group failure to make hard choices and prepare the country for a new time. People have lost their homes and their jobs, and businesses have closed. Our hospitals are too expensive. Our schools don't teach children well enough. And every day shows us that our energy use makes our enemies stronger and is bad for the earth.

These are the **indicators** of **crisis**, subject to **data** and **statistics**. Less **measurable** but no less **profound** is a **sapping** of **confidence** across our **land** — a nagging **fear** that America's **decline inevitable**, that the next **generation** must **lower** its **sights**.

Theez är thee[(y)]indəcaderz əv crysəs, səbject tə dadə and stətistəcs. Less mezhrəbəl bət no less prəfound izə sæpping əv cänfədənts əcräss är lænd — ə nægging fear thəd əmerəcəz dəcline izinevətəbəl, thət thə next genəration məst lower its sights.

These are the signs of big problems. You can see this in the numbers in the reports. It is not as easy to measure the decrease in confidence in America, but it is equally important. There is a continuing fear that America will fail and the next generation will have to accept less in life.

Today I say to **you** that the **challenges** we face are **real.** They are **serious** and they are **many.** They will not be met **easily** or in a **short** span of **time.** But **know this, America** — they **will** be **met.** On **this** day, we **gather** because we have chosen **hope** over **fear, unity** of **purpose** over **conflict** and **discord.** On this **day,** we come to **proclaim** an **end** to the petty **grievances** and false **promises,** the **recriminations** and worn-out **dogmas,** that for far too **long** have **strangled** our **politics.**

Təday I say də you thət thə chælləngəz we face är real. They är siree[(y)]us and they är many. They will nät be met eezəly or innə short span of time. But know this, əmerəcə — they will be met. Än this day, we gæther bəcəz we həv chozən ho po ver fir, yunədy əv prpəs over cänflict and discord. Än this day, we cəm tə prəclaim ənend tə thə peddy grieevəncəz and false präməsəz, thə rəcrimənashənz and wor nout dägməz, that fr fär too läng həv stræ̈ngəld är pälətics.

I am telling you today that we are facing real challenges. They are serious and there are a lot of them. It will not be easy to fix these problems and it will take a long time. But we will fix them. We are here together today because we think hope is better than fear. We think that we should all work together instead of fighting and arguing. We are here to say that this is the end of small complaints and false promises. We have to stop blaming each other and using old ideas. This has held our politics back.

We remain a young **nation,** but in the words of **Scripture,** the **time** has **come** to set **aside** childish **things.** The **time** has **come** to **reaffirm** our enduring **spirit;** to **choose** our better **history;** to carry **forward that precious gift**, that noble **idea, passed** on from generation to **generation**: the **God**-given **promise** that **all** are **equal**, **all** are **free**, and **all** deserve a chance to pursue their **full** measure of **happiness**.

We rəmainə yəng nation, bəddin thə wrrdz əv Scripchər, thə time həz cəm tə sedə side childish thingz. Thə time həz cəme tə ree⁽ʸ⁾əffirm är endyuring spirət; tə choozar bedder histry; tə carry forwrrd thæt preshəs gift, thæt nobəl idea, pæst än frəm genəration tə genəration: thə Gäd-givən präməs thədäller eekəl, äller free, and äll dəzervə chænts tə prrsue their füll mezher əv hæppinəss.

We are still a young country. As it says in the Bible, it is time to stop acting like children. It is time to talk about our lasting spirit. It is time to choose a better path for our history. It is time to carry forward that valuable gift, that noble idea, that has been passed on from generation to generation. It is a promise from God that all people are equal, everyone is free, and we all should have the chance of as much happiness as possible.

Synonyms
同义词

A synonym is a word with a meaning that is similar to another word. For example, synonyms for sarcastic are ironic, sardonic, mocking, and satirical. These are all words indicating mockery, but there are important nuances.

某个单词的同义词就是与其意义相似的单词。例如，sarcastic的同义词是ironic，sardonic，mocking 和satirical。这几个词都表示嘲弄，但又存在重要的细微差别。

One of the first things a child learns in elementary school is to use synonyms in order to avoid repeating the same word over and over again. The following is a student writing sample. You'll notice that the word **cook** is used in various forms 13 times. In the rewrite, the word has been replaced all but twice.

小学生在学校里要学的第一件事就包括使用同义词，因为只有学会了这个，才不会一遍遍地重复同样的单词。下面是某个学生的写作实例，你会发现cook这个词以不同的形式出现了13次。在修改后的文章中，这个词只用了两次，其他的全部被替换掉了。

Repetitive Wording

Have I ever told you how lucky I am? Yesterday my husband **cooked** a cake! It was the most delicious cake I had ever eaten in my life. You may know that I'm not good at **cooking**. If I had had to **cook**, I would have **cooked** instant noodles. When I was in Thailand, my dad and my two sisters did all the **cooking**. If I had wanted to eat something and I didn't know how to **cook** it, I just told them what it looked like, and they would **cook** it and it always turned out very delicious. When I decided to get married, everyone got worried. That was because I knew nothing about **cooking.** First I told my husband-to-be that I didn't know how to **cook,** but he said that was OK, he would teach me. Do you know what Thai potato curry looks like? Steve **cooked** it for me. It was so good and I liked it. He taught me how to **cook**. Today I can **cook** almost everything he likes and also some Thai foods. I hope I will be a perfect **cook** soon. When I visit my family in Thailand, I will show them how good I am.

With Synonyms

Have I ever told you how lucky I am? Yesterday my husband **made** a cake! It was the most delicious cake I had ever eaten in my life. You may know that I'm not a good **cook**. If I had had to **make dinner**, I would have **heated up** instant noodles. When I was in Thailand, my dad and my two sisters **made** all the meals. If I wanted to eat something and I didn't know how to **prepare** it, I just told them what it looked like, and they would **take care of** it and it always turned out very delicious. When I decided to get married, everyone got worried. That was because I knew nothing about **the kitchen**. I told my husband-to-be that, but he said that was OK, he would teach me. Do you know what Thai potato curry looks like? He **fixed** it for me once. It was so good and I liked it. He taught me how to **cook**. Today I can **make** almost everything he likes and also some Thai foods. When I visit my family in Thailand, I will show them how good I am.

VERBS

In this section, you will learn the true passive and the various imitation passives, as well as six useful verbs, and the past and future real duo.

在这部分，你要学习真正的被动语态、各种仿被动语态、6个有用的动词，以及过去真实双重时态和将来真实双重时态。

	Passive		
	Past	Present	Future
Simple	It was done.	It is done.	It will be done.
Real Duo	A had been done before B was done.	A has been done many times.	A will be done before B is done.
Unreal Duo	If A had been done, B would've been done.	If A were done, B would be done.	If A is done, B will be done.

The Passive
被动语态

There are two ways of giving information. The most direct is called the **active voice** (SVO), as in **The dogs ate the bones**. With the active voice, the subject(the dogs) does something to the object(the bones). You can flip this order so the subject receives the action (**The bones were eaten by the dogs**).

呈现信息有两种方式。最直接的一种叫做主动语态(SVO)，比如：The dogs ate the bones。在主动语态中，主语(the dogs)对宾语(the bones)做了一些事。你也可以把顺序颠倒过来，这样主语就变成了受动者(The bones were eaten by the dogs)。

The passive voice always includes a form of be, such as am, is, was, were, are, or been. Another way to recognize it is that it may include "by," such as It was developed by a team of engineers.

被动语态始终包含be动词的某种形式，如：am，is，was，were，are 或been。确认句子是不是被动语态还有一种方法，那就是被动句中很可能含有"by"这个词，例如：It was developed by a team of engineers。

The active voice is more common and is generally preferred as it makes your communications stronger and more dynamic. Overuse of the passive voice will make you sound flat and uninteresting. There are instances where the passive voice should be used, however, such as in scientific writing, where it gives the appearance of objectivity.

　　主动语态更加常见，也更加受到人们的偏爱，因为它会让你的话更有力、更有动感。如果你过多地使用被动语态，只会让人觉得你平淡无味。但是，在有些情况下必须要用被动语态，比如在写科学文章的时候，因为它能呈现出事物的客观性。

1 Let's start with the active voice. You did something and you admit it. 我们先从主动语态开始。你做了某事，并且承认了。 I **broke** the cup.	**3** One step further away, it turns into a description, and doesn't involve you at all. 再下一步，它变成了一个描述性的句子，跟你一点关系也没有了。 The cup **is broken**.
2 Next, you remove yourself a bit. This is the true passive voice. 接下来，你把自己的位置挪动了一下。这是真正的被动语态。 The cup **was broken**（by me）. The cup **got broken**（by me）.	**4** Finally, you blame the cup. 最后，你把责任推给了杯子。 The cup **broke**.

With these particular verbs, it's common to put the focus on the **action**, rather than on the **cause**. 对这几个动词来说，我们一般关注的是动作而不是原因。	It broke. It bent. It creased. It crinkled. It crumpled. It folded. It rumpled. It wrinkled. It chipped. It cracked. It crumbled.	It crashed. It crushed. It fractured. It ripped. It shattered. It smashed. It snapped. It splintered. It split. It tore. It healed.

Exercise 10-11: Switching Between Active and Passive

Change to the opposite form. Then check the Answer Key.

A watched B.　　　　　　　　　　　　**B was watched by A.**
A was folded by B.　　　　　　　　　　**B folded A.**

1.　The boys washed the cars.

2.　The papers were handed out by the teacher.

3.　The dentist cleaned her teeth.

4.　Everyone was upset by his remarks.

5. Gold was discovered by the miners.

6. Snow covered the fields.

7. The plan will be revised by the committee.

8. Our intelligence has been insulted by the media.

9. The patient should have been informed by the doctor.

10. The mailman will have delivered the package by 5:00 p.m.

Exercise 10-12: Active to No-Blame Passive

*Change to **no-blame**. Then check the Answer Key.*

They opened it.   It opened.

1. Joe tore the paper.

2. Sammy rocked the boat.

3. Edna crashed the car.

4. Gloria fractured her leg.

5. The suspect burned the evidence.

6. Angela overflowed the tub.

7. Ben tipped over the vase.

8. The drycleaner wrinkled his shirt.

9. Edgar chipped his tooth.

10. The wind snapped the branch.

Exercise 10-13: Passive Voice

Fill in the blanks using the appropriate words from the following list. Then check the Answer Key.

Soybeans ____ in Asia more than 3,000 years ago. A mural shows tofu and soy milk ____ in northern China. The earliest written reference to soy milk didn't occur for another 1,200 years, when soy milk ____ in a Chinese poem, "Ode to Tofu."

Travelers from Europe ____ with soybeans and the foods ____ them — especially miso, soy sauce, and tofu. Soybeans arrived in the United States in the 1700s, ____ Europe by several people including Benjamin Franklin.

Soy-based infant formulas ____ in the United States in 1909, and in 1910 the world's first soy dairy ____ by a Chinese biologist. By the end of the first World War, soy milk ____ commercially in New York. Within 15 years, manufacturers ____ with added nutrients such as calcium.

became acquainted	was started	brought from	made from
was mentioned	being made	were first cultivated	were introduced
were experimenting	was being produced		

Six Useful Verbs
六个有用的动词

MANAGE	TURN OUT
He **managed** to pay his bills, even though he didn't earn very much.	He thought he had no cash, but it **turned out** that he had $5 in his back pocket.
HAPPEN TO	**USED TO**
By chance, he **happened to** forget his wallet that day.	This kind of thing **used to** happen to him all the time.
END UP	**WOUND UP**
He thought he would have to write a check, but he **ended up** doing dishes to pay his bill.	He started out in the kitchen, but somehow **wound up** in the back office working on the company taxes.

Exercise 10-14: 6 Useful Verbs

Select the most appropriate of the six verbs. Then check the Answer Key.

1. It was hard, but we ▓▓▓▓ to find a spot.
2. Did anyone ▓▓▓▓ pick up the dry-cleaning?
3. When she was young, she ▓▓▓▓ hike a lot.
4. He seemed honest, but he ▓▓▓▓ not to be.
5. They started out in L.A., but ▓▓▓▓ in New York.
6. It didn't ▓▓▓▓ the way we expected.
7. If you ▓▓▓▓ see him, say hello for me.
8. Didn't you ▓▓▓▓ live in L.A.?
9. He wanted to be a doctor, but ▓▓▓▓ working as an auto mechanic.
10. They ▓▓▓▓ to scrape together the basic costs.

Past Duo
过去双重时态

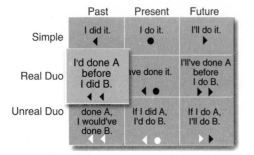

	Past	Present	Future
Simple	I did it. ◀	I do it. ●	I'll do it. ▶
Real Duo	I'd done A before I did B. ◀◀	...ve done it. ◀●	I'll've done A before I do B. ▶▶
Unreal Duo	done A, I would've done B. ◀◀	If I did A, I'd do B. ◀●	If I do A, I'll do B. ▶▶

As you learned with the present duo, you can link two events in time.

就像你学过的现在双重时态一样，你可以在时间上把两件事联系起来。

The **past duo** expresses the idea that something happened before another action in the past. It can also show that something happened before a specific time in the past.

过去双重时态表示某件事发生在过去的另一个动作之前。它也可以表示某件事发生在过去的某个具体时间之前。

This is traditionally called the past perfect.

在传统语法体系中，这被叫做过去完成时。

Exercise 10-15: Past Duo

Using the provided phrase, change the past or present to the past duo. Then check the Answer Key.

1. He has never been to Los Angeles.

   Until he was invited by the university last year,

2. He lost his wallet.

   He didn't have any money because

3. He frequently traveled there.

   Ron was very familiar with Paris as

4. We didn't make a reservation.

   We couldn't get a hotel room since

5. Fred was in college for ten years.

   By the time he graduated,

6. They owned their house for 20 years.

   They felt bad about moving because

Present and Past Duo Review
复习现在双重时态和过去双重时态

Exercise 10-16: Past Duo and Present Duo

Fill in the blanks with the most appropriate verb form, including the simple past and the present and past duo. Then check the Answer Key.

1. You may ____ (hear) of Ernest Hemingway. He ____ (be) an American novelist who ____ (die) in 1961. Prior to his death, he ____ (write) over a dozen novels.

2. Every year, Joyce and Blake ____ (spend) a few days at a hotel in Fiji. They ____ (go) there for years.

3. Sam ____ (go) for a bike ride after school yesterday. He ____ (want) some exercise because he ____ (sit) in a stuffy classroom all day.

4. It ____ (be) six months since I've seen my cousins.

5. Lee was driving over to pick up his wife. Outside her office, he met a couple of people he knew. They wanted to go out for coffee, but he ____ (arrange) to meet his wife for dinner and didn't have time.

Exercise 10-17: When Did Those Two Things Happen?

Select the correct answer. Then check the Answer Key.

1. We ____ to Paris.

    ☐ have never been
    ☐ had never been

2. We ____ to Paris **before** the Olympics.

    ☐ have never been
    ☐ had never been

3. Oh, dear! The sink ____!

    ☐ has overflowed
    ☐ had overflowed

4. The house ____ **by the time** the plumber arrived.

    ☐ has flooded
    ☐ had flooded

5. We ____ time to clean it up **yet**.

    ☐ haven't had
    ☐ hadn't had

6. We____ such a mess **before** that event.

    ☐ haven't ever seen
    ☐ hadn't ever seen

7. ____ thinking about moving out.

    ☐ We've already started
    ☐ We'd already started

8. ____ of moving **until** that happened.

    ☐ We've never thought
    ☐ We'd never thought

9. ____ in 20 years.

    ☐ We haven't moved
    ☐ We hadn't moved

10. At the beginning of the year, we ____ this possibility!

    ☐ haven't foreseen
    ☐ hadn't foreseen

Future Real Duo
将来真实双重时态

So far, you have learned the ***present*** duo (I have never done that before.) and the ***past*** duo (I had never done that before last year).

到目前为止，你已经学习了现在双重时态（I have never done that before.）和过去双重时态（I had never done that before last year）。

Now, we are going to add the **future** duo, which is two completed actions in the future. Key words are *by*, *by the time*, and *before*.

现在，我们要接着讲将来双重时态，它包含两个在将来将会完成的动作。关键词是by，by the time和before。

	Past	Present	Future
Simple	I did it. ◀	I do it. ●	I'll do it. ▶
Real Duo	I'd done A before I did B. ◀◀	I've done it. ◀●	I'll've done A before I do B. ▶▶
Unreal Duo	If I had done A, I would've done B. ◀◀	If I did A, I'd do B. ◀●	If I do A, I'll do B. ▶▶

Exercise 10-18: Future Real Duo

Using the provided phrase, change the future or present duo to the future duo. Use the supporting words where provided. Check the Answer Key when you're done.

He **has saved** enough to buy a car.
By next year, he **will have saved** enough to buy a car.

1. Will she learn French before she goes to Paris?

2. I have figured out when I'll graduate.
   By Christmas,

3. He'll finish it.
   by midnight.

4. They'll turn it in.
   before the deadline.

5. She's running out of options.
   before she hears back about the decision.

Future Review
复习将来时态

Exercise 10-19: Three Futures

Select the correct tense. Then check the Answer Key.

1. We _____ tomorrow.
   ☐ will finish
   ☐ will have finished

2. Do you think you _____ over it by then?
   ☐ will get
   ☐ will have gotten

3. If you tell me when, _____ sure to be there.
   ☐ I'll be
   ☐ I'll have been

4. _____ you at 8:00 sharp.
   ☐ I'll call
   ☐ I'll have called

5. Hurry, or they ____ all the food by the time we get there!

☐ will eat
☐ will have eaten

6. If you hurry, ____ the train.

☐ you'll catch
☐ you'll have caught

7. ____ through six meetings by the time you get here.

☐ We'll sit
☐ We'll have sat

8. Do you think ____ this time?

☐ they'll help
☐ they'll have helped

9. Don't worry, ____ all about it by tomorrow.

☐ he'll forget
☐ he'll have forgotten

10. He thinks that if he's fair, everyone ____ him.

☐ will like
☐ will have liked

Exercise 10-20: Verb Review

Select the correct answer. Then check the Answer Key.

1. Joseph ____ groceries last week.

☐ buys
☐ bought

2. I think he ____ it tomorrow.

☐ do
☐ will do

3. Let's ____ him on Friday.

☐ call
☐ to call
☐ calling

4. He ____ out the warehouse right now.

☐ vacuums
☐ is vacuuming

5. Shirley ____ supplies once a month.

☐ orders
☐ is ordering

6. The rec center ____ since 1998.

☐ is open
☐ has been open

7. The hard drive ____.

☐ is corrupt
☐ has corrupted

8. My car ____ many times since May.

☐ stalls
☐ has stalled

9. Ted and Marge ____ away ten years ago.

☐ moved
☐ have moved

10. Joanie ____ on the rowing team since Tuesday.

☐ was
☐ has been

11. I hope ____ this by Wednesday.

☐ finish
☐ to finish
☐ finishing

12. We wish he ____ be more open about it.

☐ will
☐ would

13. Everyone hopes they ____ succeed.
- [ ] will
- [ ] would

14. The insurance company ____ by the new agent.
- [ ] is called
- [ ] was called

15. We will ____ by his assistant no later than 5:00.
- [ ] be informed
- [ ] have been informed

16. "I will go," said Tom. He said that he ____.
- [ ] will go
- [ ] would go

17. She ____ here for two years next month.
- [ ] will be
- [ ] will have been

18. If he had taken an aspirin, he ____ have a headache.
- [ ] won't
- [ ] wouldn't

19. If the report ____ clear, we could act on it.
- [ ] was
- [ ] were

20. I'm not sure if I ____ help you.
- [ ] can
- [ ] could

21. He is very motivated, ____ he?
- [ ] isn't
- [ ] doesn't

22. Stewart arranges things very well, ____ he?
- [ ] isn't
- [ ] doesn't

23. The weather has been great, ____ it?
- [ ] isn't
- [ ] hasn't

24. George broke his promise, ____ he?
- [ ] wasn't
- [ ] didn't

25. Candy won't be there, ____ she?
- [ ] will
- [ ] won't

26. That would be nice, ____ it?
- [ ] won't
- [ ] wouldn't

27. Maurice had never been there, ____ he?
- [ ] has
- [ ] had
- [ ] hasn't
- [ ] hadn't

28. Benny wanted to play. The coach ____ play.
- [ ] let him
- [ ] let him to

29. They intended ____ the board soon.
- [ ] notify
- [ ] to notify
- [ ] notifying

30. Someone suggested ____ the subway.
- [ ] take
- [ ] to take
- [ ] taking

Let's review everything you have learned in Chapter 10. Check your work using the Answer Key.

我们来复习一下在第十章中学过的全部内容。请参照答案检查正误。

Part 1: *Select the proper form.*

1. By summer, he _____ in Somalia for a decade.
    - ☐ will be
    - ☐ will have been

2. Next time, they _____ before they come over.
    - ☐ call
    - ☐ will call

3. She isn't sure if she _____ help us.
    - ☐ can
    - ☐ could

4. They have several _____. Would you mind if they asked them?
    - ☐ doubts
    - ☐ questions

5. The commissioner had grave _____ about the testing process.
    - ☐ doubts
    - ☐ questions

6. When I was 16, I _____ in swim meets.
    - ☐ participated
    - ☐ was participated

7. I was _____ English by a college professor.
    - ☐ learned
    - ☐ taught

8. When I was in college, I _____ my husband.
    - ☐ met
    - ☐ was met

9. When I got off the train, I _____ by my sister.
    - ☐ met
    - ☐ was met

10. The product _____ the rigorous standards.
    - ☐ didn't meet
    - ☐ wasn't met

Part 2: *Select the proper form.*

1. I hope you _____ it.
    - ☐ like
    - ☐ would like

2. I hope he _____ find it.
    - ☐ will
    - ☐ would

3. I hoped he _____ take it, but he didn't.
    - ☐ will
    - ☐ would

4. I wish he _____ go.
    - ☐ can
    - ☐ could

5. I wished he _____, but he didn't.
    - ☐ went
    - ☐ had gone

6. I hope he _____ interested.
    - ☐ is
    - ☐ were

7. I wish he _____ interested, but he's not.
    - ☐ is
    - ☐ were

8. I hoped he _____ interested.
    - ☐ was
    - ☐ were

9. I wished he ____ interested.

☐ has been

☐ had been

10. I had hoped that he ____ interested, but he wasn't.

☐ will be

☐ would be

Part 3: *Fill in the proper tag ending.*

1. They have to change the rules,   ?
2. They have changed the rules,   ?
3. They had to change the rules,   ?
4. They had the rules changed,   ?
5. They had already changed the rules,   ?
6. They'd better change the rules,   ?
7. They'd rather change the rules,   ?
8. The rules have changed,   ?
9. The rules will be changed,   ?
10. The rules have been changed,   ?

Part 4: *Select the proper form.*

1. "I will do it." I said that I ____ it.

☐ will do

☐ would do

2. They found it. They thought they ____ it.

☐ found

☐ had found

3. She isn't ready. She told us that she ____ ready.

☐ isn't

☐ wasn't

4. If you have time, we ____ to the park.

☐ will go

☐ would go

☐ would have gone

5. If you had time, we ____ to the park.

☐ will go

☐ would go

☐ would have gone

6. If you'd had time, we ____ to the park.

☐ will go

☐ would go

☐ would have gone

7. If they ____ interested, they would join.

☐ are

☐ were

☐ had been

8. If they ____ interested, they would've joined.

☐ are

☐ were

☐ had been

9. If they ____ interested, they will join.

☐ are

☐ were

☐ had been

296

10. People will be happy if that _____ true.

☐ is
☐ was
☐ were

ESSAY

Using what you have learned, write an essay using the following topics:
利用你学过的知识写两段话，话题如下：

1. What childhood friends would you like to reconnect with?
   你想跟哪几个儿时的伙伴重新联系？

2. If you had to move, what would you miss most about your home?
   如果你不得不搬家，你会最想念家里的什么？

You can handwrite your essay below or e-mail it to **para@grammar.bz** to be stored. These paragraphs are not graded or reviewed, but simply by writing them, your English will improve. For this final essay, review the outline format, the writing structure checklist, and the technical editing checklist.

你可以把作文写在下方，也可以把它们发送到邮箱 para@grammar.bz 以存档。我们不会对你的作文进行打分或点评，但只要你写了，你的英语水平就会提高。在写这最后一篇作文之前，请先重温一下提纲样式、文章结构注意事项，以及文章细节注意事项。

Student Paragraph
Send Chat Attach Address Fonts Colors Save As Draft Photo Browser Show Stationery

To: para@grammar.bz
Cc:
Bcc:
Subject: Chapter 10
Signature: Corporate

My name is _____

Outline Format
大纲样式

You'll notice that this is the same format you first learned in Chapter 1: Introduction, Body, and Conclusion. The number of main points, subpoints, and sub-subpoints will change depending on how much information you have and how much detail and supporting material you need to use. Don't use more than five main points in your essay.

你会注意到这个样式跟你在第一章学过的一样：开头，主体和结尾。主要论点，分论点，分论点下的分论点都根据你有的信息量与使用的详略程度，和你需要使用的支持材料的多少而变化。文章不要超过五个主要论点。

Introduction

I. Attention-getting statement — Get the reader's attention by telling a short or humorous story, asking a question, using a quotation, etc.

II. Thesis statement — State the specific purpose of your essay.

III. Preview statement — Give an overview of all of your main points.

Body

   I. First main point

      A. Subpoint

            1. Sub-subpoint

            2. Sub-subpoint

      B. Subpoint

            1. Sub-subpoint

            2. Sub-subpoint

            3. Sub-subpoint

   II. Second main point

      A. Subpoint

            1. Sub-subpoint

            2. Sub-subpoint

      B. Subpoint

            1. Sub-subpoint

            2. Sub-subpoint

            3. Sub-subpoint

      C. Subpoint

Conclusion

I. Summary statement — Review all of your main points.

II. Concluding statement — Prepare a closing statement that ends your presentation smoothly.

Writing Structure Checklist
写作注意事项

1. ☐ There are at least 200 words.
2. ☐ There are at least 15 periods (i.e., 15 complete sentences).
3. ☐ The introduction has 2–3 sentences, the main paragraph 10–11, and the conclusion 2–3.
4. ☐ The introduction captures the reader's interest.
5. ☐ There is a clear topic sentence in the first paragraph. This is an opinion that needs support and is not just a simple fact.
6. ☐ The introduction does not use the words **I agree**, **I disagree**, **I think**, **in my opinion**, etc.
7. ☐ The main body paragraph gives 2–3 different reasons or a combination of reasons and examples that support the topic sentence in the introduction.
8. ☐ There is a single voice, with no shifting between I / you / we / they.
9. ☐ Vocabulary, idioms, prepositions, and word order sound natural.
10. ☐ Every sentence connects to the sentence before and after it in some way; synonym, antonym, repeated word, word form, etc.
11. ☐ There are at least four different sentence types.

Technical Editing Checklist
修改注意事项

1. ☐ The mechanical aspects of punctuation, spelling, capitalization, and indenting are correct.
2. ☐ There are no sentence fragments. Every sentence can be turned into a yes/no question.
   Complete: I was tired. (Was I tired?)
   Fragment: Because I was tired. (You can't ask, I was tired because?)
3. ☐ Every two-part sentence has a joiner (for, and, but, or, yet, so).
4. ☐ All future time clauses use the simple present tense.
   Correct: When I go...
   Incorrect: When I will go...
5. ☐ There is an **article** (a, an, the) or other **modifier** (my, one, that, etc.) before every **single** countable noun.
6. ☐ There are proper plural noun modifiers such as **these** and **those**.
7. ☐ There is an **-s ending** on every plural noun, with the few exceptions of **men**, **women**, **people**, **children**, etc.
8. ☐ **The** is only used to mean something specific. It is not used with general things, such as **life**, **nature**, **kindness**.
9. ☐ Each **he / she / it / they** refers back to a specific noun that it matches (i.e., singular / singular & plural / plural).
10. ☐ The simple form is used after these helping verbs: can / could / will / would / may / might / must / shall / should (e.g., I can **go**).
11. ☐ The simple form is used after **do**, **does**, or **did** (Did he **go**?, not Did he **went**?).
12. ☐ A comma is used with **which**, but not with **that**.

FINAL

Let's review everything you've learned in Chapters 6 through 10. Check your work using the Answer Key.

我们来复习一下你从第六章到第十章所学的全部内容。请参照答案检查正误。

Part 1: *Join the two statements using* **that**.

1. We are sad. We lost the game.

2. He is happy. His friends arrived safely.

Part 2: *Rewrite each sentence starting with the indicated phrase.*

1. They finished it.
    It's not clear who
2. It's wonderful.
    She said that
3. They can't swim.
    I thought that

Part 3: *Change the statement to an indirect question by adding the statement to the intro phrase.*

1. She bought groceries.
    Do you remember that
2. They got married.
    Did you know that
3. The new store opened.
    Did you hear that

Part 4: *Change the statement to an indirect question, using your own intro phrase.*

1. They went **there**.

2. **That girl** won an award.

3. He drove to California **on Wednesday**.

Part 5: *Fill in the blank with* **so** *or* **such**.

1. He was _____ worried about his lost dog.
2. We are _____ good friends.
3. Her teacher is _____ prepared to teach class every day.
4. I had _____ an amazing time at the concert!

Part 6: *Fill in the blank with the proper form of* **hope** *or* **wish**.

1. She _____ she had a million dollars.
2. She _____ you will give her a million dollars.
3. We _____ you have a nice day.
4. We _____ it were a nice day.

Part 7: *Complete the sentence with the appropriate probability verb.*

1. I _____ be able to go with you.   0% probability
2. You _____ finish your homework before you go out   strong probability
   tonight.
3. She _____ help you.   slight possibility
4. We _____ complete the sale tomorrow.   100% probability
5. He _____ know the answer; let's ask him.   50% possibility

Part 8: *Complete the sentence with the appropriate verb of obligation.*

1. We _____ followed directions.   past advice
2. She _____ catch up, or she'll be left behind!   obligation
3. You _____ be four feet tall to go on this ride.   strong obligation
4. I _____ only bench-press fifty pounds.   ability
5. You _____ eat dessert after you finish your meal.   permission

Part 9: *Fill in the blank with the proper form of* **say**, **tell**, **speak**, *or* **talk**.

1. Please _____ your sister that I called.
2. Don't _____ that! It's not true!
3. You should _____ with the sales associate if you have a question.
4. We were _____ loudly in the library.

Part 10: *Select the proper word.*

1. Did you _____ that noise? It surprised me!   ☐ listen to
                                                                 ☐ hear
2. We should _____ his advice; he knows what he's talking   ☐ listen to
   about.   ☐ hear
3. It _____ like a UFO! I'm serious!   ☐ appeared
                                                                 ☐ looked
4. We _____ everywhere but couldn't find it.   ☐ looked
                                                                 ☐ saw
5. The babysitter _____ the children while their parents   ☐ looked at
   were out.   ☐ watched
6. Your singing _____ very professional.   ☐ looks
                                                                 ☐ sounds

Part 11: *Flip the adjective in each of the following sentences.*

1. The **very hungry** caterpillar wouldn't stop eating.

2. The **bright red** car was the fastest at the race.

3. A person **who is funny** can make other people laugh.

4. Water **that has frozen** is called ice.

Part 12: *Compact the sentences.*

1. **The flowers** are blooming. **They** grow in the garden.

2. I know **a girl**. **She** can speak three languages.

Part 13: *Convert the following statement to **Who**, **What**, **Where**, **When**, **Why**, and **How** questions.*

My grandmother eagerly takes the bus to the market every day to sell scarves that she has knitted.

1. Who
2. What
3. Where
4. When
5. Why
6. How

Part 14: *Change the **bold words** to an **else** phrase.*

1. We went to **the other store** to find milk.

2. He talked to **the other salesperson**.

Part 15: *Select the proper form.*

1. He hasn't worked there _____ three years. ☐ for ☐ ago ☐ in
2. We moved into this house two weeks _____. ☐ for ☐ ago ☐ in
3. She listens to music _____ she rides the bus. ☐ during ☐ while
4. You weren't paying attention _____ the meeting. ☐ during ☐ while
5. You have to turn in your paper _____ Friday. ☐ by ☐ until
6. She won't give up _____ they find her purse. ☐ by ☐ until
7. I've known about that _____ yesterday. ☐ for ☐ since
8. We'll call you _____ lunch. ☐ in ☐ after

9. The judge has not _____ heard all of the arguments.

☐ yet   ☐ already
☐ still

10. Have you _____ finished eating?

☐ yet ☐ already ☐ still

Part 16: *Fill in the proper* **tag ending**.

1. They have to listen to you,   ?
2. They haven't changed,   ?
3. They had already done it,   ?
4. She will have finished it by then,   ?
5. We've been good,   ?

Part 17: *Convert each statement to a* **how** *question.*

1. That ride was so scary!
2. We bought 60 pounds of potatoes.
3. There are 60 minutes in an hour.

Part 18: *Convert each statement from the -en verb to* **make** *and an* **adjective**.

1. He lifts weights to strengthen his body.
2. This lamp lightens the room.
3. This polish hardens the surface.

Part 19: *Fill in the blank with* **to**, **for**, **of**, **on**, **with**, **about**, **at**, **in**, **out**, **than**, **up**, *or* **from**.

1. I like to think   all the good times with my friends.
2. We need to get   the store before it closes.
3. We want to take advantage   the sale before it ends.
4. Who does this purse belong   ?
5. He is preparing   his trip to Hawaii.
6. She is getting ready   the dance tonight.
7. Who is taking care   the children after school?
8. He refuses to ask   help.
9. I am looking forward   my upcoming vacation.
10. They work   at the gym three days a week.

Part 20: *Indicate if each sentence is grammatically correct.*

1. We made them to stand up.   ☐ Yes   ☐ No
2. We allow them to stand up.   ☐ Yes   ☐ No
3. We force them to stand up.   ☐ Yes   ☐ No
4. We permit them to stand up.   ☐ Yes   ☐ No
5. We let them to stand up.   ☐ Yes   ☐ No

Part 21: Change the direct statement to a reported statement.

1. She calls her sister every day.
   I thought that
2. They will talk to him tomorrow.
   We believed that
3. He'll wake up early when he has to work.
   He said that

Part 22: Fill in the blank with **their / they're / there**.

1. Have you seen _____ house? It's gorgeous.
2. _____ not coming back until Saturday.
3. _____ is something wrong with that picture.

Part 23: Fill in the blank with **to / too / two**.

1. I ate _____ much last night!
2. I ate _____ pieces of pie.
3. I didn't mean _____ eat so much, but I couldn't help myself!

Part 24: Check the box with the appropriate meaning of the sentence.

1. We were the only ones at the party.
   - ☐ Nobody else was having a party.
   - ☐ Nobody else was at the party.

2. He is only hosting the party in town.
   - ☐ He is not doing anything but hosting.
   - ☐ Nobody else is hosting the party.

Part 25: Select the appropriate response.

1. If I _____ his judgment, he will become defensive.
   - ☐ doubt
   - ☐ question
2. If you have any _____, I will answer them.
   - ☐ doubts
   - ☐ questions
3. I _____ that she would arrive on time.
   - ☐ doubted
   - ☐ questioned

Part 26: Change to the opposite form (*passive or active*).

1. The stylist cut the girl's hair.

2. The newspapers were distributed by the paperboy.

3. We vacuumed all of the carpets.

Part 27: *Change to no-blame.*

1. Leslie broke the plate.

2. We burned the wood.

3. Joe rolled the tire down the street.

Part 28: *Fill in the blank with the proper form of* **take** *or* **have**.

1. The baby _____ three naps a day.
2. We're _____ company at four.
3. They _____ a short coffee break at ten.
4. Everyone _____ a good time at the party.
5. We're _____ a trip next month.

Part 29: *Fill in the blank with the appropriate preposition.*

1. We got lost and wound _____ 30 miles from our destination.
2. People who succeed don't give _____ easily.
3. I have faith that my lost watch will turn _____ sooner or later.
4. The cake didn't turn _____ the way I had hoped. Oops!
5. If you happen _____ be in the area, stop by and see us.
6. They turned _____ our offer to buy their house.
7. Everyone booed when he gave _____ the ending of the story.
8. She used _____ go there all the time.
9. After the fight, he ended _____ with a black eye.
10. The athlete's knee finally gave _____ after sustaining multiple injuries.

Answer Key

Dictation Placement Test (100 words)

Soccer, a team sport played between two teams of eleven players, is considered to be the most popular sport in the world. It is played on a rectangular grass or artificial turf field, with a goal at each end. The object of the game is to score by maneuvering the ball into the opposing goal. In general play, the goalkeepers are the only players allowed to use their hands or arms to touch the ball. The rest of the team use their feet, head or body. The team that scores the most goals by the end of the match wins.

Placement Test: Basic Grammar

1. a. am b. are c. is
2. a. These tests are easy.
   b. The trees are tall.
3. Shelly is not in Europe.
4. Is your brother in college?
5. a. I am always late.
   b. I am late every day.
6. a. feeds   b. tell
7. a. He reads it.   b. They fly it.
   c. She plans them.
8. a. on b. on c. in d. under
9. a. and b. but c. so
10. a. Lou does not know Ed. / Lou doesn't know Ed.
    b. The cars do not go fast. / The cars don't go fast.
11. a. Does it rain every day?
    b. Do you like it?
12. the worst
13. a. into b. away
14. a. They thought about it.
    b. We saw him at the gym.
    c. We had enough time.
15. Morgan did not hear a noise. / Morgan didn't hear a noise.
16. a. Did James drive to New York?
    b. Did Andrea and Sarah walk to work?
17. James frequently drove to New York.
18. a. wasn't he   b. aren't I?
19. a. didn't they   b. did she?
20. a. some   b. a
21. a. a   b. the
22. a.—   b. a
23. a. much   b. many
24. a. is sleeping   b. work
25. Is the store being remodeled?
26. a. up   b. off
27. a. Charlie will go to France.
    b. Marcus won't order shoes from Italy. / Marcus will not order shoes from Italy.c. Will Larry fix my computer?
28. Timmy will not answer your questions. / Timmy won't answer your questions.
29. Will the cell phone need to be charged?
30. a. do   b. make   c. make
31. a. talking   b. told
32. a. for   b. with

Placement Test: Advanced Grammar

1. a. We don't know who did it.
   b. We don't know who makes them.
   c. We don't know who will take care of it.
2. a. What did he do?
   b. What will they buy?
   c. Where did he do it?
   d. When did he do it?
   e. How did he do it?
   f. How does she paint?
3. a. I'm not sure if he did it.
   b. I'm not sure if we need one.
4. a. I thought that he did it.
   b. I thought that she would buy one.
   c. I thought that we were trying our hardest.
5. a. must be   b. may be
   c. could be   d. has to
   e. May   f. can
   g. should   h. to see
   i. going   j. manage
   k. to give   l. to keep
   m. going   n. to tell
   o. leaving   p. take
   q. try   r. see
   s. look   t. hear
   u. listen   v. who
   w. that   x. whose
   y. what   z. will
   aa. were   bb. were
   cc. is   dd. had been
   ee. should have been
   ff. could dance
   gg. could have called
6. a. don't we   b. didn't they
   c. hasn't she   d. had they
   e. won't it   f. doesn't she
   g. hadn't he / shouldn't he
   h. wouldn't they
7. a. ago   b. for
   c. in   d. during

e. during   f. While
g. during   h. while
i. until   j. by
k. for   l. since
m. in   n. after
o. yet   p. already
q. still   r. any more

8.   a. for   b. on
    c. to   d. of
    e. on   f. with
    g. to   h. to

9.   a. They have done the dishes. / They've done the dishes.
    b. Things have fallen in earthquakes.
    c. The situation has gotten better.
    d. The competitors have brought their own gear.
    e. Everyone has seen that movie.
    f. The students have learned the lessons.
    g. The CEO has been thinking about it.
    h. Many people have forgotten the answer.

10.   a. has thought   b. bought
    c. have never seen
    d. has done   e. has already gone
    f. has thought   g. have needed
    h. lived   i. has lived

11.   a. They do it perfectly.
    b. They usually do it.
    c. They do it here.
    d. They do it at night.
    e. They definitely do it.

12.   a. let   b. allow
    c. permit   d. had
    e. make   f. get
    g. looks   h. sounds
    i. feels

13.   a. The ancient Egyptians built the pyramids.
    b. The accusation stunned our friends.
    c. The design committee selected the colors.
    d. A professional speaker will present your ideas.

14.   a. have always been
    b. had reported
    c. will have really thought this through
    d. wouldn't have missed
    e. will all be promoted
    f. would have
    g. will definitely take
    h. let   i. we'd walk
    j. we would've walked

Exercise 1–1: Dictation

1. She is very nice.
2. This is an apple.
3. You and I are in this together.
4. He's in the other room.
5. They're not available for comment right now.

Exercise 1–20: *A* or *An*

1. a
2. an
3. A, an
4. an
5. a

Exercise 1–24: *A* or *The*

1. The   6. The/A
2. a   7. the/a
3. the   8. a
4. a   9. the
5. a   10. a

Exercise 1–27: *Here* or *There*

1. This   6. These
2. That   7. Those
3. These   8. These
4. Those   9. Those
5. These   10. That

Exercise 1–29: Asking Questions

1. That is Ed.
2. This is a garden.
3. Those are paper clips.
4. Those people are men.
5. That is a donut.
6. These are coffee cups.
7. This is my friend.
8. This is a teapot.
9. These are cowboys.
10. Those are teachers.

Exercise 1–31: Replacing Subject Nouns with Pronouns

1. They   6. They
2. She   7. You
3. They   8. It
4. They   9. It
5. We   10. She

Exercise 1–34: Replacing Nouns with Pronouns

1.	it	6.	us
2.	them	7.	you
3.	him	8.	us
4.	her	9.	it
5.	them	10.	it

Exercise 1–36: Replacing Nouns with Pronouns — *It* or *One*

1.	it	6.	it
2.	one	7.	it
3.	it	8.	it
4.	one	9.	one
5.	one	10.	one

Exercise 1–38: Replacing the Nouns

1. They are in it.
2. He is watching it.
3. She is near it.
4. They are on it.
5. He is holding one.
6. He is in a good one.
7. They are in it.
8. We/They are in it.
9. We are good ones.
10. You are on one.
11. It is in his back one.
12. They are in it.
13. It is on it.
14. They are in a different one.
15. They are in it.

Exercise 1–40: Possessive Modifiers

1.	their	6.	his	11.	his
2.	his	7.	His	12.	my
3.	her	8.	our	13.	Her
4.	Her	9.	our	14.	its
5.	his	10.	your	15.	their

Exercise 1–41: Possessive Pronouns

1.	theirs	6.	his	11.	his
2.	his	7.	his	12.	mine
3.	hers	8.	ours	13.	hers
4.	hers	9.	ours	14.	its
5.	his	10.	theirs	15.	ours

Exercise 1–43: The Verb *To Be* — *Is* or *Are*

1.	is	6.	is	11.	are
2.	is	7.	are	12.	are
3.	are	8.	are	13.	are
4.	is	9.	are	14.	is
5.	are	10.	is	15.	are

Exercise 1–44: The Verb *To Be* — *Am, Is, Are*

1.	is	6.	am
2.	are	7.	is
3.	are	8.	are
4.	is	9.	are
5.	is	10.	is

Exercise 1–46: Contractions

1. They're happy.
2. It's here.
3. They're dirty.
4. It's wet.
5. They're late.
6. It's fast.
7. He's French.
8. They're easy.
9. She's your friend.
10. It's fun.

Exercise 1–48: Negatives

1. The teachers are not happy.
2. My bus is not here.
3. The dogs are not dirty.
4. My hair is not wet.
5. You are not silly.
6. The clock is not fast.
7. Tom is not French.
8. These reports are not easy.
9. I am not your friend.
10. This is not fun.

Exercise 1–49: Negative Contractions

1. They are not happy. They aren't happy.
2. It is not here. It isn't here.
3. They are not dirty. They aren't dirty.
4. It is not wet. It isn't wet.
5. You are not silly. You aren't silly.
6. It is not fast. It isn't fast.
7. He is not French. He isn't French.
8. They are not easy. They aren't easy.
9. I am not your friend. (*This verb form does not have a contraction.*)
10. This is not fun. This isn't fun.

Exercise 1–50: Questions

1. Are the teachers happy?
2. Is my bus here?

3. Are the dogs dirty?
4. Is my hair wet?
5. Are you silly?
6. Is the clock fast?
7. Is Tom French?
8. Are these reports easy?
9. Am I your friend?
10. Is this fun?

Exercise 1–51: Questions with Pronouns

1. Are they happy?
2. Is it here?
3. Are they dirty?
4. Is it wet?
5. Are you silly?
6. Is it fast?
7. Is he French?
8. Are they easy?
9. Am I one?
10. Is this fun?

Exercise 1–52: Making a Tag Question

1. aren't they?
2. is it?
3. aren't they?
4. isn't it?
5. aren't you?
6. isn't it?
7. isn't he?
8. are they?
9. aren't I?
10. isn't it?

Exercise 1–53: Contractions, Negatives, and Questions

	Statement	Negative	Question
I	I am here.	I am not here.	Am I here?
You	You are here.	You aren't here.	Are you here?
He	He is here.	He isn't here.	Is he here?
She	She is here.	She isn't here.	Is she here?
It	It is here.	It isn't here.	Is it here?
We	We are here.	We aren't here.	Are we here?
They	They are here.	They aren't here.	Are they here?

Chapter 1 Test

Part 1:
1. He
2. She
3. They

Part 2:
1. They are in it.
2. They are in it.

Part 3:
1. am
2. are
3. are
4. are
5. is
6. is
7. is
8. am
9. is
10. are

Part 4:
1. These tests are easy.
2. There are books.
3. Those men are hungry.
4. The trees are tall.
5. My sisters are nurses.

Part 5:
1. It's a good idea.
2. That's old.
3. We're here.
4. You're there.
5. I'm in class.
6. She's late.
7. He's funny.

Part 6:
1. Shelly is not in Europe.
2. Paul and Larry are not here.
3. The girls are not tired.

Part 7:
1. The boys aren't outside.
2. Charlie isn't happy.
3. My eyes aren't closed.

Part 8:
1. Is your brother in college?
2. Is his bike in the shop?
3. Is my watch fast?

Part 9:
1. Is it in it (there)?
2. Is he in it (there)?
3. Is it in it (there)?

Part 10:
1. He is <u>never</u> rude.
2. I am late <u>every day</u>.
3. We are <u>often</u> confused.
4. She is sleepy <u>in the morning</u>.
5. You are <u>usually</u> right.

Part 11:
1. Bob, friend
2. boys, car
3. teacher, room
4. students, happy
5. dogs, yard

Part 12:
1. æ
2. ə
3. ä

Exercise 2–1: Dictation

1. They don't even want to think about it.
2. We can't afford to make any more mistakes.
3. They don't know about the plan to start over again.
4. Does he know how to set the access code for the front door?
5. Do you know how to work the new coffee machine?

Exercise 2–11: Noun and Pronoun Review

1. She studies it.
2. They need long ones.
3. They ask hard ones.
4. He breaks it.
5. They make it.
6. He forgets it.
7. They take it.
8. She wants one.
9. She likes to cook them.
10. They need warm ones.

Exercise 2–13: Replacing Nouns

1. They saw it.
2. She plays it.
3. We took one.
4. He married her.
5. They gave it to us.

Exercise 2–14: Prepositions of Location

1.	under	11.	in
2.	over	12.	in front of
3.	through	13.	on
4.	beside	14.	in
5.	behind	15.	under
6.	behind	16.	for
7.	next to	17.	in
8.	under	18.	at
9.	on	19.	on
10.	from	20.	in

Exercise 2–16: Conjunctions — And, But, So, Or, Because

1.	so	6.	but
2.	and	7.	and
3.	so	8.	but
4.	because	9.	so
5.	so	10.	and

Exercise 2–17: Changing Main Verbs (Regular)

1.	speaks	6.	wants
2.	lives in	7.	make
3.	need	8.	sends
4.	seems	9.	gets
5.	give	10.	takes

Exercise 2–18: Changing Main Verbs (Adding-es)

1.	goes	5.	kisses
2.	does	6.	catches
3.	boxes	7.	pushes
4.	buzzes		

Exercise 2–19: Changing Main Verbs (Adding-ies)

1.	studies	4.	flies
2.	cries	5.	fries
3.	tries	6.	denies

Exercise 2–20: Changing Main Verbs (Go)

1. goes
2. go
3. go
4. goes
5. go

Exercise 2–21: Changing Main Verbs (Do)

1. do
2. do
3. does
4. does
5. do

Exercise 2–22: Changing Main Verbs (Have)

1. has
2. have
3. have
4. have
5. has

Exercise 2–23: Adding Do for Emphasis (I, You, We, They)

1. The kids do play at the park.
2. The dogs do get dirty.
3. You do forget many things.

4. These reports do need work.
5. I do work too hard.

Exercise 2–24: Adding *Does* for Emphasis (He, She, It)

1. My bus does come late.
2. My boss does need this done.
3. The clock does cost a lot.
4. Tom does make mistakes.
5. The car does run well.

Exercise 2–25: Adding *Do* or *Does* for Emphasis

1. The kids do play at the park.
2. My bus does come late.
3. The dogs do get dirty.
4. My boss does need this done.
5. You do forget many things.
6. The clock does cost a lot.
7. Tom does make mistakes.
8. These reports do need work.
9. I do work too hard.
10. The car does run well.

Exercise 2–26: Adding *Can*

1. The kids can play at the park.
2. My bus can come late.
3. The dogs can get dirty.
4. My boss can get things done.
5. You can forget many things.
6. The clock can cost a lot.
7. Tom can make mistakes.
8. These reports can change every day.
9. I can work too hard.
10. The car can run well.

Exercise 2–27: Adding a Verb + To

1. like to, hope to, want to
2. needs to, has to, tries to, wants to
3. want to, like to
4. wants to, has to, needs to, tries to, likes to
5. try to, have to, need to, like to
6. wants to, likes to, tries to, hopes to
7. wants to, likes to, hopes to, tries to
8. hope to, try to, need to, like to
9. try to, have to, need to, want to
10. tries to, likes to

Exercise 2–28: Adding *Not*

1. The kids do not play at the park.
2. My bus does not come late.
3. The dogs cannot get dirty.
4. My boss does not need this done.
5. You do not forget many things.
6. The clock does not cost a lot.
7. Tom cannot make mistakes.
8. These reports do not need work.
9. I do not work too hard.
10. The car cannot run well.
11. My sister does not want to help him.
12. I do not have to study.
13. We do not need to practice.
14. They do not like to dance together.
15. He does not want to take the test.

Exercise 2–29: Changing to a Contraction

1. The kinds don't play at the park.
2. My bus doesn't come late.
3. The dogs don't get dirty.
4. My boss doesn't need this done.
5. You don't forget many things.
6. The clock doesn't cost a lot.
7. Tom doesn't make mistakes.
8. These reports don't need work.
9. I don't work too hard.
10. The car doesn't run well.
11. My sister doesn't want to help him.
12. I don't have to study.
13. We don't need to practice.
14. They don't like to dance together.
15. He doesn't want to take the test.

Exercise 2–30: Making a Question from an Emphatic Statement

1. Do the kids play at the park?
2. Does my bus come late?
3. Can the dogs get dirty?
4. Does my boss need this done?
5. Do you forget many things?
6. Does the clock cost a lot?
7. Can Tom make mistakes?
8. Do these reports need work?
9. Do I work too hard?
10. Does the car run well?
11. Can my sister help him?
12. Do I have to study?
13. Do we need to practice?

14. Do they like to dance together?
15. Does he hope to pass the test?

Exercise 2–31: Making a Question from a Regular Statement

1. Can the kids play at the park?
2. Does my bus come late?
3. Can the dogs get dirty?
4. Does my boss need this done?
5. Do you forget many things?
6. Does the clock cost a lot?
7. Can Tom make mistakes?
8. Do these reports need work?
9. Do I work too hard?
10. Does the car run well?
11. Can my sister help him?
12. Do I have to study?
13. Do we need to practice?
14. Do they like to dance together?
15. Does he hope to pass the test?

Exercise 2–32: Making a Question with Pronouns

1. Do they play there?
2. Does it come late?
3. Can they get dirty?
4. Does he/she need this done?
5. Do you forget them?
6. Does it cost a lot?
7. Can he make them?
8. Do they need work?
9. Does he work too hard?
10. Does it run well?
11. Does she want to help him/her?
12. Do I have to study it?
13. Do we need to practice it?
14. Do they like to dance together?
15. Does he hope to pass it?

Exercise 2–34: Making a Tag Question

1. do they
2. doesn't it?
3. can't they?
4. doesn't he/she?
5. don't you?
6. doesn't it?
7. can't he?
8. don't they?
9. don't I?
10. does it?
11. isn't he?
12. is she?
13. aren't they?
14. aren't I?
15. am I?

Exercise 2–35: Making a Tag Assertion

1. do they!
2. doesn't it!
3. can't they!
4. doesn't he/she!
5. don't you!
6. doesn't it!
7. can't he!
8. don't they!
9. don't I!
10. does it!
11. isn't he!
12. is she!
13. aren't they!
14. aren't I!
15. am I!

Exercise 2–36: Identifying Intent

1. ?
2. !
3. !
4. ?
5. ?
6. !
7. ?
8. ?
9. !
10. !

Exercise 2–37: Contractions, Negatives, and Questions

	Statement	Negative	Question
I	I do it.	I don't do it.	Do I do it?
You	You do it.	You don't do it.	Do you do it?
He	He does it.	He doesn't do it.	Does he do it?
She	She does it.	She doesn't do it.	Does she do it?
It	It does it.	It doesn't do it.	Does it do it?
We	We do it.	We don't do it.	Do we do it?
They	They do it.	They don't do it.	Do they do it?

Exercise 2–38: Commands

1. Don't give up!
2. They aren't to be informed!
3. Don't try again!
4. Let's not think about it!
5. Don't bring it back!

Chapter 2 Test

Part 1:
1. He buys a new one.
2. They fly it.
3. She plans them.
4. It tells a good one.
5. They bark at him.

Part 2:
1. on
2. under
3. in

4. besides, next to, near
5. under

Part 3:
1. and
2. but
3. so
4. or
5. because

Part 4:
1. speaks
2. eat
3. goes to
4. likes
5. bark at
6. feeds
7. has
8. tell
9. doesn't speak
10. is

Part 5:
1. They do see him every day.
2. He does tell the truth.
3. We do have fun.

Part 6:
1. The boy can see the toys.
2. The girl can speak well.
3. This book can be helpful.

Part 7:
1. Lou does not know Ed.
2. It does not work well.
3. The cars do not go fast.
4. The well is not dry.
5. The boys are not in the house.

Part 8:
1. George doesn't work in Las Vegas.
2. Sandy doesn't sell seashells.
3. The team members don't play every day.
4. Big cities aren't often crowded.
5. It isn't really hot today.

Part 9:
1. Does it rain every day?
2. Does he call us all of the time?
3. Do you like it?
4. Are they very kind?
5. Is he in trouble?

Part 10:
1. doesn't he
2. isn't she
3. don't they
4. aren't they

Part 11:
3, 2, 1

Exercise 3–1: Dictation

1. His latest plan was even more dangerous than any of the ones in the past.

2. The kids learned the hard way that there was an easier solution.
3. She didn't understand the instructions on the package.
4. They didn't even try to clarify the situation.
5. I pretended that everything was OK.

Exercise 3–4: *A* or *Some*

1. some
2. some
3. a
4. a
5. a
6. some
7. a
8. some
9. some
10. a

Exercise 3–5: *A/An* or *The*

1. the
2. a
3. a
4. the, the
5. the
6. a
7. a
8. the
9. the
10. a
11. the
12. the
13. an, a, a, the, a
14. the
15. a
16. the
17. the
18. the
19. a, the
20. The, a
21. the, the
22. the, the
23. the
24. a
25. the
26. the
27. a
28. the
29. the
30. the, a
31. a, the
32. the
33. a
34. An, a, the
35. a, the

Exercise 3–6: Short Comparison Words

1. the best
2. cheaper
3. the worst
4. hot
5. smarter
6. the tallest
7. warm
8. colder
9. better
10. easier
11. the oldest
12. happy
13. harder
14. nice
15. big
16. faster
17. the best
18. more
19. richer
20. farther

Exercise 3–7: Long Comparison Words

1. the most interesting
2. a delicious
3. more obedient
4. difficult
5. more expensive
6. wonderful
7. the most unusual
8. more complicated
9. the most important
10. a wonderful

Exercise 3–8: Long and Short Comparison Words

1. more effective
2. cheaper
3. more dangerous
4. the most important
5. richer
6. better
7. scarier
8. the longest
9. earlier
10. the closest

Exercise 3–12: Change to the Past

1. The teachers wrote on the blackboard.
2. Larry rode his bike everywhere.
3. Your cousin flew first class.
4. The managers arranged meetings.
5. I gave many presents.
6. We thought about it all the time.
7. They threw it away every day.
8. Virginia had long hair.
9. Happy people had good luck.
10. Her sister said hello.
11. The kids wanted to ride their bikes.
12. Students tried to pass tests.
13. Ed liked to go to the gym.
14. The class hoped to have a party.
15. Everyone needed to have more fun.

Exercise 3–13: Change to the Emphatic

1. The teachers did write on the blackboard!
2. Larry did ride his bike everywhere!
3. Your cousin did fly first class!
4. The managers did arrange meetings!
5. I did give many presents!
6. We did think about it all of the time!
7. They did throw it away every day!
8. Virginia did have long hair!
9. Happy people did have good luck!
10. Her sister did say hello!
11. The kids did want to ride their bikes!
12. The students did try to pass the tests!
13. Ed did like to go to the gym!
14. The class did hope to have a party!
15. Everyone did need to have more fun!

Exercise 3–14: Change to the Negative

1. The teachers did not write on the blackboard.
2. Larry did not ride his bike everywhere.
3. Your cousin did not fly first class.
4. The managers did not arrange meetings.
5. I did not give many presents.
6. We did not think about it all of the time.
7. They did not throw it away every day.
8. Virginia did not have long hair.
9. Happy people did not have good luck.
10. Her sister did not say hello.
11. The kids did not want to ride their bikes.
12. The students did not try to pass the tests.
13. Ed did not like to go to the gym.
14. The class did not hope to have a party.
15. Everyone did not need to have more fun.

Exercise 3–15: Change to Negative Contractions

1. The teachers didn't write on the blackboard.
2. Larry didn't ride his bike everywhere.
3. Your cousin didn't fly first class.
4. The managers didn't arrange meetings.
5. I didn't give many presents.
6. We didn't think about it all of the time.
7. They didn't throw it away every day.
8. Virginia didn't have long hair.
9. Happy people didn't have good luck.
10. Her sister didn't say hello.
11. The kids didn't want to ride their bikes.
12. Students didn't try to pass tests.
13. Ed didn't like to go to the gym.
14. The class didn't hope to have a party.
15. Everyone didn't need to have more fun.

Exercise 3–16: Change the Positive to Negative Contractions

1. They didn't write on it.
2. He didn't ride it everywhere.
3. He/She didn't fly first class.
4. They didn't arrange them.
5. I didn't give them.
6. We didn't think about it all of the time.
7. They didn't throw it away every day.
8. She didn't have it.
9. They didn't have it.
10. She didn't say hello.
11. They didn't want to ride them.
12. They didn't try to pass them.
13. He didn't like to go to it.
14. They didn't need to have one.
15. Everyone didn't need to have it.

Exercise 3–17: Change the Emphatic to a Question

1. Did the teachers write on the blackboard?
2. Did Larry ride his bike everywhere?
3. Can your cousin fly first class?
4. Did the managers arrange meetings?
5. Can I give many presents?
6. Did we think about it all of the time?
7. Did they throw it away every day?
8. Did Virginia have long hair?
9. Can happy people have good luck?
10. Did her sister say hello?
11. Did the kids want to ride their bikes?
12. Did students try to pass tests?
13. Did Ed like to go to the gym?
14. Did the class hope to have a party?
15. Did everyone need to have more fun?

Exercise 3–18: Change a Regular Statement to a Question

1. (Did / Didn't / Could / Couldn't) the teachers write on the blackboard?
2. (Did / Didn't / Could / Couldn't) Larry ride his bike everywhere?
3. (Did / Didn't / Could / Couldn't) your cousin fly first class?
4. (Did / Didn't / Could / Couldn't) the managers arrange meetings?
5. (Did / Didn't / Could / Couldn't) I give many presents?
6. (Did / Didn't / Could / Couldn't) we think about it all of the time?
7. (Did / Didn't / Could / Couldn't) they throw it away every day?
8. (Did / Didn't / Could / Couldn't) Virginia have long hair?
9. (Did / Didn't / Could / Couldn't) happy people have good luck?
10. (Did / Didn't / Could / Couldn't) her sister say hello?
11. (Did / Didn't) the kids want to ride their bikes?
12. (Did / Didn't / Could / Couldn't) the students try to pass the tests?
13. (Did / Didn't) Ed like to go to the gym?
14. (Did / Didn't) the class hope to have a party?
15. (Did / Didn't) everyone need to have more fun?

Exercise 3–19: Change to Pronouns

1. Did they write on it?
2. Did he ride it everywhere?
3. Did he/she fly first class?
4. Can they arrange them?
5. Did I give them?
6. Did he think about her all of the time?
7. Can he throw it away every day?
8. Did she have it?
9. Did they have it?
10. Can she say it?
11. Did they want to ride them?
12. Can they try to pass them?
13. Did he like to go to it?
14. Did they hope to have one?
15. Did everyone need to do them?

Exercise 3–20: Change a Regular Statement to a Question

1. (Do / Don't / Could / Couldn't) they write on it?
2. (Did / Didn't / Could / Couldn't) he ride it everywhere?
3. (Does/Doesn't/Can/Can't) he/she fly first class?
4. (Did / Didn't / Could / Couldn't) they arrange them?
5. (Did / Didn't / Could / Couldn't) I give them?
6. (Do / Don't / Can / Can't) we think about it all of the time?
7. (Did / Didn't / Could / Couldn't) they throw it away every day?
8. (Does / Doesn't / Can / Can't) she have it?
9. (Did / Didn't / Could / Couldn't) they have it?
10. (Does/Doesn't/Can/Can't) she say hello?
11. (Did / Didn't) they want to ride them?
12. (Do / Don't / Can / Can't) they try to pass them?
13. (Did / Didn't) he like to go to it?
14. (Do / Don't) they hope to have it?
15. (Did / Didn't) everyone need to do them?
16. (Did / Didn't / Could / Couldn't) they jump over it?
17. (Does / Doesn't) she like it?
18. (Does / Doesn't) he want it?
19. (Does / Doesn't) he always lose it with him?
20. (Did / Didn't / Could / Couldn't) they get in trouble again?
21. (Did / Didn't / Could / Couldn't) he burn it?
22. (Does / Doesn't / Can / Can't) it get it?
23. (Did / Didn't / Could / Couldn't) he/she drop out of it?

24. (Did / Didn't / Could / Couldn't) they fall in it?
25. (Do / Don't / Can / Can't) they give them?
26. (Did / Didn't / Could / Couldn't) they find them?
27. (Did / Didn't / Could / Couldn't) it burn it?
28. (Did / Didn't / Could / Couldn't) they lose it?
29. (Did / Didn't / Could / Couldn't) he forget to get it?
30. (Did / Didn't / Could / Couldn't) she change it?

Exercise 3–21: Change to a Tag Question

1. didn't they?
2. didn't he?
3. didn't he/she?
4. didn't they?
5. didn't I?
6. didn't we?
7. didn't they?
8. didn't she?
9. didn't they?
10. didn't she?
11. didn't they?
12. didn't they?
13. didn't he?
14. didn't it? / didn't they?
15. didn't they?

Exercise 3–22: Change to a Tag Question —All Verbs

1. don't I?
2. don't you?
3. didn't you?
4. do you?
5. did you?
6. didn't we?
7. can't they?
8. isn't she?
9. aren't I?
10. didn't she?
11. are they?
12. am I?
13. weren't there?
14. wasn't there?
15. was there?

Exercise 3–23: Past Tense Review

thought, was, was, wanted, tried, worked, invented, was, handled, replied, were, taught

Exercise 3–26: *Get*

1. along
2. back
3. fired
4. used
5. sick
6. down
7. together
8. even
9. upset
10. ahead
11. excited
12. bored
13. off
14. away
15. divorced
16. tired
17. together
18. impatient
19. lost
20. dressed
21. ahead
22. worried
23. back
24. into
25. tired of
26. in an accident
27. undressed
28. rid of
29. in trouble
30. better
31. there
32. up
33. bored
34. down
35. in an argument
36. along
37. worse
38. started
39. rid of
40. back
41. drunk
42. hired
43. hungry

Chapter 3 Test

Part 1:

1. the best
2. bigger
3. nice
4. the warmest
5. more interesting

Part 2:

1. over / above / on top of
2. through / into / by / inside of

Part 3:

1. Sam lived in Chicago.
2. We thought about it.
3. We saw him at the gym.
4. You found many good opportunities.
5. I knew the answer.
6. She said anything!
7. Charlie did not make mistakes.
8. Did Laura get in trouble?
9. We had enough time.
10. It took too long!
11. I was hungry.
12. You were right.
13. He was over there.
14. We were not on the committee.
15. She was going to the party.

Part 4:

1. Morgan did not hear the news.
2. Gordon did not follow the rules.
3. The girl was not confused.
4. The boys were not late again.

Part 5:

1. He didn't buy it.
2. She didn't go with him.
3. She wasn't on it.
4. They weren't in it.

Part 6:

1. Did James drive to New York?
2. Is Susie in back?
3. Did Andrea say hello?
4. Were Fred and Jim outside?
5. Do I like pie?

Part 7:

1. Edgar buys groceries all the time.
2. Sam and Charlie never fly the kite.
3. Moira organized her schedule every once in a while.
4. The book often tells a good story.
5. The dogs barked at passers-by all day.

Part 8:

1. wasn't he?
2. aren't you?
3. weren't they?
4. aren't I?
5. isn't it?
6. didn't they?
7. don't you?
8. didn't they?
9. don't I?
10. did she?

Part 9:

1. a
2. a
3. the
4. a, some

Part 10:

1. tired
2. used to
3. done
4. together
5. lost

Exercise 4–1: Dictation

1. They're thinking about having a meeting and making a final decision.
2. Sam thinks that Ed won't know what to say about the latest business development.
3. He was talking to his boss about the increase in sales for the month of May.
4. I needed to buy some fruit and other groceries for the meeting.
5. We are thinking about trying the new plan.

Exercise 4–5: Countable and Uncountable Nouns (*A / —*)

1. —, (All)
2. —, (Some)
3. —, (All)
4. —, (Some)
5. a
6. —, (Some)
7. a
8. —, (Some)
9. —
10. a

Exercise 4–6: Countable and Uncountable Nouns (*A / An / Some / —*)

1. a
2. some
3. —
4. some
5. a
6. an

7. —, —
8. a
9. A, —
10. a, —

Exercise 4–7: *Much* or *Many*

1. many
2. much
3. much
4. many
5. many
6. much
7. much
8. many
9. many
10. much

Exercise 4–9: Prepositions of Time

1. in
2. on
3. on
4. in
5. on
6. in
7. at
8. in
9. at
10. in

Exercise 4–10: Prepositions of Manner

1. in
2. by
3. in
4. in
5. in
6. by
7. by
8. on
9. for
10. to
11. of

Exercise 4–11: Jack and the Beanstalk

Once upon **a** time, there was **a** poor widow and her son Jack. One day, **the** widow said, "Jack, we don't have **any** food . Take **the** cow to — town and sell her so that we can have **some** money for___— food." Jack said OK and went to ___— town, leading **the** cow behind him. Very soon, he came back all alone. "See what I got for our cow, Mother," he said happily. "I sold her to **a** man for ____ three magic beans." When Jack's mother heard that he traded **the** cow for three beans, she was very angry. "Jack! " she yelled. "Three beans can't keep us from starving! "She threw **the** beans out of **the** window. Jack went to — bed.

The next morning, they saw **a** huge vine. **The** vine rose above **the** house and disappeared into **the** clouds. Jack climbed up **the** vine and soon disappeared into **the** clouds, too. At **the** top of **the** vine, Jack saw a huge castle. **The** door was ten times his size. He called out, "Excuse me, do you have **any** food for **a** hungry boy?" **The** door opened, and Jack saw **a** woman who was as tall as **a** tree. She picked him up by his shirt and put him on **the** table. "So, you're hungry? Well, I'll give you **a** bite to eat. But watch out for my husband!" She handed Jack a slice of bread as big as **a** mattress, and **a** piece of __—__ _ cheese high enough to sit on. But before Jack could eat, he heard __—__ giant-sized footsteps and **a** voice said, "Wife, where's my dinner?" Jack hid out of sight in **the** shadows. Then he heard **the** giant say, "Fee, fie, fo, fum, I smell the blood of an Englishman! "

...

The giant didn't want Jack to take **the** goose that laid golden eggs. One thing led to another, and there was **a** huge fight between Jack and **the** giant. Jack grabbed the goose and ran. **The** giant ended up chasing Jack down the beanstalk. Fortunately, Jack got to **the** bottom first, grabbed **an** ax, and chopped it down. **The** giant fell to his death and Jack and his mother lived happily ever after with the goose.

Exercise 4–14: Reading Comprehension

Synonyms:

1. hearing-impaired
2. hard of hearing

True or False:

1.	False	4.	False
2.	True	5.	False
3.	False	6.	False

How do most languages convey information: Spoken word

What does sign language use: Visual signals

List three reasons why people who can hear might also need to learn sign language:

1. Scuba divers for use underwater
2. Firefighters and policemen to communicate silently
3. Dog-trainers to train dogs

Exercise 4–18: Present Continuous

1. I'm having lunch right now.
2. Bob's sick right now.
3. It's raining in California today.
4. It's not/It isn't raining in California right now.
5. He's working hard for a change.
6. She's dancing well this week.
7. He's thinking about it at the moment.
8. He's not/He isn't thinking about it for the moment.
9. She's making cookies tonight.
10. They're not/They aren't drinking coffee these days.

Exercise 4–19: Past Continuous

1. The teachers were writing on the blackboard

when the bell rang.
2. Larry was riding his bike when it started raining.
3. Your cousin was flying first class until he ran out of money.
4. The managers were still arranging the meetings before the conference.
5. I was not working hard last year, but I am now.
6. We were thinking about it before the situation changed.
7. They were throwing it away until they realized its value.
8. Virginia was not selling her car until she won the lottery.
9. The candles were burning steadily even though it was windy.
10. Her sister was saying hello when he rudely interrupted.

Exercise 4–20: Continuous Negative Contractions

1. They aren't writing on it. They're not writing on it.
2. He isn't riding it. He's not riding it.
3. He/She isn't flying first class. He's/She's not flying first class.
4. They aren't arranging them. They're not arranging them.
5. I'm not giving them.
6. We aren't thinking about it. We're not thinking about it.
7. They aren't throwing it away. They're not throwing it away.
8. She isn't selling it. She's not selling it.
9. They aren't burning steadily. They're not burning steadily.
10. She wasn't saying hello.

Exercise 4–21: Continuous Questions

1. Are they writing on it?
2. Are they riding them?
3. Is he/she flying first class?
4. Are they arranging them?
5. Am I giving them?
6. Were we thinking about it?
7. Were they throwing it away?
8. Was she selling it?
9. Are they burning steadily?
10. Was she saying hello?

Exercise 4–23: Simple Present vs. Continuous Present

1. go
2. are going
3. has
4. is wearing
5. is having
6. has
7. likes
8. wants
9. think
10. is thinking
11. am
12. is
13. is being
14. is being
15. is making
16. do you make
17. are you making
18. Are you waiting
19. Will you wait
20. is having
21. has
22. are having
23. had/were having
24. is having
25. had
26. is having
27. are having
28. have
29. gets
30. take
31. am taking
32. buys
33. is buying
34. is selling
35. sells
36. is walking
37. walks
38. dances
39. is dancing
40. works
41. is working
42. are eating
43. eat
44. plays
45. is playing
46. is writing
47. writes
48. does
49. is doing
50. doesn't

Exercise 4–24: Getting It Right

1. along, divorced
2. up
3. on
4. away
5. used
6. excited
7. better
8. rid of
9. back
10. annoyed
11. confused
12. behind
13. dressed
14. even
15. together

Exercise 4–26: *Who* and *What* — *To Be* *Subject*

1. Who is worried?
2. What was expensive?
3. What were filled in?
4. Who was on duty?
5. What is playing?

Exercise 4–27: *Who* and *What* — Main Verbs Subject

1. Who told Lou/him?
2. What closed early?
3. Who left early?
4. What left the station/it?
5. What rang loudly?

Exercise 4–28: Yes / No Question Review — *To Be Subject*

1. Is she excited about the party?
2. Is the party very exciting?
3. Weren't we invited?
4. Isn't he ready yet?
5. Is Bob sick?

Exercise 4–29: Yes / No Question Review — Main Verbs *Subject*

1. Do they like to swim?
2. Can he tell you the answer?
3. Didn't you eat breakfast?
4. Does Bob have a headache?
5. Doesn't Ella want one?

Exercise 4–30: *5 W* Questions *To Be* Object

1. What is he jumping on?
2. Where is the book?
3. When was he here?
4. What time was he here?
5. Why isn't he tired?

Exercise 4–31: *5 W* Questions — Main Verbs Object

1. Where does she shop?
2. Who did Janice tell?
3. When did he start work?
4. Why did he stop?
5. Where does he want to move?

Exercise 4–32: *How* Questions — *To Be*

1. How were they?
2. How is she?
3. How were they?
4. How is it?
5. How will it be?

Exercise 4–33: *How* Questions — *To Be*

1. How excited were they?
2. How happy is she?
3. How bad were they?
4. How burned is it?
5. How old is it?

Chapter 4 Test

Part 1:
1. an
2. a
3. an
4. an
5. a

Part 2:
1. some
2. a
3. some
4. a
5. some

Part 3:
1. a
2. the
3. the
4. a
5. the

Part 4:
1. —
2. a
3. —
4. —
5. —

Part 5:
1. on, at
2. to

Part 6:
1. much
2. many
3. many
4. much
5. many

Part 7:
1. He is being silly.
2. They are working hard.
3. You were choosing one.
4. He was losing the race.
5. I was writing to him.

Part 8:
1. is sleeping
2. works
3. was thinking
4. is / was
5. is being

Part 9:
1. Lou does not know Ed.
2. The cars do not go fast.

Part 10:
1. Does it rain every day?
2. Is it raining?
3. Do you like it?
4. Are you in charge?

Part 11:
1. but your brother may.
2. but my sister may.
3. he really, really doesn't like dogs.
4. but he tolerates them.
5. but he does like cats.

Part 12:
1. Who is starting the game now?
2. What fell off the shelf?

Part 13:
1. Where are they sitting?

2. When did we leave?
3. What did she look at?
4. Why did he laugh?

Exercise 5–1: Dictation

1. I'm going to have to think about it a little bit more.
2. We'll wait around for them to make the delivery.
3. We're going to Hawaii for the first time next week.
4. They'll let you know your schedule in the morning.
5. If it weren't so difficult, we'd do it ourselves.

Exercise 5–3: Noun Intonation

1.	time	11.	truck	21.	egg
2.	time	12.	truck	22.	egg
3.	hair	13.	hot	23.	butter
4.	hair	14.	coffee	24.	knife
5.	hot	15.	wedding	25.	towels
6.	deal	16.	cake	26.	towels
7.	cell	17.	house	27.	house
8.	plan	18.	key	28.	house
9.	note	19.	hair	29.	base
10.	walk	20.	brush	30.	ball

Exercise 5–4: Noun Intonation

1. short, alley, super
2. air, Angeles
3. school, amusement, hours, sun
4. President, White, C.
5. math, book, text
6. swim, day, summer
7. recipes, junk
8. boy, ring, birth
9. dog, look, porch, day
10. break, down

Exercise 5–5: Word Order

1. His three Chinese rugs
2. my big red leather couch
3. a tiny French notebook
4. the old, brown wooden bookshelf
5. ten black Thai chopsticks

Exercise 5–6: Word Order

1. I saw the three young Japanese English students.
2. We're on the only long, black Italian train in China.

3. Where are Todd's ten tiny Tunisian tin tabletops?
4. *Answers will vary.*
5. *Answers will vary.*

Exercise 5–8: Conjunctions

1. until
2. because
3. but then
4. as soon as
5. whenever
6. unless
7. even though
8. right after
9. ever since
10. after

Exercise 5–9: *How + Many*

1. How many cars were on the road?
2. How many problems did we have?
3. How many alternatives did she want?
4. How many mistakes did they make?
5. How many sugars did he put in his coffee?
6. How many doors does this car have?
7. How many pairs of shoes does my aunt have?
8. How many dogs does that boy have?
9. How many minutes do I have to finish this?
10. How many units is the student taking?

Exercise 5–10: *How + Much*

1. How much ink do I have?
2. How much does this ink cost?
3. How much do they cost this year?
4. How much does it cost this year?
5. How much did they cost last year?
6. How much did it cost last year?
7. How much energy does she have?
8. How much rice was left over?
9. How much fun was it?
10. How much smoke is in the air?

Exercise 5–11: *How Much / How Many*

1. How much noise is out here?
2. How many singers are there?
3. How much cloth is there for that dress?
4. How many dresses are you making?
5. How much gas do I have in the car?
6. How many gas stations are there?
7. How much hair do I have?
8. How many hairs were in my sink?

9. How much did you learn today?
10. How many classes did you go to today?

Exercise 5–12: *How + Often — To Be*

1. How often are they in trouble?
2. How often is the weather nice?
3. How often is the staff out of the office?
4. How often are our dogs dirty?
5. How often were his comments ignored?
6. How often is she on the road?
7. How often are swans vicious?
8. How often is history repeated?
9. How often are we confused?
10. How often is he in L.A.?

Exercise 5–13: *How + Often — Main Verbs*

1. How often do we plan for the future?
2. How often did she have a Plan B?
3. How often do I eat donuts?
4. How often do ants get into the kitchen?
5. How often do commuters take shortcuts?
6. How often do I do the right thing?
7. How often is she direct?
8. How often is it cold in Alaska?
9. How often is the car reliable?
10. How often does he change his mind?

Exercise 5–15: *Two* Terminology — Fill in the Blanks

The following are sample answers. Your answers will differ.

1. There are two animals.
2. These are both quadrupeds.
3. They both have four legs. Neither of them can fly.
4. They each have a specific type of coloring.
5. One of them is striped, but the other isn't.
6. Can either of them fly? No, neither of them can fly, but both of them can run fast.
7. One of them is wild. It is either the horse or the zebra. Neither of them is native to Alaska.
8. The one on the left is a horse. The one on the right is a zebra.
9. The horse is a quadruped, and the zebra is, too. The horse is a quadruped and so is the zebra.
10. The horse runs fast, and the zebra does, too. The horse runs fast and so does the zebra.

Exercise 5–16: *Two* Terminology — Make Up Your Own Sentences

The following are sample answers. Your answers will differ.

1. These are two places to live.
2. Both usually have four walls and a roof.
3. Both are common in the United States, but neither is considered to be a luxury home.
4. Each has its own different attraction for people.
5. One of them has wheels. The other doesn't.
6. Either can be found anywhere in the United States. Neither is typically used for schools. Both of them are legal residences.
7. One of them is made of metal. Either can be used as a permanent home. Neither of them is usually more than one story tall.
8. The one on the left is a mobile home. The one on the right is a cabin.
9. A mobile home is a house, and a cabin is, too. A mobile home is a house, and so is a cabin.
10. A cabin has a front door, and a mobile home does, too. A cabin has a front door, and so does a mobile home.
11. Both of them are usually fairly small.

Exercise 5–17: *Use*

1. use
2. am used to
3. used to
4. use
5. is used
6. uses
7. are used to
8. used to
9. uses
10. is used

Exercise 5–19: *Much* or *Many* with Countables and Uncountables

1.	much	6.	many
2.	many	7.	much
3.	much	8.	many
4.	many	9.	much
5.	much	10.	many

Exercise 5–20: Half Is ... Half Are ...

1.	are	2.	is
3.	Is	7.	were
4.	Are	8.	were
5.	was	9.	has been
6.	was	10.	have been

Exercise 5–21: *Much* or *Many* with Countables and Uncountables

1.	much	8.	many
2.	many	9.	much
3.	many	10.	many
4.	much	11.	much
5.	much	12.	many
6.	many	13.	much
7.	much	14.	many

Exercise 5–22: Eureka!

Here is **a** famous experiment; **a** king buys **a** new crown from **a** craftsman. **The** craftsman says that **the** crown is — pure gold, but **the** king thinks that **a** cheaper, lighter metal like — silver is in it, too. He asks his friend, Archimedes, to find out if **the** craftsman is telling **the** truth. — silver is lighter than — gold, so you need more than one cup of silver to weigh **the** same as one cup of gold. If he mixes silver into **the** crown, there will be more cups of — metal in it than in **the** same weight of pure gold. Archimedes says, "I have to figure out if there are more cups of metal in **the** crown than in **the** same weight of pure gold. But, if I melt **the** crown to find out, it won't be **a** crown anymore. **The** king will be angry. How can I find out how many cups there are without melting **the** crown?"

Archimedes decides to take **a** bath. He steps into his tub and **the** overflowing water gives him **an** idea. He fills **a** bucket with water. He puts **a** pound of gold in **the** bucket. **A** cupful of water spills out. Then he puts a pound of silver in **the** bucket. Two cupfuls of water spill out! This is because silver weighs less than gold, so **a** pound of it (weight) takes up more room (volume) than **a** pound of gold and pushes out more water. **The** king's crown weighs **a** pound. Archimedes puts it into **a** full bucket. If one cupful of water spills out, there is **a** pound of gold in **the** crown. If more than one cupful of water spills out, it can't be pure gold. This way, he doesn't have to melt **the** crown. All he has to do is measure **the** water that spills out. It's **a** great idea! Archimedes gets so excited that he jumps out of **the** tub, and runs naked down **the** street shouting "Eureka!" In Greek, this means, "I found it!"

When Archimedes does **the** experiment, he finds that **the** crown pushes out more water than **an** equal weight of gold does. That means that the gold is mixed with silver. **The** craftsman is cheating **the** king.

Exercise 5–24: Simple Future

1. The teachers will write on the blackboard.
2. Larry will ride his bike everywhere.
3. Your cousin will fly first class.
4. The managers will arrange meetings.
5. I will give many presents.
6. We will think about it.
7. They will throw it away.
8. Virginia will sell her car.
9. The candles will burn steadily.
10. Her sister will say hello.

Exercise 5–25: Negatives

1. The teachers will not write on the blackboard.
2. Larry will not ride his bike everywhere.
3. Your cousin will not fly first class.
4. The managers will not arrange meetings.
5. I will not give many presents.
6. We will not think about it.
7. They will not throw it away.
8. Virginia will not sell her car.
9. The candles will not burn steadily.
10. Her sister will not say hello.

Exercise 5–26: Negative Contractions

1. The teachers won't write on the blackboard.
2. Larry won't ride his bike everywhere.
3. Your cousin won't fly first class.
4. The managers won't arrange meetings.
5. I won't give many presents.
6. We won't think about it.
7. They won't throw it away.
8. Virginia won't sell her car.
9. The candles won't burn steadily.
10. Her sister won't say hello.

Exercise 5–27: Negative Contractions

1. They're not writing on it.
2. He's not riding it.
3. She's not flying in one.
4. They're not arranging them.
5. He's not giving them.
6. We're not thinking about it.
7. They're not throwing it away.

8. Virginia's not selling it.
9. They're not burning steadily.
10. She's not saying hello.

Exercise 5–29: Changing Future Forms

1. We're going to think about it.
2. They're going to throw it away.
3. She's going to sell it.
4. They're going to burn steadily.
5. She's going to say hello.

Exercise 5–30: Questions

1. Will the teachers write on the blackboard?
2. Will Larry ride his bike everywhere?
3. Will your cousin fly first class?
4. Will the managers arrange meetings?
5. Will I give many presents?
6. Will we think about it?
7. Will they throw it away?
8. Will Virginia sell her car?
9. Will the candles burn steadily?
10. Will her sister say hello?

Exercise 5–31: Questions with Pronouns

1. Will they write on it?
2. Will he ride it everywhere?
3. Will he/she fly in it?
4. Will they arrange them?
5. Will I give them?
6. Will he think about them?
7. Will they throw it away?
8. Will she sell it?
9. Will they sit in one?
10. Will she say hello?

Exercise 5–32: Present Tense to Indicate the Future

1. She's making the decision when she is here.
2. I'm not telling you until she gets here.
3. We're leaving when it's over.
4. He's not getting up until it's time to go.
5. Everyone's working until the bell rings.
6. They're going home after the stores close.
7. I'm taking a walk even if it's raining.
8. We're going to bed when the sun sets.
9. She was very rude to me. I'm refusing to speak to her again until she apologizes.
10. I'm starting after I get organized.
11. We're doing something soon, before it's too late.

12. I'm not calling him unless I need to.
13. We're going shopping even if it's snowing.
14. I'm going to be a nurse when I pass the exam.
15. I'm not telling you until after we finish class.

Exercise 5–34: The Unreal — *To Be*

1. If the boxes are full, they'll be heavy.
2. If the boxes are empty, they won't be heavy.
3. If it's raining, you'll be cold.
4. If he's lying, he'll be in trouble.
5. If he is sorry, his friends will be understanding.
6. If they are on time, they'll be satisfied.
7. If the wheel is loose, the driver will be scared.
8. If he is here, he'll be helpful.
9. If he isn't here, he won't be helpful.
10. If they are tired, they'll stay home.

Exercise 5–35: The Unreal — Main Verbs

1. If he has time, he'll go to the party.
2. If she runs a red light, she'll get a ticket.
3. If she knows all the answers, she'll pass the test.
4. If he tries hard, he'll succeed.
5. If you tell the truth, he'll appreciate it.
6. If they get to work late, they'll get fired.
7. If she drives too fast, she'll have an accident.
8. If he forgets to pay, he'll get in trouble.
9. If I lose the ring, he'll be upset.
10. If we are hungry, we'll stop for lunch.

Exercise 5–36: Future Tags

1. won't she?
2. aren't you?
3. won't they?
4. won't they?
5. are they?

Exercise 5–43: *Do* or *Make*

1.	do	6.	do
2.	make	7.	make
3.	do	8.	do
4.	made	9.	make
5.	do	10.	Make

Exercise 5–44: *Stand*

1. for
2. up to
3. up for

4. a chance
5. ground

Chapter 5 Test

Part 1:

1.	walk	6.	fax
2.	lap	7.	shirt
3.	paper	8.	leg
4.	day	9.	expiration
5.	house	10.	sun

Part 2:
1. after
2. unless
3. as soon as

Part 3:

We were walking down **a** dark street. **The** moon wasn't out, so we couldn't see **a** thing. **The** sidewalk was uneven, and I almost took **a** fall. We were lost, so we figured that **the** best thing would be to go back **the** way we had come. **None** of us knew where we were, so it took quite **some** time to get back home.

Part 4:
1. Charlie will go to France.
2. Sam will give a speech.
3. John will read a book.
4. Marcus will not order shoes from Italy.
5. Will Larry fix my computer?

Part 5:
1. Timmy won't answer your questions.
2. Lea won't be dancing in Fresno.
3. Jill isn't going to facilitate the file transfer. / Jill's not going to facilitate the file transfer.
4. The clown won't joke with the crowd.
5. Twenty trees won't crash to the ground in the storm.
6. The secretary isn't going to file the forms. / The secretary's not going to file the forms.

Part 6:
1. Will Shorty eat his dog food?
2. Will the cell phone need to be charged?
3. Is Nate going to make a big announcement?

Part 7:
1. do
2. make
3. make
4. do
5. do

Part 8:
1. up
2. for
3. on
4. still
5. out

Chapters 1–5 Midterm

Part 1:
1. dogs, yard

2. taxi, suit, trunk

3. earth, Francisco, week

Part 2:

1. æ

2. ə

3. ä

Part 3:

1. but you might have.

2. but that's not true at all.

3. but he put it in an e-mail to me.

4. but I did hear someone else say it.

5. but I know that's what he thinks.

6. but I heard him say something else.

Part 4:

1. Who came to visit?

2. What were painted again?

Part 5:

1. Where was she dancing?

2. When did he graduate?

3. What did they order?

4. Who cried because it was so sad?

Part 6:

1. They were cancelled because of it.

2. She is going to visit us.

Part 7:

1. These buildings were poorly built.

2. Can the children have some more?

3. Those people were not ready.

Part 8:   *Part 9:*

1. a   1. or

2. the   2. so

3. an   3. but

4. a   4. and

5. the

Part 10:   *Part 11:*

1. to   1. best

2. in   2. bigger

3. on   3. happier

4. with   4. less

5. by, on   5. worst

Part 12:

1. much

2. many

3. much

4. many

Part 13:

1. We used to go to the beach all the time.

2. They always talk about it.

3. Let's do it today.

Part 14:

1. I drove fast.

2. She thought about it every day.

Part 15:

1. She was laughing.

2. He won't be helping us this time.

3. She was dancing and singing well.

Part 16:

1. He will work on it all the time.

2. They will need more time.

Part 17:

1. They started the new system yesterday.

2. She eats lunch at the same restaurant every day.

3. They were watching TV when the phone rang.

4. He will be here tomorrow.

Part 18:

1. He doesn't know how to do it.

2. She didn't understand.

3. They won't try it again.

4. She's not ready. / She isn't ready.

Part 19:

1. Were they ready?

2. Did she buy one?

Part 20:

1. She won't tell you.

2. They can't get here in time.

3. He's not coming. / He isn't coming.

Part 21:   *Part 22:*

1. will you?   1. make

2. wasn't he?   2. do, make

3. doesn't she?   3. make

Part 23:

2, 3, 1

Exercise 6–1: Dictation

1. Who even knows if they should've used 93658321 as the registration number?

2. None of the e-mails got answered, so the account was closed by the bank.

3. You've got to want to talk about the process and how to fix it.

4. I really hope you know what you're doing.

5. I wish it were possible, but it's not.

Exercise 6–3: Joining Phrases and Sentences with That

1. They are happy that they won the lottery.

2. You are concerned that they are working too hard.

3. The farmers were happy that it was finally raining.

4. It's not clear that they're telling the truth.

5. We aren't worried that things aren't going well.

Exercise 6–4: Indirect Statement

1. I'm not sure who they saw.
2. They are confused about what she did.
3. It's not clear where they went.
4. Please confirm when they did it.
5. It's clear why they were in trouble.
6. Let us know how they got there.
7. It isn't obvious why she didn't ask him.
8. The note didn't indicate what they thought about.
9. In your astronomy class, you learned where Rigel is located.
10. We don't want to know who Jane gave her coat to.
11. It's not posted when the post office closes.
12. Tell me where I put my keys.
13. Ask her when she moved to France.
14. Show me the record of what they bought.
15. You know why we never watch TV.

Exercise 6–5: Indirect Yes / No Questions — Subject

1. Do you remember who took the test?
2. Did they find out what happened?
3. Does he know who saved him?
4. Do they understand what is going on?
5. Did they realize who was there?

Exercise 6–6: Indirect Yes / No Questions — Object

1. Do you remember who they saw?
2. Can you tell me what she did?
3. Do you know where they went?
4. Does anyone know when they did it?
5. Is it clear why they were in trouble?
6. Are we clear on how they got there?
7. Isn't it obvious why she didn't ask him?
8. Did the note indicate what they thought about?
9. In your astronomy class, will you learn where Rigel is located?
10. Will you confirm who Jane gave her coat to?
11. Do you know when the post office closes?
12. Do you know where I put my keys?
13. Will you be asking her when she moved to France?
14. Do you have a record of what they bought?
15. Isn't it apparent why we never watch TV?
16. Will they be able to get back what they lost?
17. Do you know where he is?

18. Did he explain where it was?
19. Can you guess how I got there?
20. Did you tell them how you figured it out?

Exercise 6–7: Subject and Object

1. Do you know what was in the garage?
2. Do you know where the car was?
3. Do you know who ran quickly to the pool?
4. Do you know how the man ran to the pool?
5. Do you know where the man ran quickly?
6. Do you know who played baseball?
7. Do you know what the boys played?
8. Do you know what cost $10?
9. Do you know what the book cost?

Exercise 6–8: *So or Such*?

1.	such	6.	so	11.	so
2.	so	7.	so	12.	such
3.	so	8.	such	13.	such
4.	such	9.	such	14.	such
5.	such	10.	so	15.	so

Exercise 6–9: Unreal Duo — Present / *To Be*

1. If it were obvious, I would understand it completely.
2. If they were in good shape, they would win the competition.
3. If we were prepared, she would hire us.
4. If I were working on it, I would make the deadline.
5. If she were honest, she would not lie.
6. If you were not available, you wouldn't offer to help.
7. If he were running late, he would call us.
8. If it were hot, we would be sweating.
9. If you were sincere, I would trust you completely.
10. If I were I sure about it, I would recommend it to everyone.

Exercise 6 –10: Unreal Duo — Present / Main Verbs

1. If you liked to ski, you would go as often as possible.
2. If I told you, you wouldn't remember.
3. If we practiced every day, we would get better.
4. If he ate a lot, he would be overweight.
5. If I studied every day, I would speak English well.
6. If they talked too much, they would get in trouble.
7. If it worked well, we would use it every day.

8. If they paid attention, they would understand.
9. If everyone knew how to do it, we wouldn't need the instruction manual.
10. If it made us mad, we would complain about it.

Exercise 6–11: Intro Phrases

1. I'm not sure if it works.
2. I'm not sure if it will work.
3. I'm not sure if it worked.
4. He doesn't know if he'll be there.
5. I don't know if he was there.
6. I don't know if he is here.

Exercise 6–12: *Hope* or *Wish*?

1. hope
2. wish
3. hope
4. wish
5. hoped
6. wished
7. hoped/wish(ed)
8. hope
9. wishes
10. hopes
11. hope
12. wish
13. hope
14. wish
15. hopes

Exercise 6–13: Probability

1. will
2. won't
3. may/might
4. could
5. must
6. would
7. must
8. would
9. could
10. might/may
11. would
12. must
13. could
14. won't
15. will

Exercise 6–14: Obligation

1. have to / must
2. had better
3. had better
4. can
5. could
6. should
7. may
8. can
9. Could
10. had better
11. has to
12. can
13. had better
14. should / had better
15. may

Exercise 6–15: Three Verb Forms

1. to do
2. doing
3. to tell, doing
4. to accomplish
5. helping
6. help
7. studying
8. paying
9. to submit
10. registering
11. to go
12. using
13. to drive
14. take
15. to play
16. seeing
17. come
18. to ask, to work
19. telling
20. to avoid, telling
21. hearing
22. shipping
23. to practice
24. complaining
25. worrying
26. to do
27. do
28. helping
29. helping
30. saw
31. told
32. heard
33. to see
34. seeing
35. meeting
36. be
37. to see
38. to show
39. to eat
40. eating
41. deciding
42. to finish
43. go
44. to go
45. go
46. go
47. do

Exercise 6–16: *Say, Tell, Speak, Talk*

1. tell
2. say
3. talk
4. tell
5. speak
6. tell
7. talk
8. say, talking
9. tell
10. tell

Exercise 6–18: *Look / See / Watch*

1. Look
2. watch
3. look
4. watch
5. see
6. look
7. see
8. watch
9. see
10. look

Exercise 6–19: *Hear / Listen*

1. hear
2. listen
3. listen
4. heard
5. hear
6. Listen
7. hear
8. listening
9. Listen, hear
10. heard

Exercise 6–20: Verbs of Perception

1. looks
2. sounds
3. feel
4. saw
5. heard
6. appear
7. feel
8. looks
9. touch
10. listening to

Exercise 6–21: Linking Verbs of Perception

1. looks
2. sound
3. appears

4. feel
5. sound

Exercise 6–22: Verbs of Perception

1. hear
2. see
3. watching
4. listening
5. looks
6. look at
7. sounded
8. feel
9. touch
10. watch

Exercise 6–23: *Have* or *Take*

1. having
2. take
3. have
4. take
5. took
6. had
7. take
8. Take, have
9. take
10. taking

Exercise 6–24: Take It Easy! Take Five!

1. up
2. advantage
3. advantage of
4. take
5. time
6. place
7. notes
8. bribes
9. advice
10. turns

Chapter 6 Test

Part 1:
1. he did.
2. he didn't.
3. they won't.
4. they can.
5. she wouldn't.

Part 2:
1. He/She did it.
2. He/She should do it.

Part 3:
1. I don't know who did it.
2. I don't know who likes them. / I don't know who they like.

Part 4:
1. We can't figure out who did it.
2. We can't figure out who makes them.

Part 5:
1. What did he do?
2. What will they buy?

Part 6:
1. Where did he do it?
2. Where will they go?

Part 7:
1. When did he do it?
2. When do we dance?

Part 8:
1. How did he do it?
2. How does she paint?

Part 9:
1. I'm not sure if he did it.
2. I'm not sure if we need one.
3. I'm not sure if he'll do it.

Part 10:
  Answers may vary.

Part 11:
1. say
2. tell
3. talking
4. tells / told
5. speak

Part 12:
1. must be
2. may be
3. could be
4. has to be
5. May
6. can
7. should

Exercise 7–1: Dictation

1. There should have been some kind of explanation during the meeting while everyone was together.
2. They must have forgotten to lock the storage door when they left.
3. We shouldn't have listened in on their conversation while they were discussing private matters.
4. You didn't really think they were going to let you get away with it, did you?
5. He hopes he can deal with it on his own, doesn't he?

Exercise 7–5: Regular Adjective to Reverse Adjective

1. The bomb that is ticking loudly is about to go off.
2. The facts that are well known are not in dispute. / The facts that are known well are not in dispute.
3. The audience that was recently admitted clapped loudly.
4. A child who is two years old can't read.
5. The salesmen who were downsized protested loudly. / The salesmen who had been downsized protested loudly.

Exercise 7–6: Reverse Adjective to Regular Adjective

1. An illiterate person can't work for the government.
2. An unidentified object flew over the city.
3. The recently purchased car runs really well.

4. The eliminated players cheered for the remaining contestants.

5. The retired detective has written a book about his experiences.

Exercise 7–7: Compacting Subjects

1. The kids who are playing on the swings are having a great time. / The kids, who are having a great time, are playing on the swings.

2. The house that was painted blue is next door to us. / The house that is next door to us was painted blue.

3. My sister who is married is very happy. / My sister, who is married, is very happy. / My sister who is very happy is married. / My sister, who is very happy, is married.

4. The teacher who gave us a test today will grade it later. / The teacher, who gave us a test today, will grade it later.

5. The dress that doesn't fit anymore would be better off given to someone else. / The dress that would be better off given to someone else doesn't fit anymore.

Exercise 7–8: Compacting Objects

1. I met a man who had nine kids.
2. We heard a rumor that wasn't true at all.
3. I like people who are nice.
4. There was a mistake in his report that caused a lot of problems.
5. They'll organize a protest that will change everything.

Exercise 7–9: It's All Relative

I'd like to welcome you to our company, introduce you to the people **who** work here, and tell you about the job **that** you'll be doing. Mr. Edwards is the man **who** started this company. This room is **where** we hold our weekly meetings at 8:00 am, although morning is usually **when** we make most of our calls. This is Mr. Roberts, **who(m)** you'll be working with. Finally, here's the room **where** you will be working and the ID card **that** you'll need to carry at all times. This is the best company **that** I've ever worked for.

Exercise 7–10: *How* Questions of Manner

1. How does it work?
2. How did she get rich?
3. How does he drive?
4. How did we open it?

5. How did they find it?
6. How did he do it?
7. How did he do it?
8. How did he do it?
9. How did we travel?
10. How did he make friends?

Exercise 7–11: *How* Questions of Extent

1. How well does it work?
2. How rich did she get?
3. How fast does he drive?
4. How slowly did we open it?
5. How late did they find it?
6. How dumb was he?
7. How ridiculous was it?
8. How furious were they?
9. How modern was her house?
10. How small were his hands?

Exercise 7–12: 5 W Review

1. Who landed on it? What did he land on? Where did he land? When did he land on it? Why did he land on it? How did he land on it? Did he land on it?

2. Who sailed across it? What did he sail across? Where did he sail? When did he sail? Why did he sail? How did he sail? Did he sail (across it)?

3. Who discovered it? What did he discover? Where did he discover it? When did he discover it? Why did he discover it? How did he discover it? Did he discover it?

Exercise 7–13: Something Else

1. someone else
2. nothing else
3. When else
4. Who else
5. everything else
6. somewhere else
7. Why else
8. anywhere else
9. everyone else
10. How else
11. Everywhere else
12. someone else
13. anything else
14. anywhere else
15. Someone else

Exercise 7–14: *Ago / For / In*

It's six o'clock now. I'll eat dinner **in** an hour, at seven o'clock. I was supposed to meet Tom an hour **ago** at five o'clock, but he wasn't there. I waited **for** fifteen minutes, (from 5:00 to 5:15) and then I had to leave without him. He'll probably call me **in** a couple of minutes, at 6:15.

Exercise 7–15: *During* or *While*

1.	while	11.	While
2.	during	12.	during
3.	During	13.	During
4.	while	14.	while
5.	during	15.	while
6.	while	16.	while
7.	while	17.	while
8.	During	18.	while
9.	during	19.	during
10.	while	20.	during

Exercise 7–16: *By / Until*

1.	until	9.	until
2.	by	10.	By
3.	until	11.	until
4.	by	12.	by
5.	until	13.	until
6.	by	14.	by
7.	until	15.	until
8.	By		

Exercise 7–17: *For* or *Since*

1.	for	6.	for
2.	since	7.	for
3.	for	8.	since
4.	since	9.	for
5.	for	10.	since

Exercise 7–18: *Ago / Before / In / After / Later*

1.	in	6.	after
2.	ago	7.	before
3.	before	8.	Before / After
4.	After	9.	After
5.	later	10.	ago

Exercise 7–19: *Yet / Already / Still / Anymore*

1.	yet	6.	already
2.	yet	7.	anymore
3.	already	8.	already
4.	anymore / yet	9.	still
5.	yet, still	10.	still

Exercise 7–20: *Yet / Already / Still / Anymore*

The Cubans and the Americans haven't settled their differences **yet**. They are **still** arguing about communism and capitalism. They've **already** discussed it many times. Most people don't hope for a speedy resolution **anymore** because it has gone on for so long.

Exercise 7–21: "Have You Ever Been to Mexico?"

I **have been** to Mexico three times this year. My brother **has** never **been** there. We **have talked** about it several times, but he **has**n't ever **found** the time to go. He **has been waiting** for a long time! We **have made** plans to go later this year, but he **has**n't **decided** when. When we do go, it'll be great.

Exercise 7–22: "A Has-Been or a Wannabe?"

America is a good country, but it **has been** slowly crumbling ever since the Vietnam War. **Have** we **learned** the lessons of the past? Can we say that we **have provided** all of our children with a good education? We **have devoted** far, far too much time, energy and money on the military. This country **has arrived** at a crossroads, and we can either survive and become stronger, or fall by the wayside in global significance.

Exercise 7–23: Present Duo vs. Simple Past

1. have lived
2. moved
3. has never tried
4. drove
5. took
6. has happened
7. started / haven't finished
8. finished
9. have finished
10. worked
11. has been working
12. rained
13. has been raining
14. Have you seen
15. have been sitting
16. sat
17. drove / have driven / have been driving
18. drove
19. have seen
20. saw

Exercise 7–24: Present Duo vs. Simple Present

1. have liked
2. like
3. finish / have finished
4. finish
5. grows
6. have grown
7. have managed
8. manage / have managed
9. have grown
10. grows

Exercise 7–26: *There* or *Have*

1. There is not enough time.
2. There was a lot of exciting stuff to do.
3. There is no need to buy new clothes.
4. There was no reason to arrange the meeting.
5. There were many reasons to arrange the meeting.
6. There was a lot of trouble with the fax machine.
7. There were many hardworking people in the office.
8. There is no need to go to work today.
9. There were a lot of seals on the beach.
10. There will be peace someday.
11. There was no class on Friday.
12. There are a lot of butterflies in that town.
13. There was a shirt on the floor.
14. There was no need to do that.
15. There were a lot of balloons in the room.

Exercise 7–27: *There* or *It*

1. There is, There are
2. Is there, there is
3. there was
4. Is it, it's
5. There's
6. there was, It was, There was, There were
7. There are
8. it was, There was, It was
9. there will be
10. There's
11. There is / There must be
12. There are
13. There was, it was, there were
14. it was
15. There will be
16. There's, It's
17. there will be
18. there would be, there was
19. There was
20. it is/ it would be
21. It was
22. There was
23. it were, there were, it were
24. there is
25. it is
26. is it
27. It is / It would be
28. There
29. It
30. There
31. there was
32. Is it
33. There isn't
34. There was
35. There was
36. there are / there might be

Exercise 7–28: Verb Review

1. is
2. was
3. have been
4. will be
5. may be / might be
6. should be
7. could be
8. must be
9. would be
10. will have been
11. might have been
12. must have been
13. should have been
14. have been
15. could have been
16. had been
17. were
18. had been
19. must have been
20. were, would be

Exercise 7–29: Change to the Past

1. He must have been able to think quickly.
2. He had to be able to think quickly.
3. It might have been better to wait for them.
4. He said that they shouldn't have gone.
5. If they took my car, they wouldn't have to wait for the bus.
6. If they had taken my car, they wouldn't have had to wait for the bus.
7. You were able to go home at five today.
8. He wasn't supposed to take Jim's car without asking.
9. They said that they would be here until next week.
10. Al may have used your car for the rest of the week.
11. Al was allowed to use your car for the rest of the week.

12. I wish I had known what he wanted.
13. He knew what he was doing.
14. I forgot why we had done it.

Exercise 7–30: Tag Endings

1. isn't he/she
2. can't he
3. does she
4. didn't they
5. do you
6. do I
7. aren't I
8. will you
9. doesn't he
10. could you
11. don't we
12. haven't we
13. didn't we
14. didn't we
15. hadn't we
16. hadn't we / shouldn't we
17. hasn't it
18. isn't it
19. won't it
20. hasn't it
21. won't you
22. haven't we
23. shouldn't he
24. shouldn't he
25. did I
26. will I
27. don't you
28. aren't you
29. didn't you
30. can't I
31. do we
32. don't they
33. wouldn't he
34. did you
35. would it
36. have they
37. hadn't I / shouldn't I
38. isn't it
39. did they
40. wouldn't they

Exercise 7–31: *Turn*

1. out
2. down
3. up
4. out
5. into
6. up
7. out
8. thirty
9. turnover
10. over

Chapter 7 Test

Part 1:
1. who
2. that
3. whose
4. what
5. will
6. were
7. were
8. is
9. had been
10. should have been
11. could dance
12. could have called

Part 2:
1. don't we
2. didn't they
3. hasn't she
4. had they
5. won't it
6. doesn't she
7. hadn't he
8. wouldn't they

Part 3:
1. ago
2. for
3. in
4. during
5. during
6. While
7. during
8. while
9. until
10. by
11. for
12. since
13. in
14. after
15. yet
16. already
17. still
18. anymore

Part 4:
1. I have watched TV.
2. They have done the dishes.
3. People have made mistakes.
4. Things have fallen in an earthquake.
5. The situation has gotten better.
6. The shredder has torn the paper.
7. The children have been well behaved.
8. The competitors have brought their own gear.
9. The cats have drunk the milk.
10. Dennis has broken his leg.

Part 5:
1. Everyone has seen that movie.
2. Joe has stolen the books.
3. Louise has taken the test.
4. The teacher has chosen the participants.
5. The idea has become more popular.
6. The students have learned the lessons.
7. His parents have been informed of the decision.
8. The CEO has been thinking about it.
9. Many people have forgotten to answer.
10. The horses have eaten the hay.

Part 6:
1. has thought
2. bought
3. drove
4. have never seen
5. talked
6. they've always used
7. has done
8. barked
9. gone
10. has already gone
11. thinks
12. has thought
13. need
14. have needed
15. lived
16. has lived
17. worked
18. has worked

Exercise 8–1: Dictation

1. Let's have him get a haircut and then make him make an appointment for a job interview.
2. We can't let her see what the house looks like or she'll get really mad.
3. If he'd been paying attention, this never would have happened.
4. They would never have acted like that if you hadn't been so demanding.
5. If you'd thought about it, you would have come to a different conclusion.

Exercise 8–17: *How* + Adjective

1. How wide is it?
2. How much does it weigh?
3. How many pages does it have?
4. How old is it?
5. How much is it?
6. How often do you brush it?
7. How many did she eat?
8. How much did she eat?
9. How tall is it?
10. How long was it?

Exercise 8–18: Nouns to Verbs

1. Make this dress longer.
2. It made the system weaker.
3. We need to make our industries stronger.
4. Could you make this knot tighter?
5. I need to make my tie looser.
6. It only made my love for them deeper.
7. It will make the suspense higher.
8. We hope it will make the damage less.
9. Let's try to make its appeal broader.
10. Try to make the gap between them wider.
11. You should make the sauce a little thicker.
12. This lamp will make the room brighter.
13. Use this to make your teeth whiter.
14. Could you make the room darker, please?
15. The farmer made the turkey fatter.

Exercise 8–19: *To*

I'd like to **introduce** you to my cousin, and **invite** you to our company party. If you **agree** to do this, you'll be able to **talk** to a lot of fun people. If you **happen** to be busy that day, let me know. I'm having trouble **getting used** to your new schedule! Anyway, I **look forward** to seeing you there!

Exercise 8–20: *For*

Could I **ask** you for a favor? I **apologize** for the inconvenience, but I have a good **reason** for asking. I'm **looking** for a new apartment and I can't **wait** for the real estate agent. I **applied** for three apartments, but I wasn't able to get any of them. I wasn't **prepared** for this, and I'm starting a new job on Monday, so I really hope this **works out** for me!

Exercise 8–21: *Of* and *About*

1. hear
2. accused

3. got rid / thinking
4. talk / become

Exercise 8–22: *On*

I'd like to **congratulate** you on your recent promotion. I hear that the bosses **decided** on you for the position at the last meeting. As a matter of fact, the CEO **insisted** on your being selected, and said that future contracts depended on your continued involvement, and that you need to **concentrate** on the big projects. They really **rely** on you!

Exercise 8–23: *With*

Have you noticed that the new chef doesn't **get along** with the rest of the staff? I think he has a problem **communicating** with others. Whether you **agree** with a person or not, you don't have to **argue** with them. He needs to have more **patience** with everyone and **deal** with them as individuals.

Exercise 8–24: *From*

So, when did you **get back** from your vacation? I hear you had a pretty bad cold at the beginning. Have you **recovered** from it? It's hard to **prevent** yourself from getting sick, but it helps to wash your hands a lot. With children, you need to **stop** them from touching their faces. Hey, are you still under the weather? Are you **keeping** something from me?

Exercise 8–25: Preposition Review

1.	to	24.	for
2.	for	25.	to
3.	with	26.	with
4.	on	27.	for
5.	about	28.	to
6.	from	29.	of
7.	of	30.	about
8.	to	31.	in
9.	of	32.	on
10.	for	33.	on
11.	to	34.	to
12.	for	35.	to
13.	for	36.	out
14.	to	37.	to
15.	to	38.	with
16.	about	39.	of
17.	from	40.	on
18.	to	41.	with
19.	with	42.	on
20.	to	43.	to
21.	to	44.	for
22.	about	45.	of
23.	to	46.	to

47.	in	74.	in
48.	of	75.	on
49.	to	76.	at
50.	at	77.	on
51.	for	78.	in
52.	at	79.	on
53.	in	80.	in
54.	of	81.	By
55.	of	82.	in
56.	to	83.	at
57.	to	84.	to
58.	from	85.	on
59.	than	86.	about
60.	to	87.	to
61.	out	88.	from
62.	in	89.	on
63.	up	90.	for
64.	of	91.	with
65.	about	92.	to
66.	about	93.	at
67.	at	94.	to
68.	in	95.	up
69.	on	96.	of
70.	at	97.	up
71.	in	98.	to
72.	in	99.	up
73.	on	100.	at

Exercise 8–26: Past Unreal Duo — Main Verbs

1. If you had liked to ski, you would have gone as often as possible.
2. If I had told you, you wouldn't have remembered.
3. If we had practiced every day, we would have gotten better.
4. If he had eaten too much, he would have been overweight.
5. If I had studied every day, I would have spoken English well.
6. If they had talked too much, they would have gotten in trouble.
7. If it had worked well, we would have used it every day.
8. If they had paid attention, they would have understood.
9. If everyone had known how to do it, we would not have needed the instruction manual.
10. If it had made us mad, we would have complained about it.

Exercise 8–28: That's a Big If!

1. would have ridden
2. will ride
3. would ride

4. are ready
5. were ready
6. had been ready
7. They'd be happy
8. They'd have been happy
9. They'll be happy
10. were

Exercise 8–29: Giving Permission

He wants to go to the beach. She says OK.
She lets him go to the beach.
She allows him to go to the beach.
She permits him to go to the beach.

I would like to think about it. He says OK.
He lets me think about it.
He allows me to think about it.
He permits me to think about it.

We need to try again. They said OK.
They let us try again.
They allow us to try again.
They permit us to try again.

Exercise 8–30: Causing an Action

We want them to come back later.
We have them come back later.
We make them come back later.
We get them to come back later.

They wanted him to change the settings.
They had him change the settings.
They made him change the settings.
They got him to change the settings.

She needed us to work on it.
She had us work on it.
She made us work on it.
She got us to work on it.

Exercise 8–31: Causing an Action

1.	having	6.	get	11.	got
2.	made	7.	had	12.	let
3.	got	8.	made	13.	made
4.	had	9.	let	14.	had
5.	get	10.	had	15.	get

Chapter 8 Test

Part 1:

1.	to	11.	to
2.	for	12.	for
3.	of	13.	of
4.	about	14.	about
5.	on	15.	on
6.	to	16.	with
7.	from	17.	from
8.	to	18.	to
9.	for	19.	for
10.	to	20.	to

Part 2:

1. How far is it?
2. How old is it?
3. How much is it?
4. How often is it?
5. How much is it?
6. How many are there?
7. How long is it?
8. How long is it?
9. How wide is it?
10. How tall is it?
11. How thick is it?

Part 3:

1. would have sent
2. will send
3. would send
4. were
5. had been
6. is

Part 4:

1. True
2. False
3. False
4. True
5. True

Part 5:

1. had, finished
2. had, thought
3. had, thought
4. had, understood
5. had, realized

Part 6:

1. If you had studied, you would have learned.
2. If it had been impossible, you would have stopped trying.
3. If they had shown me how to do it, it wouldn't have been scary anymore.

Part 7:

1. went
2. has spoken
3. had spoken
4. always said / had always said
5. had known
6. studied

Part 8:

1. Could you make this essay shorter?

2. Let's make this row straighter.
3. She tried to make the knot looser.

Exercise 9–1: Dictation

1. Bob said he didn't understand how to operate the fax machine.
2. Bill indicated that he wasn't interested in upgrading to a better system.
3. Do you think they knew who the developer of the process was?
4. Nobody can figure out who took the access code to the private elevator.
5. The notes indicated that more resources would have been helpful.

Exercise 9–3: The Story of Human Language

"I **never met a person** who is not interested in language," wrote the bestselling author and psychologist Steven Pinker. **There are good reasons** that language fascinates us so. It not **only defines humans as a species**, placing us head and **shoulders above even** the most proficient animal communicators, but it also beguiles us with its endless mysteries.

For example, **how did different languages come to be?** Why isn't there just one language? **How does a language** change, **and when it does**, is that change **indicative of decay or** growth? **How does a language become** extinct? Consider how a single tongue spoken 150,000 years ago has evolved into the estimated 6,000 languages **used around the world today.**

Exercise 9–4: Polar Bears and Global Warming

1. endangered species
2. become extinct
3. protections
4. jeopardize
5. measures
6. dioxide
7. stemmed
8. 25,000
9. 4,700
10. white

Exercise 9–5: Physics

"It doesn't **take an Einstein** to understand modern physics," says Professor Richard Wolfson. **Relativity and quantum physics** touch the very basis of physical reality, altering our commonsense notions of **space and time, cause and effect.** Both have reputations for being bewilderingly complex. But the basic ideas behind relativity and quantum physics are, in fact, simple **and**

comprehensible by anyone. The essence of relativity is summed up in a single, concise sentence: **The laws of physics are the same for all observers in** uniform motion.

Exercise 9–6: The History of the English Language

1. True
2. False
3. False
4. True
5. True

Exercise 9–7: Economics

Economic issues play a large part in our everyday lives, and it's important to have a deeper understanding of the fundamentals.

Exercise 9–8: The Joy of Science

People should be acquainted with the second **law** of thermodynamics. This law deals with the diffusion of **heat** and has many **profound** consequences. Also important are Newton's laws, the periodic table of elements, the double-helix **structure of** DNA, and scores of other masterpieces of **scientific discovery**.

Exercise 9–9: Drawing a Conclusion

The fundamental questions in our lives pertain to value.

Exercise 9–10: Listening for Specific Facts

1. True
2. False
3. False
4. True
5. True

Exercise 9–11: John F. Kennedy

1. John Fitzgerald Kennedy
2. JFK and Richard Nixon
3. 43
4. assassinated
5. Lee Harvey Oswald
6. He may have been, but there is a probability of a conspiracy.
7. He was murdered two days later by Jack Ruby.
8. deeply
9. He continues to rank highly in public opinion ratings of former U.S. presidents.

Exercise 9–12: Rice

What are the two edible parts of rice? **The grain and the husk.**

Rice grows in all the countries with climates that are: **C. warm and moist**

What is another word for **consumed** in the first sentence? **eaten**

Why is rice husk important? **B. because it has many vitamins**

Why do people who don't eat rice husk suffer from various deficiencies? (**Answers may vary.**)

Exercise 9–13: Gin–Soaked Raisins

In your own words, what is the main idea of the article? **Eating raisins soaked in gin is a remedy for arthritic pain.**

What ingredient in gin helps healing and reduces swelling? **Juniper berries**

Exercise 9–15: Preposition Review

1.	over	16.	off
2.	off	17.	away
3.	—	18.	up
4.	off	19.	up for
5.	into	20.	down
6.	out of	21.	have
7.	up	22.	take
8.	out	23.	make
9.	away	24.	take
10.	down	25.	make
11.	at	26.	make
12.	out	27.	take
13.	do	28.	let
14.	off	29.	had
15.	out	30.	got

Exercise 9–16: Reported or Indirect Speech

1. I thought that she did that every day.
2. He said that he would do it later.
3. She believed that they had left early.
4. I thought that your friends had left.
5. He said that he would call you when he had time.
6. She believed that you needed to take a bath.
7. I thought that she wanted him to do his homework.
8. He said that these shoes were too small.
9. She believed that she looked great in that dress.
10. I thought that the computer had crashed.

Exercise 9–17: Past Unreal Duo

1. If she had saved her money, she would / could have lived comfortably.
2. If they had considered all of the options, they would / could have been prepared.
3. If we had planted a garden, we would / could have had a lot of vegetables.
4. If I hadn't watched the road, I would / could have gotten in an accident.
5. If we hadn't done the laundry, we wouldn't have had anything to wear.

Exercise 9–18: Verb Tense Understanding

1. happened
2. knows
3. will call
4. have tried
5. may be
6. has never gone
7. did
8. have done
9. did/had done
10. drink
11. was
12. used to
13. is used to
14. is
15. was
16. will be able to
17. didn't
18. fell
19. cry
20. painted

Exercise 9–19: Three *Theres*

1. There
2. their
3. they're

Exercise 9–20: Four *2s*

1. 4 (too)
2. 2 (too)
3. 3 (two)
4. 1 (to)

Exercise 9–21: Four *Hads*

1. 3 (obligation)
2. 2 (causative)
3. 1 (possession)
4. 4 (past real duo)

Exercise 9–22: Four *Woulds*

1. 2 (polite)
2. 4 (reported speech)
3. 3 (repeated past)
4. 1 (unreal duo)

Exercise 9–23: Seven *Bes*

1. 3 (-ed)
2. 2 (adjective)
3. 1 (-ing)
4. 4 (noun/pronoun)

5. 6 (passive)
6. 5 (preposition)
7. 7 (conjunction)
8. 5 (preposition)
9. 2 (adjective)
10. 2 (adjective)
11. 4 (noun/pronoun)
12. 4 (noun/pronoun)
13. 5 (preposition)
14. 1 (-ing)
15. 2 (adjective)
16. 2 (adjective)
17. 3 (-ed)
18. 6 (passive)
19. 2 (adjective)
20. 6 (passive)

Exercise 9–25: *Give*

1. in
2. up
3. opinion
4. it's given that
5. benefit of the doubt
6. away
7. away
8. out
9. back
10. off

Chapter 9 Test

Part 1:
1. Did
2. Will
3. Is
4. Has
5. Would

Part 2:
1. Do
2. will inform
3. has
4. would've
5. would
6. will

Part 3:
1. I said that he did it. / I thought that he did it.
2. I said that she would buy one. / I thought that she would buy one.
3. I said that they had opened a new branch. / I thought that they had opened a new branch.
4. I said that they had designed a wonderful plaza. / I thought that they had designed a wonderful plaza.
5. I said that we were trying our hardest. / I thought that we were trying our hardest.

Part 4:
1. out
2. up

Part 5:
1. off
2. out

Part 6:
1. If he had thought about it, he would/could have reconsidered.
2. If they had brought their laptops, they would/could have gotten a little work done.

Part 7:
1. There
2. their
3. they're

Part 8:

1. to
2. two
3. too

Exercise 10–1: Dictation

1. Sam couldn't explain why he had done it, could he?
2. The alarm had been turned off by the time the police arrived.
3. All but one of the teams will have been eliminated by the end of the tournament.
4. I hope you'll have learned your lesson by then.
5. She'll have mastered the intermediate level by August of next year.
6. It was reported in the news last Friday that many of the schools that had been built in the 1950s were being closed due to problems with the structure and condition of the classrooms.
7. Nobody was more surprised than the chairman about the sudden and rapid drop in the value of the stocks of the printing company.
8. Long before it was popular, there were many people who took advantage of trading goods and property among themselves instead of buying things new at the various stores in the neighborhood.
9. It seems unbelievable now, but people really used to believe that the earth was flat and that you would fall off if you sailed out past the horizon.
10. They say that travel is broadening, but there are people who have never been anywhere except between the covers of a book and they can be considered as informed and as experienced as anyone who has traveled around the world.

Exercise 10–7: *Only*

1. It's for your viewing.
2. He doesn't have any siblings.
3. He is very young.
4. No one else calls.
5. That's the only day we call.

Exercise 10–8: *Doubt / Question*

1. doubt
2. question
3. question
4. doubt

5. doubt
6. questioned
7. questioned
8. doubts
9. questions
10. question

Exercise 10–11: Switching Between Active and Passive

1. The cars were washed by the boys.
2. The teacher handed out the papers.
3. Her teeth were cleaned by the dentist.
4. His remarks upset everyone.
5. The miners discovered gold.
6. The fields were covered with/by snow.
7. The committee will revise the plan.
8. The media has insulted our intelligence.
9. The doctor should have informed the patient.
10. The package will have been delivered by the mailman by 5:00 p.m.

Exercise 10–12: Active to No-Blame Passive

1. The paper tore.
2. The boat rocked.
3. The car crashed.
4. Her leg fractured.
5. The evidence burned.
6. The tub overflowed.
7. The vase tipped over.
8. His shirt wrinkled.
9. His tooth chipped.
10. The branch snapped.

Exercise 10–13: Passive Voice

Soybeans **were first cultivated** in Asia more than 3,000 years ago. A mural shows tofu and soy milk **being made** in northern China. The earliest written reference to soy milk didn't occur for another 1,200 years, when soy milk **was mentioned** in a Chinese poem, "Ode to Tofu."

Travelers from Europe **became acquainted** with soybeans and the foods **made from** them — especially miso, soy sauce, and tofu. Soybeans arrived in the United States in the 1700s, **brought from** Europe by several people including Benjamin Franklin.

Soy-based infant formulas **were introduced** in the United States in 1909, and in 1910 the world's first soy dairy **was started** by a Chinese biologist. By the end of the first World War, soy milk **was being produced** commercially in New York. Within 15 years, manufacturers **were experimenting** with added nutrients such as calcium.

Exercise 10–14: Six Useful Verbs

1. managed
2. happen to
3. used to
4. turned out
5. ended up / wound up
6. turn out
7. happen to
8. used to
9. wound up
10. managed

Exercise 10–15: Past Duo

1. Until he was invited by the university last year, he had never been to Los Angeles.
2. He didn't have any money because he had lost his wallet.
3. Ron was very familiar with Paris as he had frequently traveled there.
4. We couldn't get a hotel room since we hadn't made a reservation.
5. By the time he graduated, Fred had been in college for ten years.
6. They felt bad about moving because they had owned their house for 20 years.

Exercise 10–16: Past Duo and Present Duo

1. have heard, was, died, had written
2. spend, have gone
3. went, wanted, had sat
4. has been
5. had arranged

Exercise 10–17: When Did Those Two Things Happen?

1. have never been
2. had never been
3. has overflowed
4. had flooded
5. haven't had
6. hadn't ever seen
7. We've already started
8. We'd never thought
9. We haven't moved
10. hadn't foreseen

Exercise 10–18: Future Real Duo

1. Will she have learned French before she goes to Paris?
2. By Christmas, I'll have figured out when I'll graduate.
3. He'll have finished it by midnight.
4. They'll have turned it in before the deadline.
5. She'll have run out of options before she hears back about the decision.

Exercise 10–19: Three Futures

1. will finish
2. will have gotten

3. I'll be
4. I'll call
5. will have eaten
6. you'll catch
7. We'll have sat
8. they'll help
9. he'll have forgotten
10. will like

Exercise 10–20: Verb Review

1. bought
2. will do
3. call
4. is vacuuming
5. orders
6. has been open
7. is corrupt
8. has stalled
9. moved
10. has been
11. to finish
12. would
13. will
14. was called
15. have been informed
16. would go
17. will have been
18. wouldn't
19. were
20. can
21. isn't
22. doesn't
23. hasn't
24. didn't
25. will
26. wouldn't
27. had
28. let him
29. to notify
30. taking

Chapter 10 Test

Part 1:

1. will have been
2. will call
3. can
4. questions
5. doubts
6. participated
7. taught
8. met
9. was met
10. didn't meet

Part 2:

1. like
2. will
3. would
4. could
5. had gone
6. is
7. were
8. was
9. had been
10. would be

Part 3:

1. don't they
2. haven't they
3. didn't they
4. didn't they
5. hadn't they
6. hadn't they
7. wouldn't they
8. haven't they
9. won't they
10. haven't they

Part 4:

1. would do
2. had found
3. wasn't
4. will go
5. would go
6. would've gone
7. were
8. had been
9. are
10. is

Chapters 6–10 Final

Part 1:

1. We are sad that we lost the game.
2. He is happy that his friends arrived safely.

Part 2:
1. It's not clear who finished it.
2. She said that it was wonderful.
3. I thought that they couldn't swim.

Part 3:
1. Do you remember that she bought groceries?
2. Did you know that they got married?
3. Did you hear that the new store opened?

Part 4:
Intro phrases will vary. Your answer will differ.
1. Do you know where they went?
2. Do you know who won an award?
3. Do you remember when he drove to California?

Part 5:
1. so
2. such
3. so
4. such

Part 6:
1. wishes
2. hopes
3. hope
4. wish

Part 7:
1. won't
2. must
3. could
4. will
5. may / might

Part 8:
1. should have
2. had better / should
3. must
4. can
5. may

Part 9:
1. tell
2. say
3. speak
4. talking

Part 10:
1. hear
2. listen to
3. looked
4. looked
5. watched
6. sounds

Part 11:
1. The caterpillar that was very hungry wouldn't stop eating.
2. The car that was bright red was the fastest at the race.

3. A funny person can make other people laugh.
4. Frozen water is called ice.

Part 12:
1. The flowers that grow in the garden are blooming. / The flowers that are blooming grow in the garden.
2. I know a girl who can speak three languages.

Part 13:
1. Who takes the bus?
2. What does she take? / What does she sell?
3. Where does she take it? / Where does she go?
4. When does she take it? / When does she go to the market?
5. Why does she take it?
6. How does she take it?

Part 14:
1. We went somewhere else to find milk.
2. He talked to someone else.

Part 15:
1. in
2. ago
3. while
4. during
5. by
6. until
7. since
8. after
9. yet
10. already

Part 16:
1. don't they
2. have they
3. hadn't they
4. won't she
5. haven't we

Part 17:
1. How scary was it?
2. How much did you buy? / How many pounds did you buy?
3. How many are there?

Part 18:
1. He lifts weights to make his body stronger.
2. This lamp makes the room lighter.
3. This polish makes the surface harder.

Part 19:
1. about
2. to
3. of
4. to
5. for
6. for

7. of
8. for
9. to
10. out

Part 20:
1. No
2. Yes
3. Yes
4. Yes
5. No

Part 21:
1. I thought that she called her sister every day.
2. We believed that they would talk to him tomorrow.
3. He said that he would wake up early when he had to work.

Part 22:
1. their
2. They're
3. There

Part 23:
1. too
2. two
3. to

Part 24:
1. Nobody else was at the party.
2. He is not doing anything but hosting.

Part 25:

1. question
2. questions
3. doubted

Part 26:
1. The girl's hair was cut by the stylist.
2. The paperboy distributed the newspapers.
3. All of the carpets were vacuumed by us.

Part 27:
1. The plate broke.
2. The wood burned.
3. The tire rolled down the street.

Part 28:
1. takes
2. having
3. took
4. had
5. taking

Part 29:
1. up
2. up
3. up
4. out
5. to
6. down
7. away
8. to
9. up
10. out

Grammar Glossary

5 Ws – 五个以W开头的疑问词（谁、什么、哪里、何时、为何）*Who, what, where, when, why.* This general category of question words also includes *how.*

ability – 能力 The capacity to do something, which is important in the selection of the helping verb, such as *can* or *could.* See *helping verb.*

absolute –（形容词）原级 An adjective used when not comparing, such as *good.* See *comparative* and *superlative.*

acronym – 首字母缩略词 Initial letters representing an entire phrase, such as *ASAP* for *as soon as possible.*

active voice – 主动语态 Where the subject does something to the object, such as *The rain damaged the crops.* This is considered to be more powerful and straightforward than the passive voice. It also uses fewer words, which is generally good. See *passive voice.*

adjective – 形容词 A type of modifier, specifically for nouns (*a* **nice** *day*). Possessive adjectives indicate ownership, such as **his** *book* or **her** *plan.*

adverb – 副词 A type of modifier, specifically for verbs (*He ran* **fast**) or adjectives (*They are* **very** *upset*). There are five types of adverbs (manner, time, frequency, extent, degree). See *5 Ws.*

alveolar ridge – 牙槽嵴 The bumpy ridge just behind the top teeth, where *T, D, N, L, S, Z, Sh, Zh, J, Ch* are formed.

antonym – 反义词 A word opposite in meaning from another, such as *good* and *bad.* See *synonym.*

aptitude – 能力 See *test.*

article – 冠词 A specific type of noun modifier that lets you know if the thing is *singular* (a book, an apple, the car) or *plural* (the cars); or *new information* (a book, an apple) or *known information* (the books, the apples). See *modifier.*

auxiliary verb – 助动词 See *helping verb*, *verb*, and *modal.*

base form – 动词原形 Another name for the *plain form.* See *verb.*

brackets – 方括号 [ ] A way to set off information [ ], similar to parentheses ( ).

cadence – 节奏；韵律 Rhythm of a spoken sentence, the use of pitch changes to create a noticeable and informative pattern of information. See *intonation.*

capitalize – 把…首字母大写 To use a capital for the first letter of a personal or place name, such as *Bob* or *New York.*

causative – 使役动词 Verbs that produce an effect or cause someone or something to do something, such as

let, permit, allow, make, have, get. The causative involves a combination of *desire* and *power.* *Let* indicates that the *doer* has the desire to do something and the *permitter* has the power to grant permission. *Force* indicates that the doer doesn't want to participate, but doesn't have the power to resist.

clause – 从句 A group of words containing a subject and a verb. Some clauses are *independent*, which means they express a complete thought (*I laughed* or *Sam walked into the room*). Some clauses are *dependent*, which means they cannot stand alone without an independent clause (**Although I laughed**, *I was crying on the inside* or *Sam walked into the room,* **unaware that he had forgotten to button his shirt**). See *sentence.*

colloquial – 口头的 Familiar way of speaking, not formal or literary.

colon – 冒号 A punctuation mark (:) that separates lists or clauses. Also used in time (10:00) and ratios (10:1).

comma – 逗号 A punctuation mark (,) indicating a pause between parts of a sentence. Also used with large numbers, such as 1,000.

command – 命令句 To give an order, such as *Help!*, *Stop!*, or *Come here!*

comparative –（形容词）比较级 An adjective used when comparing two things, such as *A is* **better** *than* **B.** See *absolute* and *superlative.*

complement – 表语 Similar to the *object* of a sentence, but it comes after the verb **to be**, not a main verb. With a main verb, you have the SVO pattern, but with the verb **to be**, it's SVC, because objects are always nouns (*Bob sees* **Betty**) and the complement after the verb **to be** can be a noun (*I am a* **teacher**), an adjective (*I am* **happy**), or an adverb (*I am* **here**). In this book, complements are treated as objects.

complex intonation – 综合语调 Going beyond the basic SVO pattern, where the subject and the object are stressed for new information, complex intonation can stress a single noun up through a five-word pattern such as **bright** *red* **fire** *truck paint.*

compound noun – 复合名词 Two nouns that form a new word such as talk show. The stress always goes on the first word, **talk** *show.* The first word can also be a gerund, **swimming** *pool*, or an adjective, **hot** *dog.*

conditional – 条件句 See *duo.*

conjugate – 对动词进行词形变化 To change verb tenses (*he is, they are; he was, they were*) based on time and person. This includes past, present, future, simple, and duo forms, real and unreal.

conjunction – 连词 A word such as *and, but, if,* or *or,* used to connect nouns, verbs, clauses, or sentences.

consonant – 辅音 A speech sound where the air flow is blocked at some point, as opposed to a vowel, where the air flows freely. This is why *Y* and *W* are sometimes considered vowels. The American *R* acts like a vowel, whereas the British *R* does not. There are two types of consonant, *voiced* and *unvoiced.* When the vocal cords vibrate, the consonant is spoken or voiced. When they don't, it is whispered or unvoiced. See *vowel.*

continuous – (动词的)进行时 A verb form that indicates an ongoing action or something that is happening right now, such as He **is reading** a book. Also known as *progressive.* See *-ing.*

contraction – 缩写形式 A shortened form of a verb plus another word, generally a noun or a pronoun. Examples are *I'm, he's, you've, can't, isn't.*

countable noun – 可数名词 A noun that can have a number attached, such as *one chair* or *ten minutes.* See *uncountable noun.*

dangling participle – 垂悬分词 A present participle is a verb ending in *-ing.* It is called *dangling* when the subject of the *-ing* verb and the subject of the sentence do not agree, such as *Hurrying to get to work, Bob's car broke down.* The subject is *Bob's car,* but the car isn't doing the *hurrying.* It would be better to say, *While Bob was hurrying to work, his car broke down.* This term is often used humorously. See *participle* and *verb.*

dash – 破折号 A punctuation mark (—), slightly longer than a hyphen, used to indicate a pause.

definite article – 定冠词 *The* is called *definite* because it refers to something specific, known, or previously mentioned, as opposed to *a* or *an.* See *article* and *modifier.*

demonstrative – 指示词 One of four noun modifiers that indicate proximity and number (how far and how many): *this, that, these, those.* See *modifier.*

descriptive – 描述性的 A style of instruction that focuses on how things actually *are,* rather than how they *should be,* or how traditional rules would dictate. The program in this book is descriptive. See *prescriptive.* Also a noun modified with an adjective, as opposed to a *compound noun.*

determiner – 限定词 See *modifier.*

diagnostic – 诊断的 See *test.*

direct speech – 直接引语 Uses quotation marks and a person's exact words, such as *Tom said,* "*I have to go.*" See *indirect speech.*

directional preposition – 方向介词 See *preposition.*

duo – 双重时态 Any of the six forms that require two separate events or states, such as the future real duo(*He will have finished*[1] *by the time you are ready to go*[2].) or the past unreal duo (*He would have gone*[1] *if he had been ready*[2].) The second event or state is often unmentioned in the present real duo (*I've never been there before.*).

The three real duo forms are also known as the *present, past,* and *future perfect.*

emphatic form – 强调句 An intense way to present information. With the verb *to be,* the verb is stressed but not changed (*She is* happy!). With main verbs, the verb *to do* is added and stressed (She *does* like it!).

exclamation – 感叹语 A short remark indicating surprise, joy, anger, excitement, pain, or a command, such as *Hey!, Wow!, Ouch!, Oh, no!,* or *Stop!*

exclamation mark – 感叹号 A punctuation mark (!) used to indicate urgency, such as *Hey!* or *Stop!*

figurative – 比喻的 Departing from the literal, actual meaning of a word to a metaphorical meaning, such as *His heart turned to stone.* See *literal.*

future tense – 将来时 A time frame that has not yet happened and can use *will*(*I* **will** *call you tomorrow*), *going to* (*He***'s going** *to try again*), or even the *simple present*(*I* **have** *a doctor's appointment next week*).

gerund – 动名词 An *-ing* form, where the verb works like a noun, such as ***Swimming** is fun* (subject), *I like **swimming*** (object), *She is afraid of **swimming***(object of the preposition), *a **swimming** pool* (compound noun). See *-ing.*

grammar – 语法 The whole structure and system of a language, including syntax, morphology, phonology, and semantics. In plain English, it is the rules of a language.

helping verb – 助动词 Any of the 23 verbs that go along with the main verb: *may, might, must, be, being, been, am, are, is, was, were, do, does, did, should, could, would, have, had, has, will, can, shall.* Also called *auxiliary verbs.*

hyphen – 连字符 A punctuation mark (-), used to join words, such as *third-grader.*

if clause – if从句 The conditional half of the unreal duo, such as ***If I were you,** I wouldn't do that.*

-ing – 动词的-ing形式 There are three *-ing* forms. 1) The **continuous**, where the verb acts like a **verb** (*He is swimming.*) 2) A **participle**, where the verb acts like an **adjective** (*a **speeding** car* or ***hoping** to go*). 3) A **gerund**, where the verb works like a **noun**(***Swimming** is fun* or *a **swimming** pool*).

indefinite article – 不定冠词 *A* and *an* are called indefinite because they refer to any member of a group, as opposed to *the.* See *article* and *modifier.*

indirect speech – 间接引语 Does not use quotation marks and adjusts the words a person used, such as *Tom said that he had to go* or *I'm not sure if he is still here.* See *direct speech.*

infinitive – 不定式 *To* + the basic form of a verb, such as *to go.*

inflection – 音调的抑扬变化;(动词词尾的) 屈折变化 In speech, inflection is the modulation of intonation or pitch when speaking. For verbs, it is the changing of the base form to indicate time, person, or number. For speech, see *intonation*. For verbs, see *conjugate*.

interjection – 感叹词 See *exclamation*.

intonation – 声调 This is a broad category that encompasses speech, music, pitch change, word and syllable stress, cadence, rhythm, phrasing, inflection, and the staircase. Intonation is initially used to introduce new information via the nouns, or to indicate if a noun is compound or not. It is used secondarily to indicate contrast or opinion.

intransitive verb – 不及物动词 A verb that cannot have an object, such as *I laughed*. See *verb*.

lax vowel – 松元音 One of the vowels produced with relaxed muscles, such as *ih, eh, uh*. See *vowel*.

liaison – 连音，(单词) 连读 A word connection, such as *Gotcha* for *Got you*.

literal – 字面的 The use of words in their actual meaning. See *figurative*.

locational preposition – 方位介词 See *preposition*.

main verb – 主动词 A verb that expresses action, such as *go* or *have*, as contrasted with the verb *to be* or a *helping verb*. Every sentence needs a main verb. See *verb*.

manner – 方式 The way something is done or how it happens. See *adverb*.

manner adverb – 方式副词 See *adverb*.

modal – 情态动词 Traditionally, this is not actually a *tense*, but rather a *mood*. Modals are a type of helping verb. They indicate probability, potential, ability, duty, obligation: *can, could, have to, have got to, had better, may, might, must, ought to, shall, should, will, would*. *Would* is used with the present and past unreal duo.

modifier – 修饰语 A broad term that includes articles, adjectives, adverbs, and demonstratives. Also called a *determiner*. See *reverse modifier*.

morpheme – 词素 The smallest possible sound unit with meaning, such as *break*. In plain English, it is a word, a prefix, or a suffix. For instance, *unbreakable* is made up of three morphemes - *un, break, able*. See *phoneme*.

negative – 否定句 Expressing negation through denial, refusal, or refutation, using words such as *no, not, never, nor, neither, none*. See *positive*.

non-standard – 不标准的；不规范的 Any formulation of speech that is not commonly heard; generally considered to be unacceptable. See *standard*.

noun – 名词 A person, place, thing, or idea.

noun, singular – 单数名词 One thing, such as *a chair*. See *noun, plural*.

noun, plural – 复数名词 When there is more than one thing, it's most common to add an S, such as *book / books*. Irregular plural nouns include *children, mice, men,* and *feet*. Plurals include *these* and *those*. See *modifier*.

noun, countable – 可数名词 See *countable noun*.

noun, uncountable – 不可数名词 See *uncountable noun*.

noun, common – 普通名词 A general item，such as *country* or *woman*. Common nouns are not capitalized.

noun, proper – 专有名词 The name of a specific person, place, or thing such as *United States* or *Mary*. Proper nouns are capitalized.

object – 宾语 In plain English, it's the back end of the SVO sentence, such as *Bob sees **Betty***. The object is always a noun. See *subject*.

object pronoun – 宾格代词 See *pronoun*.

obligation – 义务 Duty, which is important in the selection of the helping verb, such as *have to, should,* or *must*. See *helping verb*.

paragraph – 段落 A section of writing in a larger essay or letter, with its own idea or theme, set off by an indent or a line space.

parentheses – 圆括号 ( ) Punctuation marks ( ) that enclose a phrase or sentence as an explanation or afterthought.

participle – 分词 A verb ending in *-ing*, differing from the *-ing* of the continuous, which tells time. A participle is timeless, as in *Hoping to pass the test, Fred studied hard. Hoping* has no time reference. It also appears with the *-ed* and *-tten* endings, as in *Forgotten by everyone, Fred sank into a deep depression*.

parts of speech – 词类 The eight grammatical terms: verb, noun, pronoun, adjective, adverb, preposition, conjunction, and exclamation.

passive voice – 被动语态 Where the subject is acted upon by the object, such as *The crops were damaged by the rain*. This form is used when the doer is unknown or if responsibility is being avoided. See *active voice* and *verb*.

past perfect – 过去完成时 Another name for the *past real duo*, such as *had done*. See *duo*.

past tense – 过去时 A verb tense that indicates that something happened before now. See *verb*.

perfect – 完成时 Another name for the three *real duos*, present, past, and future.

period – 句号 A punctuation mark at the end of a sentence(.). Also used in .com, but it is called *dot*. Used with numbers, such as 10.5, it is called a point or a decimal point.

person – 人称 The individual identified by the verb tense, such as *first person plural: we*.

phoneme – 音素，音位 The smallest possible sound unit with no actual meaning, such as the P in *pit*. In plain English, it is simply a consonant sound or a vowel sound. Two letters can also form a single phoneme, such as SH or CH because they make a single sound. See *morpheme*.

phrase – 短语 A partial sentence. See *sentence* and *clause*.

pitch – 音高 The degree of highness or lowness of the voice, used to indicate a stressed syllable or an important word. See *intonation*.

placement – 摸底 See *test*.

plain form – 动词原形 The base form of the main verb, such as the *go* of *to go*. It is used with helping verbs, such as *He should go.* See *verb* and *main verb*.

pluperfect – 过去完成时 Another word for the *past real duo*, such as *had done*.

plural – 复数名词 When there is more than one thing, it's most common to add an S, such as *book / books*. Irregular plural nouns include *children, mice, men*, and *feet*. Plural modifiers include *these and those*. See *modifier*.

polarity – 极性 This term is used to explain how tag questions and tag endings work. To form a tag, change the polarity from positive to negative or negative to positive, as in *He is here, isn't he?*

positive – 肯定句 Expressing affirmation through agreement or permission, using words such as *yes, always, or, either, some, all*. Also known as *affirmative*. See *negative*.

possessive – 所有格的 See *pronoun* and *adjective*.

possibility – 可能性 Something that may happen, which is important in the selection of the helping verb, such as *will, may, could*. See *helping verb*.

preposition – 介词 A word that indicates direction (*to*), location (*in*), possession (*of*).

prescriptive – 规定性的 An approach to teaching grammar and pronunciation based on what *ought to be*, as contrasted with *descriptive*, which is based on what actually *is*. The program in this book is descriptive.

present perfect – 现在完成时 Another name for the *present real duo*, such as *has done*. See *duo* or *verb*.

present tense – 一般现在时 A verb tense that indicates that something is happening in the general sense of now, such as *is* and *does*. See *verb*.

probability – 可能性 Something that most likely will happen, which is important in the selection of the helping verb, such as *will, may, could*. See *helping verb*.

progressive – 进行时的 See *continuous* and *-ing*.

pronoun – 代词 A word used to replace a noun, both as a subject(*I, you, he, she, it, we, they*) and the object(*me, you, him, her, it, us, them*). The possessive pronoun is used to indicate that something belongs to someone, such as **his**, **hers**, **mine**, **ours**, etc. The reflexive pronoun refers back to the subject, such as *I taught* **myself** *how to knit*. The relative pronoun is another name for the linking word in a *reverse modifier*, such as *He is the man* **who** *danced all night*.

punctuation mark – 标点符号 Any of the symbols, such as the period, comma, or parentheses, used to separate sentences into their elements or to clarify meaning.

question flip – 疑问句的词序颠倒 The grammatical structure of reversing the position of the subject and the verb from a statement to a question, such as *He is here* to *Is he here?* This symbol is used to indicate the question flip ↻, and this one to indicate its absence ↺.

question mark – 问号 A mark used to indicate that the previous statement is asking a question (？).

reduced sounds – 弱读音 Unstressed vowels that lose their clear pronunciation.

reflexive – 反身的 See *pronoun*.

relative pronoun – 关系代词 See *pronoun*.

reported speech – 间接引语 See *indirect speech*.

reverse modifier – 后置修饰语 A group of words that follow the noun that they describe, such as *He is the man* **who danced all night**. Also called an adjective clause or relative clause.

rhythm – 韵律 The pitch changes of a spoken sentence, creating a noticeable and informative pattern of information. See *intonation and word stress*.

schwa – 非重读央元音 The most common sound in English, the schwa is a neutral vowel sound, pronounced *uh* and represented with the symbol ə. It can be used with any of the vowel sounds: *w<u>a</u>s, en<u>e</u>my, possible, some, m<u>u</u>ch, s<u>y</u>ringe*, or even when there is no vowel present, such as *ch<u>a</u>sm*. Some dictionaries use an upside-down V for stressed neutral sounds, such as *cup*, but this method only uses the schwa.

semi-colon – 分号 A punctuation mark (；) used to separate clauses. It's stronger than a comma, but weaker than a colon.

sentence – 句子 A complete group of words in a grammatical order. See *clause, phrase, statement, question flip, command*.

simple form – 一般式；动词原形 See *plain form*.

singular noun – 单数名词 One thing, such as *a chair*. See *plural noun*.

speech music – 语音语调 The pitch changes in spoken English. See *intonation*.

staircase – 阶梯状 The up-and-down pitch changes in spoken English. See *intonation*.

standard – 标准的 Widely accepted as the correct form. Words such as *ain't* are considered non-standard.

statement – 陈述句 A type of sentence that gives information, as opposed to a question, which requests information. See *sentence*.

stress – 重音 The application of pitch change to a syllable or word. See *intonation*.

subject – 主语 In plain English, it's the front end of the SVO sentence, such as **Bob** *sees Betty*. The subject is always a noun. See *object*.

subject pronoun – 主格代词 See *pronoun*.

subjunctive – 虚拟的；虚拟语气的 See *duo*.

superlative – （形容词）最高级 An adjective used when

comparing and determining the highest order, such as *A is the best of all*. See *absolute* and *comparative*.

syllable stress – 重读音节 The syllable that carries the emphasis. This can change the meaning of a word, such as ***con**tent*(n) and *con**tent*** (adj). See *word stress* and *intonation*.

symbol – （用来解释读音的非字母表上的）符号 One of the non-alphabet characters used here to explain pronunciation: ə ä ü æ ɛ.

synonym – 同义词 Words with similar meanings, such as *teacher* and *instructor*. See *antonym*.

syntax – 句法 The arrangement of words and sentences to make well-formed sentences. Syntax is the rules of English, differing from grammar by being just one part of it, along with morphology, phonology, and semantics.

tag ending – 反意疑问句 A type of statement or question ending, such as *isn't he*! or *isn't he*?

tag question – 反意疑问句 A type of question ending, such as *isn't he*?

tense （verb） – 时态 One of the grammatical markers that indicate what time the action took place, such as *run**s**, want**ed**, **will** go*. See *verb*.

tense （vowel） – 紧（元音） One of the vowels produced with tensed muscles, such as *ee, oh, ooh*. Also called *long vowels*. See *vowel*.

test – 测试 There are four types of tests, *aptitude* （to see what a person is naturally good at）, *diagnostic* （to show what a person does wrong）, *placement* (to determine

what level a person should be within a program), and *achievement* （to demonstrate what a person has accomplished so far）.

transitive verb – 及物动词 A verb that can have an object, such as *He opened the window*. See *verb*.

uncountable noun – 不可数名词 A noun that cannot have a number attached, such as *beauty* or *water*. See *countable noun*.

unvoiced consonant – 清辅音 See *consonant* and *voiced consonant*.

verb – 动词 Either an action word such as *to run*, or a state, *to have* or *to be*. See *tense* （verb）, *modal, helping verb, active, passive, transitive, intransitive*.

voice – 语态 A way that a verb acts. If the subject is in charge, it is called the active voice, such as *The rain **damaged** the crops*. If the subject is acted upon, it is called the passive voice, such as *The crops **were damaged** by the rain*.

voiced consonant – 浊辅音 See *consonant*.

vowel – 元音 A, E, I, O, U are the vowel letters. English has 14 vowel sounds. See *tense, lax, consonant*.

word connection – 单词连读 See *liaison*.

word stress – （句子中）重读的单词 The word(s) in a sentence that carries the emphasis. The primary form is ***Subject**-Verb-**Object*** (SVO). Secondary forms include contrast, emphasis, and complex intonation. See *syllable stress* and *intonation*.

终极英语单词系列：

《终极英语单词12000—变身口语达人3000词》
《终极英语单词12000—成为英语学霸3000词》
《终极英语单词12000—畅读英文报刊3000词》
《终极英语单词12000—英语母语水平3000词》

（日）ALC Press Inc. 著

（免费下载图书相关音频文件）

"终极英语单词12000系列"由新东方从日本ALC集团独家引进，从40年累积的各类英文语料中精选而出，并根据英美人的使用频率，由浅入深分为四册。该系列已经在日本和中国台湾地区持续畅销10年，深受好评。

《英语词组全书》（全两册）

（韩）金正基 编著

英语词组量轻松过万，突破词汇学习难关！

◎ 英语词组大容量
◎ 词义溯源易熟记
◎ 丰富实例好素材
◎ 练习、测试重实用
◎ 词汇书、词典集一身

定价：49.8元　开本：32开　页码：832页

读美国中小学课本学各科词汇系列：（1-6册、全6册套装）

（免费下载图书相关音频文件）

M. A. Putlack/e-Creative Contents 编著

◎ 掌握美国中小学生必备学科词汇，读懂英文课本很轻松
◎ 读过这套书，用英文学习数学、物理、化学、历史、地理，一点都不难
◎ 读美国课本，和美国学生同步学习，像学母语一样学英文
◎ 体验美国课堂，不必远赴重洋

《200个一定要学的英文词根词缀》

新东方词汇研究中心 编著

（免费下载图书相关音频文件）

◎ 共收录100个常用词根、50个常用前缀和50个常用后缀
◎ 深度剖析词根、词缀的起源及含义，拆解例词，给出精到例句
◎ 所选词汇均为四六级难度，刚需实用
◎ 配有拓展词汇和阶段检测题

定价：28元　开本：32开　页码：352页

《英语易混词辨析——用不对词，写作怎么拿高分？》高凌 主编

◎ 共收录443组易混词，包含单词近1000个
◎ 深度剖析每组易混词在意义和用法上的异与同
◎ 搭配简明、实用的例句，并根据单词的典型应用语境精心设计小测验
◎ 适用于有一定英语基础的英语爱好者、高中生，同时为英语四六级考生提供帮助

定价：35元　开本：32开　页码：464页

《英语词缀词典》/《英语词根词典》

（韩）金正基 编著

◎ 适合中国学生使用的词汇学习书！
◎ TOEFL、GRE、SAT、IELTS词汇，一本搞定！
◎ 两本书为相辅相成的姊妹篇，共收录了33,000多个单词和习语，词汇量之大在同类书中名列前茅，收词全面，科学，实用。

英语词汇速记大全系列：

《英语词汇速记大全1——词根+词缀记忆法》
《英语词汇速记大全2——词形记忆法》
《英语词汇速记大全3——同类记忆法》
《英语词汇速记大全4——语境记忆法》

（免费下载图书相关音频文件）

俞敏洪 编著

新东方创始人俞敏洪多年词汇研究之精华，自1999年问世以来，持续畅销，长盛不衰。囊括绝大部分常考单词，适用于各类英语考试，所选词汇具有较强的实用性和发散性，对词汇的研究独到而深刻。

新东方词汇进阶系列：

《Vocabulary Basic》/《Vocabulary 6000》
《Vocabulary 12000》/《Vocabulary 23000》

（免费下载图书相关音频文件）

包凡一 王玉梅 编著

◎ 明确针对性！涵盖四六级、考研、TOEFL等考试应掌握的全部核心词汇
◎ 记忆全方位！释义从多个角度详细讲解，提供多种记忆方法，帮助读者理解掌握
◎ 练习高密度！每课设置多样习题，并附有参考答案，便于随时检测学习效果
◎ 改版多亮点！例句增加准确翻译，更加贴合读者需求，进一步提升学习体验

BEC词汇精选系列：

《剑桥商务英语(BEC)初级词汇精选》
《剑桥商务英语(BEC)中级词汇精选》
《剑桥商务英语(BEC)高级词汇精选》
新东方考试研究中心 编著

（免费下载图书相关音频文件）

◎ 精选BEC考试高频核心商务词汇，制订30天学习计划
◎ 参考历年真题，释义详尽准确
◎ 采用"词根+联想记忆法"，方法科学
◎ 给出词汇的商务例句、搭配、派生词等丰富实例，加深理解
◎ 设置听说小站、写作小站，将词汇应用于商务场景，学以致用
◎ 免费赠送英音录音，同步学习

《BEC词汇词根＋联想记忆法》

《BEC词汇词根＋联想记忆法：乱序版》
《BEC词汇词根＋联想记忆法：便携版》
（免费下载图书相关音频文件） 俞敏洪 编著

◎ 参考BEC考试真题，精选商务英语常用词汇
◎ 标注词汇商务释义，总结常用商务短语和缩略语，扫清专业术语障碍
◎ 分别按正序、乱序排列单词，并推出精简便携版，方便不同读者选用

《21世纪办公室书信大全》

（美）Francis J. Kurdyla 著

本书精选278封商务书信，包括致谢、推销、订货、投诉、邀请、祝贺等20余种常用商务书信类型，涵盖建筑、贸易、教育、出版、金融、服务等行业，涉及经管、研发、销售、宣传等业务种类，另特别增加3封传真和13份常用商务文书，可供繁忙的商务人士随时查阅，直接套用。

定价：58元 开本：32开 页码：808页

商务英语跟我学系列：

《商务英语应急600词》 金利 主编
《商务英语应急900句》 金利 主编
《情境商务口语应急一本通》
（韩）Myungsoo Park, Jinkyu Lee 编著

三个分册系统讲解600个商务英语核心必备词汇、900个难度递增的经典商务语句和商务情境口语，可免费下载MP3录音文件，助你迅速提升商务英语水平，补充重点商务知识。

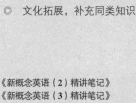

新概念英语之全新全绎系列：

（1-4册）（各含光盘1张）
周成刚 翁云凯 主编

◎ 按图索骥，追溯字根词源
◎ 说文解字，洞悉语句内涵
◎ 语法简述，化解疑难考点
◎ 文化拓展，补充同类知识

《新概念英语（2）精讲笔记》
《新概念英语（3）精讲笔记》
张少云 编著

◎ 遵照语言学习的普遍规律，单词入手，语法铺陈，实例巩固，步步为营
◎ 根据知识点的重要性及考查频率来安排编写体例，大而全面，精到明晰

英语语法新思维系列：

《英语语法新思维初级教程——走近语法》
《英语语法新思维中级教程——通悟语法》
《英语语法新思维高级教程——驾驭语法》
《英语语法新思维——名词从句超精解》
《英语语法新思维——定语从句超精解》
《英语语法新思维——句子成分超精解》
《英语语法新思维——语法难点妙解》
张满胜 著

◎ 张满胜老师多年教学实践经验和深入研究的成果
◎ 从全新的思维角度讲解和剖析各类语法知识点，帮你轻松攻克语法学习难关
◎ 探求语法规则背后深层本质，助你把语法规则内化成英语思维

《英文语法有规则：151个一学就会的语法规则》
《英文语法有规则：151个一学就会的语法规则（练习册）》
（日）石黑昭博 著

◎ 品牌保障：引进自培生教育出版集团，特别为亚洲英语学习者编排，在日本畅销多年
◎ 定位明确：适合初中生、高中生和一般基础语法学习者
◎ 版式编排：简明图片阐释语法内容，直观而易于理解
◎ 有学有练：配套练习册，先简述每一章的语法要点，再设置练习，方便巩固和检测